Using ActiveX™ Technology to Create
Programmable Applications

Automation
Programmer's Reference

Microsoft®*Press*

PUBLISHED BY
Microsoft Press
A Division of Microsoft Corporation
One Microsoft Way
Redmond, Washington 98052-6399

Copyright © 1997 by Microsoft Corporation

Library of Congress Cataloging-in-Publication Data pending.

Printed and bound in the United States of America.

1 2 3 4 5 6 7 8 9 MLML 2 1 0 9 8 7

Distributed to the book trade in Canada by Macmillan of Canada, a division of Canada Publishing Corporation.

A CIP catalogue record for this book is available from the British Library.

Microsoft Press books are available through booksellers and distributors worldwide. For further information about international editions, contact your local Microsoft Corporation office. Or contact Microsoft Press International directly at fax (206) 936-7329.

Apple, Macintosh, and Power Macintosh are registered trademarks of Apple Computer, Inc.

Microsoft, Microsoft Press, MS, MS-DOS, Visual Basic, Visual C++, Win32, Windows, and Windows NT are registered trademarks and ActiveX is a trademark of Microsoft Corporation.

Acquisitions Editor: David Clark
Project Editor: Saul Candib

Contents

Introduction

This book provides procedural and reference information for Automation (formerly called OLE Automation). While Automation runs on other platforms, the focus of this book is applications that use the Microsoft® Windows® 32-bit operating system. To get the most out of this book, you should be familiar with:

- The C++ and Microsoft Visual Basic® programming languages.

- The Microsoft Windows 95 and Windows NT® programming environments.

- The OLE protocols that are implemented through dynamic-link libraries (DLLs) and used in conjunction with other Microsoft Windows programs.

- The Component Object Model (COM).

The information in this book is also available in the Win32® Software Development Kit (SDK), which is contained on the Microsoft Developer Network (MSDN).

About This Book

This book is divided into three parts:

Part 1 About Automation

Chapter 1, "Overview of Automation," introduces the basic concepts of Automation and identifies the components.

Chapter 2, "Exposing ActiveX Objects," shows how to write and expose programmable objects for use by ActiveX™ clients, and demonstrates programming techniques with sample code.

Chapter 3, "Accessing ActiveX Objects," explains how to write applications and programming tools that access exposed objects.

Chapter 4, "Standard Objects and Naming Guidelines," lists the standard ActiveX objects that are recommended for most applications, and describes naming conventions for objects.

Part 2 Reference Information

Chapter 5, "Dispatch Interface and API Functions," describes the interfaces and functions that support access to exposed objects.

Chapter 6, "Data Types, Structures, and Enumerations," describes functions that manipulate arrays, strings, and variant types of data within Automation.

Chapter 7, "Conversion and Manipulation Functions," describes Automation API functions.

Chapter 8, "Type Libraries and the Object Description Language," describes the Microsoft Interface Definition Language (MIDL) compiler and the MkTypLib tool and its source file language. MIDL and MkTypLib create type libraries according to the descriptions you provide.

Chapter 9, "Type Description Interfaces," describes the interfaces and functions that allow programs to read and bind to the descriptions of objects in a type library.

Chapter 10, "Type Building Interfaces," describes interfaces and functions that build type libraries.

Chapter 11, "Error Handling Interfaces," describes how Automation error handling interfaces define and return error information.

Part 3 Appendixes

Appendix A, "National Language Support Functions," describes functions for 32-bit and 16-bit systems that support multiple national languages.

Appendix B, "File Requirements," lists the files you and your customers need to run Automation applications.

Appendix C, "Information for Visual Basic Programmers," lists the Automation Application Programming Interfaces (APIs) that are called by Visual Basic statements.

Appendix D, "String Comparisons," describes the string comparison rules applied by Automation.

Appendix E, "Managing GUIDs," provides supplemental information on globally unique identifiers.

The **Glossary** defines some of the terms that are useful in understanding Automation.

Other Sources of Information

Automation and ActiveX technologies are implementations of the OLE COM, which provides mechanisms for in-place activation, structured file storage, and many other application features. These parts of OLE are fully described in the following sources:

- *OLE Programmer's Reference* describes the COM, in-place activation, visual editing, structured file storage, and application registration in terms of the APIs and interfaces provided by OLE.

- *Microsoft Interface Definition Language Programmer's Guide and Reference*, contained in the Win32 SDK on the MSDN, describes the MIDL compiler.

- *Inside OLE, Second Edition,* by Kraig Brockschmidt, published by Microsoft Press®, provides introductory and how-to information about implementing OLE objects and containers.

- If you are developing C++ applications, the *ActiveX Control Developer's Kit* and Microsoft Visual C++® version 4.x product documentation describes how to develop Automation applications using C++.

For technical support, see the *OLE Programmer's Reference* and the documentation for the product with which you received OLE. Support for Automation is also provided on the World Wide Web on the Microsoft home page at www.microsoft.com.

Note ActiveX is Microsoft's brand name for the technologies that enable interoperability using the COM. OLE is a special-purpose subset of ActiveX. In this document, we use OLE to refer specifically to cases where an object is linked or embedded. We use ActiveX to encompass the broader technology that includes OLE, the Internet, and multimedia.

Document Conventions

The following typographical conventions are used throughout this book.

Convention	Meaning
bold	Indicates a word that is a function name, method, property, attribute, or other fixed part of a programming language, the Microsoft Windows operating system, or an API. For example, **DispInvoke** is an OLE-specific function. These words must always be typed exactly as they are printed.
italic	Indicates a word that is a placeholder or variable. For example, *ClassName* would be a placeholder for any ActiveX object class name. Function parameters in API reference material are italic to indicate that any variable name can be used. In addition, ActiveX and OLE terms are italicized at first use to highlight their definition.
UPPERCASE	Indicates a constant or data structure. For example, E_INVALIDARG is a constant.
InitialCaps	Indicates the name of an object, event, or file name. For example, the Application object.
monospace	Indicates source code and syntax spacing. For example: `*pdwRegisterCF = 0;`

Note The interface syntax in this book follows the variable-naming convention known as Hungarian notation, invented by programmer Charles Simonyi. Variables are prefixed with lowercase letters indicating their data type. For example, *lpszNewDocname* would be a long pointer to a zero-terminated string named *NewDocname*. For more information about Hungarian notation, refer to *Programming Windows* by Charles Petzold.

About Automation

Overview of Automation

Automation (formerly called OLE Automation) is a technology that allows software packages to expose their unique features to scripting tools and other applications. Automation uses the Component Object Model (COM), but may be implemented independently from other OLE features, such as in-place activation. Using Automation, you can:

- Create applications and programming tools that expose objects.
- Create and manipulate objects exposed in one application from another application.
- Create tools that access and manipulate objects. These tools can include embedded macro languages, external programming tools, object browsers, and compilers.

The objects an application or programming tool exposes are called *ActiveX objects*. Applications and programming tools that access those objects are called *ActiveX clients*. ActiveX objects and clients interact as follows:

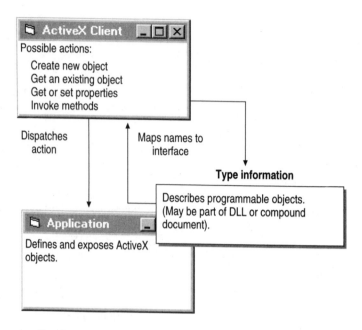

Applications and other software packages that support ActiveX technology define and expose objects which can be acted on by *ActiveX components*. ActiveX components are physical files (for example .exe and .dll files) that contain classes, which are definitions of objects. Type information describes the exposed objects, and can be used by ActiveX components at either compile time or at run time.

Why Expose Objects?

Exposing objects provides a way to manipulate an application's tools programmatically. This allows customers to use a programming tool that automates repetitive tasks that might not have been anticipated.

For example, Microsoft Excel exposes a variety of objects that can be used to build applications. One such object is the Workbook, which contains a group of related worksheets, charts, and macros—the Microsoft Excel equivalent of a three-ring binder. Using Automation, you could write an application that accesses Microsoft Excel Workbook objects, possibly to print them, as in the following diagram:

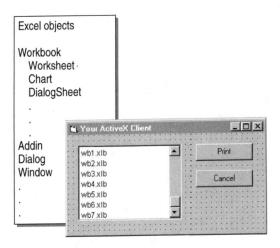

With Automation, solution providers can use your general-purpose objects to build applications that target a specific task. For example, you could use a general-purpose drawing tool to expose objects that draw boxes, lines, and arrows, insert text, and so forth. Another programmer could build a flowchart tool by accessing the exposed objects and then adding a user interface and other application-specific features.

Exposing objects to Automation or supporting Automation within a macro language offers several benefits.

- Exposed objects from many applications are available in a single programming environment. Software developers can choose from these objects to create solutions that span applications.

- Exposed objects are accessible from any macro language or programming tool that implements Automation. Systems integrators are not limited to the programming language in which the objects were developed. Instead, they can choose the programming tool or macro language that best suits their own needs and capabilities.

- Object names can remain consistent across versions of an application, and can conform automatically to the user's national language.

What Is an ActiveX Object?

An ActiveX object is an instance of a class that exposes properties, methods, and events to ActiveX clients. ActiveX objects support the COM. An ActiveX component is an application or library that is capable of creating one or more ActiveX objects. For example, Microsoft Excel exposes many objects that you can use to create new applications and programming tools. Within Microsoft Excel, objects are organized hierarchically, with an object named Application at the top of the hierarchy.

The following figure shows some of the objects in Microsoft Excel.

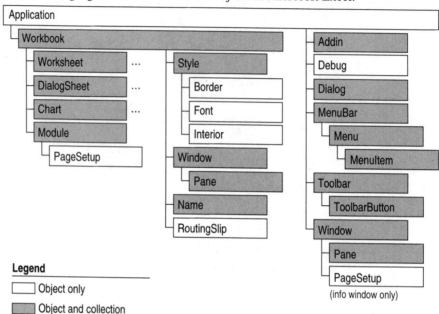

Each ActiveX object has its own unique member functions. When the member functions are exposed, it makes the object programmable by ActiveX clients. Three types of members for an object can be exposed:

- *Methods* are actions that an object can perform. For example, the Worksheet object in Microsoft Excel provides a **Calculate** method that recalculates the values in the worksheet.

- *Properties* are functions that access information about the state of an object. The Worksheet object's **Visible** property determines whether the worksheet is visible.

- *Events* are actions recognized by an object, such as clicking the mouse or pressing a key. You can write code to respond to such actions. In Automation, an event is a method that is called, rather than implemented, by an object.

For example, you might expose the following objects in a document-based application by implementing these methods and properties:

ActiveX object	Methods	Properties
Application	Help Quit Save Repeat Undo	ActiveDocument Application Caption DefaultFilePath Documents Height Name Parent Path Printers StatusBar Top Value Visible Width
Document	Activate Close NewWindow Print PrintPreview RevertToSaved Save SaveAs	Application Author Comments FullName Keywords Name Parent Path ReadOnly Saved Subject Title Value

Often, an application works with several instances of an object which together make up a *collection object*. For example, an ActiveX application based on Microsoft Excel might have multiple workbooks. To provide an easy way to access and program the workbooks, Microsoft Excel exposes an object named Workbooks, which refers to all of the current Workbook objects. Workbooks is a collection object.

In the preceding figure, collection objects in Microsoft Excel are shaded. Collection objects let you work iteratively with the objects they manage. If an application is created with a multiple-document interface (MDI), it might expose a collection object named Documents with the methods and properties in the following table.

Collection object	Methods	Properties
Documents	Add Close Item Open	Application Count Parent

What Is an ActiveX Client?

An ActiveX client is an application or programming tool that manipulates one or more ActiveX objects. The objects can exist in the same application or in another application. Clients can use existing objects, create new instances of objects, get and set properties, and invoke methods supported by the object.

Visual Basic is an ActiveX client. You can use Visual Basic and similar programming tools to create packaged scripts that access Automation objects. You can also create clients by doing the following:

- Writing code within an application that accesses another application's exposed objects through Automation.

- Revising an existing programming tool, such as an embedded macro language, to add support for Automation.

- Developing a new application, such as a compiler or type information browser, that supports Automation.

How Do Clients and Objects Interact?

ActiveX clients can access objects in two different ways:

- By using the **IDispatch** *interface*.
- By calling one of the member functions directly in the object's *virtual function table* (VTBL).

An Automation interface is a group of related functions that provide a service. All ActiveX objects must implement the **IUnknown** interface because it manages all of the other interfaces that are supported by the object. The **IDispatch** interface, which derives from the **IUnknown** interface, consists of functions that allow access to the methods and properties of ActiveX objects.

A *custom interface* is a COM interface that is not defined as part of OLE. Any user-defined interface is a custom interface.

The VTBL lists the addresses of all the properties and methods that are members of an object, including the member functions of the interfaces that it supports. The first three members of the VTBL are the members of the **IUnknown** interface. Subsequent entries are members of the other supported interfaces.

The following figure shows the VTBL for an object that supports the **IUnknown** and **IDispatch** interfaces.

IUnknown::QueryInterface
IUnknown::AddRef
IUnknown::Release
IDispatch::GetIDsOfNames
IDispatch::GetTypeInfo
IDispatch::GetTypeInfoCount
IDispatch::Invoke

If an object does not support **IDispatch**, the member entries of the object's custom interfaces immediately follow the members of **IUnknown**. For example, the following figure shows the VTBL for an object that supports a custom interface named IMyInterface.

.
IUnknown::AddRef
IUnknown::Release
IMyInterface::Member1
IMyInterface::Member2
. Remaining members . of IMyInterface

When an object for Automation is exposed, you must decide whether to implement an **IDispatch** interface, a VTBL interface, or both. Microsoft strongly recommends that objects provide a *dual interface*, which supports both access methods.

In a dual interface, the first three entries in the VTBL are the members of **IUnknown**, the next four entries are the members of **IDispatch**, and the subsequent entries are the addresses of the members of the dual interface.

The following figure shows the VTBL for an object that supports a dual interface named IMyInterface:

IUnknown::QueryInterface
IUnknown::AddRef
IUnknown::Release
IDispatch::GetIDsOfNames
IDispatch::GetTypeInfo
IDispatch::GetTypeInfoCount
IDispatch::Invoke
IMyInterface::Member1
IMyInterface::Member2
. . . Remaining members of IMyInterface

In addition to providing access to objects, Automation also provides information about exposed objects. By using **IDispatch** or a *type library*, an ActiveX client or programming tool can determine which interfaces an object supports, as well as the names of its members. Type libraries, which are files or parts of files that describe the type of one or more ActiveX objects, are especially useful because they can be accessed at compile time. For information on type libraries, refer to "What Is a Type Library?" later in this chapter, and "Type Libraries" in Chapter 2, "Exposing ActiveX Objects."

Accessing an Object Through the IDispatch Interface

ActiveX clients can use the **IDispatch** interface to access objects that implement the interface. The client must first create the object, and then query the object's **IUnknown** interface for a pointer to its **IDispatch** interface.

Although programmers might know objects, methods, and properties by name, **IDispatch** keeps track of them internally with a number called the *dispatch identifier* (DISPID). Before an ActiveX client can access a property or method, it must have the DISPID that maps to the name of the member.

With the DISPID, a client can call the member **IDispatch::Invoke** to access the property or invoke the method, and then package the parameters for the property or method into one of the **IDispatch::Invoke** parameters.

The object's implementation of **IDispatch::Invoke** must then unpackage the parameters, call the property or method, and handle any errors that occur. When the property or method returns, the object passes its return value back to the client through an **IDispatch::Invoke** parameter.

DISPIDs are available at run time, and, in some circumstances, at compile time. At run time, clients get DISPIDs by calling the **IDispatch::GetIDsOfNames** function. This is called *late binding* because the controller binds to the property or method at run time instead of compile time.

The DISPID of each property or method is fixed, and is part of the object's type description. If the object is described in a type library, an ActiveX client can read the DISPIDs from the type library at compile time, and avoid calling **IDispatch::GetIDsOfNames**. This is called *ID binding*. Because it requires only one call to **IDispatch** (the call to **Invoke**), rather than the two calls required by late binding, it is generally about twice as fast. Late-binding clients can improve performance by caching DISPIDs after retrieving them, so that **IDispatch::GetIDsOfNames** is called only once for each property or method.

Accessing an Object Through the VTBL

Automation allows an ActiveX client to call a method or property accessor function directly, either within or across processes. This approach, called *VTBL binding*, does not use the **IDispatch** interface. The client obtains type information from the type library at compile time, and then calls the methods and functions directly. VTBL binding is faster than both ID binding and late binding because the access is direct, and no calls are made through **IDispatch**.

In-Process and Out-of-Process Server Objects

ActiveX objects can exist in the same process as their controller, or in a different process. *In-process server* objects are implemented in a dynamic-link library (DLL) and are run in the process space of the controller. Because they are contained in a DLL, they cannot be run as stand-alone objects. *Out-of-process server* objects are implemented in an executable file and are run in a separate process space. Access to in-process objects is much faster than to out-of-process server objects because Automation does not need to make remote procedure calls across the process boundary.

The access mechanism (**IDispatch** or VTBL) and the location of an object (in-process or out-of-process server) determine the fixed overhead required for access. The most important factor in performance, however, is the quantity and nature of the work performed by the methods and procedures that are invoked. If a method is time consuming or requires remote procedure calls, the overhead of the call to **IDispatch** may make a call to VTBL more appropriate.

What Is a Type Library?

A type library is a file or part of a file that describes the type of one or more ActiveX objects. Type libraries do not store objects; they store type information. By accessing a type library, applications and browsers can determine the characteristics of an object, such as the interfaces supported by the object and the names and addresses of the members of each interface. A member can also be invoked through a type library. For details about the interfaces, refer to Chapter 9, "Type Description Interfaces."

When ActiveX objects are exposed, you should create a type library to make objects easily accessible to other developers. The simplest way to do this is to describe objects in an Object Description Language file (.odl), and then compile the file using the MIDL compiler (preferred) or with the MkTypLib utility, as described in Chapter 8, "Type Libraries and the Object Description Language."

For information about the MIDL compiler, refer to the *Microsoft Interface Definition Language Programmer's Guide and Reference* in the Win32 Software Development Kit (SDK) section of the Microsoft Developer's Network (MSDN).

CHAPTER 2

Exposing ActiveX Objects

Exposing objects makes them available for programmatic use by other applications and programming tools. This chapter discusses how to design an application that exposes objects, and then uses various samples from the *OLE Programmer's Reference* in the Win32 Software Development Kit (SDK) to demonstrate how to implement the design.

Note Throughout this chapter, the file names of sample applications appear in parentheses before the sample code.

Exposing Objects

To expose ActiveX objects, you write code to initialize the objects, implement the objects, and then release OLE when the application terminates.

▶ **To initialize exposed objects**

1. Initialize OLE.

2. Register the class factories of the exposed objects.

3. Register the active object.

▶ **To implement exposed objects**

1. Implement the **IUnknown**, **IDispatch**, and virtual function table (VTBL) interfaces for the objects.

2. Implement the properties and methods of the objects.

▶ **To release OLE when the application terminates**

1. Revoke the registration of the class factories and revoke the active object.

2. Uninitialize OLE.

▶ **To retrieve active objects for use by others**

1. Use the Object Description Language (ODL) to create an .odl file, or use the Interface Definition Language (IDL) to create a library section in an .idl file that describes the properties and methods of the exposed objects. Use the MkTypLib utility to compile the .odl file into a type library or use the Microsoft Interface Definition Language (MIDL) compiler for both the .idl file and .odl file.

2. Create a registration (.reg) file for the application.

Initializing Exposed Objects

To initialize OLE and the exposed objects, use the following functions:

- **OleInitialize**—Initializes OLE.

- **CoRegisterClassObject**—Registers the object's class factory with OLE so other applications can use it to create new objects.

- **RegisterActiveObject**—Registers the active object so other applications can connect to an existing object.

For more information on **OleInitialize** and **CoRegisterClassObject**, see the *OLE Programmer's Reference* in the Win32 SDK.

Implementing Exposed Objects

The following figure shows the interfaces that you should implement to expose ActiveX objects.

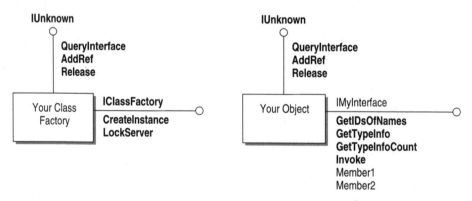

The member functions are listed under each interface name.

Implementing a Class Factory

Before OLE can create an object, it needs access to the object's *class factory*. The class factory implements the **IClassFactory** interface. For detailed information about this interface, see the *OLE Programmer's Reference* and *Inside OLE, Second Edition,* published by Microsoft Press®. This chapter describes only what you must do to expose objects for Automation.

It is important to implement a class factory for objects that may be created explicitly through the OLE function **CoCreateInstance,** or through the Visual Basic **New** keyword. For example, an application can expose an Application object for creation, but may have many other programmable objects that can be created or destroyed by referencing a member of the Application object. In this case, only the Application object would need a class factory.

For each class factory, you need to implement the following two member functions of the **IClassFactory** interface, which provide services for OLE API functions. The prototypes for the member functions reside in the file Ole2.h.

- **CreateInstance**—Creates an instance of the object's class.
- **LockServer**—Prevents the object's server from shutting down, even if the last instance of the object is released. **LockServer** can improve the performance of applications that frequently create and release objects.

In general, the **CreateInstance** method should create a new instance of the object's class. For the Application object, however, the **CreateInstance** method should return the existing instance of the Application object, which is registered in the running object table (ROT).

The class factory object implements the **IClassFactory** and **IUnknown** interfaces. All objects must implement **IUnknown**, which allows ActiveX clients to determine which interfaces the object supports. A class factory can create instances of a class.

The object implements two interfaces: **IUnknown** and IMyInterface. The interface IMyInterface is a **dual** interface, which supports both late binding through **IDispatch,** and early binding through the VTBL. The **dual** interface provides two ways to invoke the object's methods and properties. **IDispatch** includes the member functions **GetIDsOfNames, GetTypeInfo, GetTypeInfoCount,** and **Invoke.**

Member1 and Member2 are the members of IMyInterface. These members are available as direct entry points through the object's VTBL. They can also be accessed through **IDispatch::Invoke.**

You must decide how to handle errors that occur in the exposed objects. If an object supports a **dual** interface and needs to return detailed, contextual error information, you also need to implement the Automation error interface, **IErrorInfo.**

In addition to writing code to implement objects, you must create a type library and a registration file. Describe the types of exposed objects in the library section of the MIDL file or create an .odl file. Use the MIDL compiler or the MkTypLib tool to compile the .odl file. A type library (.tlb) file and a header (.h) file are created. The registration file provides information that the operating system and OLE need to locate objects.

Exposing the Application Object

Any document-based, user-interactive applications that expose ActiveX objects should have one top-level object named the Application object. This object is initialized as the active object when an application starts.

The Application object identifies the application and provides a way for ActiveX clients to bind to and navigate the application's exposed objects. All other exposed objects are subordinate to the Application object; it is the root-level object in the object hierarchy.

The names of the Application object's members are part of the global namespace, so ActiveX clients do not need to qualify them. For example, if MyApplication is the name of the Application object, a Visual Basic program can refer to a method of MyApplication as MyApplication.MyMethod or simply MyMethod. However, you should be careful not to overload the Application object with too many members because it can cause ambiguity and decrease performance. A large, complicated application with many members should be organized hierarchically, with a few generalized objects at the top, branching out into smaller, more specialized objects.

The following chart shows how applications should expose their Application and Document objects.

Command line	Multiple-document interface application	Single-document interface application
/Embedding	Expose class factories for document classes, but not for the application.	Expose class factories for document class, but not for the application.
	Call **RegisterActiveObject** for the Application object.	Call **RegisterActiveObject** for the Application object.
/Automation	Expose class factories for document classes.	Do not expose class factory for document class.
	Expose class factory for the application using **RegisterClassObject**.	Expose class factory for the Application object using **RegisterClassObject**.
	Call **RegisterActiveObject** for the Application object.	Call **RegisterActiveObject** for the Application object.

Command line	Multiple-document interface application	Single-document interface application
No OLE switches	Expose class factories for document classes, but not for the application. Call **RegisterActiveObject** for the Application object.	Call **RegisterActiveObject** for the Application object.

The call to **RegisterActiveObject** enters the Application object in OLE's running object table (ROT), so ActiveX clients can retrieve the active object instead of creating a new instance. Visual Basic applications can use the **GetObject** statement to access an existing object.

Creating a Registration File

Before an application can use OLE and Automation, the OLE objects must be registered with the user's system registration database. OLE provides sample registration files to perform this task for the OLE objects and the sample applications. Registration makes the following possible:

- ActiveX clients can create instances of the objects through **CoCreateInstance**.

- Automation tools can find the type libraries that are installed on the user's computer.

- OLE can find remoting code for the interfaces.

You can use the **DLLRegisterServer** function to register all objects implemented by a dynamic-link library (DLL). This function registers the class identifiers (CLSIDs) for each object, the programmatic identifiers (ProgIDs) for each application, and the type library. For details, refer to the description of **DLLRegisterServer** in *Programming with MFC*, provided with Microsoft Visual C++ version 4.1 and later product documentation.

The following sections give a brief overview of the syntax used in registering ActiveX objects. Descriptions of the process are provided later in this chapter. For detailed information, refer to the *OLE Programmer's Reference* in the Win32 SDK, which can be found on the Microsoft Developer's Network (MSDN).

Registering the Application

Registration maps the ProgID of the application to a unique CLSID, so that you can create instances of the application by name, rather than by CLSID. For example, registering Microsoft Excel associates a CLSID with the ProgID Excel.Application. In Visual Basic, you use the ProgID to create an instance of the application as follows:

```
SET xl = CreateObject("Excel.Application")
```

By passing the ProgID to **CLSIDFromProgID**, you can get the corresponding CLSID for use in **CoCreateInstance**. Only applications that will be used in this way need to be registered.

The registration file uses the following syntax for the application:

\ *AppName*.*ObjectName*[.*VersionNumber*] = *human_readable_string*
\ *AppName*.*ObjectName***CLSID** = {*UUID*}

AppName
>   The name of the application.

ObjectName
>   The name of the object to be registered (in this case, Application).

VersionNumber
>   The optional version number of the object.

human_readable_string
>   A string that describes the application to users. The recommended maximum length is 40 characters.

UUID
>   The universally unique identifier for the application CLSID. To generate a UUID for your class, run the utility Guidgen.exe.

Registering Classes

Objects that can be created with **CoCreateInstance** must also be registered with the system. For these objects, registration maps a CLSID to the Automation component file (.dll or .exe) in which the object resides. The CLSID also maps an ActiveX object back to its application and ProgID.

The following figure shows how registration connects ProgIDs, CLSIDs, and ActiveX components.

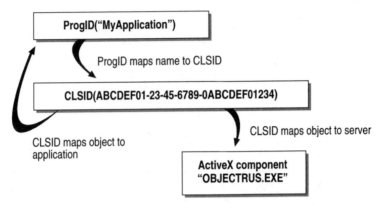

The type library can be obtained from its CLSID using the following syntax:

\CLSID\TypeLib = {*UUID of type library*}

The following syntax indicates that the server is an ActiveX component:

\CLSID\Programmable

The following shows the resulting example code; these COM class registry keys are required:

```
HKEY_CLASSES_ROOT\CLSID\{F37C8061-4AD5-101B-B826-00DD01103DE1} = Hello 2.0 Application
HKEY_CLASSES_ROOT\CLSID\{F37C8061-4AD5-101B-B826-00DD01103DE1}\ProgID = Hello.Application.2
HKEY_CLASSES_ROOT\CLSID\{F37C8061-4AD5-101B-B826-00DD01103DE1}\VersionIndependentProgID =
Hello.Application
HKEY_CLASSES_ROOT\CLSID\{F37C8061-4AD5-101B-B826-00DD01103DE1}\LocalServer32 = hello.exe
/Automation
HKEY_CLASSES_ROOT\CLSID\{F37C8061-4AD5-101B-B826-00DD01103DE1}\TypeLib = {F37C8060-4AD5-
101B-B826-00DD01103DE1}
HKEY_CLASSES_ROOT\CLSID\{F37C8061-4AD5-101B-B826-00DD01103DE1}\Programmable
```

The registration file uses the following syntax for each class of each object that the application exposes.

\CLSID\{*UUID*} = *human_readable_string*
\CLSID\{*UUID*}\ProgID = *AppName.ObjectName.VersionNumber*
\CLSID\{*UUID*}\VersionIndependentProgID = *AppName.ObjectName*
\CLSID\{*UUID*}\LocalServer[32] = *filepath*[/**Automation**]
\CLSID\{*UUID*}\InProcServer[32] = *filepath*[/**Automation**]

human_readable_string
>A string that describes the object to users. The recommended maximum length is 40 characters.

AppName
>The name of the application, as specified previously in the application registration string.

ObjectName
>The name of the object to be registered.

VersionNumber
>The version number of the object.

UUID
>The universally unique identifier for the application CLSID. To generate a UUID for your class, run the utility Guidgen.exe.

filepath
>The full path and name of the file that contains the object. The optional **/Automation** switch tells the application it was launched for Automation purposes. The switch should be specified for the Application object's class. For more information on **/Automation**, see "Initializing the Active Object" later in this chapter.

The ProgID and VersionIndependentProgID are used by other programmers to gain access to the objects you expose. These identifiers (IDs) should use consistent naming guidelines across all your applications as follows:

- Can contain up to 39 characters.

- Must not contain any punctuation (except for the period).

- Must not start with a digit.

Version-independent names consist of an *AppName.ObjectName*, without a version number. For example, `Word.Document` or `Excel.Chart`.

Version-dependent names consist of an *AppName.ObjectName.VersionNumber*, such as `Excel.Application.5`.

LocalServer[32]
>Indicates that the ActiveX component is an .exe file and runs in a separate process from the ActiveX client. The optional 32 specifies a server intended for use on 32-bit Windows systems.

InProcServer[32]
>Indicates that the ActiveX component is a DLL and runs in the same process space as the ActiveX client. The optional 32 specifies a server intended for use on 32-bit Windows systems.
>
>The *filepath* you register should give the full path and name. Applications should not rely on the MS-DOS PATH variable to find the object.

Releasing OLE and Objects

To release OLE and the exposed objects, use the following functions:

- **RevokeActiveObject**—Ends an object's status as the active object.
- **CoRevokeClassObject**—Informs OLE that a class factory is no longer available for use by other applications.
- **OLEUninitialize**—Releases OLE.

For more information on **OleUninitialize** and **CoRevokeClassObject**, see the *OLE Programmer's Reference* in the Win32 SDK.

Retrieving Objects

Automation provides several functions to identify and retrieve the active instance of an object or application, so you can make the object available to others.

- **RegisterActiveObject**—Sets the active object for an application. (Use when the application starts.)
- **RevokeActiveObject**—Revokes the active object. (Use when the application ends.)
- **GetActiveObject**—Retrieves a pointer to the active object. (In Visual Basic, this pointer is implemented by the **GetObject** function.)

Applications can have more than one active object at a time. To be initialized as active, an object must:

- Have a class factory (that is, the object provides an interface for creating instances of itself).
- Identify its class factory by a ProgID in the system registry.
- Be registered by a call to **RegisterActiveObject** when the object is created, or when it becomes active.

The Application object must be registered as an active object.

Returning Objects

To return an object from a property or method, the application should return a pointer to the object's implementation of the **IDispatch** interface. The data type of the return value should be VT_DISPATCH, or if the object does not support **IDispatch,** VT_UNKNOWN. The .odl file for the object should specify the name of the interface, rather than **IDispatch***, as follows:

```
ICustom * MyMember(...) {...};
```

The example declares a member that returns a pointer to a custom interface named **ICustom**.

Shutting Down Objects

ActiveX objects must shut down in the following way:

- If the object's application is visible, the object should shut down only in response to an explicit user command (for example, clicking **Exit** on the **File** menu) or the equivalent command from an ActiveX client.

- If the object's application is not visible, the object should shut down only when the last external reference is gone.

- If the object's application is visible and is controlled by an ActiveX client, it should become invisible when the user shuts it down (for example, clicking **Exit** on the **File** menu). This behavior allows the controller to continue to control the object. The controller should shut down only when the last external reference to the object has disappeared.

Application Design Considerations

When you expose objects to Automation, you need to decide which interfaces to implement and how to organize your objects. You should also create a type library. This section provides information to guide you in designing an Automation application.

Creating the Programmable Interface

An object's programmable interface comprises the properties, methods, and events that it defines. Organizing the objects, properties, and methods that an application exposes is like creating an object-oriented framework for an application. Chapter 4, "Standard Objects and Naming Guidelines," discusses some of the concepts behind naming and organizing the programmable elements that an application can expose.

Creating Methods

A *method* is an action that an object can perform, such as drawing a line or clearing the screen. Methods can take any number of arguments (including optional arguments), and they can be passed either by value or by reference. A method may or may not return a value.

Creating Properties

A *property* is a member function that sets or returns information about the state of the object, such as color or visibility. Most properties have a pair of accessor functions— a function to get the property value and a function to set the property value. Properties that are read-only or write-only, however, have only one accessor function.

Accessor Functions

The accessor functions for a single property have the same dispatch identifier (DISPID). The purpose of each function is indicated by attributes that are set for the function. These attributes are set in the .odl file description of the function, and are passed in the *wFlags* parameter to **Invoke** in order to set the context for the call. The attributes and flags are shown in the following table.

Purpose of function	ODL attribute	wFlags
Returns a value.	**propget**	DISPATCH_PROPERTYGET
Sets a value.	**propput**	DISPATCH_PROPERTYPUT
Sets a reference.	**propputref**	DISPATCH_PROPERTYPUTREF

The **propget** attribute designates the accessor function that gets the value of a property. When the ActiveX client needs to get the value of the property, it passes the DISPATCH_PROPERTYGET flag to **Invoke**.

The **propput** attribute designates the accessor function that sets the value of a property. When an ActiveX client needs to set a property by value, it passes the DISPATCH_PROPERTYPUT flag to **Invoke**. In Visual Basic, **Let** statements set properties by value.

The **propputref** attribute indicates that the property should be set by reference, rather than by value. In these cases, ActiveX clients that need to set a reference to a property pass DISPATCH_PROPERTYPUTREF. Visual Basic treats the **Set** statement as a by-reference property assignment.

Implementing the Value Property

The **Value** property defines the default behavior of an object when no property or method is specified. It is typically used for the property that users associate most closely with the object. For example, a cell in a spreadsheet might have many properties (**Font, Width, Height,** and so on), but its **Value** property defines the value of the cell. To refer to this property, a user does not need to specify the property name `Cell(1,1).Value`, but can simply use `Cell(1,1)`. The **Value** property is identified by the DISPID named DISPID_VALUE. In an .odl file, the **Value** property for an object has the attribute **id(0)**.

Handling Events

In addition to supporting properties and methods, ActiveX objects can be a source of events. In Automation, an *event* is a method that is called by an ActiveX object, rather than implemented by the object. For example, an object might include an event method named Button that retrieves clicks of the mouse button. Instead of being implemented by the object, the Button method returns an object that is a source of events.

In Automation, you use the **source** attribute to identify a member that is a source of events.

Details of the Automation event interfaces are provided in *Programming with MFC*, provided with Visual C++ version 4.1 or later product documentation.

Creating the IUnknown Interface

The **IUnknown** interface defines three member functions that must be implemented for each object that is exposed. The prototypes for these functions reside in the header file, Ole2.h.

- **QueryInterface**—Identifies which OLE interfaces the object supports.
- **AddRef**—Increments a member variable that tracks the number of references to the object.
- **Release**—Decrements the member variable that tracks the instances of the object. If an object has zero references, **Release** frees the object.

These functions provide the fundamental interface through which OLE can access objects. The *OLE Programmer's Reference* describes in detail how to implement the functions.

Creating the IDispatch Interface

The **IDispatch** interface provides a late-bound mechanism to access and retrieve information about an object's methods and properties. In addition to the member functions inherited from **IUnknown**, the following member functions should be implemented within the class definition of each object that will be exposed through Automation.

- **GetTypeInfoCount**—Returns the number of type descriptions for the object. For objects that support **IDispatch**, the type information count is always 1.
- **GetTypeInfo**—Retrieves a description of the object's programmable interface.
- **GetIDsOfNames**—Maps the name of a method or property to a DISPID, which can later be used to invoke the method or property.
- **Invoke**—Calls one of the object's methods, or gets or sets one of its properties.

You can implement **IDispatch** by any of the following means:

- Delegating to the **DispInvoke** and **DispGetIDsOfNames** functions, or to **ITypeInfo::Invoke** and **ITypeInfo::GetIDsOfNames**. This is the recommended approach, because it supports multiple locales and allows exceptions to be returned.
- Calling the **CreateStdDispatch** function. This approach is the simplest, but it does not provide for rich error handling or multiple national languages.
- Implementing the member functions without delegating to the dispatch functions. This approach is seldom necessary. Because **Invoke** is a complex interface with many subtle semantics that are difficult to emulate, it is strongly recommended that code delegate to **ITypeInfo::Invoke** to implement this mechanism.

Implementing Dual Interfaces

Although Automation allows you to implement an **IDispatch** interface, a VTBL interface, or a **dual** interface (which encompasses both), it is strongly recommended that you implement **dual** interfaces for all exposed ActiveX objects. **Dual** interfaces have significant advantages over **IDispatch**-only or VTBL-only interfaces.

- Binding can take place at compile time through the VTBL interface, or at run time through **IDispatch**.
- ActiveX clients that can use the VTBL interface may benefit from improved performance.
- Existing ActiveX clients that use the **IDispatch** interface will continue to work.
- The VTBL interface is easier to call from C++.
- **Dual** interfaces are required for compatibility with Visual Basic object support features.

Converting Existing Objects to Dual Interfaces

If you have already implemented exposed objects that support only the **IDispatch** interface, you should convert them to support **dual** interfaces. Use the following steps:

1. Edit the .odl file to declare a **dual** interface instead of an **IDispatch**-only interface.

2. Rearrange the parameter lists so that the methods and properties of your exposed objects return an HRESULT and pass their return values in a parameter.

3. If your object implements an exception handler, revise your code to use the Automation error handling interface. This interface provides detailed, contextual error information through both **IDispatch** and VTBL interfaces.

Registering Interfaces

Applications that add interfaces need to register the interfaces so OLE can find the appropriate remoting code for interprocess communication. By default, Automation registers dispinterfaces that appear in the .odl file. It also registers remote Automation-compatible interfaces that are not registered elsewhere in the system registry under the label **ProxyStubClsid32** (or **ProxyStubClsid** on 16-bit systems).

The syntax of the information registered for an interface is as follows:

\Interface\{_UUID_**}** = _InterfaceName_
\Interface\{_UUID_**}\Typelib** = _LIBID_
\Interface\{_UUID_**}\ProxyStubClsid[32]** = _CLSID_

UUID
    The universally unique ID of the interface.

InterfaceName
    The name of the interface.

LIBID
    The universally unique ID associated with the type library in which the interface is described.

CLSID
    The universally unique ID associated with the proxy/stub implementation of the interface, used internally by OLE for interprocess communication. ActiveX objects use the proxy/stub implementation of **IDispatch**.

Note To obtain a universally unique identifier ID, use the Guidgen.exe utility, which is a random number generator for creating unique identifiers. For more information about this utility, refer to Appendix E, "Managing GUIDs."

Creating Class Identifiers

Each object that is exposed for creation must have a unique CLSID. CLSIDs are universally unique identifiers (UUIDs, also called globally unique identifiers, or GUIDs) that identify class objects to OLE. The CLSID is included in an application, and must be registered with the operating system when an application is installed.

To generate UUIDs, run the Guidgen.exe utility. By default, Guidgen.exe puts a DEFINE_GUID macro on the Windows Clipboard, which can then be pasted into your source code.

Passing Formatted Data

Often, an application needs to accept formatted data as an argument to a method or property. Examples include a bitmap, formatted text, or a spreadsheet range. When handling formatted data, the application should pass an object that implements the OLE **IDataObject** interface. For detailed information about the interface, see the *OLE Programmer's Reference* in the Win32 SDK.

By using this interface, applications can retrieve the data of any Clipboard format. Because an **IDataObject** instance can provide data of more than one format, a caller can provide data in several formats, and let the called object choose which format is most appropriate.

If the data object implements **IDispatch**, it should be passed using the VT_DISPATCH flag. If the data object does not support **IDispatch**, it should be passed with the VT_UNKNOWN flag.

Implementing the IEnumVARIANT Interface

Automation defines the **IEnumVARIANT** interface to provide a standard way for ActiveX clients to iterate over collection objects. Every collection object must expose a read-only property named **_NewEnum** to let ActiveX clients know that the object supports iteration. The **_NewEnum** property returns an enumerator object that supports **IEnumVARIANT**.

The **IEnumVARIANT** interface provides a way to iterate through the items contained by a collection object. This interface is supported by an enumerator object that is returned by the **_NewEnum** property of the collection object, as in the following figure.

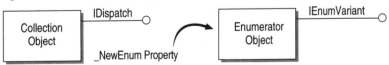

The **IEnumVARIANT** interface defines these member functions:

- **Next**—Retrieves one or more elements in a collection, starting with the current element.
- **Skip**—Skips over one or more elements in a collection.
- **Reset**—Resets the current element to the first element in the collection.
- **Clone**—Copies the current state of the enumeration so you can return to the current element after using **Skip** or **Reset**.

Implementing the _NewEnum Property

The **_NewEnum** property identifies an object as supporting iteration through the **IEnumVARIANT** interface. This property has the following requirements:

- Must be named **_NewEnum** and must not be localized.
- Must return a pointer to the enumerator object's **IUnknown** interface.
- Must include DISPID = DISPID_NEWENUM (-4).

Type Libraries

You must create a type library for each set of exposed objects. Because VTBL references are bound at compile time, exposed objects that support VTBL binding must be described in a type library.

Type libraries provide these important benefits:

- Type checking can be performed at compile time. This may help developers of ActiveX clients to write fast, correct code to access objects.
- You can describe an interface with type information and implement **IDispatch::Invoke** for the interface using a single call to **DispInvoke**.
- Visual Basic applications can create objects with specific interface types, rather than the generic **Object** type, to take advantage of early binding.
- ActiveX clients that do not support VTBLs can read and cache DISPIDs at compile time, improving run-time performance.
- Type browsers can scan the library, allowing others to see the characteristics of objects.
- The **RegisterTypeLib** function can be used to register exposed objects in the registration database.

- The **UnRegisterTypeLib** function can be used to completely uninstall an application from the system registry.
- Local server access is improved because Automation uses information from the type library to package the parameters that are passed to an object in another process.

Creating a Type Library

Most ActiveX components create *type libraries*. Type libraries contain type information, Help file names and contexts, and function-specific documentation strings. Access to this information is available at both compile time and run time.

Type information is the Automation standard for describing the objects, properties, and methods exposed by the ActiveX component. Browsers and compilers use the type information to display and access the exposed objects.

Type libraries are described in ODL and are compiled by the MIDL compiler or the MkTypLib utility.

▶ **To create a type library**

1. Write an object description script for the objects you expose. An object description script is essentially an annotated header file written in ODL.

2. Using the MIDL compiler or the MkTypLib utility, build the type library (.tlb) file and class description header (.h) file from the object description script.

Object Description Script Example

```
/* TDATA.ODL */
AppName library{
    dispinterface ObjeNamePro {
        interface ObjName
        }
}
```

Automation also supports the creation of alternative tools that compile and access type information. For information about creating these tools, refer to Chapter 9, "Type Description Interfaces."

A type library stores complete type information for all of an application's exposed objects. It may be included as a resource in a DLL or executable file, or remain as a stand-alone file (.tlb).

MIDL Library Statement Example

```
[
    uuid(F37C8060-4AD5-101B-B826-00DD01103DE1),    // LIBID_Hello.
    helpstring("Hello 2.0 Type Library"),
    lcid(0x0409),
    version(2.0)
]
library Hello
{
    importlib("stdole.tlb");
  [
        uuid(F37C8062-4AD5-101B-B826-00DD01103DE1),    // IID_Ihello.
        helpstring("Application object for the Hello application."),
        oleautomation,
        dual
    ]
    interface IHello : IDispatch
    {
        [propget, helpstring("Returns the application of the object.")]
        HRESULT Application([in, lcid] long localeID,
            [out, retval] IHello** retval)
    }
}
```

Building a Type Library

The MIDL compiler and the MkTypLib utility build type libraries. These tools are described in Chapter 8, "Type Libraries and the Object Description Language."

▶ To create a type library from an object description script

Run the MIDL compiler or MkTypLib tool on the script. For example:

```
MIDL /TLB output.tlb /H output.h inscript.odl
```
or
```
MKTYPLIB /TLB output.tlb /H output.h inscript.odl
```

Based on the object description script inscript.odl, the example creates a type library named output.tlb and a header file named output.h.

After creating the type library, you can include it in the resource step of building your application, or leave it as a stand-alone file. In either case, be sure to specify the file name and path of the library in the application's registration (.reg) file, so Automation can find the type library when necessary. See the following section for information on registering the type library.

▶   **To build an application that uses a type library**

1. Include the header file in the project.

2. Compile the project.

3. Optionally, use the Resource Compiler (RC) to bind the type library with the compiled project. The type library can bind with DLLs or executable files. For example, to bind a type library named `output.tlb` with a DLL, use the following statement in the .rc file for the DLL:

```
1 typelib output.tlb
```

   A DLL that contains a type library resource usually has the .olb (object library) extension.

Registering a Type Library

Tools and applications that expose type information must register the information so that it is available to type browsers and programming tools. The correct registration entries for a type library can be generated by calling the **RegisterTypeLib** function on the type library. Regedit.exe, which is supplied with the Win32 SDK as well as Windows NT and Windows 95, can then be used to write the registration entries to a text file from the system registration database.

The following information is registered for a type library:

\TypeLib\\{*libUUID***}**
\TypeLib\\{*libUUID***}***major.minor* = *human_readable_string*
\TypeLib\\{*libUUID***}***major.minor***\HELPDIR** = [*helpfile_path*]
\TypeLib\\{*libUUID***}***major.minor***\Flags** = *typelib_flags*
\TypeLib\\{*libUUID***}***major.minor******lcid******platform* = *localized_typelib_filename*

libUUID
   The universally unique ID of the type library.

major.minor
   The two-part version number of the type library. If only the minor version number increases, all the features of the previous type library are supported in a compatible way. If the major version number changes, code that compiled against the type library must be recompiled. The version number of the type library may differ from the version number of the application.

human_readable_string
   A string that describes the type library to users. The recommended maximum length is 40 characters.

helpfile_path
   The directory where the Help file for the types in the type library is located. If the application supports type libraries for multiple languages, the libraries may refer to different file names in the Help file directory.

typelib_flags
> The hexadecimal representation of the type library flags for this type library. These are the values of the LIBFLAGS enumeration, and are the same flags specified in the *uLibFlags* parameter to **ICreateTypeLib::SetLibFlags**. These flags cannot have leading zeros or the *0x* prefix.

lcid
> The hexadecimal string representation of the locale identifier (LCID). It is one to four hexadecimal digits with no *0x* prefix and no leading zeros. The LCID may have a neutral sublanguage ID.

platform
> The target operating system platform: 16-bit Windows, 32-bit Windows, or Apple® Macintosh®.

localized_typelib_filename
> The full name of the localized type library.

Using the LCID specifier, an application can explicitly register the file names of type libraries for different languages. This allows the application to find the desired language without having to open all type libraries with a given name.

For example, to find the type library for Australian English (309), the application first looks for it. If that fails, the application looks for an entry for standard English (a primary identifier of 0x09). If there is no entry for standard English, the application looks for LANG_SYSTEM_DEFAULT (0). For more information on locale support, refer to your operating system documentation for the national language support (NLS) interface. For 16-bit systems, see Appendix A, "National Language Support Functions."

Type Library Registration Example

```
; Type library registration information.

HKEY_CLASSES_ROOT\TypeLib\{F37C8060-4AD5-101B-B826-00DD01103DE1}
HKEY_CLASSES_ROOT\TypeLib\{F37C8060-4AD5-101B-B826-00DD01103DE1}\2.0 = Automation Hello 2.0
Type Library.
HKEY_CLASSES_ROOT\TypeLib\{F37C8060-4AD5-101B-B826-00DD01103DE1}\2.0\HELPDIR =

; U.S. English.

HKEY_CLASSES_ROOT\TypeLib\{F37C8060-4AD5-101B-B826-00DD01103DE1}\2.0\9\win32 = hello.tlb
```

Returning an Error

ActiveX objects typically return rich contextual error information, which includes an error number, a description of the error, and the path of a Help file that supplies more information. Objects that do not need to return detailed error information can simply return an HRESULT that indicates the nature of the error.

Passing Exceptions Through IDispatch

When an error occurs, objects invoked through **IDispatch** can return DISP_E_EXCEPTION and pass the details in the *pexcepinfo* parameter (an EXCEPINFO structure) to **IDispatch::Invoke**. Refer to the EXCEPINFO structure in Chapter 5, "Dispatch Interface and API Functions," and see "Passing Exceptions Through VTBLs" later in this chapter.

"Hello" Sample

The Hello sample is an Automation application with one object. It has these characteristics:

- Supports VTBL binding.
- Permits multiple instances of its exposed object to exist at the same time.
- Implements **IErrorInfo** for exception handling.

This sample has been simplified for demonstration purposes. It has the following limitations:

- Has only one object.
- Uses only scalar argument types. Automation also supports methods and properties that accept arguments of complex types, including arrays, references to objects, and formatted data, but not structures.
- Supports one national language.

The sections that follow demonstrate how the Hello sample exposes a simple class. The code is abridged to illustrate the essential parts. For a complete listing, see the source code in the *OLE Programmer's Reference* in the Win32 SDK.

Initializing OLE

When the Hello application starts, it initializes OLE and then creates the object to be exposed through Automation. For example (Main.cpp):

```
BOOL InitInstance (HINSTANCE hinst)
{
    HRESULT hr;
    TCHAR ach[STR_LEN];

    // Intialize OLE.

    hr = OleInitialize(NULL);
    if (FAILED(hr))
        return FALSE;

    // Create an instance of the Hello Application object.
    // The object is created with refcount 0.

    LoadString(hinst, IDS_HelloMessage, ach, sizeof(ach));
    hr = CHello::Create(hinst, ach, &g_phello);
    if (FAILED(hr))
        return FALSE;
    return TRUE;
}
```

This function calls **OleInitialize** to initialize OLE. It loads the string ach with the initial Hello message, obtained from the string table through the constant IDS_HelloMessage. Then it calls CHello::Create to create a single, global instance of the application object, passing it the initial Hello message and receiving a value for g_phello, a pointer to the instance. If the function is successful, it returns a value of **True**.

Registering the Active Object

After Hello creates an instance of the object, it exposes and registers the class factory (if necessary) and registers the active object (Main.cpp):

```
BOOL ProcessCmdLine(LPSTR pCmdLine,
                    LPDWORD pdwRegisterCF,
                    LPDWORD pdwRegisterActiveObject,
                    int nCmdShow)
{
    LPCLASSFACTORY pcf = NULL;
    HRESULT hr;

    *pdwRegisterCF = 0;
    *pdwRegisterActiveObject = 0;

    // Expose class factory for application object if command line
    // contains the /Automation switch.
    if (_fstrstr(pCmdLine, "-Automation") != NULL
        || _fstrstr(pCmdLine, "/Automation") != NULL)
```

```
{
        pcf = new CHelloCF;
        if (!pcf)
            goto error;
        pcf->AddRef();
        hr = CoRegisterClassObject(CLSID_Hello, pcf,
                               CLSCTX_LOCAL_SERVER,
                               REGCLS_SINGLEUSE,
                               pdwRegisterCF);
        if (hr != NOERROR)
            goto error;
        pcf->Release();
    }
    else g_phello->ShowWindow(nCmdShow); //Show if started stand-alone.

RegisterActiveObject(g_phello, CLSID_Hello, ACTIVEOBJECT_WEAK,
                pdwRegisterActiveObject);
    return TRUE;

error:
    if (!pcf)
        pcf->Release();
    return FALSE;
}
```

The sample first checks the command line for the **/Automation** switch. This switch indicates that the application should be started for programmatic access, so that ActiveX clients can create additional instances of the application's class. In this case, the class factory must be created and registered. If the switch is present, the Hello sample creates a new CHelloCF object and calls its **AddRef** method, thereby creating the class factory.

Next, the sample calls **CoRegisterClassObject** to register the class factory. It passes the object's CLSID (CLSID_Hello), a pointer to the CHelloCF object (pcf), and two constants (CLSCTX_LOCAL_SERVER and REGCLS_SINGLEUSE) that govern the class factory's use.

- CLSCTX_LOCAL_SERVER indicates that the executable code for the object runs in a separate process space from the controller.

- REGCLS_SINGLEUSE allows only one ActiveX client to use each instance of the class factory. The value returned through pdwRegisterCF must later be used to revoke the class factory.

The example specifies weak registration (ACTIVEOBJECT_WEAK), which means that OLE will release the object when all external connections to it have disappeared. You should always give ActiveX objects weak registration. For more information, see "RegisterActiveObject" in Chapter 5, "Dispatch Interface and API Functions."

The *OLE Programmer's Reference* provides more information on the functions **OleInitialize** and **CoRegisterClassObject**. *Inside OLE, Second Edition,* published by Microsoft Press, provides more information about verifying application entries in the registration database.

Registering the Hello Application

Finally, the sample registers the Hello application object in the running object table (ROT). Registering an active object allows ActiveX clients to retrieve an object that is already running, rather than create a new instance of the object. Use weak registration (ACTIVEOBJECT_WEAK) so that the running object table releases its reference when all external references are released. If strong registration is used (the default), the running object table will not release the reference until **RevokeActiveObject** is called. For more information, refer to Chapter 5, "Dispatch Interface and API Functions."

The following sample shows the registration entries for the Hello object.

```
REGEDIT

; Registration information for Automation Hello 2.0 Application.
; Version independent registration. Points to Version 2.0.

HKEY_CLASSES_ROOT\Hello.Application = Automation Hello Application
HKEY_CLASSES_ROOT\Hello.Application\Clsid = {F37C8061-4AD5-101B-B826-00DD01103DE1}

; Version 2.0 registration.

HKEY_CLASSES_ROOT\Hello.Application.2 = Automation Hello 2.0 Application
HKEY_CLASSES_ROOT\Hello.Application.2\Clsid = {F37C8061-4AD5-101B-B826-00DD01103DE1}
```

Implementing IDispatch

The **IDispatch** interface provides access to and information about an object. The interface requires the member functions **GetTypeInfoCount, GetTypeInfo, GetIdsOfNames,** and **Invoke.** The Hello sample implements **IDispatch** as follows (Hello.cpp):

```
STDMETHODIMP
CHello::GetTypeInfoCount(UINT FAR* pctinfo)
{
    *pctinfo = 1;
    return NOERROR;
}


STDMETHODIMP
CHello::GetTypeInfo(
        UINT itinfo,
        LCID lcid,
        ITypeInfo FAR* FAR* pptinfo)
```

```
{
    *pptinfo = NULL;

    if(itinfo != 0)
        return ResultFromScode(DISP_E_BADINDEX);

    m_ptinfo->AddRef();
    *pptinfo = m_ptinfo;

    return NOERROR;
}

STDMETHODIMP
CHello::GetIDsOfNames(
        REFIID riid,
        OLECHAR FAR* FAR* rgszNames,
        UINT cNames,
        LCID lcid,
        DISPID FAR* rgdispid)
{
    return DispGetIDsOfNames(m_ptinfo, rgszNames, cNames, rgdispid);
}

STDMETHODIMP
CHello::Invoke(
        DISPID dispidMember,
        REFIID riid,
        LCID lcid,
        WORD wFlags,
        DISPPARAMS FAR* pdispparams,
        VARIANT FAR* pvarResult,
        EXCEPINFO FAR* pexcepinfo,
        UINT FAR* puArgErr)
{
    {
        return DispInvoke(
        this, m_ptinfo,
        dispidMember, wFlags, pdispparams,
        pvarResult, pexcepinfo, puArgErr);
}
}
```

Automation includes two functions, **DispGetIdsOfNames** and **DispInvoke**, which provide standard implementations for **IDispatch::GetIDsOfNames**, and **IDispatch::Invoke**. The Hello sample uses these two functions to simplify the code.

Implementing IUnknown

Every OLE object must implement the **IUnknown** interface, which allows controllers to query the object to find out what interfaces it supports. **IUnknown** has three member functions: **QueryInterface**, **AddRef**, and **Release**. The Hello sample implements these functions for the CHello object as follows (Hello.cpp):

```
STDMETHODIMP
CHello::QueryInterface(REFIID iid, void FAR* FAR* ppv)
{
    *ppv = NULL;
    if (iid == IID_IUnknown || iid == IID_IDispatch || iid == IID_IHello
        *ppv = this;
    else if (iid == IID_ISupportErrorInfo)
        *ppv = &m_SupportErrorInfo;
    else return ResultFromScode(E_NOINTERFACE);

    AddRef();
    return NOERROR;
}


STDMETHODIMP_(ULONG)
CHello::AddRef(void)
{
    return ++m_cRef;
}


STDMETHODIMP_(ULONG)
CHello::Release(void)
{
if (--m_cRef == 0)
    {
        delete this;
        return 0;
    }
    return m_cRef;
}
```

Implementing IClassFactory

A class factory is a class that is capable of creating instances of another class. The Hello sample implements a single class factory named CHelloCF, as follows (HelloCf.cpp):

```
CHelloCF::CHelloCF(void)
{
    m_cRef = 0;
}
```

```
STDMETHODIMP
CHelloCF::QueryInterface(REFIID iid, void FAR* FAR* ppv)
{
    *ppv = NULL;
    if (iid == IID_IUnknown || iid == IID_IClassFactory)
        *ppv = this;
    else
        return ResultFromScode(E_NOINTERFACE);
    AddRef();
    return NOERROR;
}


STDMETHODIMP_(ULONG)
CHelloCF::AddRef(void)
{
    return ++m_cRef;
}
STDMETHODIMP_(ULONG)
CHelloCF::Release(void)
{
    if (--m_cRef == 0)
    {
        delete this;
        return 0;
    }
    return m_cRef;
}


STDMETHODIMP
CHelloCF::CreateInstance(IUnknown FAR* punkOuter,
                         REFIID riid,
                         void FAR* FAR* ppv)
{
    HRESULT hr;

    *ppv = NULL;

    // This implementation doesn't allow aggregation.
    if (punkOuter)
        return ResultFromScode(CLASS_E_NOAGGREGATION);

    hr = g_phello->QueryInterface(riid, ppv);
    if (FAILED(hr))
    {
        g_phello->Quit();
        return hr;
    }
    return NOERROR;
}
```

```
STDMETHODIMP
CHelloCF::LockServer(BOOL fLock)
{
    CoLockObjectExternal(g_phello, fLock, TRUE);
    return NOERROR;
}
```

The function CHelloCF::CHelloCF is a C++ constructor function. By default, the constructor function initializes the object's VTBLs; CHelloCF::CHelloCF also initializes the reference count for the class.

The class factory supports six member functions. **QueryInterface**, **AddRef**, and **Release** are the required **IUnknown** members, and **CreateInstance** and **LockServer** are the required **IClassFactory** members.

Implementing VTBL Binding

In addition to the **IDispatch** interface, the Hello sample supports VTBL binding. When a member is invoked, objects that support a VTBL interface return an HRESULT instead of a value, and pass their return value as the last parameter. Objects may also accept a LCID parameter, which allows them to parse strings correctly for the local language. The following example shows how the **Visible** property is implemented (Hello.cpp):

```
STDMETHODIMP
CHello::put_Visible(BOOL bVisible)
{
    ShowWindow(bVisible ? SW_SHOW : SW_HIDE);
    return NOERROR;
}


STDMETHODIMP
CHello::get_Visible(BOOL FAR* pbool)
{
    *pbool = m_bVisible;
    return NOERROR;
}
```

Additional information must be specified in the .odl file to create a **dual** interface, as shown in "Creating Type Information" later in this chapter.

Registering the Interface for VTBL Binding

The following lines from the Hello.reg file register the interface for VTBL binding. In the example, **ProxyStubClsid** refers to the proxy and stub implementation of **IDispatch**.

```
HKEY_CLASSES_ROOT\Interface\{F37C8062-4AD5-101B-B826-00DD01103DE1} = IHello
HKEY_CLASSES_ROOT\Interface\{F37C806 2-4AD5-101B-B826-00DD01103DE1}\TypeLib = {F37C8060-
4AD5-101B-B826-00DD01103DE1}
HKEY_CLASSES_ROOT\Interface\{F37C8062-4AD5-101B-B826-00DD01103DE1}\ProxyStubClsid32 =
{00020424-0000-0000-C000-000000000046}
```

Handling Errors

The Hello sample includes an exception handler that passes exceptions through **IDispatch::Invoke,** and supports rich error information through VTBLs (Hello.cpp):

```
STDMETHODIMP
CHello::RaiseException(int nID)
{
    extern return value g_scodes[];
    char szError[STR_LEN];
    ICreateErrorInfo *pcerrinfo;
    IErrorInfo *perrinfo;
    HRESULT hr;
    BSTR bstrDescription = NULL;

if (LoadString(g_phello->m_hinst,nID, szError, sizeof(szError)))
    bstrDescription = SysAllocString(TO_OLE_STRING(szError));

// Set ErrorInfo object so that VTBL binding controller can get
// rich error information. If the controller is using IDispatch
// to access properties or methods, DispInvoke will fill the
// EXCEPINFO structure using the values specified in the ErrorInfo
// object, and Dispinvoke will return DISP_E_EXCEPTION. The
// property or method must return a failure return value for DispInvoke
// to do this.

hr = CreateErrorInfo(hr))
{

    pcerrinfo->SetGUID(rguid);
    pcerrinfo->SetSource(g_phello->m_bstrProgID);
    if (bstrDescription)
        pcerrinfo->SetDescription(bstrDescription);
    hr = pcerrinfo->QueryInterface(IID_IErrorInfo,
    (LPVOID FAR*) &perrinfo);
    if (succeeded(hr))
```

```
        {

            SetErrorInfo(0,perrinfo);
            perrinfo->Release();
    }

if (bstrDescription)
        SysFreeString(bstrDescription);
    return ResultFromScode(g_scodes[nID-1001]);
}
```

The member functions of the Hello sample call this routine when an exception occurs. **RaiseException** sets the system's error object so that controller applications that call through VTBLs can retrieve rich error information. Controllers that call through **IDispatch::Invoke** will be returned with this error information by **DispInvoke** through the EXCEPINFO structure.

Hello also implements the **ISupportErrorInfo** interface, which allows ActiveX clients to query whether an error object will be available (Hello.cpp):

```
CSupportErrorInfo::CSupportErrorInfo(IUnknown FAR* punkObject,
                                     REFIID riid)
{
    m_punkObject = punkObject;
    m_iid = riid;
}

STDMETHODIMP
CSupportErrorInfo::QueryInterface(REFIID iid, void FAR* FAR* ppv)
{
    return m_punkObject->QueryInterface(iid, ppv);
}

STDMETHODIMP_(ULONG)
CSupportErrorInfo::AddRef(void)
{
    return m_punkObject->AddRef();
}

STDMETHODIMP_(ULONG)
CSupportErrorInfo::Release(void)
{
    return m_punkObject->Release();
}

STDMETHODIMP
CSupportErrorInfo::InterfaceSupportsErrorInfo(REFIID riid)
{
    return (riid == m_iid) ? NOERROR : ResultFromScode(S_FALSE);
}
```

Releasing Objects and OLE

When the Hello application ends, it revokes the class factory and the active object, and uninitializes OLE. For example (Main.cpp):

```
void Uninitialize(DWORD dwRegisterCF, DWORD dwRegisterActiveObject)
{
    if (dwRegisterCF != 0)
        CoRevokeClassObject(dwRegisterCF);
    if (dwRegisterActiveObject != 0)
        RevokeActiveObject(dwRegisterActiveObject, NULL);
    OleUninitialize();
}
```

Creating Type Information

Type information for the Hello sample is described in ODL. The MIDL compiler and MkTypLib utility use the .odl file to create a type library (Hellotl.tlb) and a header file (Hellotl.h).

The following example shows the description for the Hello type library, interface, and Application object (Hello.odl):

```
[
    uuid(F37C8060-4AD5-101B-B826-00DD01103DE1),        // LIBID_Hello.
    helpstring("Hello 2.0 Type Library"),
    lcid(0x009),
    version(2.0)
]
library Hello
{
    importlib("stdole32.tlb");
    [
    uuid(F37C8062-4AD5-101B-B826-00DD01103DE1),    // IID_Ihello.
    helpstring("Application object for the Hello application."),
    oleautomation,
    dual
    ]
    interface IHello : IDispatch
    {
        [propget, helpstring("Returns the application of the object.")]
        HRESULT Application([out, retval] IHello** retval);

    [propget,
        helpstring("Returns the full name of the application.")]
        HRESULT FullName([out, retval] BSTR* retval);

        [propget, id(0),
        helpstring("Returns the name of the application.")]
        HRESULT Name([out, retval] BSTR* retval);
```

```
     [propget, helpstring("Returns the parent of the object.")]
     HRESULT Parent([out, retval] IHello** retval);

     [propput]
     HRESULT Visible([in] boolean VisibleFlag);
     [propget,
     helpstring
     ("Sets or returns whether the main window is visible.")]
     HRESULT Visible([out, retval] boolean* retval);

     [helpstring("Exits the application.")]
     HRESULT Quit();

     [propput,
     helpstring("Sets or returns the hello message to be used.")]
     HRESULT HelloMessage([in] BSTR Message);
     [propget]
     HRESULT HelloMessage([out, retval] BSTR *retval);

     [helpstring("Say Hello using HelloMessage.")]
     HRESULT SayHello();
  }


  [
     uuid(F37C8061-4AD5-101B-B826-00DD01103DE1),     // CLSID_Hello.
     helpstring("Hello Class"),
     appobject
  ]
  coclass Hello
  {
     [default]          interface IHello;
                           interface IDispatch;
  }
}
```

The items enclosed by square brackets are *attributes*, which provide further information about the objects in the file. The **oleautomation** and **dual** attributes, for example, indicate that the IHello interface supports both **IDispatch** and VTBL binding. The **appobject** attribute indicates that Hello is the Application object.

For more information about attributes, refer to Chapter 8, "Type Libraries and the Object Description Language."

Creating the Hello Registration File

The system registration database lists all the OLE objects in the system. OLE uses this database to locate objects and determine their capabilities. The registration file registers the application, the type library, and the exposed classes of the sample (Hello.reg):

```
REGEDIT

; Registration information for Automation Hello 2.0 Application.
; Version independent registration. Points to Version 2.0.

HKEY_CLASSES_ROOT\Hello.Application = Hello 2.0 Application
HKEY_CLASSES_ROOT\Hello.Application\Clsid = {F37C8061-4AD5-101B-B826-00DD01103DE1}

; Version 2.0 registration.

HKEY_CLASSES_ROOT\Hello.Application.2 = Hello 2.0 Application
HKEY_CLASSES_ROOT\Hello.Application.2\Clsid = {F37C8061-4AD5-101B-B826-00DD01103DE1}
HKEY_CLASSES_ROOT\CLSID\{F37C8061-4AD5-101B-B826-00DD01103DE1} = Hello 2.0 Application
HKEY_CLASSES_ROOT\CLSID\{F37C8061-4AD5-101B-B826-00DD01103DE1}\ProgID = Hello.Application.2
HKEY_CLASSES_ROOT\CLSID\{F37C8061-4AD5-101B-B826-00DD01103DE1}\VersionIndependentProgID =
Hello.Application
HKEY_CLASSES_ROOT\CLSID\{F37C8061-4AD5-101B-B826-00DD01103DE1}\LocalServer = hello.exe
/Automation
HKEY_CLASSES_ROOT\CLSID\{F37C8061-4AD5-101B-B826-00DD01103DE1}\TypeLib = {F37C8061-4AD5-
101B-B826-00DD01103DE1}
HKEY_CLASSES_ROOT\CLSID\{F37C8061-4AD5-101B-B826-00DD01103DE1}\Programmable

; Type library registration information.

HKEY_CLASSES_ROOT\TypeLib\{F37C8060-4AD5-101B-B826-00DD01103DE1}
HKEY_CLASSES_ROOT\TypeLib\{F37C8060-4AD5-101B-B826-00DD01103DE1}\2.0 = Hello 2.0 Type
Library
HKEY_CLASSES_ROOT\TypeLib\{F37C8060-4AD5-101B-B826-00DD01103DE1}\2.0\HELPDIR =

; English

HKEY_CLASSES_ROOT\TypeLib\{F37C8060-4AD5-101B-B826-00DD01103DE1}\2.0\9\win32 = hello.tlb
```

```
; Interface registration. All interfaces that support VTBL binding
; must be registered as follows. RegisterTypeLib & LoadTypeLib will do
; this automatically.
; IID_IHello = {F37C8062-4AD5-101B-B826-00DD01103DE1}.
; LIBID_Hello = {F37C8060-4AD5-101B-B826-00DD01103DE1}.

HKEY_CLASSES_ROOT\Interface\{F37C8062-4AD5-101B-B826-00DD01103DE1} = IHello
HKEY_CLASSES_ROOT\Interface\{F37C8062-4AD5-101B-B826-00DD01103DE1}\TypeLib = {F37C8060-
4AD5-101B-B826-00DD01103DE1}
HKEY_CLASSES_ROOT\Interface\{F37C8062-4AD5-101B-B826-00DD01103DE1}\ProxyStubClsid32 =
{00020424-0000-0000-C000-000000000046}
```

To merge an object's registration information with the system registry, the object should expose the **DLLRegisterServer** API, as described in the *OLE Programmer's Reference*. **DLLRegisterServer** should call **RegisterTypeLib** to register the type library and the interfaces supported by the application. This only applies to in-process servers. Out-of-process servers such as the Hello sample do not export **DLLRegisterServer**.

"Lines" Sample

The Lines sample is an ActiveX component application that implements collections. This sample file allows a collection of lines to be drawn on a pane using Automation. This sample implements the following features:

- **Dual** interfaces that allow access to automation properties and methods through VTBL binding and **IDispatch**.
- Rich error information for VTBL-binding controllers implemented by **ISupportErrorInfo** and **IErrorInfo**.
- Two collections.
- Active object registration using **RegisterActiveObject** and **RevokeActiveObject**.
- Correct shutdown behavior.
- A registration file that contains Lines.Application as the ProgID.
- Initial invisibility.

The following routine initializes OLE, and then creates an instance of the Lines Application object (Main.cpp):

```
BOOL InitInstance (HINSTANCE hinst)
{
    HRESULT hr;

    // Intialize OLE.
    hr = OleInitialize(NULL);
    if (FAILED(hr))
        return FALSE;

    // Create an instance of the Lines Application object. The object is
    // created with refcount 0.
    hr = CApplication::Create(hinst, &g_pApplication);
    if (FAILED(hr))
        return FALSE;
    return TRUE;
}
```

Initializing the Active Object

The following function creates and registers the application's class factory, and then registers the Lines Application object as the active object (Main.cpp):

```
BOOL ProcessCmdLine(LPSTR lpCmdLine, LPDWORD pdwRegisterCF,
                    LPDWORD pdwRegisterActiveObject, int nCmdShow)
{
    LPCLASSFACTORY pcf = NULL;
    HRESULT hr;
    *pdwRegisterCF = 0;
    *pdwRegisterActiveObject = 0;

    // Expose class factory for application object if command line
    // contains the /Automation switch.
    if (_fstrstr(lpCmdLine, "-Automation") != NULL
        || _fstrstr(lpCmdLine, "/Automation") != NULL)
    {
        pcf = new CApplicationCF;
        if (!pcf)
            goto error;
        pcf->AddRef();
        hr = CoRegisterClassObject(CLSID_Lines, pcf,
                                CLSCTX_LOCAL_SERVER, REGCLS_SINGLEUSE,
                                pdwRegisterCF);
        if (hr != NOERROR)
            goto error;
        pcf->Release();
    }
    else            // Show window if started as stand-alone.
    g_pApplication->ShowWindow(nCmdShow );
```

```
// Register Lines Application object in the running object table (ROT).
// Use weak registration so that the ROT releases its reference when
// all external references are released.
    RegisterActiveObject(g_pApplication, CLSID_Lines, ACTIVEOBJECT_WEAK,
            pdwRegisterActiveObject);
    return TRUE;

error:
    if (pcf)
        pcf->Release();
    return FALSE;
}
```

Registering the Active Object

The sample application exposes the class factory for the Lines application, **CApplicationCF**, if the command line contains the **/Automation** switch. The switch indicates that the application was started for programmatic access, and therefore OLE needs to register the class factory and create an instance of the Application object. OLE applies this switch if it appears on the command line or in the application's registration file. OLE also supports the **/Embedding** switch, which indicates that an application has been started by a container application.

You should register the class factory for the Application object only if the application is launched with the **/Automation** switch. When **/Automation** is not specified, the application has been started for some reason other than programmatic access through Automation. If the class factory is registered under these circumstances, and a user later requests a new instance of the Application object, Automation will return the existing instance instead of creating a new one.

The sample calls **CoRegisterClassObject** to register the class factory as the active object. The CLSCTX_LOCAL_SERVER flag means the code that creates and manages Application objects will run in a separate process space.

Because the Application object's class factory is exposed, the call specifies the REGCLS_SINGLEUSE flag. When a multiple-document interface (MDI) application starts, it typically registers the class factory for its Document object, specifying REGCLS_MULTIPLEUSE. This flag, defined in the REGCLS enumeration, allows the existing application instance to be used later, when instances of the document objects need to be created. Each new Application object, however, requires a new instance of the application to be launched, and should therefore specify REGCLS_SINGLEUSE. If the application registered its class factory using REGCLS_MULTIPLEUSE, then the next **CreateObject** call that tries to create the application will get an existing copy.

In the following example, the macro defines a CLSID for Lines (Tlb.h):

```
DEFINE_GUID(CLSID_Lines,0x3C591B21,0x1F13,0x101B,0xB8,0x26,0x00,0xDD,0x0
1,0x10,0x3D,0xE1);
```

When the MIDL compiler to MkTypLib creates the optional header file (Tlb.h), it inserts DEFINE_GUID macros for each library, interface, and each class in an application.

Creating the Lines Registration File

The registration file provides information about the application, the Application object, classes of objects, type libraries, and interfaces. Entries for objects and interfaces start with the constant HKEY_CLASSES_ROOT, which represents the root key of the entire registration database. Entries for type libraries start with HKEY_TYPELIB_ROOT. After the constant, each entry supplies specific information about an object, type library, or interface.

Use the following steps to create the registration file:

1. Copy the file Lines.reg.

2. Rename and edit this file, adding entries for the application.

Registering the Lines Application Files

The Lines sample uses the following entries to register its Application object (Lines.Application) and its type library with the system (Lines.reg):

```
REGEDIT
; Registration information for the Lines Application object. Version
; independent registration.

HKEY_CLASSES_ROOT\Lines.Application = Lines
HKEY_CLASSES_ROOT\Lines.Application\Clsid = {3C591B21-1F13-101B-B826-00DD01103DE1}

; Version 1.0 registration.

HKEY_CLASSES_ROOT\Lines.Application.1 = Lines 1.0
HKEY_CLASSES_ROOT\Lines.Application.1\Clsid = {3C591B21-1F13-101B-B826-00DD01103DE1}

HKEY_CLASSES_ROOT\CLSID\{3C591B21-1F13-101B-B826-00DD01103DE1} = Lines 1.0
HKEY_CLASSES_ROOT\CLSID\{3C591B21-1F13-101B-B826-00DD01103DE1}\ProgID = Lines.Application.1
HKEY_CLASSES_ROOT\CLSID\{3C591B21-1F13-101B-B826-00DD01103DE1}\VersionIndependentProgID =
Lines.Application
HKEY_CLASSES_ROOT\CLSID\{3C591B21-1F13-101B-B826-00DD01103DE1}\LocalServer32 = lines.exe
/Automation
HKEY_CLASSES_ROOT\CLSID\{3C591B21-1F13-101B-B826-00DD01103DE1}\TypeLib = {3C591B20-1F13-
101B-B826-00DD01103DE1}
HKEY_CLASSES_ROOT\CLSID\{3C591B21-1F13-101B-B826-00DD01103DE1}\Programmable
```

```
; Type library registration information.

HKEY_CLASSES_ROOT\TypeLib\{3C591B20-1F13-101B-B826-00DD01103DE1}
HKEY_CLASSES_ROOT\TypeLib\{3C591B20-1F13-101B-B826-00DD01103DE1}\1.0 = Lines 1.0 Type
Library
HKEY_CLASSES_ROOT\TypeLib\{3C591B20-1F13-101B-B826-00DD01103DE1}\1.0\HELPDIR =

; English.

HKEY_CLASSES_ROOT\TypeLib\{3C591B20-1F13-101B-B826-00DD01103DE1}\1.0\9\win32 = lines.tlb

; Interface registration. All interfaces that support VTBL binding must
; be registered as follows. RegisterTypeLib will do this automatically.
; LIBID_Lines = {3C591B20-1F13-101B-B826-00DD01103DE1}.
; IID_IPoint = {3C591B25-1F13-101B-B826-00DD01103DE1}.

HKEY_CLASSES_ROOT\Interface\{3C591B25-1F13-101B-B826-00DD01103DE1} = IPoint
HKEY_CLASSES_ROOT\Interface\{3C591B25-1F13-101B-B826-00DD01103DE1}\TypeLib = {3C591B20-
1F13-101B-B826-00DD01103DE1}
HKEY_CLASSES_ROOT\Interface\{3C591B25-1F13-101B-B826-00DD01103DE1}\ProxyStubClsid32 =
{00020424-0000-0000-C000-000000000046}


; IID_ILine = {3C591B24-1F13-101B-B826-00DD01103DE1}.

HKEY_CLASSES_ROOT\Interface\{3C591B24-1F13-101B-B826-00DD01103DE1} = ILine
HKEY_CLASSES_ROOT\Interface\{3C591B24-1F13-101B-B826-00DD01103DE1}\TypeLib = {3C591B20-
1F13-101B-B826-00DD01103DE1}
HKEY_CLASSES_ROOT\Interface\{3C591B24-1F13-101B-B826-00DD01103DE1}\ProxyStubClsid32 =
{00020424-0000-0000-C000-000000000046}


; IID_ILines = {3C591B26-1F13-101B-B826-00DD01103DE1}.

HKEY_CLASSES_ROOT\Interface\{3C591B26-1F13-101B-B826-00DD01103DE1} = ILines
HKEY_CLASSES_ROOT\Interface\{3C591B26-1F13-101B-B826-00DD01103DE1}\TypeLib = {3C591B20-
1F13-101B-B826-00DD01103DE1}
HKEY_CLASSES_ROOT\Interface\{3C591B26-1F13-101B-B826-00DD01103DE1}\ProxyStubClsid32 =
{00020424-0000-0000-C000-000000000046}


; IID_IPoints = {3C591B27-1F13-101B-B826-00DD01103DE1}.

HKEY_CLASSES_ROOT\Interface\{3C591B27-1F13-101B-B826-00DD01103DE1} = IPoints
HKEY_CLASSES_ROOT\Interface\{3C591B27-1F13-101B-B826-00DD01103DE1}\TypeLib = {3C591B20-
1F13-101B-B826-00DD01103DE1}
HKEY_CLASSES_ROOT\Interface\{3C591B27-1F13-101B-B826-00DD01103DE1}\ProxyStubClsid32 =
{00020424-0000-0000-C000-000000000046}
```

```
; IID_IPane = {3C591B23-1F13-101B-B826-00DD01103DE1}.

HKEY_CLASSES_ROOT\Interface\{3C591B23-1F13-101B-B826-00DD01103DE1} = IPane
HKEY_CLASSES_ROOT\Interface\{3C591B23-1F13-101B-B826-00DD01103DE1}\TypeLib = {3C591B20-
1F13-101B-B826-00DD01103DE1}
HKEY_CLASSES_ROOT\Interface\{3C591B23-1F13-101B-B826-00DD01103DE1}\ProxyStubClsid32 =
{00020424-0000-0000-C000-000000000046}

; IID_IApplication = {3C591B22-1F13-101B-B826-00DD01103DE1}.

HKEY_CLASSES_ROOT\Interface\{3C591B22-1F13-101B-B826-00DD01103DE1} = IApplication
HKEY_CLASSES_ROOT\Interface\{3C591B22-1F13-101B-B826-00DD01103DE1}\TypeLib = {3C591B20-
1F13-101B-B826-00DD01103DE1}
HKEY_CLASSES_ROOT\Interface\{3C591B22-1F13-101B-B826-00DD01103DE1}\ProxySt
```

Creating the IUnknown Interface for the Lines Application

The **IUnknown** interface for the Lines object looks like this (Lines.cpp):

```cpp
STDMETHODIMP
CLine::QueryInterface(REFIID iid, void FAR* FAR* ppv)
{
    *ppv = NULL;

    if (iid == IID_IUnknown || iid == IID_IDispatch || iid == IID_ILine)
        *ppv = this;
    else if (iid == IID_ISupportErrorInfo)
        *ppv = &m_SupportErrorInfo;
    else return ResultFromScode(E_NOINTERFACE);

    AddRef();
    return NOERROR;
}


STDMETHODIMP_(ULONG)
CLine::AddRef(void)
{
    return ++m_cRef;
}


STDMETHODIMP_(ULONG)
CLine::Release(void)
{
    if(--m_cRef == 0)
    {
        delete this;
        return 0;
    }
    return m_cRef;
}
```

Creating the IDispatch Interface for the Lines Application

The following sections explain how to implement **IDispatch** by using **CreateStdDispatch** and **DispInvoke**.

Implementing IDispatch by Calling CreateStdDispatch

The simplest way to implement the **IDispatch** interface is to call **CreateStdDispatch**. This approach works for ActiveX objects that return only the standard dispatch exception codes, support a single national language, and do not support dual interfaces.

CreateStdDispatch returns a pointer to the created **IDispatch** interface. It takes three pointers as input: a pointer to the object's **IUnknown** interface, a pointer to the object to expose, and a pointer to the type information for the object. The following example implements **IDispatch** for an object named CCalc by calling **CreateStdDispatch** on the loaded type information:

```
CCalc FAR*
CCalc::Create()
{
    HRESULT hresult;
    CCalc FAR* pcalc;
    ITypeLib FAR* ptlib;
    ITypeInfo FAR* ptinfo;
    IUnknown FAR* punkStdDisp;

    ptlib = NULL;
    ptinfo = NULL;

    // Some error handling code omitted.

    if ((pcalc = new FAR CCalc()) == NULL)
        return NULL;
    pcalc->AddRef();

    // Load the type library from the information in the registry.

    if ((hresult = LoadRegTypeLib(LIBID_DspCalc2, 1, 0, 0x0409, &ptlib))
        != NOERROR){
        goto LError0;
    }
    if ((hresult = ptlib->GetTypeInfoOfGuid(IID_ICalculator, &ptinfo))
        != NOERROR){
        goto LError0;
    }
```

```
// Create an aggregate with an instance of the default
// implementation of IDispatch that is initialized with our
// TypeInfo.

hresult = CreateStdDispatch(
        pcalc,                    // Controlling unknown.
        &(pcalc->m_arith),        // VTBL pointer to dispatch on.
        ptinfo,
        &punkStdDisp);
```

Implementing IDispatch by Delegating

Another way to implement **IDispatch** is to use the dispatch functions **DispInvoke** and **DispGetIDsOfNames**. These functions give you the option of supporting multiple national languages and creating application-specific exceptions that are passed back to ActiveX clients.

The Lines sample implements **IDispatch::GetIDsOfNames** and **IDispatch::Invoke** using these functions (Lines.cpp):

```
STDMETHODIMP
CLines::GetIDsOfNames(
        REFIID riid,
        char FAR* FAR* rgszNames,
        UINT cNames,
        LCID lcid,
        DISPID FAR* rgdispid)
{
    return DispGetIDsOfNames(m_ptinfo, rgszNames, cNames, rgdispid);
}


STDMETHODIMP
CLines::Invoke(
        DISPID dispidMember,
        REFIID riid,
        LCID lcid,
        WORD wFlags,
        DISPPARAMS FAR* pdispparams,
        VARIANT FAR* pvarResult,
        EXCEPINFO FAR* pexcepinfo,
        UINT FAR* puArgErr)
{

    {
    return DispInvoke(
        this, m_ptinfo,
        dispidMember, wFlags, pdispparams,
        pvarResult, pexcepinfo, puArgErr);
    }
}
```

The Lines object implements the **IID_ILine dual** interface for VTBL binding. It also implements the **IID_ISupportErrorInfo** interface so that it can return rich, contextual error information through VTBLs.

Implementing the Class Factory for the Lines Application

The Lines sample implements a class factory for its Application object, as follows (Appcf.cpp):

```
STDMETHODIMP
CApplicationCF::CreateInstance(IUnknown FAR* punkOuter,
                               REFIID riid,
                               void FAR* FAR* ppv)
{
    HRESULT hr;

    *ppv = NULL;

    // This implementation doesn't allow aggregation.

    if (punkOuter)
        return ResultFromScode(CLASS_E_NOAGGREGATION);

    // This is REGCLS_SINGLEUSE class factory, so CreateInstance will be
    // called at most once. An application object has a REGCLS_SINGLEUSE
    // class factory. The global application object has already been
    // created when CreateInstance is called. A REGCLS_MULTIPLEUSE class
    // factory's CreateInstance would be called multiple times and would
    // create a new object each time. An MDI application would have a
    // REGCLS_MULTIPLEUSE class factory for its document objects.

    hr = g_pApplication->QueryInterface(riid, ppv);
    if (FAILED(hr))
    {
        g_pApplication->Quit();
        return hr;
    }
    return NOERROR;
}


STDMETHODIMP
CApplicationCF::LockServer(BOOL fLock)
{
    CoLockObjectExternal(g_pApplication, fLock, TRUE);
    return NOERROR;
}
```

The object's class factory must also implement an **IUnknown** interface. For example (Appcf.cpp):

```
STDMETHODIMP
CApplicationCF::QueryInterface(REFIID iid, void FAR* FAR* ppv)
{
    *ppv = NULL;

    if (iid == IID_IUnknown || iid == IID_IClassFactory)
        *ppv = this;
    else
        return ResultFromScode(E_NOINTERFACE);
    AddRef();
    return NOERROR;
}

STDMETHODIMP_(ULONG)
CApplicationCF::AddRef(void)
{
    return ++m_cRef;
}

STDMETHODIMP_(ULONG)
CApplicationCF::Release(void)
{
    if(--m_cRef == 0)
    {
        delete this;
        return 0;
    }
    return m_cRef;
}
```

Setting Up the VTBL Interface

The Lines sample supports VTBL binding as well as the **IDispatch** interface. By supporting this **dual** interface, the sample allows ActiveX clients both the flexibility of the **IDispatch** interface and the speed of VTBLs. Controllers that know the names of the members can compile directly against the function pointers in the VTBL. Controllers that do not have this information can use **IDispatch** at run time.

To have a **dual** interface, an interface must:

- Declare all of its members to return an HRESULT, and pass their actual return values as the last parameter.

- Have only Automation-compatible parameters and return types, as described in Chapter 7, "Conversion and Manipulation Functions."

- Specify the **dual** attribute on the interface description in the .odl file.

- Initialize the VTBLs with the appropriate member function pointers.

In the Lines sample, the interfaces **IPoint, IPoints, ILine, ILines, IPane,** and **IApplication** are all dual interfaces. The **IPoint** interface defines functions that get and put the values of the **X** and **Y** properties, as follows (Point.cpp):

```
STDMETHODIMP
CPoint::get_x(int FAR* pnX)
{
    *pnX = m_nX;
    return NOERROR;
}


STDMETHODIMP
CPoint::put_x(int nX)
{
    m_nX = nX;
    return NOERROR;
}


STDMETHODIMP
CPoint::get_y(int FAR* pnY)
{
    *pnY = m_nY;
    return NOERROR;
}


STDMETHODIMP
CPoint::put_y(int nY)
{
    m_nY = nY;
    return NOERROR;
}
```

The **get_x** and **get_y** accessor functions pass their return values in the last parameter, *pnX* and *pnY*, and return an HRESULT as the function value.

In the .odl file, the interface is described as follows (Lines.odl):

```
[
        uuid(3C591B25-1F13-101B-B826-00DD01103DE1),      // IID_IPoint.
        helpstring("Point object."),
        oleautomation,
        dual
    ]
```

```
interface IPoint : IDispatch
{
    [propget, helpstring("Returns and sets x coordinate.")]
    HRESULT x([out, retval] int* retval);
    [propput, helpstring("Returns and sets x coordinate.")]
    HRESULT x([in] int Value);

    [propget, helpstring("Returns and sets y coordinate.")]
    HRESULT y([out, retval] int* retval);
    [propput, helpstring("Returns and sets y coordinate.")]
    HRESULT y([in] int Value);
}
```

The attributes **oleautomation** and **dual** indicate that the interface supports both
IDispatch and VTBL binding. All of the member functions are declared with
HRESULT return values. The **Get** accessor functions, indicated by the **propget**
attribute, return their value in the last parameter. This parameter has the **out** and
retval attributes.

In the Lines sample, the Application object exposes the following method (App.cpp):

```
STDMETHODIMP
CApplication::CreatePoint(IPoint FAR* FAR* ppPoint)
{
    CPoint FAR* ppoint = NULL;
    HRESULT hr;

    // Create new item and QueryInterface for IDispatch.

    hr = CPoint::Create(&ppoint);
    if (FAILED(hr))
        {hr = RaiseException(IDS_OutOfMemory); goto error;}

    hr = ppoint->QueryInterface(IID_IDispatch, (void FAR* FAR*)ppPoint);
    if (FAILED(hr))
        {hr = RaiseException(IDS_Unexpected); goto error;}
    return NOERROR;

error:
    if (ppoint)
        delete ppoint;
    return hr;
}
```

The **CreatePoint** method creates a new point and returns a pointer to it in the
parameter pPoint.

In the Lines sample, the CLine object exposes the **Color** property. This property is implemented by the following accessor functions (Lines.cpp):

```
STDMETHODIMP
CLine::get_Color(long FAR* plColorref)
{
    *plColorref = m_colorref;
    return NOERROR;
}
STDMETHODIMP
CLine::put_Color(long lColorref)
{
    m_colorref = (COLORREF)lColorref;
    return NOERROR;
}
```

Implementing the Value Property

In the Lines sample, ILines.Item, IPoints.Item, and IApplication.Name are the Value properties of the objects ILines, IPoints, and IApplication, respectively. The ILines.Item object is described as follows:

```
interface ILines : IDispatch
{

// Some descriptions omitted for brevity.

    [propget, id(0), helpstring(
"Given an integer index, returns one of the lines in the collection")]
    HRESULT Item([in] long Index,[out, retval] ILine** retval);

}
```

Using this property, a user can refer to the fourth line in the collection as **ILines(4).Item** or simply as **ILines(4)**.

For more information on recommended objects, properties, and methods, see Chapter 4, "Standard Objects and Naming Guidelines."

Restricting Access to Objects

Automation provides several ways of restricting access to objects. The simplest approach is not to document the properties and methods you do not want users to see. Alternatively, you can prevent a property or method from appearing in type library browsers by specifying the **hidden** attribute in the .odl file.

The **restricted** attribute goes one step further, preventing user calls from binding to the property or method, as well as hiding it from type browsers. For example, the following restricts access to the **_NewEnum** property of the ILines object:

```
[propget, restricted, id(DISPID_NEWENUM)]          // Must be propget.
    HRESULT _NewEnum( [out, retval] IUnknown** retval);
```

Restricted properties and methods can be invoked by ActiveX clients, but are not visible to the user who may be using a language such as Visual Basic. In addition, they cannot be bound to by user calls.

Creating Collection Objects

A collection object contains a group of exposed objects of the same type and can iterate over them. Collection objects do not need an **IClassFactory** implementation, because they are accessed from elements that have their own class factories.

For example, the Lines sample has a collection object named CLines that iterates over a group of Line objects. The following routine creates and initializes the CLines collection object (Lines.cpp):

```
STDMETHODIMP
CLines::Create(ULONG lMaxSize, long lLBound, CPane FAR* pPane,
               CLines FAR* FAR* ppLines)
{
    HRESULT hr;
    CLines FAR* pLines = NULL;
    SAFEARRAYBOUND sabound[1];

    *ppLines = NULL;

    // Create new collection.

    pLines = new CLines();
    if (pLines == NULL)
        goto error;

    pLines->m_cMax = lMaxSize;
    pLines->m_cElements = 0;
    pLines->m_lLBound = lLBound;
    pLines->m_pPane = pPane;

    // Load type information for the Lines collection from type library.

    hr = LoadTypeInfo(&pLines->m_ptinfo, IID_ILines);
    if (FAILED(hr))
        goto error;

    // Create a safe array of variants used to implement the collection.

    sabound[0].cElements = lMaxSize;
    sabound[0].lLbound = lLBound;
    pLines->m_psa = SafeArrayCreate(VT_VARIANT, 1, sabound);
    if (pLines->m_psa == NULL)
    {
        hr = ResultFromScode(E_OUTOFMEMORY);
        goto error;
    }
```

```
        *ppLines = pLines;
        return NOERROR;

error:
    if (pLines == NULL)
        return ResultFromScode(E_OUTOFMEMORY);
    if (pLines->m_ptinfo)
        pLines->m_ptinfo->Release();
    if (pLines->m_psa)
        SafeArrayDestroy(pLines->m_psa);

    pLines->m_psa = NULL;
    pLines->m_ptinfo = NULL;

    delete pLines;
    return hr;
}
```

The parameters to **CLines::Create** specify the maximum number of lines that the collection can contain, the lower bound of the indexes of the collection, and a pointer to a pane, which contains the lines and points in the sample.

Implementing the IEnumVARIANT Interface for the Lines Application

In the Lines sample, **CEnumVariant** implements the **Next, Skip, Reset,** and **Clone** member functions (Enumvar.cpp):

```
STDMETHODIMP
CEnumVariant::Next(ULONG cElements, VARIANT FAR* pvar,
                    ULONG FAR* pcElementFetched)
{
    HRESULT hr;
    ULONG l;
    long l1;
    ULONG l2;

    if (pcElementFetched != NULL)
        *pcElementFetched = 0;

    // Retrieve the elements of the next cElements.

    for (l1=m_lCurrent, l2=0; l1<(long)(m_lLBound+m_cElements) &&
        l2<cElements; l1++, l2++)
    {
        hr = SafeArrayGetElement(m_psa, &l1, &pvar[l2]);
        if (FAILED(hr))
            goto error;
    }
```

```
    // Set count of elements retrieved.

    if (pcElementFetched != NULL)
        *pcElementFetched = 12;
    m_lCurrent = 11;

    return (12 < cElements) ? ResultFromScode(S_FALSE) : NOERROR;
error:
    for (l=0; l<cElements; l++)
        VariantClear(&pvar[l]);
    return hr;
}

STDMETHODIMP
CEnumVariant::Skip(ULONG cElements)
{
    m_lCurrent += cElements;
    if (m_lCurrent > (long)(m_lLBound+m_cElements))
    {
        m_lCurrent = m_lLBound+m_cElements;
        return ResultFromScode(S_FALSE);
    }
    else return NOERROR;
}

STDMETHODIMP
CEnumVariant::Reset()
{
    m_lCurrent = m_lLBound;
    return NOERROR;
}

STDMETHODIMP
CEnumVariant::Clone(IEnumVARIANT FAR* FAR* ppenum)
{
    CEnumVariant FAR* penum = NULL;
    HRESULT hr;

    *ppenum = NULL;

    hr = CEnumVariant::Create(m_psa, m_cElements, &penum);
    if (FAILED(hr))
        goto error;
    penum->AddRef();
    penum->m_lCurrent = m_lCurrent;

    *ppenum = penum;
    return NOERROR;
```

```
error:
    if (penum)
        penum->Release();
    return hr;
}
```

Implementing the _NewEnum Property for the Lines Application

The Lines sample contains two collections, Lines and Points, and implements a
_NewEnum property for each. Both are restricted properties, available to ActiveX
clients, but invisible to users of scripting or macro languages supported by ActiveX
clients. The property returns an enumerator (**IEnumVARIANT**) for the items in the
collection.

The following code implements the **_NewEnum** property for the Lines collection
(Lines.cpp):

```
STDMETHODIMP
CLines::get__NewEnum(IUnknown FAR* FAR* ppunkEnum)
{
    CEnumVariant FAR* penum = NULL;;
    HRESULT hr;

    *ppunkEnum = NULL;

    // Create a new enumerator for items currently in the collection and
    // QueryInterface for IUnknown.

    hr = CEnumVariant::Create(m_psa, m_cElements, &penum);
    if (FAILED(hr))
        {hr = RaiseException(IDS_OutOfMemory); goto error;}
    hr = penum->QueryInterface(IID_IUnknown, (VOID FAR* FAR*)ppunkEnum);
    if (FAILED(hr))
        {hr = RaiseException(IDS_Unexpected); goto error;}
    return NOERROR;

error:
    if (penum)
        delete penum;
    return hr;
}
```

Returning Errors

The Lines sample defines an exception handler that fills the EXCEPINFO structure and signals **IDispatch** to return DISP_E_EXCEPTION (App.cpp):

```
STDMETHODIMP
HRESULT RaiseException (int nID, Refguid rguid)
{
    extern return value g_scodes[];
    TCHAR szError[STR_LEN];
    ICreateErrorInfo *pcerrinfo;
    IErrorInfo *perrinfo;
    HRESULT hr;
    BSTR bstrDescription = NULL;

    if (LoadString(g_pApplication->m_hinst, nID, szError,
    sizeof(szError)));
    bstrDescription =   SysAllocString(TO_OLE_STRING(szError));

    // Set ErrInfo object so that VTBL binding controllers can get
    // rich error information. If the controller is using IDispatch to
    // access properties or methods, DispInvoke will fill the EXCEPINFO
    // structure using the values specified in the ErrorInfo object and
    // DispInvoke will return DISP_e_EXCEPTION. The property or method
    // must return a failure return value for DispInvoke to do this.

        hr = CreateErrorInfo(&pcerrinfo);
        if (SUCCEEDED(hr))
    {
        pcerrinfo->SetGUID(rguid);
        pcerrinfo->SetSource(g_pApplication->m_bstrProgID);
        if (bstrDescription)
            pcerrinfo->SetDescription(bstrDescription);
        hr = pcerrinfo->QueryInterface(IID_IerrorInfo, (LPVOID FAR*)
            &perrinfo);
        if (SUCCEEDED(hr))
    {
            SetErrorInfo(0, perrinfo);
            perrinfo->Release();
    }
    if (bstrDescription)
        SysFreeString(bstrDescription);
    return ResultFromScode(g_scodes[nID-1001]);
}
```

Properties and methods in the Lines sample call this routine when an exception occurs. **RaiseException** sets the system's error object, so that controller applications that call through VTBLs can retrieve rich error information. Controllers that call through **IDispatch::Invoke** will be returned with this error information by **DispInvoke** through the EXCEPINFO structure.

Passing Exceptions Through VTBLs

The Lines sample also provides rich error information for members invoked through VTBLs. Because VTBL-bound calls bypass the **IDispatch** interface, they cannot return exceptions through **IDispatch**. Instead, they must use the error handling interfaces in Automation. The **RaiseException** function shown in the example calls **CreateErrorInfo** to create an error object, then fills the object's data fields with information about the error. When all of the information has been successfully recorded, it calls **SetErrorInfo** to associate the error object with the current thread of execution.

ActiveX objects similar to the collection object (CApplication), which use the error interfaces, must also implement the **ISupportErrorInfo** interface. This interface identifies the object as supporting the error interfaces, and ensures that error information can be propagated correctly up the call chain. The following example shows how the Lines sample implements this interface (Errinfo.cpp):

```
STDMETHODIMP
CSupportErrorInfo::CSupportErrorInfo(IUnknown FAR* punkObject,
        REFIID riid)
{
    m_punkObject = punkObject;
    m_iid = riid;
}


CSupportErrorInfo::QueryInterface(REFIID iid, void FAR* FAR* ppv)
{
    return m_punkObject->QueryInterface(iid, ppv);
}


STDMETHODIMP_(ULONG)
CSupportErrorInfo::AddRef(void)
{
    return m_punkObject->AddRef();
}


STDMETHODIMP_(ULONG)
CSupportErrorInfo::Release(void)
{
    return m_punkObject->Release();
}
```

```
STDMETHODIMP
CSupportErrorInfo::InterfaceSupportsErrorInfo(REFIID riid)
{
    return (riid == m_iid) ? NOERROR : ResultFromScode(S_FALSE);
}
```

ISupportErrorInfo has the **QueryInterface**, **AddRef**, and Release methods
inherited from the **IUnknown** interface, along with the **InterfaceSupportsErrorInfo**
method. ActiveX clients call **InterfaceSupportsErrorInfo** to check whether the
ActiveX object supports the **IErrorInfo** interface, so they can access the error object.
For details, see Chapter 11, "Error Handling Interfaces."

Releasing OLE on Exit

The following code revokes an active Lines object, revokes the Lines class, and then
uninitializes OLE (Main.cpp):

```
void Uninitialize(DWORD dwRegisterCF, DWORD dwRegisterActiveObject)
{
    if (dwRegisterCF != 0)
        CoRevokeClassObject(dwRegisterCF);
    if (dwRegisterActiveObject != 0)
        RevokeActiveObject(dwRegisterActiveObject, NULL);
    OleUninitialize();
}
```

Writing an Object Description Script

An object description script is essentially an annotated header file, written in ODL.
The following example shows a portion of Lines.odl, the object description script for
the Lines sample.

```
[
    uuid(3C591B20-1F13-101B-B826-00DD01103DE1),     // LIBID_Lines.
    helpstring("Lines 1.0 Type Library"),
    lcid(0x09),
    version(1.0)
]

library Lines
{
    importlib("stdole.tlb");
    #define DISPID_NEWENUM -4

// Remaining code omitted for brevity.
```

The preceding entry describes the type library (Lines.tlb) created by the sample. The
items in square brackets are attributes, which provide additional information about the
library. In the example, the attributes give the library's UUID, a Help string, an LCID,
and a version number.

The **importlib** directive is similar to the C or C++ **#include** directive. It allows access to the type descriptions in the file Stdole.tlb from the Lines library. However, it does not copy those types into the Lines.tlb. To use Lines.tlb, both the Lines.tlb and Stdole.tlb files must be available.

By default, .odl files are preprocessed with the C preprocessor, so the **#include** and **#define** directives can be used.

The object description script continues with information on the objects in the type library:

```
[
    uuid(3C591B25-1F13-101B-B826-00DD01103DE1),        // IID_Ipoint.
    helpstring("Point object."),
    oleautomation,
    dual
]
interface IPoint : IDispatch
{
    [propget, helpstring("Returns and sets x coordinate.")]
    HRESULT x( [out, retval] int* retval);
    [propput, helpstring("Returns and sets x coordinate.")]
    HRESULT x([in] int Value);

    [propget, helpstring("Returns and sets y coordinate.")]
    HRESULT y( [out, retval] int* retval);
    [propput, helpstring("Returns and sets y coordinate.")]
    HRESULT y([in] int Value);
}

// Additional definitions omitted for brevity.

}
```

This entry describes the **IPoint** interface. The interface has the attributes **oleautomation** and **dual**, indicating that the types of all its properties and methods are compatible with Automation, and that it supports binding through both **IDispatch** and VTBLs. The **IPoint** interface has two pairs of property accessor functions, which set and return the **X** and **Y** properties.

The **Value** parameter of both the **X** and **Y** properties has the **in** attribute. These parameters supply a value and are read-only. Conversely, the *retval* parameter of each property has the **out** and **retval** attributes, indicating that it returns the value of the property.

Because **IPoint** supports VTBL binding and rich error information, its properties return HRESULTs and pass their function return values through *retval* parameters. For more information, see Chapter 8, "Type Libraries and the Object Description Language."

```
[
        uuid(3C591B21-1F13-101B-B826-00DD01103DE1),        // CLSID_Lines.
        helpstring("Lines Class"),
        appobject
    ]
    coclass Lines
    {
        [default] interface IApplication;
            interface IDispatch;
    }
}
```

The file concludes with the description of the Lines Application object, as specified by the **appobject** attribute. The **default** attribute applies to the **IApplication** interface, indicating that this interface will be returned by default.

Supporting Multiple National Languages

Applications sometimes need to expose objects with names that differ across localized versions of the product. The names pose a problem for programming languages that need to access these objects, because late binding will be sensitive to the locale of the application. The **IDispatch** interface provides a range of solutions that vary in cost of implementation and quality of language support. All methods of the **IDispatch** interface that are potentially sensitive to language are passed a LCID, which identifies the local language context.

The following are some of the approaches a class implementation can take:

- Accept any LCID and use the same member names in all locales. This is acceptable if the exposed interface will typically be accessed only by very advanced users. For example, the member names for OLE interfaces will never be localized.

- Accept all LCIDs supported by all versions of the product. In this case, the implementation of **GetIDsOfNames** would need to interpret the passed array of names based on the given LCID. This is the most acceptable solution because it allows users to write code in their natural language and run the code on any localized version of the application.

- Return an error (DISP_E_UNKNOWNLCID) from **GetIDsOfNames** if the caller's LCID does not match the localized version of the class. This prevents users from being able to write late-bound code that runs on machines with different localized implementations of the class.

- Recognize the particular version's localized names, as well as one language that is recognized in all versions. For example, a French version might accept French and English names, where English is the language supported in all versions. Users who want to write code that runs in all countries would have to use English names.

To provide general language support, the application should check the LCID before interpreting member names. Because **Invoke** is passed a LCID, methods can properly interpret parameters whose meaning varies by locale. The following sections provide examples and guidelines for creating multilingual applications.

Implementing IDispatch for Multilingual Applications

When creating applications that will support multiple languages, you need to create separate type libraries for each supported language, as well as for versions of the **IDispatch** member functions that include dependencies for each language. In the example below, the Hello sample code has been modified to define LCIDs for both U.S. English and German.

Implementing the IDispatch Member Functions

The following example code from the Hello sample implements language-sensitive versions of **GetTypeInfoCount, GetIDsOfNames,** and **Invoke.** Note that **Invoke** does not check the LCID, but merely passes it to **DispInvoke. GetTypeInfoCount** does not contain any language-specific information; however, **GetTypeInfo** does.

The **IDispatch** member functions must be implemented in such a way as to take into account any language-specific features. **DispInvoke** is passed only the U.S. English type information pointer.

```
STDMETHODIMP
CHello::GetTypeInfoCount(UINT FAR* pctinfo)
{
    *pctinfo = 1;
    return NOERROR;
}

STDMETHODIMP
CHello::GetTypeInfo(
        UINT itinfo,
        LCID lcid,
        ITypeInfo FAR* FAR* pptinfo)
{
    LPTYPEINFO ptinfo;
    *pptinfo = NULL;

    if(itinfo != 0)
        return ResultFromScode(DISP_E_BADINDEX);

    if(lcid == LOCALE_SYSTEM_DEFAULT || lcid == 0)
        lcid = GettSystemDefaultLCID();

    if(lcid == LOCALE_USER_DEFAULT)
        lcid = GetUserDefaultLCID();
```

```
        switch(lcid)
        {
            case LCID_GERMAN:
                ptinfo = m_ptinfoGerman;
                break;

            case LCID_ENGLISH:
                ptinfo = m_ptinfoEnglish;
                break;

            default:
                return ResultFromScode(DISP_E_UNKNOWNLCID);
        }

        ptinfo->AddRef();
        *pptinfo = ptinfo;
        return NOERROR;
}

STDMETHODIMP
CHello::GetIDsOfNames(
        REFIID riid,
        OLECHAR FAR* FAR* rgszNames,
        UINT cNames,
        LCID lcid,
        DISPID FAR* rgdispid)
{
    LPTYPEINFO ptinfo;

    if(lcid == LOCALE_SYSTEM_DEFAULT || lcid == 0)
        lcid = GetSystemDeraultLCID();

    if(lcid == LOCALE_USER_DEFAULT)
        lcid = GetUserDefaultLCID();

    switch(lcid)
    {
        case LCID_GERMAN:
            ptinfo = m_ptinfoGerman;
            break;

        case LCID_ENGLISH:
            ptinfo = m_ptinfoEnglish;
            break;

        default:
            return ResultFromScode(DISP_E_UNKNOWNLCID);
    }
    return DispGetIDsOfNames(ptinfo, rgszNames, cNames, rgdispid);
}
```

```
STDMETHODIMP
CHello::Invoke(
    DISPID dispidMember,
    REFIID riid,
    LCID lcid,
    WORD wFlags,
    DISPPARAMS FAR* pdispparams,
    VARIANT FAR* pvarResult,
    EXCEPINFO FAR* pexcepinfo,
    UINT FAR* puArgErr)
{

    return DispInvoke(
    this, m_ptinfoEnglish,
    dispidMember, wFlags, pdispparams,
    pvarResult, pexcepinfo, puArgErr);
}


}
```

Creating Separate Type Libraries

For each supported language, write and register a separate type library. The type libraries use the same DISPIDs and globally unique identifiers, but you should localize names and Help strings based on the language. You must also define the LCIDs for the supported languages.

The following registration file example includes entries for U.S. English and German.

```
; Type library registration information.

HKEY_CLASSES_ROOT\TypeLib\{F37C8060-4AD5-101B-B826-00DD01103DE1}
HKEY_CLASSES_ROOT\TypeLib\{F37C8060-4AD5-101B-B826-00DD01103DE1}\2.0 =Hello 2.0 Type
Library
HKEY_CLASSES_ROOT\TypeLib\{F37C8060-4AD5-101B-B826-00DD01103DE1}\2.0\HELPDIR =

; U.S. English.

HKEY_CLASSES_ROOT\TypeLib\{F37C8060-4AD5-101B-B826-00DD01103DE1}\2.0\409\win32 =
helloeng.tlb

; German.

HKEY_CLASSES_ROOT\TypeLib\{F37C8060-4AD5-101B-B826-00DD01103DE1}\2.0\407\win32 =
helloger.tlb
```

Defining the Locale IDs

Refer to the next section to obtain the language identifiers (LANGIDs) for the supported languages.

```
// Locale IDs for the languages that are supported.

#define LCID_ENGLISH MAKELCID(MAKELANGID(0x09, 0x01))
#define LCID_GERMAN  MAKELCID(MAKELANGID(0x07, 0x01))
```

Using the example code from the Hello sample, define member variables that can be used to contain U.S. English and German type information.

```
class FAR CHello : public IHello
{
public:

// Code omitted for brevity.

private:
    LPTYPEINFO m_ptinfoEnglish; // English type information of Hello
                                // application interface.
    LPTYPEINFO m_ptinfoGerman;  // German type information of Hello
                                // application interface.
    // Remaining code omitted for brevity.
};
```

Loading Type information

The following example uses the Hello sample code to illustrate the **LoadTypeInfo** function that loads locale-specific type library information when an object is created.

```
LoadTypeInfo(&phello->m_ptinfoEnglish, IID_IHello, LCID_ENGLISH);
LoadTypeInfo(&phello->m_ptinfoGerman, IID_IHello, LCID_GERMAN);

// LoadTypeInfo - Gets type information of an object's interface from
// the type library.

// Parameters:
// ppunkStdDispatch - Returns type information.
// clsid - Interface ID of object in type library.
// lcid - Locale ID of type information to be loaded.

// Return Value:
// HRESULT
```

```
HRESULT LoadTypeInfo(ITypeInfo FAR* FAR* pptinfo, REFCLSID clsid,
LCID lcid)
{
    HRESULT hr;
    LPTYPELIB ptlib = NULL;
    LPTYPEINFO ptinfo = NULL;

    *pptinfo = NULL;

    // Load type library.

    hr = LoadRegTypeLib(LIBID_Hello, 2, 0, lcid, &ptlib);
    if (FAILED(hr))
        return hr;

    // Get type information for interface of the object.

    hr = ptlib->GetTypeInfoOfGuid(clsid, &ptinfo);
    if (FAILED(hr))
    {
        ptlib->Release();
        return hr;
    }

    ptlib->Release();
    *pptinfo = ptinfo;
    return NOERROR;
}
```

Interpreting Arguments and Strings Based on the Locale ID

Some methods or properties need to interpret arguments based on the LCID. These methods or properties can require that an LCID be passed as an argument. Therefore, properties should be designed to have an LCID parameter.

The following example code of an object description language file implements a property that takes a LCID.

```
[
    uuid(83219430-CB36-11cd-B774-00DD01103DE1),
    helpstring("Bank Account object."),
    oleautomation,
    dual
    ]
```

```
interface IBankAccount : IDispatch
{
    [propget, helpstring("Returns account balance formatted for the
        country described by localeID.")]
    HRESULT CheckingBalance([in, lcid] long localeID, [out, retval]
    BSTR* retval);

    // Remaining code omitted for brevity.
}
```

In this example, **get_CheckingBalance** returns a currency string that contains the balance in the checking account. The currency string should be correctly formatted depending on the locale that is passed in. **ConvertCurrency** is a private function that converts the checking balance to the currency of the country described by the LCID. The string form of converted currency is placed in **m_szBalance**. **GetCurrencyFormat** is a 32-bit Windows function that formats a currency string for the given locale.

The following represents the information contained in the header file:

```
class FAR CBankAccount : public IBankAccount
{
    public:

    // IUnknown methods (omitted).


    // IDispatch methods (omitted).

    // IBankAccount methods.

    STDMETHOD(get_CheckingBalance)(long llcid, BSTR FAR* pbstr);

    // Remaining code omitted for brevity.
}
```

The following represents the .cpp file:

```
STDMETHODIMP
CBankAccount::get_CheckingBalance(long llcid, BSTR FAR* pbstr)
{
    TCHAR ach[100];
    ConvertCurrency(llcid);
        GetCurrencyFormat(llcid, 0, m_szBalance, NULL, ach,
        sizeof(ach));
        *pbstr = SysAllocString(ach);           // Return currency string
                                                // formatted according to
                                                // locale ID.


        return NOERROR;
}
```

The LCID is commonly used to parse strings that contain locale-dependent information. For example, a function that takes a string such as "6/11/96" needs the LCID to determine whether the month is June (6) or November (11). You should not use the LCID for output strings, including error strings. These strings should always be displayed in the current system language.

Locale, Language, and Sublanguage IDs

The following macro is defined for creating LCIDs (Winnt.h for 32-bit systems; Olenls.h for 16-bit systems and Macintosh):

```
// LCID creation/extraction macros:
// MAKELCID - construct locale ID from language ID and
// country code.

#define MAKELCID(1) ((DWORD)(((WORD)(1)) | (((DWORD)((WORD)(0))) <<
16)))
```

There are two predefined LCID values. The system default locale is LOCALE_SYSTEM_DEFAULT, and the current user's locale is LOCALE_USER_DEFAULT.

Another macro constructs a LANGID:

```
// Language ID creation/extraction macros:
// MAKELANGID - Construct language ID from primary language ID and
// sublanguage ID.

#define MAKELANGID(p, s)        (((((USHORT)(s)) << 10) | (USHORT)(p))
```

The following three combinations of primary LANGID and sublanguage identifier (SUBLANGID) have special meanings:

Primary LANGID	SUBLANGID	Result
LANG_NEUTRAL	SUBLANG_NEUTRAL	Language neutral
LANG_NEUTRAL	SUBLANG_SYS_DEFAULT	System default language
LANG_NEUTRAL	SUBLANG_DEFAULT	User default language

For primary LANGIDs, the range 0x200 to 0x3ff is user definable. The range 0x000 to 0x1ff is reserved for system use. For SUBLANGIDs, the range 0x20 to 0x3f is user definable. The range 0x00 to 0x1f is reserved for system use.

Language Tables

The following table lists the primary LANGIDs supported by Automation. For more information about national language support for 16-bit Windows systems, refer to Appendix A, "National Language Support Functions." For information about 32-bit Windows systems, see your operating system documentation.

Language	PRIMARYLANGID
Neutral	0x00
Chinese	0x04
Czech	0x05
Danish	0x06
Dutch	0x13
English	0x09
Finnish	0x0b
French	0x0c
German	0x07
Greek	0x08
Hungarian	0x0e
Icelandic	0x0F
Italian	0x10
Japanese	0x11
Korean	0x12
Norwegian	0x14
Polish	0x15
Portuguese	0x16
Russian	0x19
Slovak	0x1b
Spanish	0x0a
Swedish	0x1d
Turkish	0x1F

The following table lists the SUBLANGIDs supported by Automation. For more information about national language support for 16-bit systems, refer to Appendix A, "National Language Support Functions." For information about 32-bit Windows systems, see your operating system documentation.

Sublanguage	SUBLANGID
Neutral	0x00
Default	0x01
System Default	0x02
Chinese (Simplified)	0x02
Chinese (Traditional)	0x01
Czech	0x01
Danish	0x01
Dutch	0x01
Dutch (Belgian)	0x02
English (U.S.)	0x01
English (UK)	0x02
English (Australian)	0x03
English (Canadian)	0x04
English (Irish)	0x06
English (New Zealand)	0x05
Finnish	0x01
French	0x01
French (Belgian)	0x02
French (Canadian)	0x03
French (Swiss)	0x04
German	0x01
German (Swiss)	0x02
German (Austrian)	0x03
Greek	0x01
Hungarian	0x01
Icelandic	0x01
Italian	0x01
Italian (Swiss)	0x02
Japanese	0x01
Korean	0x01
Norwegian (Bokmal)	0x01
Norwegian (Nynorsk)	0x02
Polish	0x01

Sublanguage	SUBLANGID
Portuguese	0x02
Portuguese (Brazilian)	0x01
Russian	0x01
Slovak	0x01
Spanish (Castilian)[1]	0x01
Spanish (Mexican)	0x02
Spanish (Modern)[1]	0x03
Swedish	0x01
Turkish	0x01

[1] The only difference between Spanish (Castilian) and Spanish (Modern) is the sort ordering. The LCType values are the same.

CHAPTER 3

Accessing ActiveX Objects

To access exposed objects, you can create ActiveX clients using Visual Basic, Visual C++, Microsoft Excel, and other applications and programming languages that support the Automation technology. This chapter discusses several strategies for accessing exposed objects.

- Creating scripts with Visual Basic.
- Creating controllers that manipulate objects.
- Creating type information browsers.

Regardless of your strategy, an ActiveX client needs to follow these steps:

▶ **To initialize and create the object**

1. Initialize OLE.
2. Create an instance of the exposed object.

▶ **To manipulate methods and properties**

1. Get information about the object's methods and properties.
2. Invoke the methods and properties.

▶ **To release OLE when the application or programming tool terminates**

1. Revoke the active object.
2. Uninitialize OLE.

Note Throughout this chapter, the file names of sample applications appear in parentheses before the sample code.

Creating Scripts Using Visual Basic

Visual Basic provides a complete programming environment for creating Windows applications with which you can manipulate the exposed ActiveX objects of other applications. Internally, Visual Basic fully supports Automation dual interfaces.

For the syntax and semantics of the Automation features, see the Visual Basic Help file, Vb.hlp. To see how the Visual Basic statements translate into ActiveX application programming interfaces (APIs), refer to Appendix C, "Information for Visual Basic Programmers."

Note   Visual Basic is not necessary to use Automation. It is presented here as an example of a programming tool that supports Automation and is convenient for packaging Automation scripts. Optionally, a different ActiveX client can be used for testing.

Exposed objects can be called directly from programs written with Visual Basic. The following figure shows how this was done for the sample program Hello.exe.

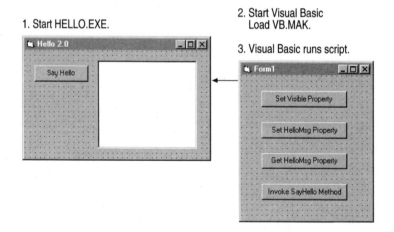

▶ **To access an exposed object**

1. Start Visual Basic. (Initialization and release of OLE is handled automatically by Visual Basic.)

2. To select the type library of the object, click **Tools** on the **References** menu.

3. Add code to declare a variable of the interface type. For example:

```
Dim HelloObj As IHello
```

4. Add code in event procedures to create an instance of the object and to manipulate the object using its properties and methods. For example:

```
Sub Form_Load ( )
    Set HelloObj = New Hello.Hello
End Sub
Sub SetVisible_Click ( )
    HelloObj.Visible = True
End Sub
```

5. Click **Start** on the **Run** menu, and then trigger the event by clicking the form.

The following figure shows the interfaces you use when accessing exposed objects through Visual Basic.

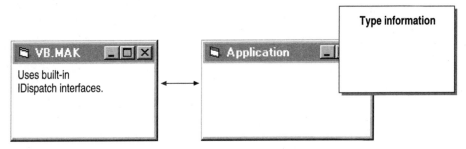

Accessing a Remote Object

With Visual Basic, accessing a remote object requires only that the program declare an object variable and assign the return of a **New** statement to the variable. The following is the syntax for the statements:

***Dim** ObjectVar **As** InterfaceName*
***Set** ObjectVar = **New** CoClassName*

The **Dim** statement declares a variable of an interface type. The **New** keyword creates an instance of an object. Used together, the two declare and create an instance of an ActiveX object. For example:

```
Dim MyLines As ILines
Set MyLines = New Lines.Lines
```

The **Dim** statement declares the object variable MyLines of the interface type **ILines.** The **Set** statement assigns a new object of the *component object class* (coclass) Lines to the variable MyLines. When you use the **Dim** statement to set a variable to an interface type, subsequent uses of the variable will execute faster than with the generic Object syntax.

The **New** keyword applies only to creating coclasses of interface or dispinterface types. To create other types of objects, the variable must be declared with the **Dim** statement, and the **CreateObject** function used as follows:

Set ObjectVar = *CreateObject(*ProgID*)*

CreateObject creates an ActiveX object, based on the specified programmatic identifier (ProgID). The ProgID has the form:

AppName.ObjectName

The *AppName* is the name of the application, and the *ObjectName* identifies the type of object to create. For more information about ProgIDs, see "Registering the Application" in Chapter 2, "Exposing ActiveX Objects."

You can use the **GetObject** function to re-establish the reference to the most recently used object that corresponds to the *Filename* and *AppName.ObjectName* specification, as follows:

Set ObjectVar = *GetObject("*Filename*",* ProgID*)*

For example, if the ActiveX client needs an existing instance of an object instead of a new instance, it can use the **GetObject** function.

The Hello sample application, included in the Win32 Software Development Kit (SDK), displays a Hello message in response to a mouse click. You can add a simple form that accesses the Hello application's exposed object from another process.

▶ **To add a form**

1. Start Visual Basic.
2. Click **Open Project** on the **File** menu.
3. In the dialog box, click Vb.mak in the Sample directory.
4. In the **Forms** box, click **View Form** to see the form, or click **View Code** to see the Visual Basic code.

```
' Module-level declarations

Dim HelloObj As IHello

Sub Form_load ( )
    Set HelloObj = New Hello.Hello
End Sub

Sub Invoke_SayHello_Method_Click ( )
    HelloObj.SayHello

End Sub
```

```
Sub Get_HelloMsg_Property_Click ()
    Debug.Print HelloObj.HelloMessage
End Sub

Sub Set_HelloMsg_Property_Click ( )
    HelloObj.HelloMessage = "Hello Universe"
End Sub

Sub SetVisible_Click ( )
    HelloObj.Visible = True
End Sub
```

The **Form_Load** subroutine creates the Hello Application object. Other subroutines manipulate the Hello Application object through the **Visible** and HelloMessage properties and the SayHello method.

To program an object in Visual Basic, you need its class name and the names and parameters of its properties and methods. For the Hello sample application, you need to know the exact names of the SayHello method, and the **Visible** and HelloMsg properties, along with the types of their arguments. This information is provided in the documentation for many objects, such as those exposed by Microsoft Excel. You can also get the information by viewing the object's type library with an object browser, such as the one included in Visual Basic. A sample browser, Browse, is provided in the Win32 SDK.

Creating an Invisible Object

In the preceding section, Visual Basic was used to access and program a form-based interface for the Hello sample. The Hello Application object was started as invisible, and was later displayed when its **Visible** property was set to **True**. Some objects are not visible, and some objects are never displayed to the user.

For example, a word-processing application may expose its spelling checker engine as an object. This object might support a method called CheckWord that takes a string as an argument. If the string is spelled correctly, the method returns **True**; otherwise, the method returns **False**. If the string is spelled incorrectly, it could be passed to another (hypothetical) method called SuggestWord that returns a suggestion for its correct spelling. The code might look something like this.

```
Sub CheckSpelling ()
    Dim ObjVar As New SpellChecker
    Dim MyWord, Result

    MyWord = "potatoe"

    ' Check the spelling.

    Result = ObjVar.CheckWord MyWord
```

```
' If False, get suggestion.

If Not Result Then
    MyWord = ObjVar.SuggestWord MyWord
End If
End Sub
```

In this example, the spelling checker is never displayed to the user. Its capabilities are exposed through the properties and methods of the spelling checker object.

As shown in the example, invisible objects can be created and referenced in the same way as any other type of object.

Activating an Object from a File

Many Automation applications let the user save objects in files. For example, a spreadsheet application that supports Worksheet objects lets the user save the worksheet in a file. The same application may also support a Chart object that the user can save in a file.

To activate an object from a file, first declare an object variable, and then call the **GetObject** function using the following syntax:

GetObject (filename[, ProgID])

The *filename* argument is a string containing the full path and name of the file to be activated. For example, an application named SpdSheet.exe creates an object that was saved in a file named Revenue.spd. The following code invokes Spdsheet.exe, loads the file Revenue.spd, and assigns Revenue.spd to an object variable:

```
Dim Ss As Spreadsheet
Set Ss = GetObject("C:\Accounts\Revenue.spd")
```

If the *filename* argument is omitted, then **GetObject** returns the currently active object of the specified ProgID. For example:

```
Set Ss = GetObject (,"SpdSheet.Application")
```

If there is no active object of the class SpdSheet.Application, an error will occur.

In addition to activating an entire file, some applications let you activate part of a file. To activate part of a file, add an exclamation point (!) or a backslash (\) to the end of the file name, followed by a string that identifies the part of the file you want to activate. For information on how to create this string, refer to the object's documentation.

For example, if SpdSheet.exe is a spreadsheet application that uses R1C1 syntax, the following code could be used to activate a range of cells within Revenue.spd:

```
Set Ss = GetObject("C:\Accounts\Revenue.spd!R1C1:R10C20")
```

These examples invoke an application and activate an object. In these examples, the application name (SpdSheet.exe) is never specified. When **GetObject** is used to activate an object, the registry files determine the application to invoke and the object to activate based on the file name or ProgID that is provided. If a ProgID is not provided, Automation activates the default object of the specified file.

Some ActiveX components, however, support more than one class of object. Suppose the spreadsheet file, Revenue.spd, supports three different classes of objects: an Application object, a Worksheet object, and a Toolbar object, all of which are part of the same file. To specify which object to activate, an argument must be supplied for the optional ProgID parameter. For example:

```
Set Ss = GetObject("C:\Revenue.spd", "SpdSheet.Toolbar")
```

This statement activates the SpdSheet.Toolbar object in the file Revenue.spd.

Accessing Linked and Embedded Objects

Some applications that supply objects support linking and embedding as well as Automation. Using the ActiveX control (Msole2.vbx) from the OLE toolkit, you can create and display embedded objects in a Visual Basic application. If the objects also support Automation, you can access their properties and methods by using the **Object** property. The **Object** property returns the object in the ActiveX control. This property refers to an ActiveX object in the same way an object variable created with the functions **New**, **CreateObject**, or **GetObject** refers to the object.

For example, an ActiveX control named Ole1 contains an object that supports Automation. This object has an **Insert** method, a **Select** method, and a **Bold** property. In this case, the following code could be written to manipulate the ActiveX control's object:

```
' Insert text in the object.
Ole1.Object.Insert "Hello, world."
' Select the text.
Ole1.Object.Select
' Format the text as bold.
Ole1.Object.Bold = True
```

Manipulating Objects

Once a variable has been created that references an ActiveX object, the object can be manipulated in the same way as any other Visual Basic object. To get and set an object's properties, or to perform an object's methods, use the *object.property* or *object.method* syntax. Multiple objects, properties, and methods can be included on the same line of code using the following syntax:

```
ObjVar.Cell(1,1).FontBold = True
```

Accessing the Properties of an Object

To assign a value to a property of an object, put the object variable and property name on the left side of an assignment, and the desired property setting on the right side. For example:

```
Dim ObjVar As IMyInterface
Dim RowPos, ColPos
Set ObjVar = New MyObject

ObjVar.Text = "Hello, world"
ObjVar.Cell(RowPos, ColPos) = "This property accepts two arguments."

' Sets the font for ObjVar.Selection.

ObjVar.Selection.Font = 12
```

Property values can also be retrieved from an object:

```
Dim X As Object

X = ObjVar.Text
X = ObjVar.Range(12, 32)
```

Invoking Methods

In addition to getting and setting properties, an object can be manipulated using the methods it supports. Some methods may return a value, as in the following example:

```
X = ObjVar.Calculate(1,2,3)
```

Methods that do not return a value behave like subroutines. For example:

```
' This method requires two arguments.
ObjVar.Move XPos, YPos
```

If such a method is assigned to a variable, an error will occur.

Creating Applications and Tools That Access Objects

Automation provides interfaces for accessing exposed objects from an application or programming tool written in C or C++. The following sections show C++ code that uses the same type of access method as the Visual Basic code, which is described earlier in this chapter. Although the process is more complex with C++ than with Visual Basic, the approach is similar. This section shows the minimum code necessary to access and manipulate a remote object.

You can use the **IDispatch** interface to access ActiveX objects, or you can access objects directly through the VTBL. Because VTBL references can be bound at compile time, VTBL access is generally faster than through **IDispatch**. Whenever possible, use the **ITypeInfo** or **ITypeInfo2** interfaces to get information about an object, including the VTBL addresses of the object's members. Then, use this information to access ActiveX objects through the VTBL.

To create compilers and other programming tools that use information from type libraries, use the **ITypeComp** interface. This interface binds to exposed objects at compile time. For details on **ITypeComp**, see Chapter 9, "Type Description Interfaces."

Accessing Members Through VTBLs

For objects that have dual interfaces, the first seven members of the VTBL are the members of **IUnknown** and **IDispatch**, and the subsequent members are standard COM entries for the interface's member functions. You can call these entries directly from C++.

▶ **To access a method or property through the VTBL**

1. Initialize OLE.

2. Create an instance of the exposed object.

3. Manipulate the properties and methods of the object.

4. Uninitialize OLE.

The code sample that follows shows how to access a property of the Hello object. Error handling has been omitted for brevity (Hello.vbp).

```
HRESULT hr;
CLSID clsid;                        // Class ID of Hello object.
LPUNKNOWN punk = NULL;              // Unknown of Hello object.
IHello* phello = NULL;             // IHello interface of Hello object.

// Initialize OLE.
hr = OleInitialize(NULL);

// Retrieve CLSID from the ProgID for Hello.
hr = CLSIDFromProgID("Hello.Application", &clsid);

// Create an instance of the Hello object and ask for its
// IDispatch interface.
hr = CoCreateInstance(clsid, NULL, CLSCTX_SERVER,
                      IID_IUnknown, (void FAR* FAR*)&punk);
```

```
hr = punk->QueryInterface(IID_IHello, (void FAR* FAR*)&pHello);

punk->Release();                    // Release when no longer needed.

hr = pHello->put_Visible (TRUE);

// Additional code to work with other methods and properties
// (omitted).

OleUninitialize();
```

The example initializes OLE, and then calls the **CLSIDFromProgID** function to obtain the class identifier (CLSID) for the Hello application. With the CLSID, the example can call **CoCreateInstance** to create an instance of the Hello Application object. **CoCreateInstance** returns a pointer to the object's **IUnknown** interface (punk), and this, in turn, is used to call **QueryInterface** to get pHello, a pointer to the IID_IHello dual interface. The punk is no longer needed, so the example releases it. The example then sets the value of the **Visible** property to **True**.

If the function returns an error HRESULT, you can get detailed, contextual information through the **IErrorInfo** interface. For details, see Chapter 11, "Error Handling Interfaces."

Accessing Members Through IDispatch

To bind to exposed objects at run time, use the **IDispatch** interface.

▶ **To create an ActiveX client using IDispatch**

1. Initialize OLE.

2. Create an instance of the object you want to access. The object's ActiveX component creates the object.

3. Obtain a reference to the object's **IDispatch** interface (if it has implemented one).

4. Manipulate the object through the methods and properties exposed in its **IDispatch** interface.

5. Terminate the object by invoking the appropriate method in its **IDispatch** interface, or by releasing all references to the object.

6. Uninitialize OLE.

The following table shows the minimum set of functions necessary to manipulate a remote object.

Function	Purpose	Interface
OleInitialize	Initializes OLE.	OLE API function
CoCreateInstance	Creates an instance of the class represented by the specified CLSID, and returns a pointer to the object's **IUnknown** interface.	Component object API function
QueryInterface	Checks whether **IDispatch** has been implemented for the object. If so, returns a pointer to the **IDispatch** implementation.	**IUnknown**
GetIDsOfNames	Returns dispatch identifiers (DISPIDs) for properties and methods and their parameters.	**IDispatch**
Invoke	Invokes a method, or sets or gets a property of the remote object.	**IDispatch**
Release	Decrements the reference count for an **IUnknown** or **IDispatch** object.	**IUnknown**
OleUninitialize	Uninitializes OLE.	OLE API function

The code that follows is extracted from a generalized Windows-based ActiveX client. The controller relies on helper functions provided in the file Invhelp.cpp, which is available in the Browse directory of the samples. Error checking is omitted to save space, but would normally be used where an HRESULT is returned.

The two functions that follow initialize OLE, and then create an instance of an object and get a pointer to the object's **IDispatch** interface (Invhelp.cpp):

```
BOOL InitOle(void)
{
    if(OleInitialize(NULL) != 0)
        return FALSE;

    return TRUE;
}
HRESULT CreateObject(LPSTR pszProgID, IDispatch FAR* FAR* ppdisp)
{
    CLSID clsid;                    // CLSID of ActiveX object.
    HRESULT hr;
    LPUNKNOWN punk = NULL;          // IUnknown of ActiveX object.
    LPDISPATCH pdisp = NULL;        // IDispatch of ActiveX object.

    *ppdisp = NULL;
```

```
                    // Retrieve CLSID from the ProgID that the user specified.

                    hr = CLSIDFromProgID(pszProgID, &clsid);
                    if (FAILED(hr))
                        goto error;

                    // Create an instance of the ActiveX object and ask for the
                    // IDispatch interface.

                    hr = CoCreateInstance(clsid, NULL, CLSCTX_SERVER,
                                            IID_IUnknown, (void FAR* FAR*)&punk);
                    if (FAILED(hr))
                        goto error;

                    hr = punk->QueryInterface(IID_IDispatch, (void FAR* FAR*)&pdisp);
                    if (FAILED(hr))
                        goto error;

                    *ppdisp = pdisp;
                    punk->Release();
                    return NOERROR;

            error:
                if (punk) punk->Release();
                if (pdisp) pdisp->Release();
                return hr;
            }
```

The **CreateObject** function is passed a ProgID and returns a pointer to the **IDispatch** implementation of the specified object. **CreateObject** calls the OLE API **CLSIDFromProgID** to get the CLSID that corresponds to the requested object, and then passes the CLSID to **CoCreateInstance** to create an instance of the object and get a pointer to the object's **IUnknown** interface. (The **CLSIDFromProgID** function is described in the *OLE Programmer's Reference.*) With this pointer, **CreateObject** calls **IUnknown::QueryInterface,** specifying IID_IDispatch, to get a pointer to the object's **IDispatch** interface.

```
HRESULT FAR
Invoke(LPDISPATCH pdisp,
    WORD wFlags,
    LPVARIANT pvRet,
    EXCEPINFO FAR* pexcepinfo,
    UINT FAR* pnArgErr,
    LPSTR pszName,
    char *pszFmt,
    ...)
```

```
{
    va_list argList;
    va_start(argList, pszFmt);
    DISPID dispid;
    HRESULT hr;
    VARIANTARG* pvarg = NULL;

    if (pdisp == NULL)
        return ResultFromScode(E_INVALIDARG);
    // Get DISPID of property/method.

    hr = pdisp->GetIDsOfNames(IID_NULL, &pszName, 1,
        LOCALE_SYSTEM_DEFAULT, &dispid);
    if(FAILED(hr))
        return hr;

    DISPPARAMS dispparams;
    _fmemset(&dispparams, 0, sizeof dispparams);

    // Determine number of arguments.

    if (pszFmt != NULL)
        CountArgsInFormat(pszFmt, &dispparams.cArgs);

    // Property puts have a named argument that represents the value
    // being assigned to the property.

    DISPID dispidNamed = DISPID_PROPERTYPUT;
    if (wFlags & DISPATCH_PROPERTYPUT)
    {
        if (dispparams.cArgs == 0)
            return ResultFromScode(E_INVALIDARG);
        dispparams.cNamedArgs = 1;
        dispparams.rgdispidNamedArgs = &dispidNamed;
    }
    if (dispparams.cArgs != 0)
    {
        // Allocate memory for all VARIANTARG parameters.
        pvarg = new VARIANTARG[dispparams.cArgs];
        if(pvarg == NULL)
            return ResultFromScode(E_OUTOFMEMORY);
        dispparams.rgvarg = pvarg;
        _fmemset(pvarg, 0, sizeof(VARIANTARG) * dispparams.cArgs);
```

```
            // Get ready to traverse the vararg list.

            LPSTR psz = pszFmt;
            pvarg += dispparams.cArgs - 1;    // Params go in opposite order.

      while (psz = GetNextVarType(psz, &pvarg->vt))
            {
                if (pvarg < dispparams.rgvarg)
                {
                    hr = ResultFromScode(E_INVALIDARG);
                    goto cleanup;
                }
                switch (pvarg->vt)
                {
                case VT_I2:
                    V_I2(pvarg) = va_arg(argList, short);
                    break;
                case VT_I4:
                    V_I4(pvarg) = va_arg(argList, long);
                    break;

                // Additional cases omitted to save space.

                default:
                    {
                        hr = ResultFromScode(E_INVALIDARG);
                        goto cleanup;
                    }
                    break;
                }
                --pvarg;                    // Get ready to fill next argument.
            }
        }

        // Initialize return variant, in case caller forgot. Caller can pass
        // Null if no return value is expected.

        if (pvRet)
            VariantInit(pvRet);

        // Make the call.

        hr = pdisp->Invoke(dispid, IID_NULL, LOCALE_SYSTEM_DEFAULT, wFlags,
            &dispparams, pvRet, pexcepinfo, pnArgErr);
```

```
cleanup:

    // Clean up any arguments that need it.

if (dispparams.cArgs != 0)
    {
        VARIANTARG FAR* pvarg = dispparams.rgvarg;
        UINT cArgs = dispparams.cArgs;
        while (cArgs--)
        {
            switch (pvarg->vt)
            {
            case VT_BSTR:
                VariantClear(pvarg);
                break;
            }
            ++pvarg;
        }
    }
    delete dispparams.rgvarg;
    va_end(argList);
    return hr;
}
```

In this example, the **Invoke** function is a general-purpose function that calls
IDispatch::Invoke to invoke a property or method of an ActiveX object. As
arguments, it accepts the object's **IDispatch** implementation, the name of the member
to invoke, flags that control the invocation, and a variable list of the member's
arguments. It can be found in the Browse sample in the file Invelp.cpp.

Using the object's **IDispatch** implementation and the name of the member, it calls
GetIDsOfNames to get the DISPID of the requested member. The member's DISPID
must be used later, in the call to **IDispatch::Invoke**.

The invocation flags specify whether a method, PROPERTYPUT, or
PROPERTYGET function is being invoked. The helper function simply passes these
flags directly to **IDispatch::Invoke**.

The helper function next fills in the DISPPARAMS structure with the parameters of
the member. DISPPARAMS structures have the following form:

```
typedef struct FARSTRUCT tagDISPPARAMS
{
    VARIANTARG FAR* rgvarg;              // Array of arguments.
    DISPID FAR* rgdispidNamedArgs;       // DISPIDs of named arguments.
    UINT cArgs;                          // Number of arguments.
    UINT cNamedArgs;                     // Number of named arguments.
} DISPPARAMS;
```

The *rgvarg* field is a pointer to an array of VARIANTARG structures. Each element of the array specifies an argument, whose position in the array corresponds to its position in the parameter list of the method definition. The *cArgs* field specifies the total number of arguments, and the *cNamedArgs* field specifies the number of named arguments.

For methods and property get functions, all arguments can be accessed as positional, or they can be accessed as named arguments. Property put functions have a named argument that is the new value for the property. The DISPID of this argument is DISPID_PROPERTYPUT.

To build the *rgvarg* array, the **Invoke** helper function retrieves the parameter values and types from its own argument list, and constructs a VARIANTARG structure for each one. (For a description of the format string that specifies the types of the parameters, see the file Invhelp.cpp.) Parameters are put in the array in reverse order, so that the last parameter is in *rgvarg*[0], and so forth. Although VARIANTARG has the following five fields, only the first and fifth are used.

```
typedef struct FARSTRUCT tagVARIANT VARIANTARG;

struct FARSTRUCT tagVARIANT
{
    VARTYPE vt;
    unsigned short wReserved1;
    unsigned short wReserved2;
    unsigned short wReserved3;
    union
    {
        short        iVal;        // VT_I2

    // The rest of this union specifies numerous other types (omitted).

    };
} VARIANTARG;
```

The first field contains the argument's type, and the fifth contains its value. To pass a long integer, for example, the *vt* and *iVal* fields of the VARIANTARG structure would be filled with VT_I4 (long integer) and the actual value of the long integer.

In addition, for property put functions, the first element of the *rgdispidNamedArgs* array must contain DISPID_PROPERTYPUT.

After filling the DISPPARAMS structure, the **Invoke** helper function initializes pvRet, a variant in which **IDispatch::Invoke** returns a value from the method or property. The following is the actual call to **IDispatch::Invoke**:

```
hr = pdisp->Invoke(dispid, IID_NULL, LOCALE_SYSTEM_DEFAULT, wFlags,
        &dispparams, pvRet, pexcepinfo, pnArgErr);
```

The variable pdisp is a pointer to the object's **IDispatch** interface. DISPID indicates the method or property being invoked. The value IID_NULL must be specified for all **IDispatch::Invoke** calls, and LOCALE_SYSTEM_DEFAULT is a constant denoting the default locale identifier (LCID) for this system. In the final two arguments, pexcepinfo and pnArgErr, **IDispatch::Invoke** can return error information.

If the invoked member has defined an exception handler, it returns exception information in pexcepinfo. If certain errors occur in the argument vector, pnArgErr points to the errant argument. The function return value hr is an HRESULT that indicates success or various types of failure.

For more information, including how to pass optional arguments, see "**IDispatch::Invoke**" in Chapter 5, "Dispatch Interface and API Functions."

Creating Type Information Browsers

Type information browsers let users scan type libraries to determine what types of objects are available. The following figure shows the interfaces you can use when creating compilers or browsers that access type libraries.

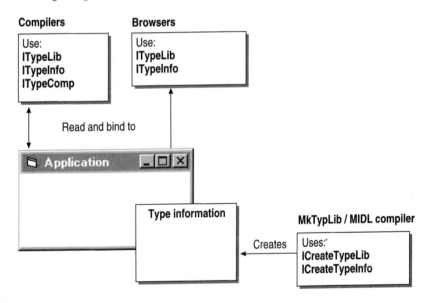

The Browse and BrowseH samples show how a browser might access a type library. The Browse sample is a Windows-based browser that presents a dialog box from which type information items can be selected to display. This example function prompts for the name of the type library, opens the library, and gathers and displays information.

C H A P T E R   4

Standard Objects and Naming Guidelines

This chapter describes the standard ActiveX objects, and discusses naming guidelines for creating objects that are unique to applications, especially user-interactive applications that support a multiple-document interface (MDI). If an ActiveX object is not user-interactive or supports only a single-document interface (SDI), the standards and guidelines should be adapted as appropriate.

- *Standard objects* comprise a set of objects defined by Automation. You can use them as appropriate to your application. The objects described in this chapter are oriented toward document-based, user-interactive applications. Other applications (such as noninteractive database servers) may have different requirements.

- *Naming guidelines* are recommendations meant to improve consistency across applications.

This chapter also provides examples in a hypothetical syntax derived from Visual Basic. The standards and guidelines are subject to change.

Using Standard Objects

The following table lists the Automation standard objects. Although none of these objects are required, user-interactive applications with subordinate objects should include an Application object.

Object name	Description
Application	Top-level object. Provides a standard way for ActiveX clients to retrieve and navigate an application's subordinate objects.
Document	Provides a way to open, print, change, and save an application document.
Documents	Provides a way to iterate over and select open documents in MDI applications.
Font	Describes fonts that are used to display or print text.

The following illustration shows how the standard objects fit into the organization of objects provided by an application.

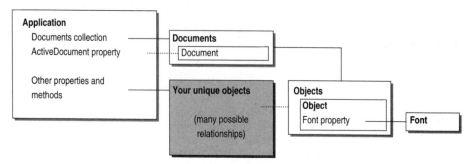

The following sections describe the standard properties and methods for all objects, all collection objects, and each of the standard objects. These sections list the standard methods and properties for each object, as well as the standard arguments for those properties and methods.

Note You can define additional application-specific properties and methods for each object. You can also provide additional optional arguments for any of the listed properties or methods; however, the optional arguments should follow the standard arguments in a positional argument list.

Object Properties

All objects, including the Application object and collection objects, must provide the following properties:

Property name	Return type	Description
Application	VT_DISPATCH	Returns the Application object; read only.
Parent	VT_DISPATCH	Returns the creator of the object; read only.

Note The **Application** and **Parent** properties of the Application object return the Application object.

Collection Object Properties

A collection provides a set of objects over which iteration can be performed. All collection objects must provide the following properties:

Property name	Return type	Description
Count	VT_I4	Returns the number of items in the collection; read only. Required.
_NewEnum	VT_DISPATCH	A special property that returns an enumerator object that implements **IEnumVARIANT**. Required.

Collection Methods

Methods for collections are described in the following table. The **Item** method is required; other methods are optional.

Method name	Return type	Description
Add	VT_DISPATCH or VT_EMPTY	Adds an item to a collection. Returns VT_DISPATCH if object is created (object cannot exist outside the collection) or VT_EMPTY if no object is created (object can exist outside the collection).
Item	Varies with type of collection	Returns the indicated item in the collection. Required. The **Item** method may take one or more arguments to indicate the element within the collection to return. This method is the default member (DISPID_VALUE) for the collection object.
Remove	VT_EMPTY	Removes an item from a collection. Uses indexing arguments in the same way as the **Item** method.

All collection objects must provide at least one form of indexing through the **Item** method. The dispatch identifier (DISPID) of the **Item** method is DISPID_VALUE. Because it is the default member, it can be used in the following form:

```
ThirdDef = MyWords(3).Definition
```

Which is equivalent to:

```
MyWords.Item(3).Definition
```

The **Item** method takes one or more arguments to indicate the index. Indexes can be numbers, strings, or other types. For example:

```
DogDef = MyWords("dog").Definition
```

Note Within the application's type library, the **_NewEnum** property has a special DISPID: DISPID_NEWENUM. The name **_NewEnum** should not be localized.

The **Add** method may take one or more arguments. For example, if **MyWord** is an object with the properties **Letters** and **Definition**:

```
Dim MyWord As New Word
Dim MyDictionary As Words
MyWord = "dog"
MyWord.Letters = "Dog"
MyWord.Definition = "My best friend."
MyDictionary.Add MyWord
MyDictionary.Remove("Dog")
```

For more information about creating collection objects, see Chapter 2, "Exposing ActiveX Objects."

Kinds of Collections

The standard for collections lets you describe two kinds of collections, depending on whether it makes sense for the collected objects to exist outside the collection.

In some cases, it is not logical for an object to exist independently of its collection. For example, an application's Documents collection contains all Document objects currently open. Opening a document means adding it to the collection, and closing the document means removing it from the collection. All open documents are part of the collection. The application cannot have open documents that are not part of the collection. The relationship between the collection and the members of the collection can be shown in the following ways:

- **Documents.Add** creates an object (an open document) and adds it to the collection. Because an object is created, a reference to it is returned.

  ```
  Set MyDoc = Documents.Add
  ```

- **Document.Close** removes an object from the collection.

  ```
  Set SomeDoc = Documents(3)
  SomeDoc.Close
  ```

In other cases, it is logical for the objects to exist outside the collection. For example, a Mail application might have Name objects, and many collections of these Name objects. Each Name object would have a user's e-mail name, full name, and possibly other information. The e-mail name and full name would likely be properties named EmailName and FullName.

Additionally, the application might have the following collections of Name objects.

- A collection for the "To" list on each piece of e-mail.
- A collection of the names of the people to whom a user has sent e-mail.

The collections of Name objects could be indexed by using either EmailName or FullName.

For these collections, the **Add** method does not create an object because the object already exists. Therefore, the **Add** method should take an object as an argument, and should not return a value.

Assuming the existence of two collections (AddressBook and ToList), a user might execute the following code to add a Name object to the ToList collection:

```
Dim Message As Object
Dim AddressBook As Object
Dim NameRef As Object

' Code omitted for brevity.

Set NameRef = AddressBook.Names("Fred Funk")
Message.ToList.Add    NameRef
```

The Name object already exists and is contained in the AddressBook collection. The first line of code obtains a reference to the Name object for "Fred Funk" and points to NameRef. The second line of code adds a reference to the object to the ToList collection. No new object is created, so no reference is returned from the **Add** method.

Unlike the relationship between Documents and Document, there is no way for the collected object (the Name) to know how to remove itself from the collections in which it is contained. To remove an item from a collection, use the **Remove** method, as follows:

```
Message.ToList.Remove("Fred Funk")
```

This line of code removes the Name object that has the FullName "Fred Funk." The "Fred Funk" object may exist in other collections, but they will be unaffected.

Using the Application Object in a Type Library

If you use a type library, the Application object should be the object that has the **appobject** attribute. Because some ActiveX clients use the type information to allow unqualified access to the Application object's members, it is important to avoid overloading the Application object with too many members.

The Application object should have the properties listed in the following table. The **Application, FullName, Name, Parent,** and **Visible** properties are required; other properties are optional.

Property name	Return type	Description
ActiveDocument	VT_DISPATCH, VT_EMPTY	Returns the active document object or VT_EMPTY if none; read only.
Application	VT_DISPATCH	Returns the Application object; read only. Required.
Caption	VT_BSTR	Sets or returns the title of the application window; read/write. Setting the **Caption** to VT_EMPTY returns control to the application.
DefaultFilePath	VT_BSTR	Sets or returns the default path specification used by the application for opening files; read/write.
Documents	VT_DISPATCH	Returns a collection object for the open documents; read only.
FullName	VT_BSTR	Returns the file specification for the application, including path; read only. For example, C:\Drawdir\Scribble. Required.
Height	VT_R4	Sets or returns the distance between the top and bottom edge of the main application window; read/write.
Interactive	VT_BOOL	Sets or returns True if the application accepts actions from the user, otherwise False; read/write.
Left	VT_R4	Sets or returns the distance between the left edge of the physical screen and the main application window; read/write.
Name	VT_BSTR	Returns the name of the application, such as "Microsoft Excel"; read only. The **Name** property is the default member (DISPID_VALUE) for the Application object. Required.
Parent	VT_DISPATCH	Returns the Application object; read only. Required.
Path	VT_BSTR	Returns the path specification for the application's executable file; read only. For example, C:\Drawdir if the .exe file is C:\Drawdir\Scribble.exe.
StatusBar	VT_BSTR	Sets or returns the text displayed in the status bar; read/write.

Property name	Return type	Description
Top	VT_R4	Sets or returns the distance between the top edge of the physical screen and main application window; read/write.
Visible	VT_BOOL	Sets or returns whether the application is visible to the user; read/write. The default is False when the application is started with the **/Automation** command-line switch. Required.
Width	VT_R4	Sets or returns the distance between the left and right edges of the main application window; read/write.

The Application object should have the following methods. The **Quit** method is required; other methods are optional.

Method name	Return type	Description
Help	VT_EMPTY	Displays online Help. May take three optional arguments: *helpfile* (VT_BSTR), *helpcontextID* (VT_I4), and *helpstring* (VT_BSTR). The *helpfile* argument specifies the Help file to display; if omitted, the main Help file for the application is displayed. The *helpcontextID* and *helpstring* arguments specify a Help context to display; only one of them can be supplied. If both are omitted, the default Help topic is displayed.
Quit	VT_EMPTY	Exits the application and closes all open documents. Required.
Repeat	VT_EMPTY	Repeats the previous action in the user interface.
Undo	VT_EMPTY	Reverses the previous action in the user interface.

Document Object Properties

If the application is document based, it should provide a Document object named Document. Use a different name only if Document is inappropriate (for example, if the application uses highly technical or otherwise specialized terminology within its user interface).

The Document object should have the properties listed in the table that follows. The properties **Application, FullName, Name, Parent, Path,** and **Saved** are required; other properties are optional.

Property name	Return type	Description
Application	VT_DISPATCH	Returns the Application object; read only. Required.
Author	VT_BSTR	Sets or returns summary information about the document's author; read/write.
Comments	VT_BSTR	Sets or returns summary information comments for the document; read/write.
FullName	VT_BSTR	Returns the file specification of the document, including the path; read only. Required.
Keywords	VT_BSTR	Sets or returns summary information keywords associated with the document; read/write.
Name	VT_BSTR	Returns the file name of the document, not including the file's path specification; read only.
Parent	VT_DISPATCH	Returns the **Parent** property of the Document object; read only. Required.
Path	VT_BSTR	Returns the path specification for the document, not including the file name or file name extension; read only. Required.
ReadOnly	VT_BOOL	Returns True if the file is read only, otherwise False; read only.
Saved	VT_BOOL	Returns True if the document has never been saved, but has not changed since it was created. Returns True if it has been saved and has not changed since last saved. Returns False if it has never been saved and has changed since it was created; or if it was saved, but has changed since last saved. Read only; required.
Subject	VT_BSTR	Sets or returns summary information about the subject of the document; read/write.
Title	VT_BSTR	Sets or returns summary information about the title of the document; read/write.

The Document object should have the methods listed in the following table. The methods **Activate, Close, Print, Save,** and **SaveAs** are required; other methods are optional.

Method name	Return type	Description
Activate	VT_EMPTY	Activates the first window associated with the document. Required.
Close	VT_EMPTY	Closes all windows associated with the document and removes the document from the Documents collection. Required. Takes two optional arguments, *saveChanges* (VT_BOOL) and *filename* (VT_BSTR). The *filename* argument specifies the name of the file in which to save the document.
NewWindow	VT_EMPTY	Creates a new window for the document.
Print	VT_EMPTY	Prints the document. Required. Takes three optional arguments: *from* (VT_I2), *to* (VT_I2), and *copies* (VT_I2). The *from* and *to* arguments specify the page range to print. The *copies* argument specifies the number of copies to print.
PrintOut	VT_EMPTY	Same as **Print** method, but provides an easier way to use the method in Visual Basic, because **Print** is a Visual Basic keyword.
PrintPreview	VT_EMPTY	Previews the pages and page breaks of the document. Equivalent to clicking **Print Preview** on the **File** menu.
RevertToSaved	VT_EMPTY	Reverts to the last saved copy of the document, and discards any changes.
Save	VT_EMPTY	Saves changes to the file specified in the document's **FullName** property. Required.
SaveAs	VT_EMPTY	Saves changes to a file. Required. Takes one optional argument, *filename* (VT_BSTR). The *filename* argument can include an optional path specification.

Documents Collection Object

If your application supports a multiple-document interface (MDI), you should provide a Documents collection object. Use the name Documents for this collection, unless the name is inappropriate for the application.

The Documents collection object should have all of the following properties.

Property name	Return type	Description
Application	VT_DISPATCH	Returns the Application object; read only. Required.
Count	VT_I4	Returns the number of items in the collection; read only. Required.
_NewEnum	VT_DISPATCH	A special property that returns an enumerator object that implements **IEnumVARIANT**. Required.
Parent	VT_DISPATCH	Returns the parent of the Documents collection object; read only. Required.

The Documents collection object should have all of the following methods.

Method name	Return type	Description
Add	VT_DISPATCH	Creates a new document and adds it to the collection. Returns the document that was created. Required.
Close	VT_EMPTY	Closes all documents in the collection. Required.
Item	VT_DISPATCH or VT_EMPTY	Returns a Document object from the collection or returns VT_EMPTY if the document does not exist. Takes an optional argument, *index*, which may be a string (VT_BSTR) indicating the document name, a number (VT_I4) indicating the ordered position within the collection, or either (VT_VARIANT). If *index* is omitted, returns the Document collection. The **Item** method is the default member (DISPID_VALUE). Required.
Open	VT_DISPATCH or VT_EMPTY	Opens an existing document and adds it to the collection. Returns the document that was opened, or VT_EMPTY if the object could not be opened. Takes one required argument, *filename*, and one optional argument, *password*. Both arguments have the type VT_BSTR. Required.

The Font Object

The Font object may be appropriate for some applications. The properties **Application, Bold, Italic, Parent,** and **Size** are required; other properties are optional. The Font object should have the following properties.

Property name	Return type	Description
Application	VT_DISPATCH	Returns the Application object; read only. Required.
Bold	VT_BOOL	Sets or returns True if the font is bold, otherwise False; read/write. Required.
Color	VT_I4	Sets or returns the RGB color of the font; read/write.
Italic	VT_BOOL	Sets or returns True if the font is italic; otherwise False, read/write. Required.
Name	VT_BSTR	Returns the name of the font; read only.
OutlineFont	VT_BOOL	Sets or returns True if the font is scaleable, otherwise False. For example, bitmapped fonts are not scaleable, whereas TrueType fonts are scaleable; read/write.
Parent	VT_DISPATCH	Returns the parent of the Font object; read only. Required.
Shadow	VT_BOOL	Sets or returns True if the font appears with a shadow, otherwise False; read/write.
Size	VT_R4	Sets or returns the point size of the font; read/write. Required.
Strikethrough	VT_BOOL	Sets or returns True if the font appears with a line running through it, otherwise False; read/write.
Subscript	VT_BOOL	Sets or returns True if the font is subscripted, otherwise False; read/write.
Superscript	VT_BOOL	Sets or returns True if the font is superscripted, otherwise False; read/write.

Naming Conventions

Choose names for exposed objects, properties, and methods that can be easily understood by users of the application. The guidelines in this section apply to all of the following exposed items:

- Objects — implemented as classes in an application.
- Properties and methods — implemented as members of a class.
- Named arguments — implemented as named parameters in a member function.
- Constants and enumerations — implemented as settings for properties and methods.

Use Entire Words or Syllables

It is easier for users to remember complete words than to remember whether you abbreviated Window as Wind, Wn, or Wnd.

When you need to abbreviate because an identifier would be too long, try to use complete initial syllables. For example, use AltExpEval instead of AlternateExpressionEvaluation.

Use	Don't use
Application	App
Window	Wnd

Use Mixed Case

All identifiers should use mixed case, rather than underscores, to separate words.

Use	Don't use
ShortcutMenus	Shortcut_Menus, Shortcutmenus, SHORTCUTMENUS, SHORTCUT_MENUS
BasedOn	basedOn

Use the Same Word Used in the Interface

Use consistent terminology. Do not use names like HWND that are based on Hungarian notation. Try to use the same word users would use to describe a concept.

Use	Don't use
Name	Lbl

Use the Correct Plural for the Class Name

Collection classes should use the correct plural for the class name. For example, if you have a class named Axis, store the collection of Axis objects in an Axes class. Similarly, a collection of Vertex objects should be stored in a Vertices class. In cases where English uses the same word for the plural, append the word "Collection."

Use	Don't use
Axes	Axiss
SeriesCollection	CollectionSeries
Windows	ColWindow

Using plurals rather than inventing new names for collections reduces the number of items a user must remember, and simplifies the selection of names for collections.

For some collections, however, this may not be appropriate, especially where a set of objects exists independently of the collection. For example, a Mail program might have a Name object that exists in several collections, such as ToList, CCList, and GroupList. In this case, you might specify the individual name collections as ToNames, CCNames, and GroupNames.

Exposing Programmability Interfaces

Embeddable objects, including ActiveX controls, often require access to the programmabilty interfaces of their containers. Similarly, containers often require access to the programmabilty interfaces of their embedded objects.

The following sections describe the standards for exposing the programmability interfaces from various components. With the advent of document objects and ActiveX controls on the Internet, adhering to these standards will become increasingly important.

Accessing the Containing Document

Objects that are embedded in a container often require access to that container's programmability interface (for example, its **IDispatch** implementation). The container should implement its document-level programmabity interface (for example, the Document object) that matches the one used by **IOleContainer** (either VTBL or **IDispatch**). To access the containing document, an object can call **IOleClientSite::GetContainer**, which returns a pointer to **IOleContainer**, and can then call **QueryInterface** for the appropriate interface (usually **IID_IDispatch**).

Embedded objects can also access type information by using VTBL binding to dual interfaces, calling **QueryInterface** to **IOleContainer** for **IProvideClassInfo**.

Accessing the Containing Application

Embedded objects that require access to the Application object of their container (the top-level programmability object for the process) should use the **ServiceProvider** interfaces to access it.

Containers should implement **IServiceProvider** with the same implementation as with **IOleClientSite**, and at the minimum, should support **SID_Application**. If the container can also be embedded, use its container's **IServiceProvider** implementation to access the Application object. If an error occurs, embedded objects should perform a **QueryInterface** on **IOleClientSite** for **IServiceProvider** and use **IServiceProvider** to request **SID_Application**.

The standards for Automation specify that document-level objects in an application's programmability model should support the **Parent** and **Application** properties. If this also doesn't work (because the immediate container does not support **IServiceProivder,** or **SID_Application**), an embedded object can access the containing application by calling **IOleClientSite::GetContainer, QueryInterface(IID_IDispatch,** followed by **IDispatch::GetIDsOfNames**. This gets the DISPID for the **Parent** or **Application** property.

Reference Information

C H A P T E R 5

Dispatch Interface and API Functions

The dispatch interfaces provide a way to expose and access objects within an application. Automation defines the following dispatch interfaces and functions.

- **IDispatch** interface—Exposes objects, methods, and properties to Automation programming tools and other applications.
- Dispatch API functions—Simplifies the implementation of the **IDispatch** interface. Use these functions to generate an **IDispatch** interface automatically.
- **IEnumVARIANT** interface—Provides a way for ActiveX clients to iterate over collection objects. This is a dispatch interface.

Overview of the IDispatch Interface

The following table describes the member functions of the **IDispatch** interface.

Interface	Member function	Purpose
IDispatch	**GetIDsOfNames**	Maps a single member name and an optional set of argument names to a corresponding set of integer dispatch identifiers (DISPIDs), which can then be used on subsequent calls to **Invoke**.
	GetTypeInfo	Retrieves the type information for an object.
	GetTypeInfoCount	Retrieves the number of type information interfaces that an object provides (either 0 or 1).
	Invoke	Provides access to properties and methods exposed by an object.

Implementing the IDispatch Interface

IDispatch is located in the Oleauto.h header file on 32-bit systems, and in Dispatch.h on 16-bit systems.

ActiveX or OLE objects can implement the **IDispatch** interface for access by ActiveX clients, such as Visual Basic. The object's properties and methods can be accessed using **IDispatch::GetIDsOfNames** and **IDispatch::Invoke**.

The following examples show how to access an ActiveX or OLE object through the **IDispatch** interface. The code is abbreviated for brevity, and omits error handling.

```
// Declarations of variables used.
    DEFINE_GUID(CLSID_Hello,     // Portions omitted for brevity.

    HRESULT hresult;
    IUnknown * punk;
    IDispatch * pdisp;
    OLECHAR FAR* szMember = "SayHello";
    DISPID dispid;
    DISPPARAMS dispparamsNoArgs = {NULL, NULL, 0, 0};
    EXCEPINFO excepinfo;
    UINT nArgErr;
```

In the following code, the **OleInitialize** function loads the OLE dynamic-link libraries (DLLs), and the **CoCreateInstance** function initializes the ActiveX or OLE object's class factory. For more information on these two functions, see the *OLE Programmer's Reference* in the Win32 Software Development Kit (SDK).

```
// Initialize OLE DLLs.
hresult = OleInitialize(NULL);

// OLE function CoCreateInstance starts application using GUID.
hresult = CoCreateInstance(CLSID_Hello, NULL, CLSCTX_SERVER,
IID_IUnknown, (void FAR* FAR*)&punk);
```

QueryInterface checks whether the object supports **IDispatch**. (As with any call to **QueryInterface**, the returned pointer must be released when it is no longer needed.)

```
// Call QueryInterface to see if object supports IDispatch.
hresult = punk->QueryInterface(IID_IDispatch, &pdisp);
```

GetIDsOfNames retrieves the DISPID for the indicated method or property, in this case, szMember.

```
// Retrieve the dispatch identifier for the SayHello method.
// Use defaults where possible.
hresult = pdisp->GetIDsOfNames(
    IID_NULL,
    &szMember,
    1,
    LOCALE_USER_DEFAULT,
    &dispid);
```

In the following call to **Invoke**, the DISPID indicates the property or method to invoke. The **SayHello** method does not take any parameters, so the fifth argument (*&dispparamsNoArgs*), contains a Null and 0, as initialized at declaration.

To invoke a property or method that requires parameters, supply the parameters in the DISPPARAMS structure.

```
// Invoke the method. Use defaults where possible.
hresult = pdisp->Invoke(
    dispid,
    IID_NULL,
    LOCALE_SYSTEM_DEFAULT,
    DISPATCH_METHOD,
    &dispparamsNoArgs,
    NULL,
    NULL,
    NULL);
```

IDispatch::GetIDsOfNames

HRESULT GetIDsOfNames(

REFIID *riid*,

OLECHAR FAR* FAR* *rgszNames*,

unsigned int *cNames*,

LCID *lcid*,

DISPID FAR* *rgDispId*

);

Maps a single member and an optional set of argument names to a corresponding set of integer DISPIDs, which can be used on subsequent calls to **IDispatch::Invoke**. The dispatch function **DispGetIDsOfNames** provides a standard implementation of **GetIDsOfNames**.

Parameters

riid
Reserved for future use. Must be IID_NULL.

rgszNames
Passed-in array of names to be mapped.

cNames
Count of the names to be mapped.

lcid
The locale context in which to interpret the names.

rgDispId
Caller-allocated array, each element of which contains an identifier (ID) corresponding to one of the names passed in the *rgszNames* array. The first element represents the member name. The subsequent elements represent each of the member's parameters.

Return Value

The return value obtained from the returned HRESULT is one of the following:

Return value	Meaning
S_OK	Success.
E_OUTOFMEMORY	Out of memory.
DISP_E_UNKNOWNNAME	One or more of the names were not known. The returned array of DISPIDs contains DISPID_UNKNOWN for each entry that corresponds to an unknown name.
DISP_E_UNKNOWNLCID	The locale identifier (LCID) was not recognized.

Comments

An **IDispatch** implementation can associate any positive integer ID value with a given name. Zero is reserved for the default, or **Value** property; –1 is reserved to indicate an unknown name; and other negative values are defined for other purposes. For example, if **GetIDsOfNames** is called, and the implementation does not recognize one or more of the names, it returns DISP_E_UNKNOWNNAME, and the *rgDispId* array contains DISPID_UNKNOWN for the entries that correspond to the unknown names.

The member and parameter DISPIDs must remain constant for the lifetime of the object. This allows a client to obtain the DISPIDs once, and cache them for later use.

When **GetIDsOfNames** is called with more than one name, the first name (*rgszNames*[0]) corresponds to the member name, and subsequent names correspond to the names of the member's parameters.

The same name may map to different DISPIDs, depending on context. For example, a name may have a DISPID when it is used as a member name with a particular interface, a different ID as a member of a different interface, and different mapping for each time it appears as a parameter.

The **IDispatch** interface binds to names at run time. To bind at compile time instead, an **IDispatch** client can map names to DISPIDs by using the type information interfaces described in Chapter 9, "Type Description Interfaces." This allows a client to bind to members at compile time and avoid calling **GetIDsOfNames** at run time. For a description of binding at compile time, see Chapter 9, "Type Description Interfaces."

The implementation of **GetIDsOfNames** is case insensitive. Users that need case-sensitive name mapping should use type information interfaces to map names to DISPIDs, rather than call **GetIDsOfNames**.

Examples

The following code from the Lines sample file Lines.cpp implements the **GetIDsOfNames** member function for the CLine class. The ActiveX or OLE object uses the standard implementation, **DispGetIDsOfNames**.

```
STDMETHODIMP
CLine::GetIDsOfNames(
        REFIID riid,
        OLECHAR FAR* FAR* rgszNames,
        UINT cNames,
        LCID lcid,
        DISPID FAR* rgDispId)
{
        return DispGetIDsOfNames(m_ptinfo, rgszNames, cNames, rgDispId);
}
```

The following code might appear in an ActiveX client that calls **GetIDsOfNames** to get the DISPID of the **CLine Color** property.

```
HRESULT hresult;
IDispatch FAR* pdisp = (IDispatch FAR*)NULL;
DISPID dispid;
OLECHAR FAR* szMember = "color";

// Code that sets a pointer to the dispatch (pdisp) is omitted.

hresult = pdisp->GetIDsOfNames(
    IID_NULL,
    &szMember,
    1, LOCALE_SYSTEM_DEFAULT,
    &dispid);
```

See Also

CreateStdDispatch, DispGetIDsOfNames, ITypeInfo::GetIDsOfNames

IDispatch::GetTypeInfo

HRESULT GetTypeInfo

unsigned int *iTInfo*,

LCID *lcid*,

ITypeInfo FAR* FAR* *ppTInfo*

);

Retrieves the type information for an object, which can then be used to get the type information for an interface.

Parameters

iTInfo

The type information to return. Pass 0 to retrieve type information for the **IDispatch** implementation.

lcid

The locale identifier for the type information. An object may be able to return different type information for different languages. This is important for classes that support localized member names. For classes that do not support localized member names, this parameter can be ignored.

ppTInfo

Receives a pointer to the requested type information object.

Return Value

The return value obtained from the returned HRESULT is one of the following:

Return value	Meaning
S_OK	Success; the type information element exists.
DISP_E_BADINDEX	Failure; *iTInfo* argument was not 0.
TYPE_E_ELEMENTNOTFOUND	Failure; *iTInfo* argument was not 0.

Example

The following code from the sample file Lines.cpp loads information from the type library and implements the member function **GetTypeInfo**:

```
// These lines are from CLines::Create load type information for the
// Lines collection from the type library.

    hr = LoadTypeInfo(&pLines->m_ptinfo, IID_ILines);
    if (FAILED(hr))
        goto error;

// Additional code omitted for brevity.
// This function implements GetTypeInfo for the CLines collection.
```

```
STDMETHODIMP
CLines::GetTypeInfo(
        UINT iTInfo,
        LCID lcid,
        ITypeInfo FAR* FAR* ppTInfo)
{
    *ppTInfo = NULL;

    if(iTInfo != 0)
        return ResultFromScode(DISP_E_BADINDEX);

    m_ptinfo->AddRef();
    *ppTInfo = m_ptinfo;

    return NOERROR;
}
```

See also   **CreateStdDispatch, CreateDispTypeInfo.**

IDispatch::GetTypeInfoCount

HRESULT GetTypeInfoCount(

unsigned int FAR* *pctinfo*

);

Retrieves the number of type information interfaces that an object provides (either 0 or 1).

Parameter   *pctinfo*
                   Points to a location that receives the number of type information interfaces provided by the object. If the object provides type information, this number is 1; otherwise the number is 0.

Return Value   The return value obtained from the returned HRESULT is one of the following:

Return value	Meaning
S_OK	Success.
E_NOTIMPL	Failure.

Comments   The function may return zero, which indicates that the object does not provide any type information. In this case, the object may still be programmable through **IDispatch**, but does not provide type information for browsers, compilers, or other programming tools that access type information. This can be useful for hiding an object from browsers or for preventing early binding on an object.

Example

This code from the Lines sample file Lines.cpp implements the **GetTypeInfoCount** member function for the **CLines** class (ActiveX or OLE object).

```
STDMETHODIMP
CLines::GetTypeInfoCount(UINT FAR* pctinfo)
{
    *pctinfo = 1;
    return NOERROR;
}
```

See Also

CreateStdDispatch

IDispatch::Invoke

HRESULT Invoke(

DISPID *dispIdMember,*

REFIID *riid,*

LCID *lcid,*

WORD *wFlags,*

DISPPARAMS FAR* *pDispParams,*

VARIANT FAR* *pVarResult,*

EXCEPINFO FAR* *pExcepInfo,*

unsigned int FAR* *puArgErr*

);

Provides access to properties and methods exposed by an object. The dispatch function **DispInvoke** provides a standard implementation of **IDispatch::Invoke**.

Parameters

dispIdMember

Identifies the member. Use **GetIDsOfNames** or the object's documentation to obtain the dispatch identifier.

riid

Reserved for future use. Must be IID_NULL.

lcid

The locale context in which to interpret arguments. The *lcid* is used by the **GetIDsOfNames** function, and is also passed to **Invoke** to allow the object to interpret its arguments specific to a locale.

Applications that do not support multiple national languages can ignore this parameter. For more information, refer to "Supporting Multiple National Languages" in Chapter 2, "Exposing ActiveX Objects."

wFlags

Flags describing the context of the **Invoke** call, include:

Value	Description
DISPATCH_METHOD	The member is invoked as a method. If a property has the same name, both this and the DISPATCH_PROPERTYGET flag may be set.
DISPATCH_PROPERTYGET	The member is retrieved as a property or data member.
DISPATCH_PROPERTYPUT	The member is changed as a property or data member.
DISPATCH_PROPERTYPUTREF	The member is changed by a reference assignment, rather than a value assignment. This flag is valid only when the property accepts a reference to an object.

pDispParams

Pointer to a structure containing an array of arguments, an array of argument DISPIDs for named arguments, and counts for the number of elements in the arrays. See the Comments section that follows for a description of the DISPPARAMS structure.

pVarResult

Pointer to the location where the result is to be stored, or Null if the caller expects no result. This argument is ignored if DISPATCH_PROPERTYPUT or DISPATCH_PROPERTYPUTREF is specified.

pExcepInfo

Pointer to a structure that contains exception information. This structure should be filled in if DISP_E_EXCEPTION is returned. Can be Null.

puArgErr

The index within *rgvarg* of the first argument that has an error. Arguments are stored in *pDispParams->rgvarg* in reverse order, so the first argument is the one with the highest index in the array. This parameter is returned only when the resulting return value is DISP_E_TYPEMISMATCH or DISP_E_PARAMNOTFOUND. For details, see "Returning Errors" in the following Comments section.

Return Value

The return value obtained from the returned HRESULT is one of the following:

Return value	Meaning
S_OK	Success.
DISP_E_BADPARAMCOUNT	The number of elements provided to DISPPARAMS is different from the number of arguments accepted by the method or property.

Return value	Meaning
DISP_E_BADVARTYPE	One of the arguments in *rgvarg* is not a valid variant type.
DISP_E_EXCEPTION	The application needs to raise an exception. In this case, the structure passed in *pExcepInfo* should be filled in.
DISP_E_MEMBERNOTFOUND	The requested member does not exist, or the call to **Invoke** tried to set the value of a read-only property.
DISP_E_NONAMEDARGS	This implementation of **IDispatch** does not support named arguments.
DISP_E_OVERFLOW	One of the arguments in *rgvarg* could not be coerced to the specified type.
DISP_E_PARAMNOTFOUND	One of the parameter DISPIDs does not correspond to a parameter on the method. In this case, *puArgErr* should be set to the first argument that contains the error.
DISP_E_TYPEMISMATCH	One or more of the arguments could not be coerced. The index within *rgvarg* of the first parameter with the incorrect type is returned in the *puArgErr* parameter.
DISP_E_UNKNOWNINTERFACE	The interface identifier passed in *riid* is not IID_NULL.
DISP_E_UNKNOWNLCID	The member being invoked interprets string arguments according to the LCID, and the LCID is not recognized. If the LCID is not needed to interpret arguments, this error should not be returned.
DISP_E_PARAMNOTOPTIONAL	A required parameter was omitted.

In 16-bit versions, you can define your own errors using the MAKE_SCODE value macro.

Comments   Generally, you should not implement **Invoke** directly. Instead, use the dispatch interface create functions **CreateStdDispatch** and **DispInvoke**. For details, refer to "CreateStdDispatch" and "DispInvoke" in this chapter, and "Creating the IDispatch Interface" in Chapter 2, "Exposing ActiveX Objects."

If some application-specific processing needs to be performed before calling a member, the code should perform the necessary actions, and then call **ITypeInfo::Invoke** to invoke the member. **ITypeInfo::Invoke** acts exactly like **IDispatch::Invoke**. The standard implementations of **IDispatch::Invoke** created by **CreateStdDispatch** and **DispInvoke** defer to **ITypeInfo::Invoke**.

In an ActiveX client, **IDispatch::Invoke** should be used to get and set the values of properties, or to call a method of an ActiveX object. The *dispIdMember* argument identifies the member to invoke. The DISPIDs that identify members are defined by the implementor of the object and can be determined by using the object's documentation, the **IDispatch::GetIDsOfNames** function, or the **ITypeInfo** interface.

The information that follows addresses developers of ActiveX clients and others who use code to expose ActiveX objects. It describes the behavior that users of exposed objects should expect.

Calling a Method With No Arguments

The simplest use of **Invoke** is to call a method that does not have any arguments. You only need to pass the DISPID of the method, a LCID, the DISPATCH_METHOD flag, and an empty DISPPARAMS structure. For example:

```
HRESULT hresult;
IUnknown FAR* punk;
IDispatch FAR* pdisp = (IDispatch FAR*)NULL;
OLECHAR FAR* szMember = "Simple";
DISPID dispid;
DISPPARAMS dispparamsNoArgs = {NULL, NULL, 0, 0};

hresult = CoCreateInstance(CLSID_CMyObject, NULL, CLSCTX_SERVER,
              IID_Unknown, (void FAR* FAR*)&punk);

hresult = punk->QueryInterface(IID_IDispatch,
              (void FAR* FAR*)&pdisp);

hresult = pdisp->GetIDsOfNames(IID_NULL, &szMember, 1,
              LOCALE_USER_DEFAULT, &dispid);

hresult = pdisp->Invoke(
        dispid,
        IID_NULL,
        LOCALE_USER_DEFAULT,
        DISPATCH_METHOD,
        &dispparamsNoArgs, NULL, NULL, NULL);
```

The example invokes a method named **Simple** on an object of the class CMyObject. First, it calls **CoCreateInstance**, which instantiates the object and returns a pointer to the object's **IUnknown** interface (punk). Next, it calls **QueryInterface**, receiving a pointer to the object's **IDispatch** interface (pdisp). It then uses pdisp to call the object's **GetIDsOfNames** function, passing the string **Simple** in szMember to get the DISPID for the **Simple** method. With the DISPID for **Simple** in dispid, it calls **Invoke** to invoke the method, specifying DISPATCH_METHOD for the wFlags parameter and using the system default locale.

To further simplify the code, the example declares a DISPPARAMS structure named `dispparamsNoArgs` that is appropriate to an **Invoke** call with no arguments.

Because the **Simple** method does not take any arguments and does not return a result, the `puArgErr` and `pVarResult` parameters are Null. In addition, the example passes Null for `pExcepInfo`, indicating that it is not prepared to handle exceptions and will handle only HRESULT errors.

Most methods, however, take one or more arguments. To invoke these methods, the DISPPARAMS structure should be filled in, as described in "Passing Parameters" later in this chapter.

Automation defines special DISPIDs for invoking an object's **Value** property (the default), and the members **_NewEnum,** and **Evaluate**. For details, see "DISPID" in Chapter 6, "Data Types, Structures, and Enumerations."

Getting and Setting Properties

Properties are accessed in the same way as methods, except you specify DISPATCH_PROPERTYGET or DISPATCH_PROPERTYPUT instead of DISPATCH_METHOD. Some languages can not distinguish between retrieving a property and calling a method. In this case, you should set the flags DISPATCH_PROPERTYGET and DISPATCH_METHOD.

The following example gets the value of a property named **On.** You can assume that the object has been created, and that its interfaces have been queried, as in the previous example.

```
VARIANT FAR *pVarResult;
// Code omitted for brevity.
szMember = "On";
hresult = pdisp->GetIDsOfNames(IID_NULL, &szMember, 1,
                LOCALE_USER_DEFAULT, &dispid);

hresult = pdisp->Invoke(
        dispid,
        IID_NULL,
        LOCALE_USER_DEFAULT,
        DISPATCH_PROPERTYGET,
        &dispparamsNoArgs, pVarResult, NULL, NULL);
```

As in the previous example, the code calls **GetIDsOfNames** for the DISPID of the **On** property, and then passes the ID to **Invoke**. Then, **Invoke** returns the property's value in `pVarResult`. In general, the return value does not set VT_BYREF. However, this bit may be set and a pointer returned to the return value, if the lifetime of the return value is the same as that of the object.

To change the property's value, the call looks like this:

```
VARIANT FAR *pVarResult;
DISPPARAMS dispparams;
DISPID mydispid = DISP_PROPERTYPUT

// Code omitted for brevity.

szMember = "On";
dispparams.rgvarg[0].vt = VT_BOOL;
dispparams.rgvarg[0].bool = FALSE;
dispparams.rgdispidNamedArgs = &mydispid;
dispparams.cArgs = 1;
dispparams.cNamedArgs = 1;
hresult = pdisp->GetIDsOfNames(IID_NULL, &szMember, 1,
                LOCALE_USER_DEFAULT, &dispid);

hresult = pdisp->Invoke(
        dispid,
        IID_NULL,
        LOCALE_USER_DEFAULT,
        DISPATCH_PROPERTYPUT,
        &dispparams, NULL, NULL, NULL);
```

The new value for the property (the Boolean value False) is passed as an argument when the **On** property's **Put** function is invoked. The DISPID for the argument is DISPID_PROPERTYPUT. This DISPID is defined by Automation to designate the parameter that contains the new value for a property's **Put** function. The remaining details of the DISPPARAMS structure are described in the next section, "Passing Parameters."

The DISPATCH_PROPERTYPUT flag in the previous example indicates that a property is being set by value. In Visual Basic, the following statement assigns the **Value** property (the default) of YourObj to the **Prop** property:

```
MyObj.Prop = YourObj
```

This statement should be flagged as a DISPATCH_PROPERTYPUT. Similarly, statements like the following assign the **Value** property of one object to the **Value** property of another object.

```
Worksheet.Cell(1,1) = Worksheet.Cell(6,6)
MyDoc.Text1 = YourDoc.Text1
```

These statements result in a PROPERTY_PUT operation on `Worksheet.Cell(1,1)` and `MyDoc.Text1`.

Use the DISPATCH_PROPERTYPUTREF flag to indicate a property or data member that should be set by reference. For example, the following Visual Basic statement assigns the pointer **YourObj** to the property **Prop,** and should be flagged as DISPATCH_PROPERTYPUTREF.

```
Set MyObj.Prop = YourObj
```

The **Set** statement causes a reference assignment, rather than a value assignment.

The parameter on the right side is always passed by name, and should not be accessed positionally.

Passing Parameters

Arguments to the method or property being invoked are passed in the DISPPARAMS structure. This structure consists of a pointer to an array of arguments represented as variants, a pointer to an array of DISPIDs for named arguments, and the number of arguments in each array.

```
typedef struct FARSTRUCT tagDISPPARAMS
{
    VARIANTARG FAR* rgvarg;             // Array of arguments.
    DISPID FAR* rgdispidNamedArgs;      // Dispatch IDs of named arguments.
    unsigned int cArgs;                 // Number of arguments.
    unsigned int cNamedArgs;            // Number of named arguments.
} DISPPARAMS;
```

The arguments are passed in the array *rgvarg*[ ], with the number of arguments passed in *cArgs*. The arguments in the array should be placed from last to first, so *rgvarg*[0] has the last argument and *rgvarg*[*cArgs* −1] has the first argument. The method or property may change the values of elements within the array *rgvarg*, but only if it has set the VT_BYREF flag. Otherwise, consider the elements as read-only.

A dispatch invocation can have named arguments as well as positional arguments. If *cNamedArgs* is 0, all the elements of *rgvarg*[ ] represent positional arguments. If *cNamedArgs* is not 0, each element of *rgdispidNamedArgs*[ ] contains the DISPID of a named argument, and the value of the argument is in the matching element of *rgvarg*[ ]. The DISPIDs of the named arguments are always contiguous in *rgdispidNamedArgs*, and their values are in the first *cNamedArgs* elements of *rgvarg*. Named arguments cannot be accessed positionally, and positional arguments cannot be named.

The DISPID of an argument is its zero-based position in the argument list. For example, the following method takes three arguments.

```
BOOL _export CDECL
CCredit::CheckCredit(BSTR bstrCustomerID,    // DISPID = 0.
                     BSTR bstrLenderID,      // DISPID = 1.
                     CURRENCY cLoanAmt)      // DISPID = 2.
{
// Code omitted for brevity.
}
```

If you include the DISPID with each named argument, you can pass the named arguments to **Invoke** in any order. For example, if a method is to be invoked with two positional arguments, followed by three named arguments (*A, B,* and *C*), using the following hypothetical syntax, then *cArgs* would be 5, and *cNamedArgs* would be 3.

```
object.method("arg1", "arg2", A := "argA", B := "argB", C := "argC")
```

The first positional argument would be in *rgvarg*[4]. The second positional argument would be in *rgvarg*[3]. The ordering of named arguments is not important to the **IDispatch** implementation, but these arguments are generally passed in reverse order. The argument *A* would be in *rgvarg*[2], with the DISPID of *A* in *rgdispidNamedArgs*[2]. The argument *B* would be in *rgvarg*[1], with the corresponding DISPID in *rgdispidNamedArgs*[1]. The argument *C* would be in *rgvarg*[0], with the DISPID corresponding to *C* in *rgdispidNamedArgs*[0]. The following diagram illustrates the arrays and their contents.

	0	1	2	3	4
rgvarg	"argC"	"argB"	"argA"	"arg2"	"arg1"
rgdispidNamedArgs	ID of C	ID of B	ID of A		

You can also use **Invoke** on members with optional arguments, but all optional arguments must be of type VARIANT. As with required arguments, the contents of the argument vector depend on whether the arguments are positional or named. The invoked member must ensure that the arguments are valid. **Invoke** merely passes the DISPPARAMS structure it receives.

Omitting named arguments is straightforward. You would pass the arguments in *rgvarg* and their DISPIDs in *rgdispidNamedArgs*. To omit the argument named *B* (in the preceding example) you would set *rgvarg*[0] to the value of *C*, with its DISPID in *rgdispidNamedArgs*[0]; and *rgvarg*[1] to the value of *A,* with its DISPID in *rgdispidNamedArgs*[1]. The subsequent positional arguments would occupy elements 2 and 3 of the arrays. In this case, *cArgs* is 4 and *cNamedArgs* is 2.

If the arguments are positional (unnamed), you would set *cArgs* to the total number of possible arguments, *cNamedArgs* to 0, and pass VT_ERROR as the type of the omitted arguments, with the status code DISP_E_PARAMNOTFOUND as the value. For example, the following code invokes ShowMe (,1).

```
VARIANT FAR *pVarResult;
EXCEPINFO FAR *pExcepInfo;
unsigned int FAR *puArgErr;
DISPPARAMS dispparams;

// Code omitted for brevity.

szMember = "ShowMe";
hresult = pdisp->GetIDsOfNames(IID_NULL, &szMember, 1,
                               LOCALE_USER_DEFAULT, &dispid);
dispparams.rgvarg[0].vt = VT_I2;
dispparams.rgvarg[0].ival = 1;
dispparams.rgvarg[1].vt = VT_ERROR;
dispparams.rgvarg[1].scode = DISP_E_PARAMNOTFOUND;
dispparams.cArgs = 2;
dispparams.cNamedArgs = 0;

hresult = pdisp->Invoke(
        dispid,
        IID_NULL,
        LOCALE_USER_DEFAULT,
        DISPATCH_METHOD,
        &dispparams, pVarResult, pExcepInfo, puArgErr);
```

The example takes two positional arguments, but omits the first. Therefore, *rgvarg*[0] contains 1, the value of the last argument in the argument list, and *rgvarg*[1] contains VT_ERROR and the error return value, indicating the omitted first argument.

The calling code is responsible for releasing all strings and objects referred to by *rgvarg*[ ] or placed in **pVarResult*. As with other parameters that are passed by value, if the invoked member must maintain access to a string after returning, you should copy the string. Similarly, if the member needs access to a passed-object pointer after returning, it must call the **AddRef** function on the object. A common example occurs when an object property is changed to refer to a new object, using the DISPATCH_PROPERTYPUTREF flag.

For those implementing **IDispatch::Invoke,** Automation provides the **DispGetParam** function to retrieve parameters from the argument vector and coerce them to the proper type. For details, see "DispGetParam" later in this chapter.

Indexed Properties

When you invoke indexed properties of any dimension, you must pass the indexes as additional arguments. To set an indexed property, place the new value in the first element of the *rgvarg*[ ] vector, and the indexes in the subsequent elements. To get an indexed property, pass the indexes in the first *n* elements of *rgvarg*, and the number of indexes in *cArg*. **Invoke** returns the value of the property in *pVarResult*.

Automation stores array data in column-major order, which is the same ordering scheme used by Visual Basic and FORTRAN, but different from C, C++, and Pascal. If you are programming in C, C++, or Pascal, you must pass the indexes in the reverse order. The following example shows how to fill the DISPPARAMS structure in C++.

```
dispparams.rgvarg[0].vt = VT_I2;
dispparams.rgvarg[0].iVal = 99;
dispparams.rgvarg[1].vt = VT_I2;
dispparams.rgvarg[1].iVal = 2;
dispparams.rgvarg[2].vt = VT_I2;
dispparams.rgvarg[2].iVal = 1;
dispparams.rgdispidNamedArgs = DISPID_PROPERTYPUT;
dispparams.cArgs = 3;
dispparams.cNamedArgs = 1;
```

The example changes the value of Prop[1,2] to 99. The new property value is passed in *rgvarg*[0]. The right-most index is passed in rgvarg[1], and the next index in rgvarg[2]. The cArgs field specifies the number of elements of rgvarg[ ] that contain data, and cNamedArgs is 1, indicating the new value for the property.

Property collections are an extension of this feature.

Raising Exceptions During Invoke

When you implement **IDispatch::Invoke,** errors can be communicated either through the normal return value or by raising an exception. An exception is a special situation that is normally handled by jumping to the nearest routine enclosing the exception handler.

To raise an exception, **IDispatch::Invoke** returns DISP_E_EXCEPTION and fills the structure passed through *pExcepInfo* with information about the cause of the exception or error. You can use the information to understand the cause of the exception and proceed as necessary.

The exception information structure includes an error code number that identifies the kind of exception (a string that describes the error in a human-readable way). It also includes a Help file and a Help context number that can be passed to Windows Help for details about the error. At a minimum, the error code number must be filled with a valid number.

If you consider **IDispatch** another way to call C++ methods in an interface, EXCEPINFO models the raising of an exception or **longjmp**() call by such a method.

Returning Errors

Invoke returns DISP_E_MEMBERNOTFOUND if one of the following conditions occurs:

- A member or parameter with the specified DISPID and matching *cArgs* cannot be found, and the parameter is not optional.
- The member is a void function, and the caller did not set *pVarResult* to Null.
- The member is a read-only property, and the caller set *wFlags* to DISPATCH_PROPERTYPUT or DISPATCH_PROPERTYPUTREF.

If **Invoke** finds the member, but uncovers errors in the argument list, it returns one of several other errors. DISP_E_BAD_PARAMCOUNT means that the DISPPARAMS structure contains an incorrect number of parameters for the property or method. DISP_E_NONAMEDARGS means that **Invoke** received named arguments, but they are not supported by the member.

DISP_E_PARAMNOTFOUND means that the correct number of parameters was passed, but the DISPID for one or more parameters was incorrect. If **Invoke** cannot convert one of the arguments to the desired type, it returns DISP_E_TYPEMISMATCH. In these two cases, if it can identify which argument is incorrect, **Invoke** sets *puArgErr* to the index within *rgvarg* of the argument with the error. For example, if an Automation method expects a reference to a double-precision number as an argument, but receives a reference to an integer, the argument is coerced. However, if the method receives a date, **IDispatch::Invoke** returns DISP_E_TYPEMISMATCH and sets *puArgErr* to the index of the integer in the argument array.

Automation provides functions to perform standard conversions of VARIANT, and these functions should be used for consistent operation. DISP_E_TYPEMISMATCH is returned only when these functions fail. For more information about converting arguments, see Chapter 7, "Conversion and Manipulation Functions."

Example

This code from the Lines sample file Lines.cpp implements the **Invoke** member function for the CLines class.

```
STDMETHODIMP
CLines::Invoke(
    DISPID dispidMember,
    REFIID riid,
    LCID lcid,
    WORD wFlags,
    DISPPARAMS FAR* pDispParams,
    VARIANT FAR* pVarResult,
    EXCEPINFO FAR* pExcepInfo,
    UINT FAR* puArgErr)
```

```
{
    return DispInvoke(
        this, m_ptinfo,
        dispidMember, wFlags, pDispParams,
        pVarResult, pExcepInfo, puArgErr);
}
```

The next code example calls the **CLines::Invoke** member function to get the value of the **Color** property:

```
HRESULT hr;
EXCEPINFO excepinfo;
UINT nArgErr;
VARIANT vRet;
DISPPARAMS FAR* pdisp;
OLECHAR FAR* szMember;
DISPPARAMS dispparamsNoArgs = {NULL, NULL, 0, 0};

// Initialization code omitted for brevity.

szMember = "Color";
hr = pdisp->GetIDsOfNames(IID_NULL, &szMember, 1, LOCALE_USER_DEFAULT,
    &dispid);

// Get Color property.

hr = pdisp->Invoke(dispid, IID_NULL, LOCALE_SYSTEM_DEFAULT,
    DISPATCH_PROPERTYGET, &dispparams, &vRet, &excepinfo, &nArgErr);
```

See Also   **CreateStdDispatch, DispInvoke, DispGetParam, ITypeInfo::Invoke**

Overview of Dispatch API Functions

For 32-bit systems, dispatch functions are provided in the file Oleaut32.dll. The header file is Oleauto.h, and the import library is Oleaut32.lib. For 16-bit systems, the dispatch functions are provided in the file Oledisp.dll. The header file is Dispatch.h, and the import library is Ole2disp.lib. These functions simplify the creation of **IDispatch** interfaces. The dispatch functions are summarized in the following table.

Category	Function name	Purpose
Dispatch interface creation	**CreateDispTypeInfo**	Creates simplified type information for an object.
	CreateStdDispatch	Creates a standard **IDispatch** implementation for an object.
	DispGetIDsOfNames	Converts a set of names to DISPIDs.

Category	Function name	Purpose
	DispGetParam	Retrieves and coerces elements from a DISPPARAMS structure.
	DispInvoke	Calls a member function of an **IDispatch** interface.
Active object initialization	**GetActiveObject**	Retrieves an instance of an object that is initialized with OLE.
	RegisterActiveObject	Initializes a running object with OLE. (Use when application starts.)
	RevokeActiveObject	Revokes a running application's initialization with OLE. (Use when application ends.)

Using API Functions with the IDispatch Interface

The following five functions are used to create and modify **IDispatch**.

CreateDispTypeInfo

> **HRESULT CreateDispTypeInfo(**
>
> **INTERFACEDATA** *pidata*,
> **LCID** *lcid*,
> **ITypeInfo FAR* FAR*** *pptinfo*
> **);**

Creates simplified type information for use in an implementation of **IDispatch**.

Parameters

pidata
  The interface description that this type information describes.

lcid
  The locale identifier for the names used in the type information.

pptinfo
  On return, pointer to a type information implementation for use in **DispGetIDsOfNames** and **DispInvoke**.

Return Value   The return value obtained from the returned HRESULT is one of the following:

Return value	Meaning
S_OK	The interface is supported.
E_INVALIDARG	Either the interface description or the LCID is invalid.
E_OUTOFMEMORY	Insufficient memory to complete the operation.

Comments   You can construct type information at run time by using **CreateDispTypeInfo** and an INTERFACEDATA structure that describes the object being exposed.

The type information returned by this function is primarily designed to automate the implementation of **IDispatch**. **CreateDispTypeInfo** does not return all of the type information described in Chapter 9, "Type Description Interfaces." The argument *pidata* is not a complete description of an interface. It does not include Help information, comments, optional parameters, and other type information that is useful in different contexts.

Accordingly, the recommended method for providing type information about an object is to describe the object using the Object Description Language (ODL), and to compile the object description into a type library using the Microsoft Interface Definition Language (MIDL) compiler or the MkTypLib utility.

To use type information from a type library, use the **LoadTypeLib** and **GetTypeInfoOfGuid** functions instead of **CreateDispTypeInfo**. For more information, see Chapter 9, "Type Description Interfaces."

Example   The code that follows creates type information from INTERFACEDATA to expose the CCalc object.

```
static METHODDATA NEARDATA rgmdataCCalc[] =
{
        PROPERTY(VALUE,    IMETH_ACCUM,     IDMEMBER_ACCUM,     VT_I4)
        PROPERTY(ACCUM,    IMETH_ACCUM,     IDMEMBER_ACCUM,     VT_I4)
        PROPERTY(OPND,     IMETH_OPERAND,   IDMEMBER_OPERAND,   VT_I4)
        PROPERTY(OP,       IMETH_OPERATOR,  IDMEMBER_OPERATOR,  VT_I2)
        METHOD0(EVAL,      IMETH_EVAL,      IDMEMBER_EVAL,      VT_BOOL)
        METHOD0(CLEAR,     IMETH_CLEAR,     IDMEMBER_CLEAR,     VT_EMPTY)
        METHOD0(DISPLAY,   IMETH_DISPLAY,   IDMEMBER_DISPLAY,   VT_EMPTY)
        METHOD0(QUIT,      IMETH_QUIT,      IDMEMBER_QUIT,      VT_EMPTY)
        METHOD1(BUTTON,    IMETH_BUTTON,    IDMEMBER_BUTTON,    VT_BOOL)
}

INTERFACEDATA NEARDATA g_idataCCalc =
{
    rgmdataCCalc, DIM(rgmdataCCalc)
}
```

```
// Use Dispatch interface API functions to implement IDispatch.
CCalc FAR*
CCalc::Create()
{
    HRESULT hresult;
    CCalc FAR* pcalc;
    CArith FAR* parith;
    ITypeInfo FAR* ptinfo;
    IUnknown FAR* punkStdDisp;
extern INTERFACEDATA NEARDATA g_idataCCalc;

    if((pcalc = new FAR CCalc()) == NULL)
        return NULL;
    pcalc->AddRef();


    parith = &(pcalc->m_arith);


    // Build type information for the functionality on this object that
    // is being exposed for external programmability.

    hresult = CreateDispTypeInfo(
        &g_idataCCalc, LOCALE_SYSTEM_DEFAULT, &ptinfo);
    if(hresult != NOERROR)
        goto LError0;

    // Create an aggregate with an instance of the default
    // implementation of IDispatch that is initialized with
    // type information.

    hresult = CreateStdDispatch(
        pcalc,              // Controlling unknown.
        parith,             // Instance to dispatch on.
        ptinfo,             // Type information describing the instance.
        &punkStdDisp);

    ptinfo->Release();

    if(hresult != NOERROR)
        goto LError0;

    pcalc->m_punkStdDisp = punkStdDisp;

    return pcalc;

LError0::
    pcalc->Release();
    return NULL;
}
```

CreateStdDispatch

HRESULT CreateStdDispatch(

IUnknown FAR* *punkOuter,*

void FAR* *pvThis,*

ITypeInfo FAR* *ptinfo,*

IUnknown FAR* FAR* *ppunkStdDisp*

);

Creates a standard implementation of the **IDispatch** interface through a single function call. This simplifies exposing objects through Automation.

Parameters

punkOuter
  Pointer to the object's **IUnknown** implementation.

pvThis
  Pointer to the object to expose.

ptinfo
  Pointer to the type information that describes the exposed object.

ppunkStdDisp
  This is the private unknown for the object that implements the **IDispatch** interface **QueryInterface** call. This pointer is Null if the function fails.

Return Value

The return value obtained from the returned HRESULT is one of the following:

Return value	Meaning
S_OK	Success.
E_INVALIDARG	One of the first three arguments is invalid.
E_OUTOFMEMORY	There was insufficient memory to complete the operation.

Comments

You can use **CreateStdDispatch** when creating an object instead of implementing the **IDispatch** member functions for the object. However, the implementation that **CreateStdDispatch** creates has these limitations:

- Supports only one national language.
- Supports only dispatch-defined exception codes returned from **Invoke**.

LoadTypeLib, GetTypeInfoOfGuid, and CreateStdDispatch comprise the minimum set of functions that you need to call to expose an object using a type library. For more information on LoadTypeLib and GetTypeInfoOfGuid, see Chapter 9, "Type Description Interfaces."

CreateDispTypeInfo and CreateStdDispatch comprise the minimum set of dispatch components you need to call to expose an object using type information provided by the INTERFACEDATA structure.

Example   The following code implements the IDispatch interface for the CCalc class using CreateStdDispatch.

```
CCalc FAR*
CCalc::Create()
{
    HRESULT hresult;
    CCalc FAR* pcalc;
    CArith FAR* parith;
    ITypeInfo FAR* ptinfo;
    IUnknown FAR* punkStdDisp;
extern INTERFACEDATA NEARDATA g_idataCCalc;

    if((pcalc = new FAR CCalc()) == NULL)
        return NULL;
    pcalc->AddRef();

    parith = &(pcalc->m_arith);

    // Build type information for the functionality on this object that
    // is being exposed for external programmability.

    hresult = CreateDispTypeInfo(
        &g_idataCCalc, LOCALE_SYSTEM_DEFAULT, &ptinfo);
    if(hresult != NOERROR)
        goto LError0;

    // Create an aggregate with an instance of the default
    // implementation of IDispatch that is initialized with
    // type information.

    hresult = CreateStdDispatch(
        pcalc,                 // Controlling unknown.
        parith,                // Instance to dispatch on.
        ptinfo,                // Type information describing the instance.
    &punkStdDisp);

    ptinfo->Release();
```

```
        if(hresult != NOERROR)
            goto LError0;

        pcalc->m_punkStdDisp = punkStdDisp;

        return pcalc;

LError0:;
        pcalc->Release();
        return NULL;
}
```

DispGetIDsOfNames

HRESULT DispGetIDsOfNames(

ITypeInfo* *ptinfo*,

OLECHAR FAR* FAR* *rgszNames*,

unsigned int *cNames*,

DISPID FAR* *rgdispid*

);

Uses type information to convert a set of names to DISPIDs. This is the recommended implementation of **IDispatch::GetIDsOfNames**.

Parameters

ptinfo
> Pointer to the type information for an interface. This type information is specific to one interface and language code, so it is not necessary to pass an interface identifier (IID) or LCID to this function.

rgszNames
> An array of name strings that can be the same array passed to **DispInvoke** in the DISPPARAMS structure. If *cNames* is greater than 1, the first name is interpreted as a method name, and subsequent names are interpreted as parameters to that method.

cNames
> The number of elements in *rgszNames*.

rgdispid
> Pointer to an array of DISPIDs to be filled in by this function. The first ID corresponds to the method name. Subsequent IDs are interpreted as parameters to the method.

Return Value   The return value obtained from the returned HRESULT is one of the following:

Return value	Meaning
S_OK	The interface is supported.
E_INVALIDARG	One of the arguments is invalid.
DISP_E_UNKNOWNNAME	One or more of the given names were not known. The returned array of DISPIDs contains DISPID_UNKNOWN for each entry that corresponds to an unknown name.
Other return codes	Any of the **ITypeInfo::Invoke** errors can also be returned.

Example   This code from the Lines sample file Points.cpp implements the member function **GetIDsOfNames** for the CPoints class using **DispGetIDsOfNames**.

```
STDMETHODIMP
CPoints::GetIDsOfNames(
        REFIID riid,
        char FAR* FAR* rgszNames,
        UINT cNames,
        LCID lcid,
        DISPID FAR* rgdispid)
{
    return DispGetIDsOfNames(m_ptinfo, rgszNames, cNames, rgdispid);
}
```

See Also   **CreateStdDispatch, IDispatch::GetIDsOfNames**

DispGetParam

HRESULT DispGetParam(

DISPPARAMS FAR* *pdispparams,*

unsigned int *position,*

VARTYPE *vtTarg,*

VARIANT FAR* *pvarResult,*

unsigned int FAR* *puArgErr*

);

Retrieves a parameter from the DISPPARAMS structure, checking both named parameters and positional parameters, and coerces the parameter to the specified type.

Parameters

pdispparams
Pointer to the parameters passed to **IDispatch::Invoke**.

position
The position of the parameter in the parameter list. **DispGetParam** starts at the end of the array, so if *position* is 0, the last parameter in the array is returned.

vtTarg
The type the argument should be coerced to.

pvarResult
Pointer to the variant to pass the parameter into.

puArgErr
On return, pointer to the index of the argument that caused a DISP_E_TYPEMISMATCH error. This pointer is returned to **Invoke** to indicate the position of the argument in DISPPARAMS that caused the error.

Return Value

The return value obtained from the HRESULT is one of the following:

Return value	Meaning
S_OK	Success.
DISP_E_BADVARTYPE	The variant type *vtTarg* is not supported.
DISP_E_OVERFLOW	The retrieved parameter could not be coerced to the specified type.
DISP_E_PARAMNOTFOUND	The parameter indicated by *position* could not be found.
DISP_E_TYPEMISMATCH	The argument could not be coerced to the specified type.
E_INVALIDARG	One of the arguments was invalid.
E_OUTOFMEMORY	Insufficient memory to complete operation.

Comments

The output parameter *pvarResult* must be a valid variant. Any existing contents are released in the standard way. The contents of the variant are freed with **VariantFree**.

If you have used **DispGetParam** to get the right side of a property put operation, the second parameter should be DISPID_PROPERTYPUT. For example:

```
DispGetParam(&dispparams, DISPID_PROPERTYPUT, VT_BOOL, &varResult)
```

Named parameters cannot be accessed positionally, and vice versa.

Example

The following example uses **DispGetParam** to set X and Y properties:

```
STDMETHODIMP
CPoint::Invoke(
    DISPID dispidMember,
    REFIID riid,
    LCID lcid,
    unsigned short wFlags,
    DISPPARAMS FAR* pdispparams,
    VARIANT FAR* pvarResult,
    EXCEPINFO FAR* pExcepInfo,
    unsigned int FAR* puArgErr)
{
    unsigned int uArgErr;
    HRESULT hresult;
    VARIANTARG varg0;
    VARIANT varResultDummy;
    UNUSED(lcid);
    UNUSED(pExcepInfo);

    // Make sure the wFlags are valid.

    if(wFlags & ~(DISPATCH_METHOD | DISPATCH_PROPERTYGET |
        DISPATCH_PROPERTYPUT | DISPATCH_PROPERTYPUTREF))
        return ResultFromScode(E_INVALIDARG);

    // This object only exposes a "default" interface.

    if(!IsEqualIID(riid, IID_NULL))
        return ResultFromScode(DISP_E_UNKNOWNINTERFACE);

    // It simplifies the following code if the caller
    // ignores the return value.

    if(puArgErr == NULL)
        puArgErr = &uArgErr;
    if(pvarResult == NULL)
        pvarResult = &varResultDummy;

    VariantInit(&varg0);

    // Assume the return type is void, unless otherwise is found.

    VariantInit(pvarResult);

    switch(dispidMember){
    case IDMEMBER_CPOINT_GETX:
        V_VT(pvarResult) = VT_I2;
        V_I2(pvarResult) = GetX();
        break;
```

```
case IDMEMBER_CPOINT_SETX:
    hresult = DispGetParam(pdispparams, 0, VT_I2, &varg0, puArgErr);
    if(hresult != NOERROR)
        return hresult;
    SetX(V_I2(&varg0));
    break;

case IDMEMBER_CPOINT_GETY:
    V_VT(pvarResult) = VT_I2;
    V_I2(pvarResult) = GetY();
    break;

case IDMEMBER_CPOINT_SETY:
    hresult = DispGetParam(pdispparams, 0, VT_I2, &varg0, puArgErr);
    if(hresult != NOERROR)
        return hresult;
    SetY(V_I2(&varg0));
    break;

default:
    return ResultFromScode(DISP_E_MEMBERNOTFOUND);
}
return NOERROR;
}
```

See Also   **CreateStdDispatch, IDispatch::Invoke**

DispInvoke

HRESULT DispInvoke(

void FAR* *_this*,

ITypeInfo FAR* *ptinfo*,

DISPID *dispidMember*,

unsigned short *wFlags*,

DISPPARAMS FAR* *pparams*,

VARIANT FAR* *pvarResult*,

EXCEPINFO *pexcepinfo*,

unsigned int FAR* *puArgErr*

);

Automatically calls member functions on an interface, given the type information for the interface. You can describe an interface with type information and implement **IDispatch::Invoke** for the interface using this single call.

Parameters

_this

Pointer to an implementation of the **IDispatch** interface described by *ptinfo*.

ptinfo

Pointer to the type information that describes the interface.

dispidMember

Identifies the member. Use **GetIDsOfNames** or the object's documentation to obtain the DISPID.

wFlags

Flags describing the context of the **Invoke** call, as follows:

Value	Description
DISPATCH_METHOD	The member is invoked as a method. If a property has the same name, both this and the DISPATCH_PROPERTYGET flag can be set.
DISPATCH_PROPERTYGET	The member is retrieved as a property or data member.
DISPATCH_PROPERTYPUT	The member is changed as a property or data member.
DISPATCH_PROPERTYPUTREF	The member is changed by a reference assignment, rather than a value assignment. This flag is valid only when the property accepts a reference to an object.

pparams

Pointer to a structure containing an array of arguments, an array of argument DISPIDs for named arguments, and counts for number of elements in the arrays.

pvarResult

Pointer to where the result is to be stored, or Null if the caller expects no result. This argument is ignored if DISPATCH_PROPERTYPUT or DISPATCH_PROPERTYPUTREF is specified.

pexcepinfo

Pointer to a structure containing exception information. This structure should be filled in if DISP_E_EXCEPTION is returned.

puArgErr

The index within *rgvarg* of the first argument that has an error. Arguments are stored in *pdispparams->rgvarg* in reverse order, so the first argument is the one with the highest index in the array. This parameter is returned only when the resulting return value is DISP_E_TYPEMISMATCH or DISP_E_PARAMNOTFOUND.

Return Value   The return value obtained from the returned HRESULT is one of the following:

Return value	Meaning
S_OK	Success.
DISP_E_BADPARAMCOUNT	The number of elements provided in DISPPARAMS is different from the number of arguments accepted by the method or property.
DISP_E_BADVARTYPE	One of the arguments in DISPPARAMS is not a valid variant type.
DISP_E_EXCEPTION	The application needs to raise an exception. In this case, the structure passed in *pexcepinfo* should be filled in.
DISP_E_MEMBERNOTFOUND	The requested member does not exist.
DISP_E_NONAMEDARGS	This implementation of **IDispatch** does not support named arguments.
DISP_E_OVERFLOW	One of the arguments in DISPPARAMS could not be coerced to the specified type.
DISP_E_PARAMNOTFOUND	One of the parameter IDs does not correspond to a parameter on the method. In this case, *puArgErr* is set to the first argument that contains the error.
DISP_E_PARAMNOTOPTIONAL	A required parameter was omitted.
DISP_E_TYPEMISMATCH	One or more of the arguments could not be coerced. The index of the first parameter with the incorrect type within *rgvarg* is returned in *puArgErr*.
E_INVALIDARG	One of the arguments is invalid.
E_OUTOFMEMORY	Insufficient memory to complete the operation.
Other return codes	Any of the **ITypeInfo::Invoke** errors can also be returned.

Comments   The parameter *_this* is a pointer to an implementation of the interface that is being deferred to. **DispInvoke** builds a stack frame, coerces parameters using standard coercion rules, pushes them on the stack, and then calls the correct member function in the VTBL.

Example

The following code from the Lines sample file Lines.cpp implements **IDispatch::Invoke** using **DispInvoke**. This function uses m_bRaiseException to signal that an error occurred during the **DispInvoke** call.

```
STDMETHODIMP
CLines::Invoke(
    DISPID dispidMember,
    REFIID riid,
    LCID lcid,
    WORD wFlags,
    DISPPARAMS FAR* pdispparams,
    VARIANT FAR* pvarResult,
    EXCEPINFO FAR* pexcepinfo,
    UINT FAR* puArgErr)
{

    return DispInvoke(
    this, m_ptinfo,
    dispidMember, wFlags, pdispparams,
    pvarResult, pexcepinfo, puArgErr);
}
```

See Also

CreateStdDispatch, IDispatch::Invoke

Registering the Active Object with API Functions

These functions let you identify a running instance of an object. Because they use the OLE object table (**GetRunningObjectTable**), they also require either Ole32.dll (for 32-bit systems) or Ole2.dll (for 16-bit systems).

When an application is started with the **/Automation** switch, it should initialize its Application object as the active object by calling **RegisterActiveObject** after it initializes OLE.

Applications can also register other top-level objects as the active object. For example, an application that exposes a Document object may want to let ActiveX clients retrieve and modify the currently active document.

For more information about registering the active object, see Chapter 2, "Exposing ActiveX Objects." The following table identifies the location of these API functions.

Implemented by	Used by	Header file name	Import library name
Oleaut32.dll (32-bit systems) Ole2disp.dll (16-bit systems)	Applications that expose or access programmable objects.	Oleauto.h Dispatch.h	Oleaut32.lib Ole2disp.lib

GetActiveObject

HRESULT GetActiveObject(
REFCLSID *rclsid,*
void FAR* *pvReserved,*
IUnknown FAR* FAR* *ppunk*
);

Retrieves a pointer to a running object that has been registered with OLE.

Parameters

rclsid
Pointer to the class identifier (CLSID) of the active object from the OLE registration database.

pvReserved
Reserved for future use. Must be Null.

ppunk
On return, a pointer to the requested active object.

Return Value

The return value obtained from the returned HRESULT is one of the following:

Return value	Meaning
S_OK	Success.
Other return codes	Failure.

RegisterActiveObject

HRESULT RegisterActiveObject(
IUnknown FAR* *punk,*
REFCLSID *rclsid,*
DWORD *dwFlags,*
unsigned long FAR* *pdwRegister*
);

Registers an object as the active object for its class.

Parameters

punk

Pointer to the **IUnknown** interface of the active object.

rclsid

Pointer to the CLSID of the active object.

dwFlags

Flags controlling registration of the object. Possible values are
ACTIVEOBJECT_STRONG and ACTIVEOBJECT_WEAK.

pdwRegister

On return, a pointer to a handle. This handle must be passed to
RevokeActiveObject to end the object's active status.

Return Value

The return value obtained from the returned HRESULT is one of the following:

Return value	Meaning
S_OK	Success.
Other return codes	Failure.

Comments

The **RegisterActiveObject** function registers the object to which *punk* points as the
active object for the class denoted by *rclsid*. Registration causes the object to be listed
in the running object table (ROT) of OLE, a globally accessible lookup table that
keeps track of objects that are currently running on the computer. (For more
information about the running object table, see the *OLE Programmer's Reference*.)
The *dwFlags* parameter specifies the strength or weakness of the registration, which
affects the way the object is shut down.

In general, ActiveX objects should behave in the following manner:

- If the object is visible, it should shut down only in response to an explicit user
  command (such as the **Exit** command on the **File** menu), or to the equivalent
  command from an ActiveX client (invoking the **Quit** or **Exit** method on the
  Application object).

- If the object is not visible, it should shut down only when the last external
  connection to it is gone.

Strong registration performs an **AddRef** on the object, incrementing the reference
count of the object (and its associated stub) in the running object table. A strongly
registered object must be explicitly revoked from the table with **RevokeActiveObject**.
The default is strong registration (ACTIVEOBJECT_STRONG).

Weak registration keeps a pointer to the object in the running object table, but does not increment the reference count. Consequently, when the last external connection to a weakly registered object disappears, OLE releases the object's stub, and the object itself is no longer available.

To ensure the desired behavior, consider not only the default actions of OLE, but also the following:

- Even though code can create an invisible object, the object may become visible at some later time. Once the object is visible, it should remain visible and active until it receives an explicit command to shut down. This can occur after references from the code disappear.

- Other ActiveX clients may be using the object. If so, the code should not force the object to shut down.

To avoid possible conflicts, you should always register ActiveX objects with ACTIVEOBJECT_WEAK, and call **CoLockObjectExternal,** when necessary, to guarantee the object remains active. **CoLockObjectExternal** adds a strong lock, thereby preventing the object's reference count from reaching zero. For detailed information about this function, refer to the *OLE Programmer's Reference*.

Most commonly, objects need to call **CoLockObjectExternal** when they become visible, so they remain active until the user requests the object to shut down. The following procedure lists the steps your code should follow to shut down an object correctly.

▶ **To shut down an active object:**

1. When the object becomes visible, make the following call to add a lock for the user:

```
CoLockObjectExternal(punk, TRUE, TRUE)
```

The lock remains in effect until a user explicitly requests the object to be shut down, such as with a **Quit** or **Exit** command.

2. When the user requests the object to be shut down, call **CoLockObjectExternal** again to free the lock, as follows:

```
CoLockObjectExternal(punk, False, True)
```

3. Call **RevokeActiveObject** to make the object inactive.

4. To end all connections from remote processes, call **CoDisconnectObject** as follows:

```
CoDisconnectObject(punk, 0)
```

This function is described in more detail in the *OLE Programmer's Reference*.

RevokeActiveObject

HRESULT RevokeActiveObject(

unsigned long *dwRegister*,

void FAR* *pvReserved*

);

Ends an object's status as active.

Parameters

dwRegister
A handle previously returned by **RegisterActiveObject**.

pvReserved
Reserved for future use. Must be Null.

Return Value

The return value obtained from the returned HRESULT is one of the following:

Return value	Meaning
S_OK	Success.
Other return codes	Failure.

IEnumVARIANT Interface

The **IEnumVARIANT** interface provides a method for enumerating a collection of variants, including heterogeneous collections of objects and intrinsic types. Callers of this interface do not need to know the specific type (or types) of the elements in the collection.

Implemented by	Used by	Header file name
Applications that expose collections of objects.	Applications that access collections of objects.	Oleauto.h (32-bit systems) Dispatch.h (16-bit systems)

The following is the definition that results from expanding the parameterized type
IEnumVARIANT:

```
interface IEnumVARIANT : IUnknown
{
    virtual HRESULT Next(unsigned long celt,
                    VARIANT FAR* rgvar,
                    unsigned long FAR* pceltFetched) = 0;
    virtual HRESULT Skip(unsigned long celt) = 0;
    virtual HRESULT Reset() = 0;
    virtual HRESULT Clone(IEnumVARIANT FAR* FAR* ppenum) = 0;
}
```

To see how to implement a collection of objects using **IEnumVARIANT,** refer to the
file Enumvar.cpp in the Lines sample code.

IEnumVARIANT::Clone

HRESULT Clone(

IEnumVARIANT FAR* FAR* *ppEnum*

);

Creates a copy of the current state of enumeration.

Parameter

ppEnum
    On return, pointer to the location of the clone enumerator.

Return Value

The return value obtained from the returned HRESULT is one of the following:

Return value	Meaning
S_OK	Success.
E_OUTOFMEMORY	Insufficient memory to complete the operation.

Comments

Using this function, a particular point in the enumeration sequence can be recorded,
and then returned to at a later time. The returned enumerator is of the same actual
interface as the one that is being cloned.

There is no guarantee that exactly the same set of variants will be enumerated the
second time as was enumerated the first. Although an exact duplicate is desirable, the
outcome depends on the collection being enumerated. You may find that it is
impractical for some collections to maintain this condition (for example, an
enumeration of the files in a directory).

Example

The following code implements **IEnumVariant::Clone** for collections in the Lines sample file Enumvar.cpp.

```
STDMETHODIMP
CEnumVariant::Clone(IEnumVARIANT FAR* FAR* ppEnum)
{
    CEnumVariant FAR* penum = NULL;
    HRESULT hr;

    *ppenum = NULL;

    hr = CEnumVariant::Create(m_psa, m_cElements, &penum);
    if (FAILED(hr))
        goto error;
    penum->AddRef();
    penum->m_lCurrent = m_lCurrent;

    *ppenum = penum;
    return NOERROR;

error:
    if (penum)
        penum->Release();
    return hr;
}
```

IEnumVARIANT::Next

HRESULT Next(

  unsigned long *celt,*

  VARIANT FAR* *rgVar,*

  unsigned long FAR* *pCeltFetched*

  );

Attempts to get the next *celt* items in the enumeration sequence, and return them through the array pointed to by *rgVar*.

Parameters

celt

  The number of elements to be returned.

rgVar

  An array of at least size *celt* in which the elements are to be returned.

pCeltFetched

  Pointer to the number of elements returned in *rgVar*, or Null.

Return Value

The return value obtained from the returned HRESULT is one of the following:

Return value	Meaning
S_OK	The number of elements returned is *celt*.
S_FALSE	The number of elements returned is less than *celt*.

Comments

If fewer than the requested number of elements remain in the sequence, **Next** returns only the remaining elements. The actual number of elements returned is passed through *pCeltFetched*, unless it is Null.

Example

The following code implements **IEnumVariant::Next** for collections in the Lines sample file Enumvar.cpp.

```
STDMETHODIMP
CEnumVariant::Next(ULONG cElements, VARIANT FAR* pvar, ULONG FAR*
pcElementFetched)
{
    HRESULT hr;
    ULONG l;
    long l1;
    ULONG l2;

    if (pcElementFetched != NULL)
        *pcElementFetched = 0;

    for (l=0; l<cElements; l++)
        VariantInit(&pvar[l]);

    // Retrieve the next cElements elements.

    for (l1=m_lCurrent, l2=0; l1<(long)(m_lLBound+m_cElements) &&
        l2<cElements; l1++, l2++)
    {
        hr = SafeArrayGetElement(m_psa, &l1, &pvar[l2]);
        if (FAILED(hr))
            goto error;
    }

    // Set count of elements retrieved.

    if (pcElementFetched != NULL)
        *pcElementFetched = l2;
    m_lCurrent = l1;

    return  (l2 < cElements) ? ResultFromScode(S_FALSE) : NOERROR;

error:
    for (l=0; l<cElements; l++)
        VariantClear(&pvar[l]);
    return hr;
}
```

IEnumVARIANT::Reset

HRESULT Reset();

Resets the enumeration sequence to the beginning.

Parameters   *None*

Return Value   The return value obtained from the returned HRESULT is one of the following:

Return value	Meaning
S_OK	Success.
S_FALSE	Failure.

Comments   There is no guarantee that exactly the same set of variants will be enumerated the second time as was enumerated the first time. Although an exact duplicate is desirable, the outcome depends on the collection being enumerated. You may find that it is impractical for some collections to maintain this condition (for example, an enumeration of the files in a directory).

Example   The following code implements **IEnumVariant::Reset** for collections in the Lines sample file Enumvar.cpp:

```
STDMETHODIMP
CEnumVariant::Reset()
{
    m_lCurrent = m_lLBound;
    return NOERROR;
}
```

IEnumVARIANT::Skip

HRESULT Skip(

unsigned long *celt*

);

Attempts to skip over the next *celt* elements in the enumeration sequence.

Parameter   *celt*
      The number of elements to skip.

Return Value   The return value obtained from the returned HRESULT is one of the following:

Return value	Meaning
S_OK	The specified number of elements was skipped.
S_FALSE	The end of the sequence was reached before skipping the requested number of elements.

Example   The following code implements **IEnumVariant::Skip** for collections in the Lines sample file Enumvar.cpp.

```
STDMETHODIMP
CEnumVariant::Skip(ULONG cElements)
{
    m_lCurrent += cElements;
    if (m_lCurrent > (long)(m_lLBound+m_cElements))
    {
        m_lCurrent = m_lLBound+m_cElements;
        return ResultFromScode(S_FALSE);
    }
    else return NOERROR;
}
```

C H A P T E R   6

Data Types, Structures, and Enumerations

Each Automation interface has associated data information. This chapter contains information on the following:

- Data types
- Data structures
- Data enumerations

The interfaces discussed are:

- **IDispatch**
- **ITypeInfo**
- **ITypeLib**
- **ITypeComp**

IDispatch Data Types and Structures

The **IDispatch** interface uses the following data types and structures. For more information on the implementation of the **IDispatch** interface, see Chapter 5, "Dispatch Interface and API Functions."

Name	Purpose
BSTR	A length-prefixed string.
CALLCONV	Identifies the calling convention used by a member function.
CURRENCY	Provides a precise data type of monetary data.
DECIMAL	Provides a decimal data type.
DISPID	Identifies a method, property, or argument to **Invoke**.
DISPPARAMS	Contains arguments passed to a method or property.
EXCEPINFO	Describes an error that occurred during **Invoke**.
INTERFACEDATA	Describes the members of an interface.

Name	Purpose
LCID	Provides locale information for international string comparisons and localized member names.
METHODDATA	Describes a method or property.
PARAMDATA	Describes a parameter to a method.
VARIANT	Describes a VARIANTARG that cannot have the VT_BYREF bit set. Because VT_BYREF is not set, the data of type VARIANT cannot be passed within DISPPARAMS.
VARIANTARG	Describes arguments that may be passed within DISPPARAMS.
VARTYPE	Identifies the available variant types.
VARENUM	Used in VARIANT, TYPEDESC, and OLE (ActiveX) property sets.

BSTR

A length-prefixed string used by Automation data manipulation functions.

```
typedef OLECHAR *BSTR;
```

BSTRs are wide, double-byte (Unicode) strings on 32-bit Windows platforms and narrow, single-byte strings on the Apple® PowerMac™ platform.

For details on the BSTR data type, see Chapter 7, "Conversion and Manipulation Functions."

CALLCONV

Identifies the calling convention used by a member function described in the METHODDATA structure.

```
typedef                           // [v1_enum]
enum tagCALLCONV
{
    CC_FASTCALL    = 0,
    CC_CDECL       = 1,
    CC_MSCPASCAL   = CC_CDECL + 1,
    CC_PASCAL      = CC_MSCPASCAL,
    CC_MACPASCAL   = CC_PASCAL + 1,
    CC_STDCALL     = CC_MACPASCAL + 1,
    CC_FPFASTCALL  = CC_STDCALL + 1,
    CC_SYSCALL     = CC_FPFASTCALL + 1,
    CC_MPWCDECL    = CC_SYSCALL + 1,
    CC_MPWPASCAL   = CC_MPWCDECL + 1,
    CC_MAX         = CC_MPWPASCAL + 1
}   CALLCONV;
```

On 16-bit Windows systems, functions implemented with the CC_CDECL calling convention cannot have a return type of **float** or **double**. This includes functions that return **DATE**, which is a floating-point type.

CURRENCY

A currency number stored as an 8-byte, two's complement integer, scaled by 10,000 to give a fixed-point number with 15 digits to the left of the decimal point and 4 digits to the right. This representation provides a range of ±922337203685477.5807. The **CURRENCY** data type is useful for calculations involving money, or for any fixed-point calculation where accuracy is particularly important.

```
typedef CY CURRENCY;
```

The data type is defined as a structure for working with currency more conveniently:

```
typedef struct  tagCY
    {
    LONGLONG int64;
    }  CY;

#else

// Real definition that works with the C++ compiler.

typedef union tagCY
{
    struct
    {
#ifdef _MAC
        long        Hi;
        unsigned long Lo;
#else
        unsigned long Lo;
        long        Hi;
#endif
    }
    LONGLONG int64;
} CY;
#endif
#endif

// Size is 8.

typedef CY CURRENCY;
```

DECIMAL

A decimal data type that provides a size and scale for a number (as in coordinates).

See also "Numeric Parsing Functions" in Chapter 7, "Conversion and Manipulation Functions."

```
typedef struct tagDEC
    {
    unsigned short wReserved;
    union {
    struct {
        char sign;
        char scale;
    }
```

DISPID

Used by **IDispatch::Invoke** to identify methods, properties, and arguments.

```
typedef LONG DISPID;
```

The following dispatch identifiers (DISPIDs) have special meaning.

DISPID	Description
DISPID_VALUE	The default member for the object. This property or method is invoked when an ActiveX client specifies the object name without a property or method.
DISPID_NEWENUM	The **_NewEnum** property. This special, restricted property is required for collection objects. It returns an enumerator object that supports **IEnumVARIANT,** and should have the **restricted** attribute specified in Object Description Language.

DISPID_EVALUATE	The **Evaluate** method. This method is implicitly invoked when the ActiveX client encloses the arguments in square brackets. For example, the following two lines are equivalent:
	
	`x.[A1:C1].value = 10`
	`x.Evaluate("A1:C1").value = 10`
	
	The **Evaluate** method has the DISPID DISPID_EVALUATE.

DISPID_PROPERTYPUT	The parameter that receives the value of an assignment in a PROPERTYPUT.
DISPID_CONSTRUCTOR	The C++ constructor function for the object.
DISPID_DESTRUCTOR	The C++ destructor function for the object.
DISPID_UNKNOWN	The value returned by **IDispatch::GetIDsOfNames** to indicate that a member or parameter name was not found.

Note
       The reserved DISPIDs are:

DISPID_Name -800
DISPID_Delete -801
DISPID_Object -802
DISPID_Parent -803

DISPPARAMS

Used by **IDispatch::Invoke** to contain the arguments passed to a method or property. For more information, see "IDispatch::Invoke" in Chapter 5, "Dispatch Interface and API Functions."

```
typedef struct FARSTRUCT tagDISPPARAMS
{
VARIANTARG FAR* rgvarg;              // Array of arguments.
    DISPID FAR* rgdispidNamedArgs;  // Dispatch IDs of named arguments.
    unsigned int cArgs;             // Number of arguments.
    unsigned int cNamedArgs;        // Number of named arguments.
} DISPPARAMS;
```

EXCEPINFO

Describes an exception that occurred during **IDispatch::Invoke**. For more information on exceptions, see "IDispatch::Invoke" in Chapter 5, "Dispatch Interface and API Functions."

```
typedef struct FARSTRUCT tagEXCEPINFO
{
    unsigned short wCode;       // An error code describing the error.
    unsigned short wReserved;
    BSTR bstrSource;            // Source of the exception.
    BSTR bstrDescription;       // Textual description of the error.
    BSTR bstrHelpFile;          // Help file path.
    unsigned long dwHelpContext; // Help context ID.
    void FAR* pvReserved;
    // Pointer to function that fills in Help and description info.
    HRESULT (STDAPICALLTYPE FAR* pfnDeferredFillIn)
            (struct tagEXCEPINFO FAR*);
    RETURN VALUE return value;   // A return value describing the error.
} EXCEPINFO, FAR* LPEXCEPINFO;
```

The following table describes the fields of the EXCEPINFO structure.

Field name	Type	Description
wCode	unsigned short	An error code identifying the error. Error codes should be greater than 1000. Either this field or the return value field must be filled in; the other must be set to 0.
wReserved	unsigned short	Reserved; should be set to 0.
bstrSource	BSTR	A textual, human-readable name of the source of the exception. Typically, this is an application name. This field should be filled in by the implementor of **IDispatch**.
BstrDescription	BSTR	A textual, human-readable description of the error intended for the customer. If no description is available, use Null.
bstrHelpFile	BSTR	The fully qualified drive, path, and file name of a Help file with more information about the error. If no Help is available, use Null.
dwHelpContext	unsigned long	The Help context ID of the topic within the Help file. This field should be filled in if and only if the bstrHelpFile field is not Null.
pvReserved	void FAR*	Must be set to Null.
PfnDeferredFillIn	STDAPICALLTYPE	Pointer to a function that takes an EXCEPINFO structure as an argument and returns an HRESULT value. If deferred, fill-in is not desired, this field should be set to Null.
scode	SCODE	A return value describing the error. Either this field or wCode (but not both) must be filled in; the other must be set to 0. (16-bit versions only)

Use the *pfnDeferredFillIn* field to allow an object to defer filling in the *bstrDescription*, *bstrHelpFile*, and *dwHelpContext* fields until they are needed. This field might be used, for example, if loading the string for the error is a time-consuming operation. To use deferred fill-in, the object puts a function pointer in this slot and does not fill any of the other fields except *wCode*, which is required.

To get additional information, the caller passes the EXCEPINFO structure back to the *pexcepinfo* callback function, which fills in the additional information. When the ActiveX object and the ActiveX client are in different processes, the ActiveX object calls *pfnDeferredFillIn* before returning to the controller.

INTERFACEDATA

Describes the ActiveX object's properties and methods.

```
typedef struct FARSTRUCT tagINTERFACEDATA
{
    METHODDATA FAR* pmethdata;    // Pointer to an array of METHODDATAs.
    unsigned int cMembers;        // Count of members.
} INTERFACEDATA;
```

LCID

Identifies a locale for national language support. Locale information is used for international string comparisons and localized member names. For information on locale identifiers (LCIDs), see "Supporting Multiple National Languages" in Chapter 2, "Exposing ActiveX Objects."

```
typedef unsigned long LCID;
```

METHODDATA

Used to describe a method or property.

```
typedef struct FARSTRUCT tagMETHODDATA
{
    OLECHAR FAR* szName;          // Member name.
    PARAMDATA FAR* ppdata;        // Pointer to array of PARAMDATAs.
    DISPID dispid;                // Member ID.
    unsigned int iMeth;           // Method index.
    CALLCONV cc;                  // Calling convention.
    unsigned int cArgs;           // Count of arguments.
    unsigned short wFlags;        // Description of whether this is a
                                  // method or a PROPERTYGET, PROPERTYPUT,
                                  // or PROPERTYPUTREF.
    VARTYPE vtReturn;             // Return type.
} METHODDATA;
```

The following table describes the fields of the METHODDATA structure.

Name	Type	Description
szName	OLECHAR FAR*	The method name.
Ppdata	PARAMDATA FAR*	The parameters for the method. The first parameter is ppdata[0], and so on.
Dispid	DISPID	The ID of the method, as used in **IDispatch**.
IMeth	unsigned int	The index of the method in the VTBL of the interface. The indexes start with 0.

Name	Type	Description
Cc	CALLCONV	The calling convention. The CDECL and Pascal calling conventions are supported by the dispatch interface creation functions, such as **CreateStdDispatch**.
CArgs	unsigned int	The number of arguments for the method.
WFlags	unsigned short	Flags that indicate whether the method is used for getting or setting a property. The flags are the same as in **IDispatch::Invoke**. DISPATCH_METHOD indicates that this is not used for a property. DISPATCH_PROPERTYGET indicates that the method is used to get a property value. DISPATCH_PROPERTYPUT indicates that the method is used to set the value of a property. DISPATCH_PROPERTYPUTREF indicates that the method is used to make the property refer to a passed-in object.
VtReturn	VARTYPE	Return type for the method.

PARAMDATA

Used to describe a parameter accepted by a method or property.

```
typedef struct FARSTRUCT tagPARAMDATA
{
    OLECHAR FAR* szName;    // Parameter name.
    VARTYPE vt;             // Parameter type.
} PARAMDATA;
```

The following table describes the fields of the PARAMDATA structure.

Name	Type	Description
szName	OLECHAR FAR*	The parameter name. Names should follow standard conventions for programming language access; that is, no embedded spaces or control characters, and 32 or fewer characters. The name should be localized because each type description provides names for a particular locale.
vt	VARTYPE	The VARTYPE that will be used by the receiver. If more than one parameter type is accepted, VT_VARIANT should be specified.

VARIANT and VARIANTARG

Use VARIANTARG to describe arguments passed within DISPPARAMS, and VARIANT to specify variant data that cannot be passed by reference. The VARIANT type cannot have the VT_BYREF bit set. VARIANTs can be passed by value, even if VARIANTARGs cannot.

```
typedef struct FARSTRUCT tagVARIANT VARIANT;
typedef struct FARSTRUCT tagVARIANT VARIANTARG;


typedef struct tagVARIANT
{
    VARTYPE vt;
    unsigned short wReserved1;
    unsigned short wReserved2;
    unsigned short wReserved3;
    union {
        unsigned char      bVal;            // VT_UI1.
        short              iVal;            // VT_I2.
        long              lVal;           // VT_I4.
        float              fltVal;          // VT_R4.
        double             dblVal;          // VT_R8.
        VARIANT_BOOL       boolVal;         // VT_BOOL.
        SCODE              scode;           // VT_ERROR.
        CY                 cyVal;           // VT_CY.
        DATE             date;            // VT_DATE.
        BSTR             bstrVal;         // VT_BSTR.
        IUnknown          FAR* punkVal;      // VT_UNKNOWN.
        IDispatch         FAR* pdispVal;     // VT_DISPATCH.
        SAFEARRAY         FAR* pparray;      // VT_ARRAY|*.
        unsigned char     FAR *pbVal;        // VT_BYREF|VT_UI1.
        short             FAR* piVal;        // VT_BYREF|VT_I2.
        long            FAR* plVal;        // VT_BYREF|VT_I4.
        float             FAR* pfltVal;      // VT_BYREF|VT_R4.
        double            FAR* pdblVal;      // VT_BYREF|VT_R8.
        VARIANT_BOOL      FAR* pboolVal;     //VT_BYREF|VT_BOOL.
        SCODE             FAR* pscode;       // VT_BYREF|VT_ERROR.
        CY                FAR* pcyVal;       // VT_BYREF|VT_CY.
        DATE            FAR* pdate;        // VT_BYREF|VT_DATE.
        BSTR            FAR* pbstrVal;     // VT_BYREF|VT_BSTR.
        IUnknown FAR*       FAR* ppunkVal;   // VT_BYREF|VT_UNKNOWN.
        IDispatch FAR*      FAR* ppdispVal;  // T_BYREF|VT_DISPATCH.
        SAFEARRAY FAR*      FAR* pparray;    // VT_ARRAY|*.
        VARIANT             FAR* pvarVal;    // VT_BYREF|VT_VARIANT.
        void              FAR* byref;      // Generic ByRef.
    }
}
```

To simplify extracting values from VARIANTARGs, Automation provides a set of functions for manipulating this type. Use of these functions is strongly recommended to ensure that applications apply consistent coercion rules.

The *vt* value governs the interpretation of the union as follows:

Value	Description
VT_EMPTY	No value was specified. If an optional argument to an Automation method is left blank, do not pass a VARIANT of type VT_EMPTY. Instead, pass a VARIANT of type VT_ERROR with a value of DISP_E_MEMBERNOTFOUND.
VT_EMPTY | VT_BYREF	Not valid.
VT_UI1	An unsigned 1-byte character is stored in *bVal*.
VT_UI1 | VT_BYREF	A reference to an unsigned 1-byte character was passed. A pointer to the value is in *pbVal*.
VT_I2	A 2-byte integer value is stored in *iVal*.
VT_I2 | VT_BYREF	A reference to a 2-byte integer was passed. A pointer to the value is in *piVal*.
VT_I4	A 4-byte integer value is stored in *lVal*.
VT_I4 | VT_BYREF	A reference to a 4-byte integer was passed. A pointer to the value is in *plVal*.
VT_R4	An IEEE 4-byte real value is stored in *fltVal*.
VT_R4 | VT_BYREF	A reference to an IEEE 4-byte real value was passed. A pointer to the value is in *pfltVal*.
VT_R8	An 8-byte IEEE real value is stored in *dblVal*.
VT_R8 | VT_BYREF	A reference to an 8-byte IEEE real value was passed. A pointer to its value is in *pdblVal*.
VT_CY	A currency value was specified. A currency number is stored as an 8-byte, two's complement integer, scaled by 10,000 to give a fixed-point number with 15 digits to the left of the decimal point and 4 digits to the right. The value is in *cyVal*.
VT_CY | VT_BYREF	A reference to a currency value was passed. A pointer to the value is in *pcyVal*.
VT_BSTR	A string was passed; it is stored in *bstrVal*. This pointer must be obtained and freed by the BSTR functions, which are described in Chapter 7, "Conversion and Manipulation Functions."
VT_BSTR | VT_BYREF	A reference to a string was passed. A BSTR* that points to a BSTR is in *pbstrVal*. The referenced pointer must be obtained or freed by the BSTR functions.

Value	Description
VT_NULL	A propagating null value was specified. (This should not be confused with the null pointer.) The null value is used for tri-state logic, as with SQL.
VT_NULL I VT_BYREF	Not valid.
VT_ERROR	An SCODE was specified. The type of the error is specified in *scodee*. Generally, operations on error values should raise an exception or propagate the error to the return value, as appropriate.
VT_ERROR I VT_BYREF	A reference to an SCODE was passed. A pointer to the value is in *pscode*.
VT_BOOL	A Boolean (True/False) value was specified. A value of 0xFFFF (all bits 1) indicates True; a value of 0 (all bits 0) indicates False. No other values are valid.
VT_BOOL I VT_BYREF	A reference to a Boolean value. A pointer to the Boolean value is in *pbool*.
VT_DATE	A value denoting a date and time was specified. Dates are represented as double-precision numbers, where midnight, January 1, 1900 is 2.0, January 2, 1900 is 3.0, and so on. The value is passed in *date*.
	This is the same numbering system used by most spreadsheet programs, although some specify incorrectly that February 29, 1900 existed, and thus set January 1, 1900 to 1.0. The date can be converted to and from an MS-DOS representation using **VariantTimeToDosDateTime**, which is discussed in Chapter 7, "Conversion and Manipulation Functions."
VT_DATE I VT_BYREF	A reference to a date was passed. A pointer to the value is in *pdate*.
VT_DISPATCH	A pointer to an object was specified. The pointer is in *pdispVal*. This object is known only to implement **IDispatch**. The object can be queried as to whether it supports any other desired interface by calling **QueryInterface** on the object. Objects that do not implement **IDispatch** should be passed using VT_UNKNOWN.
VT_DISPATCH I VT_BYREF	A pointer to a pointer to an object was specified. The pointer to the object is stored in the location referred to by *ppdispVal*.
VT_VARIANT	Invalid. VARIANTARGs must be passed by reference.

Value	Description
VT_VARIANT | VT_BYREF	A pointer to another VARIANTARG is passed in *pvarVal*. This referenced VARIANTARG will never have the VT_BYREF bit set in *vt*, so only one level of indirection can ever be present. This value can be used to support languages that allow functions to change the types of variables passed by reference.
VT_UNKNOWN	A pointer to an object that implements the **IUnknown** interface is passed in *punkVal*.
VT_UNKNOWN | VT_BYREF	A pointer to the **IUnknown** interface is passed in *ppunkVal*. The pointer to the interface is stored in the location referred to by *ppunkVal*.
VT_ARRAY | <anything>	An array of data type <anything> was passed. (VT_EMPTY and VT_NULL are invalid types to combine with VT_ARRAY.) The pointer in *pbyrefVal* points to an array descriptor, which describes the dimensions, size, and in-memory location of the array. The array descriptor is never accessed directly, but instead is read and modified using the functions described in Chapter 7, "Conversion and Manipulation Functions."

VARTYPE

An enumeration type used in VARIANT, TYPEDESC, OLE property sets, and safe arrays.

The enumeration constants listed in the following VARENUM section are valid in the *vt* field of a VARIANT structure.

```
typedef unsigned short VARTYPE;
enum VARENUM
{
    VT_EMPTY    = 0,        // Not specified.
    VT_NULL     = 1,        // Null.
    VT_I2       = 2,        // 2-byte signed int.
    VT_I4       = 3,        // 4-byte signed int.
    VT_R4       = 4,        // 4-byte real.
    VT_R8       = 5,        // 8-byte real.
    VT_CY       = 6,        // Currency.
    VT_DATE     = 7,        // Date.
    VT_BSTR     = 8,        // Binary string.
    VT_DISPATCH = 9,        // IDispatch FAR*.
    VT_ERROR    = 10,       // Scodes.
    VT_BOOL     = 11,       // Boolean; True=-1, False=0.
    VT_VARIANT  = 12,       // VARIANT FAR*.
    VT_UNKNOWN  = 13,       // IUnknown FAR*.
    VT_UI1      = 17,       // Unsigned char.
```

```
    // Other constants that are not valid in VARIANTs omitted here.

}
    VT_RESERVED = (int) 0x8000
    // By reference, a pointer to the data is passed.
    VT_BYREF    = (int) 0x4000
    VT_ARRAY    = (int) 0x2000   // A safe array of the data is passed.
```

VARENUM

An enumeration type used in VARIANT, TYPEDESC, OLE property sets, and safe arrays.

The following listing identifies the enumerations that apply to each.

```
// VARENUM usage key.
// [V] - May appear in a VARIANT.
// [T] - May appear in a TYPEDESC.
// [P] - May appear in an OLE property set.
// [S] - May appear in a safe array.
VT_EMPTY          [V]    [P]          // Not specified.
VT_NULL           [V]                 // SQL-style Null.
VT_I2             [V][T][P][S]        // 2-byte signed int.
VT_I4             [V][T][P][S]        // 4-byte-signed int.
VT_R4             [V][T][P][S]        // 4-byte real.
VT_R8             [V][T][P][S]        // 8-byte real.
VT_CY             [V][T][P][S]        // Currency.
VT_DATE           [V][T][P][S]        // Date.
VT_BSTR           [V][T][P][S]        // Automation string.
VT_DISPATCH       [V][T]    [S]       // IDispatch FAR*.
VT_ERROR          [V][T]    [S]       // Scodes.
VT_BOOL           [V][T][P][S]        // Boolean; True=-1, False=0.
VT_VARIANT        [V][T][P][S]        // VARIANT FAR*.
VT_UNKNOWN        [V][T]    [S]       // IUnknown FAR*.
VT_I1             [T]                 // Signed char.
VT_UI1            [V][T]    [S]       // Unsigned char.
VT_UI2               [T]             // Unsigned short.
VT_UI4               [T]             // Unsigned short.
VT_I8                [T][P]          // Signed 64-bit int.
VT_UI8               [T]             // Unsigned 64-bit int.
VT_INT               [T]             // Signed machine int.
VT_UINT              [T]             // Unsigned machine int.
VT_VOID              [T]             // C-style void.
VT_HRESULT           [T]
VT_PTR               [T]             // Pointer type.
VT_SAFEARRAY         [T]             // Use VT_ARRAY in VARIANT.
VT_CARRAY            [T]             // C-style array.
VT_USERDEFINED       [T]             // User-defined type.
VT_LPSTR             [T][P]          // Null-terminated string.
```

```
VT_LPWSTR              [T][P]      // Wide null-terminated string.
VT_FILETIME               [P]      // FILETIME.
VT_BLOB                   [P]      // Length-prefixed bytes.
VT_STREAM                 [P]      // Name of the stream follows.
VT_STORAGE                [P]      // Name of the storage follows.
VT_STREAMED_OBJECT        [P]      // Stream contains an object.
VT_STORED_OBJECT          [P]      // Storage contains an object.
VT_BLOB_OBJECT            [P]      // Blob contains an object.
VT_CF                     [P]      // Clipboard format.
VT_CLSID                  [P]      // A class ID.
VT_VECTOR                 [P]      // Simple counted array.
VT_ARRAY            [V]            // SAFEARRAY*.
VT_BYREF            [V]
```

ITypeInfo Data Types

ITypeInfo uses the following structures and enumerations. For more information about the **ITypeInfo** interface , refer to Chapter 9, "Type Description Interfaces."

Name	Purpose
ARRAYDESC	Array description referenced by TYPEDESC, containing the element type, dimension count, and a variable-length array.
CUSTDATA	Structure for retrieving custom data
CUSTDATAITEM	Structure containing custom data
ELEMDESC	Includes the type description and process-transfer information for a variable, a function, or a function parameter.
FUNCDESC	Describes a function.
FUNCFLAGS	Enumeration containing constants that are used to define properties of a function.
FUNCKIND	Enumeration for defining whether a function is accessed as a virtual, pure virtual, nonvirtual, static, or through **IDispatch**.
HREFTYPE	A handle identifying a type description.
IDLDESC	Contains information needed for transferring a structure element, parameter, or function return value between processes. See also ELEMDESC.

Name	Purpose
PARAMFLAGS	Identifies whether the parameter is the return value of a member, the LCID of a client, and passes information from caller to callee, or callee to caller.
IMPLTYPEFLAGS	The interface or dispinterface represents the default for the source or sink. This member of a coclass is called rather than implemented. The member should not be displayed or programmable by users, or sinks receive events through the VTBL.
INVOKEKIND	Defines how a function is called and invoked. Also passed to **IDispatch::Invoke**.
MEMBERID	Identifies the member in a type description. For **IDispatch** interfaces, this is the same as a DISPID.
TYPEATTR	Contains attributes of **ITypeInfo**.
TYPEDESC	Describes the type of a variable, the return type of a function, or the type of a function parameter.
TYPEFLAGS	Defines the properties and attributes of a type description.
TYPEKIND	Defines properties of a type.
VARDESC	Describes a variable, constant, or data member.
VARFLAGS	Used to set attributes of a variable.
VARKIND	Defines the kind of variable.

ARRAYDESC

Contained within the TYPEDESC, which describes the type of the array's elements, and information about the array's dimensions. It is defined as follows:

```
typedef struct tagARRAYDESC
{
    TYPEDESC tdescElem;              // Element type.
    unsigned short cDims;           // Dimension count.
    SAFEARRAYBOUND rgbounds[1];     // Variable length array containing
                                    // one element for each dimension.
} ARRAYDESC;
```

CUSTDATA

Used for retrieving custom data. It is defined as follows:

```
typedef struct  tagCUSTDATA
    {
    DWORD cCustData;
    LPCUSTDATAITEM prgCustData;        // [size_is].
    }  CUSTDATA;
```

The following table describes the fields of the CUSTDATA structure.

Value	Description
cCustData	Number of custom data items in prgCustData
prgCustData	Array of custom data items

CUSTDATAITEM

Contains the custom data. It is defined as follows:

```
typedef struct  tagCUSTDATAITEM
    {
    GUID guid;
    VARIANTARG varValue;
    }  CUSTDATAITEM;
```

The following table describes the fields of the CUSTDATAITEM structure.

Value	Description
guid	Unique identifier for this data item
varValue	Value of this data item

ELEMDESC

Includes the type description and process-transfer information for a variable, a function, or a function parameter. It is defined as follows:

```
typedef struct tagELEMDESC
{
    TYPEDESC tdesc;              // Type of the element.
union   {
        IDLDESC idldesc;         // Information for remoting the element
                                 // (backward compatibility)
        PARAMDESC paramdesc;     // information about the parameter.
        }
} ELEMDESC, * LPELEMDESC;
    }  ELEMDESC;
```

FUNCDESC

Describes a function, and is defined as follows:

```
typedef struct tagFUNCDESC
{
    MEMBERID memid;              // Function member ID.

/* [size_is] */ SCODE __RPC_FAR *lprgscode;
/* [size_is] */ ELEMDESC __RPC_FAR *lprgelemdescParam;   FUNCKIND

funckind;                     // Specifies whether the
                              // function is virtual, static,
                              // or dispatch-only.
    INVOKEKIND invkind;       // Invocation kind. Indicates if this is a
                              // property function, and if so, what kind.
    CALLCONV callconv;        // Specifies the function's calling
                              // convention.
    short cParams;            // Count of total number of parameters.
    short cParamsOpt;         // Count of optional parameters (detailed
                              // description follows).
    short oVft;               // For FUNC_VIRTUAL, specifies the offset in
                              // the VTBL.
    short cScodes;            // Count of permitted return values.
    ELEMDESC elemdescFunc;    // Contains the return type of the function.
    WORD wFuncFlags;          // Definition of flags follows.
}   FUNCDESC;
```

The *cParams* field specifies the total number of required and optional parameters.

The *cParamsOpt* field specifies the form of optional parameters accepted by the function, as follows:

- A value of 0 specifies that no optional arguments are supported.

- A value of −1 specifies that the method's last parameter is a pointer to a safe array of variants. Any number of variant arguments greater than *cParams* −1 must be packaged by the caller into a safe array and passed as the final parameter. This array of optional parameters must be freed by the caller after control is returned from the call.

- Any other number indicates that the last *n* parameters of the function are variants and do not need to be specified by the caller explicitly. The parameters left unspecified should be filled in by the compiler or interpreter as variants of type VT_ERROR with the value DISP_E_PARAMNOTFOUND.

For 16-bit systems (Macintosh), the fields *cScodes* and *lprgscode* store the count and the set of errors that a function can return. If *cScodes* = −1, then the set of errors is unknown. If *cScodes* = −1, or if *cScodes* = 0, then *lprgscode* is undefined.

FUNCFLAGS

Defined as follows:

```
typedef enum tagFUNCFLAGS
{
        FUNCFLAG_FRESTRICTED            =   1
        , FUNCFLAG_FSOURCE              =   0x2
        , FUNCFLAG_FBINDABLE            =   0x4
        , FUNCFLAG_FREQUESTEDIT         =   0x8
        , FUNCFLAG_FDISPLAYBIND         =   0x10
        , FUNCFLAG_FDEFAULTBIND         =   0x20
        , FUNCFLAG_FHIDDEN              =   0x40
        , FUNCFLAG_FUSESGETLASTERROR =     0x80
        , FUNCFLAG_FDEFAULTCOLLELEM =      0x100
        , FUNCFLAG_FUIDEFAULT           =   0x200
        , FUNCFLAG_FNONBROWSABLE        =   0x400
        , FUNCFLAG_FREPLACEABLE         =   0x800
        , FUNCFLAG_FIMMEDIATEBIND       =   0x1000
} FUNCFLAGS;
```

Value	Description
FUNCFLAG_FRESTRICTED	The function should not be accessible from macro languages. This flag is intended for system-level functions or functions that type browsers should not display.
FUNCFLAG_FSOURCE	The function returns an object that is a source of events.
FUNCFLAG_FBINDABLE	The function that supports data binding.
FUNCFLAG_FREQUESTEDIT	
FUNCFLAG_FDISPLAYBIND	The function that is displayed to the user as bindable. FUNC_FBINDABLE must also be set.
FUNCFLAG_FDEFAULTBIND	The function that best represents the object. Only one function in a type information can have this attribute.
FUNCFLAG_FHIDDEN	The function should not be displayed to the user, although it exists and is bindable.
FUNCFLAG_USESGETLASTERROR	tbd

Value	Description
FUNCFLAG_FDEFAULTCOLLELEM	Permits an optimization in which the compiler looks for a member named "xyz" on the type of "abc". If such a member is found and is flagged as an accessor function for an element of the default collection, then a call is generated to that member function. Permitted on members in dispinterfaces and interfaces; not permitted on modules. For more information, refer to "defaultcollelem" in Chapter 8, "Type Libraries and the Object Description Language."
FUNCFLAG_FUIDEFAULT	The type information member is the default member for display in the user interface.
FUNCFLAG_FNONBROWSABLE	The property appears in an object browser, but not in a properties browser.
FUNCFLAG_FREPLACEABLE	Tags the interface as having default behaviors.
FUNCFLAG_FIMMEDIATEBIND	Mapped as individual bindable properties.

Note FUNCFLAG_FHIDDEN means that the property should never be shown in object browsers, property browsers, and so on. This function is useful for removing items from an object model. Code can bind to the member, but the user will never know that the member exists.

FUNCFLAG_FNONBROWSABLE means that the property should not be displayed in a properties browser. It is used in circumstances in which an error would occur if the property were shown in a properties browser.

Examples

- The **IsSelected** property for a control. Setting it to False would confuse a user if the properties browser was focus-oriented.
- Properties that take a long time to evaluate (for example, a **Count** property for a database object). The time to evaluate might take longer than a user is willing to wait.
- Properties that have side effects.

FUNCFLAG_FRESRICTED means that macro-oriented programmers should not be allowed to access this member. These members are usually treated as _FHIDDEN by tools such as Visual Basic, with the main difference being that code cannot bind to those members.

FUNCKIND

The FUNCKIND enumeration is defined as follows:

```
typedef enum tagFUNCKIND
{
    FUNC_VIRTUAL,
    FUNC_PUREVIRTUAL,
    FUNC_NONVIRTUAL,
    FUNC_STATIC,
    FUNC_DISPATCH,
} FUNCKIND;
```

Value	Description
FUNC_PUREVIRTUAL	The function is accessed through the virtual function table (VTBL), and takes an implicit *this* pointer.
FUNC_VIRTUAL	The function is accessed the same as PUREVIRTUAL, except the function has an implementation.
FUNC_NONVIRTUAL	The function is accessed by static address and takes an implicit *this* pointer.
FUNC_STATIC	The function is accessed by static address and does not take an implicit *this* pointer.
FUNC_DISPATCH	The function can be accessed only through **IDispatch**.

HREFTYPE

A handle that identifies a type description.

```
typedef unsigned long HREFTYPE;
```

IMPLTYPEFLAGS

Defined as follows:

```
#define IMPLTYPEFLAG_FDEFAULT       0x1
#define IMPLTYPEFLAG_FSOURCE        0x2
#define IMPLTYPEFLAG_FRESTRICTED    0x4
#define IMPLTYPEFLAG_FDEFAULTVTABLE 0x800
```

Value	Description
IMPLTYPEFLAG_FDEFAULT	The interface or dispinterface represents the default for the source or sink.
IMPLTYPEFLAG_FSOURCE	This member of a coclass is called rather than implemented.
IMPLTYPEFLAG_FRESTRICTED	The member should not be displayed or programmable by users.
IMPLTYPEFLAG_FDEFAULTVTABLE	Sinks receive events through the VTBL.

INVOKEKIND

Defined as follows:

```
typedef enum tagINVOKEKIND
{
    INVOKE_FUNC = DISPATCH_METHOD,
    INVOKE_PROPERTYGET = DISPATCH_PROPERTYGET,
    INVOKE_PROPERTYPUT = DISPATCH_PROPERTYPUT,
    INVOKE_PROPERTYPUTREF = DISPATCH_PROPERTYPUTREF
} INVOKEKIND;
```

Value	Description
INVOKE_FUNC	The member is called using a normal function invocation syntax.
INVOKE_PROPERTYGET	The function is invoked using a normal property-access syntax.
INVOKE_PROPERTYPUT	The function is invoked using a property value assignment syntax. Syntactically, a typical programming language might represent changing a property in the same way as assignment. For example: `object.property := value`.
INVOKE_PROPERTYPUTREF	The function is invoked using a property reference assignment syntax.

In C, value assignment is written as `*pobj1 = *pobj2`, while reference assignment is written as `pobj1 = pobj2`. Other languages have other syntactic conventions. A property or data member can support only a value assignment, a reference assignment, or both. For a detailed description of property functions, see Chapter 5, "Dispatch Interface and API Functions." The INVOKEKIND enumeration constants are the same constants that are passed to **IDispatch::Invoke** to specify the way in which a function is invoked.

MEMBERID

Identifies the member in a type description. For **IDispatch** interfaces, this is the same as DISPID.

```
typedef DISPID MEMBERID;
```

This is a 32-bit integral value in the following format.

Bits	Value
0–15	Offset. Any value is permissible.
16–21	The nesting level of this type information in the inheritance hierarchy. For example:
	`interface mydisp : IDispatch`
	The nesting level of **IUnknown** is 0, **IDispatch** is 1, and MyDisp is 2.
22–25	Reserved. Must be zero.
26–28	Value of the DISPID.
29	True if this is the member ID for a FUNCDESC; otherwise False.
30–31	Must be 01.

Negative IDs are reserved for use by Automation.

PARAMDESC

Contains information needed for transferring a structure element, parameter, or function return value between processes. It is defined as follows:

```
typedef struct FARSTRUCT tagPARAMDESC
{
    unsigned long lpVarValue;
    unsigned short wPARAMFlags;
} PARAMDESC
```

The *lpVarValue* field contains a pointer to a VARIANT that describes the default value for this parameter, if the PARAMFLAG_FOPT and PARAMFLAG_FHASDEFAULT bit of *wParamFlags* is set.l.

PARAMFLAGS

Defined as follows:

```
#define PARAMFLAG_NONE          0
#define PARAMFLAG_FIN           0x1
#define PARAMFLAG_FOUT          0x2
#define PARAMFLAG_FLCID         0x4
#define PARAMFLAG_FRETVAL       0x8
#define PARAMFLAG_FOPT          0x10
#define PARAMFLAG_FHASDEFAULT   0x20
```

Value	Description
PARAMFLAG_NONE	Whether the parameter passes or receives information is unspecified. **IDispatch** interfaces can use this flag.
PARAMFLAG_FIN	Parameter passes information from the caller to the callee.
PARAMFLAG_FOUT	Parameter returns information from the callee to the caller.
PARAMFLAG_FLCID	Parameter is the LCID of a client application.
PARAMFLAG_FRETVAL	Parameter is the return value of the member.
PARAMFLAG_FOPT	Parameter is optional. The *lpVarValue* field contains a pointer to a VARIANT describing the default value for this parameter, if the PARAMFLAG_FOPT and PARAMFLAG_FHASDEFAULT bit of *wParamFlags* is set.l.
PARAMFLAG_FHASDEFAULT	Parameter has default behaviors defined. The *lpVarValue* field contains a pointer to a VARIANT that describes the default value for this parameter, if the PARAMFLAG_FOPT and PARAMFLAG_FHASDEFAULT bit of wParamFlags is set.l.

TYPEATTR

Contains attributes of an **ITypeInfo**, and is defined as follows:

```
typedef struct FARSTRUCT tagTYPEATTR
{
    GUID guid;                  // The GUID of the type information.
    LCID lcid;                  // Locale of member names and doc
                                // strings.
    unsigned long dwReserved;
    MEMBERID memidConstructor;  // ID of constructor, or MEMBERID_NIL if
                                // none.
    MEMBERID memidDestructor;   // ID of destructor, or MEMBERID_NIL if
                                // none.
    OLECHAR FAR* lpstrSchema;   // Reserved for future use.
    unsigned long cbSizeInstance;// The size of an instance of
                                // this type.
    TYPEKIND typekind;          // The kind of type this information
                                // describes.
```

```
        unsigned short cFuncs;         // Number of functions.
        unsigned short cVars;          // Number of variables/data members.
        unsigned short cImplTypes;     // Number of implemented interfaces.
        unsigned short cbSizeVft;      // The size of this type's VTBL.
        unsigned short cbAlignment;    // Byte alignment for an instance
                                       // of this type.
        unsigned short wTypeFlags;
        unsigned short wMajorVerNum;   // Major version number.
        unsigned short wMinorVerNum;   // Minor version number.
        TYPEDESC tdescAlias;           // If TypeKind == TKIND_ALIAS,
                                       // specifies the type for which
                                       // this type is an alias.
        IDLDESC idldescType;           // IDL attributes of the
                                       // described type.
} TYPEATTR, FAR* LPTYPEATTR;
```

The *cbAlignment* field indicates how addresses are aligned. A value of 0 indicates
alignment on the 64K boundary; 1 indicates no special alignment. For other values, *n*
indicates aligned on byte *n*.

TYPEDESC

Describes the type of a variable, the return type of a function, or the type of a function
parameter. It is defined as follows:

```
typedef struct FARSTRUCT tagTYPEDESC
{
    union
    {

    // VT_PTR|VT_SAFEAEEAY, the pointed-at type.

    struct FARSTRUCT tagTYPEDESC FAR* lptdesc;

    // VT_CARRAY.

    struct FARSTRUCT tagARRAYDESC FAR* lpadesc;

    // VT_USERDEFINED is used to get type information for a
    // user-defined type.

    HREFTYPE hreftype;

    }UNION_NAME(u);
    VARTYPE vt;
} TYPEDESC;
```

If the variable is **VT_SAFEARRAY** or **VT_PTR**, the union portion of the
TYPEDESC contains a pointer to a TYPEDESC that specifies the element type.

TYPEFLAGS

The TYPEFLAGS enumeration is defined as follows:

```
typedef enum tagTYPEFLAGS
{
    TYPEFLAG_FAPPOBJECT =           0x01
    , TYPEFLAG_FCANCREATE =         0x02
    , TYPEFLAG_FLICENSED =          0x04
    , TYPEFLAG_FPREDECLID =         0x08
    , TYPEFLAG_FHIDDEN =            0x10
    , TYPEFLAG_FCONTROL =           0x20
    , TYPEFLAG_FDUAL =              0x40
    , TYPEFLAG_FNONEXTENSIBLE =     0x80
    , TYPEFLAG_FOLEAUTOMATION =     0x100
    , TYPEFLAG_FRESTRICTED =        0x200
    , TYPEFLAG_FAGGREGATABLE =      0x400
    , TYPEFLAG_FREPLACEABLE =       0x800
    , TYPEFLAG_FDISPATCHABLE =      0x1000
} TYPEFLAGS;
```

Value	Description
TYPEFLAG_FAPPOBJECT	A type description that describes an Application object.
TYPEFLAG_FCANCREATE	Instances of the type can be created by **ITypeInfo::CreateInstance**.
TYPEFLAG_FLICENSED	The type is licensed.
TYPEFLAG_FPREDECLID	The type is predefined. The client application should automatically create a single instance of the object that has this attribute. The name of the variable that points to the object is the same as the class name of the object.
TYPEFLAG_FHIDDEN	The type should not be displayed to browsers.
TYPEFLAG_FCONTROL	The type is a control from which other types will be derived, and should not be displayed to users.
TYPEFLAG_FDUAL	The types in the interface derive from **IDispatch** and are fully compatible with Automation. Not allowed on dispinterfaces (dispatch interfaces).
TYPEFLAG_FNONEXTENSIBLE	The interface cannot add members at run time.

Value	Description
TYPEFLAG_FOLEAUTOMATION	The types used in the interface are fully compatible with Automation, and may be displayed in an object browser. Setting **dual** on an interface sets this flag in addition to TYPEFLAG_FDUAL. Not allowed on dispinterfaces.
TYPEFLAG_FRESTRICTED	Should not be accessible from macro languages. This flag is intended for system-level types or types that type browsers should not display
TYPEFLAG_FAGGREGATABLE	The class supports aggregation.
TYPEFLAG_FREPLACEABLE	The object supports **IConnectionPointWithDefault**, and has default behaviors.
TYPEFLAG_FDISPATCHABLE	Indicates that the interface derives from **IDispatch**, either directly or indirectly. This flag is computed. There is no Object Description Language for the flag.

TYPEFLAG_FAPPOBJECT can be used on type descriptions with TypeKind = TKIND_COCLASS, and indicates that the type description specifies an Application object.

Members of the Application object are globally accessible. The **Bind** method of the **ITypeComp** instance associated with the library binds to the members of an Application object, just as it does for type descriptions that have TypeKind = TKIND_MODULE.

The type description implicitly defines a global variable with the same name and type described by the type description. This variable is also globally accessible. When **Bind** is passed the name of an Application object, a VARDESC is returned, which describes the implicit variable. The ID of the implicitly created variable is always ID_DEFAULTINST.

The **ITypeInfo::CreateInstance** function of an Application object type description is called, and then it uses **GetActiveObject** to retrieve the Application object. If **GetActiveObject** fails because the application is not running, then **CreateInstance** calls **CoCreateInstance**, which should start the application.

When TYPEFLAG_FCANCREATE is True, **ITypeInfo::CreateInstance** can create an instance of the type. This is currently true only for component object classes for which a globally unique identifier (GUID) has been specified.

TYPEKIND

Defined as follows:

```
typedef enum tagTYPEKIND
{
      TKIND_ENUM = 0
    , TKIND_RECORD
    , TKIND_MODULE
    , TKIND_INTERFACE
    , TKIND_DISPATCH
    , TKIND_COCLASS
    , TKIND_ALIAS
    , TKIND_UNION
    , TKIND_MAX
} TYPEKIND;
```

Value	Description
TKIND_ALIAS	A type that is an alias for another type.
TKIND_COCLASS	A set of implemented component object interfaces.
TKIND_DISPATCH	A set of methods and properties that are accessible through **IDispatch::Invoke**. By default, dual interfaces return TKIND_DISPATCH.
TKIND_ENUM	A set of enumerators.
TKIND_INTERFACE	A type that has virtual functions, all of which are pure.
TKIND_MODULE	A module that can only have static functions and data (for example, a DLL).
TKIND_RECORD	A structure with no methods.
TKIND_UNION	A union, all of whose members have an offset of zero.
TKIND_MAX	End of ENUM marker.

VARDESC

Describes a variable, constant, or data member. It is defined as follows:

```
typedef struct FARSTRUCT tagVARDESC
{
    MEMBERID memid;
    OLECHAR FAR* lpstrSchema;      // Reserved for future use.
    union
    {
                                   // VAR_PERINSTANCE, the offset of this
                                   // variable within the instance.
    unsigned long oInst;

                                   // VAR_CONST, the value of the constant.
```

```
        VARIANT FAR* lpvarValue;

    } UNION_NAME(u);
    ELEMDESC elemdescVar;
    unsigned short wVarFlags;
    VARKIND varkind;
} VARDESC;
```

VARFLAGS

Defined as follows:

```
typedef enum tagVARFLAGS
{
        VARFLAG_FREADONLY         =   0x1
    ,  VARFLAG_FSOURCE           = 0x2
    ,  VARFLAG_FBINDABLE         = 0x4
    ,  VARFLAG_FREQUESTEDIT      = 0x8
    ,  VARFLAG_FDISPLAYBIND      = 0x10
    ,  VARFLAG_FDEFAULTBIND      = 0x20
    ,  VARFLAG_FHIDDEN           = 0x40
    ,  VARFLAG_FRESTRICTED       = 0x80
    ,  VARFLAG_FDEFAULTCOLLELEM = 0x100
    ,  VARFLAG_FUIDEFAULT        =    0x200
    ,  VARFLAG_FNONBROWSABLE     = 0x400
    ,  VARFLAG_FREPLACEABLE      = 0x800,
    ,  VARFLAG_FIMMEDIATEBIND    = 0x1000
} VARFLAGS;
```

Value	Description
VARFLAG_FREADONLY	Assignment to the variable should not be allowed.
VARFLAG_FSOURCE	The variable returns an object that is a source of events.
VARFLAG_FBINDABLE	The variable supports data binding.
VARFLAG_FREQUESTEDIT	
VARFLAG_FDISPLAYBIND	The variable is displayed to the user as bindable. VARFLAG_FBINDABLE must also be set.
VARFLAG_FDEFAULTBIND	The variable is the single property that best represents the object. Only one variable in type information can have this attribute.
VARFLAG_FHIDDEN	The variable should not be displayed to the user in a browser, although it exists and is bindable.

Value	Description
VARFLAG_FRESTRICTED	The variable should not be accessible from macro languages. This flag is intended for system-level variables or variables that you do not want type browsers to display.
VARFLAG_FDEFAULTCOLLELEM	Permits an optimization in which the compiler looks for a member named "xyz" on the type of abc. If such a member is found and is flagged as an accessor function for an element of the default collection, then a call is generated to that member function. Permitted on members in dispinterfaces and interfaces; not permitted on modules.
VARFLAG_FUIDEFAULT	The variable is the default display in the user interface.
VARFLAG_FNONBROWSABLE	The variable appears in an object browser, but not in a properties browser.
VARFLAG_FREPLACEABLE	Tags the interface as having default behaviors.
VARFLAG_FIMMEDIATEBIND	The variable is mapped as individual bindable properties.

VARKIND

Defined as follows:

```
typedef enum tagVARKIND
{
    VAR_PERINSTANCE,
    VAR_STATIC,
    VAR_CONST,
    VAR_DISPATCH
} VARKIND;
```

Value	Description
VAR_PERINSTANCE	The variable is a field or member of the type. It exists at a fixed offset within each instance of the type.
VAR_STATIC	There is only one instance of the variable.
VAR_CONST	The VARDESC describes a symbolic constant. There is no memory associated with it.
VAR_DISPATCH	The variable can only be accessed through **IDispatch::Invoke**.

ITypeLib Structures and Enumerations

The type building interfaces use the following structures and enumerations.

Structure	Description
LIBFLAGS	Defines flags that apply to type libraries.
REGKIND	Controls how a type library is registered.
SYSKIND	Identifies the target operating system platform.
TLIBATTR	Contains information about a type library.

LIBFLAGS

Defines flags that apply to type libraries. It is defined as follows:

```
typedef enum tagLIBFLAGS
{
      LIBFLAG_FRESTRICTED    = 0x01
    , LIBFLAG_FCONTROL       = 0x02
    , LIBFLAG_FHIDDEN        = 0x04
} LIBFLAGS;
```

Value	Description
LIBFLAG_FCONTROL	The type library describes controls, and should not be displayed in type browsers intended for nonvisual objects.
LIBFLAG_FRESTRICTED	The type library is restricted, and should not be displayed to users.
LIBFLAG_FHIDDEN	The type library should not be displayed to users, although its use is not restricted. Should be used by controls. Hosts should create a new type library that wraps the control with extended properties.

REGKIND

Controls how a type library is registered. It is defined as follows:

```
typedef enum tagREGKIND
{
    REGKIND_DEFAULT,
    REGKIND_REGISTER,
    REGKIND_NONE
} REGKIND;
```

Value	Description
REGKIND_DEFAULT	Use default register behavior
REGKIND_REGISTER	Registered type
REGKIND_NONE	Not a registered type

SYSKIND

Identifies the target operating system platform. It is defined as follows:

```
typedef enum tagSYSKIND
{
    SYS_WIN16,
    SYS_WIN32,
    SYS_MAC
} SYSKIND;
```

Value	Description
SYS_WIN16	The target operating system for the type library is 16-bit Windows systems. By default, data members are packed.
SYS_WIN32	The target operating system for the type library is 32-bit Windows systems. By default, data members are naturally aligned (for example, 2-byte integers are aligned on even-byte boundaries; 4-byte integers are aligned on quad-word boundaries, and so on).
SYS_MAC	The target operating system for the type library is Apple Macintosh. By default, all data members are aligned on even-byte boundaries.

TLIBATTR

Contains information about a type library. Information from this structure is used to identify the type library and to provide national language support for member names. It is defined as follows:

```
typedef struct FARSTRUCT tagTLIBATTR
{
    GUID guid;                      // Unique ID of the library.
    LCID lcid;                      // Language/locale of the library.
    SYSKIND syskind;                // Target hardware platform.
    unsigned short wMajorVerNum;    // Major version number.
    unsigned short wMinorVerNum;    // Minor version number.
    unsigned short wLibFlags;       // Library flags.
} TLIBATTR, FAR * LPTLIBATTR;
```

For more information on national language support, see "Supporting Multiple National Languages" in Chapter 2, "Exposing ActiveX objects," and refer to the National Language Support API reference material in the Windows NT documentation.

ITypeComp Structures and Enumerations

The **ITypeComp** interface uses the following structures and enumerations:

Structure	Description
BINDPTR	A union containing a pointer to a FUNCDESC, VARDESC, or an **ITypeComp** interface.
DESCKIND	Identifies the type description being bound to.

BINDPTR

A union containing a pointer to a FUNCDESC, VARDESC, or an **ITypeComp** interface. It is defined as follows:

```
typedef union tagBINDPTR
{
    FUNCDESC FAR* lpfuncdesc;
    VARDESC FAR* lpvardesc;
    ITypeComp FAR* lptcomp;
} BINDPTR;
```

DESCKIND

Identifies the type description being bound to, and is defined as follows:

```
typedef enum tagDESCKIND
{
    DESCKIND_NONE,
    DESCKIND_FUNCDESC,
    DESCKIND_VARDESC,
    DESCKIND_TYPECOMP,
    DESCKIND_IMPLICITAPPOBJ
} DESCKIND;
```

Value	Description
DESCKIND_NONE	No match was found.
DESCKIND_FUNCDESC	A FUNCDESC was returned.
DESCKIND_VARDESC	A VARDESC was returned.
DESCKIND_TYPECOMP	A TYPECOMP was returned.
DESCKIND_IMPLICITAPPOBJ	An IMPLICITAPPOBJ was returned.

C H A P T E R   7

Conversion and Manipulation Functions

Data manipulation and conversion functions access and manipulate the array, string, and variant data types used by Automation. This chapter contains information about the following functions:

- Array manipulation
- String manipulation
- Variant manipulation
- Data type conversion
- BSTR and vector conversion
- Numeric parsing functions
- Date and time conversion

You can locate all of the data functions and data types in the following files.

Implemented by	Used by	Header file name	Import library file name
Oleaut32.dll (32-bit systems)	Applications that expose or access programmable objects.	Oleauto.h.	Oleauto32.lib
Ole2disp.dll (16-bit systems)		Dispatch.h	Ole2disp.lib

Overview of Functions

The data manipulation functions are summarized in the following table.

Category	Function name	Purpose
Array manipulation	**SafeArrayAccessData**	Increments the lock count of an array and returns a pointer to array data.

Category	Function name	Purpose
Array manipulation	**SafeArrayAllocData**	Allocates memory for a safe array based on a descriptor created with **SafeArrayAllocDescriptor**
	SafeArrayAllocDescriptor	Allocates memory for a safe array descriptor.
	SafeArrayCopy	Copies an existing array.
	SafeArrayCopyData	Copies a source array to a target array after releasing source resources.
	SafeArrayCreate	Creates a new array descriptor.
	SafeArrayCreateVector	Creates a one-dimensional array whose lower bound is always zero.
	SafeArrayDestroy	Destroys an array descriptor.
	SafeArrayDestroyData	Frees memory used by the data elements in a safe array.
	SafeArrayDestroyDescriptor	Frees memory used by a safe array descriptor.
	SafeArrayGetDim	Returns the number of dimensions in an array.
	SafeArrayGetElement	Retrieves an element of an array.
	SafeArrayGetElemsize	Returns the size of an element.
	SafeArrayGetLBound	Retrieves the lower bound for a given dimension.
	SafeArrayGetUBound	Retrieves the upper bound for a given dimension.
	SafeArrayLock	Increments the lock count of an array.
	SafeArrayPtrOfIndex	Returns a pointer to an array element.
	SafeArrayPutElement	Assigns an element into an array.
	SafeArrayRedim	Resizes a safe array.

Category	Function name	Purpose
Array manipulation	**SafeArrayUnaccessData**	Frees a pointer to array data and decrements the lock count of the array.
	SafeArrayUnlock	Decrements the lock count of an array.
String manipulation	**SysAllocString**	Creates and initializes a string.
	SysAllocStringByteLen	Creates a zero-terminated string of a specified length (32-bit only).
	SysAllocStringLen	Creates a string of a specified length.
	SysFreeString	Frees a previously created string.
	SysReAllocString	Changes the size and value of a string.
	SysReAllocStringLen	Changes the size of an existing string.
	SysStringByteLen	Returns the length of a string in bytes (32-bit only).
	SysStringLen	Returns the length of a string.
Variant manipulation	**VariantChangeType**	Converts a variant to another type.
	VariantChangeTypeEx	Converts a variant to another type, using a locale identifier (LCID).
	VariantClear	Releases resources and sets a variant to VT_EMPTY.
	VariantCopy	Copies a variant.
	VariantCopyInd	Copies variants that may contain a pointer.
	VariantInit	Initializes a variant.
Data type conversion	**VariantChangeType** **VariantChangeTypeEx**	Converts specific types of variants to other variant types.

Category	Function name	Purpose
BSTR and vector conversion	**VectorFromBstr**	Returns a vector, assigning each character in the BSTR to an element of the vector.
	BstrFromVector	Returns a BSTR, assigning each element of the vector to a character in the BSTR.
Numeric parsing	**VarParseNumFromStr**	Parses a string, and creates a type-independent desciption of the number it represents.
	VarNumFromParseNum	Converts the parse results to a number.
Time and date conversion	**DosDateTimeToVariantTime**	Converts MS-DOS date and time representations to a variant time.
	VariantTimeToDosDateTime	Converts a variant time to MS-DOS date and time representations.
	VariantTimeToSystemTime	Converts a variant time to system date and time representations.
	GetAltMonthNames	Retrieves the secondary month names.
	SystemTimeToVariantTime	Converts system date and time representations to a variant time.
	VarDateFromUdate	Packs a date.
	VarUdateFromDate	Unpacks a date

Array Manipulation API Functions

The arrays passed by **IDispatch::Invoke** within VARIANTARGs are called *safe arrays*. Safe arrays contain information about the number of dimensions and bounds within them. When an array is an argument or the return value of a function, the *parray* field of VARIANTARG points to an array descriptor. Do not access this array descriptor directly, unless you are creating arrays containing elements with nonvariant data types. Instead, use the functions **SafeArrayAccessData** and **SafeArrayUnaccessData** to access the data.

The base type of the array is indicated by VT_ tag I VT_ARRAY. The data referenced by an array descriptor is stored in column-major order, which is the same ordering scheme used by Visual Basic and FORTRAN, but different from C and Pascal. *Column-major order* is when the left-most dimension (as specified in a programming language syntax) changes first.

The following sections define the safe array descriptor, along with the functions you use when accessing the data in the descriptor and the array.

SAFEARRAY Data Type

The definition for a safe array varies, depending on the target operating system platform. On 32-bit Windows systems, both the *cbElements* and *cLocks* parameters are **unsigned long** integers, and the *handle* parameter is omitted. On 16-bit Windows systems, *cbElements* and *cLocks* are **unsigned short** integers The *handle* parameter is retained for compatibility with earlier software. For example:

```
typedef struct FARSTRUCT tagSAFEARRAY
{
    unsigned short cDims;        // Count of dimensions in this array.
    unsigned short fFeatures;    // Flags used by the SafeArray
                                 // routines documented below.
#if defined(WIN32)
    unsigned long cbElements;    // Size of an element of the array.
                                 // Does not include size of
                                 // pointed-to data.
    unsigned long cLocks;        // Number of times the array has been
                                 // locked without corresponding unlock.
#else
    unsigned short cbElements;
    unsigned short cLocks;
    unsigned long handle;        // Unused but kept for compatibility.
#endif
    void HUGEP* pvData;          // Pointer to the data.
    SAFEARRAYBOUND rgsabound[1]; // One bound for each dimension.
} SAFEARRAY;
```

The array rgsabound is stored with the left-most dimension in rgsabound[0] and the right-most dimension in rgsabound[*cDims* – 1]. If an array was specified in a C-like syntax as a [2][5], it would have two elements in the rgsabound vector. Element 0 has an lLbound of 0 and a cElements of 2. Element 1 has an lLbound of 0 and a cElements of 5.

The fFeatures flags describe attributes of an array that can affect how the array is released. This allows freeing the array without referencing its containing variant. The bits are accessed using the following constants:

```
#define FADF_AUTO       0x0001  // Array is allocated on the stack.
#define FADF_STATIC     0x0002  // Array is statically allocated.
#define FADF_EMBEDDED   0x0004  // Array is embedded in a structure.
#define FADF_FIXEDSIZE  0x0010  // Array may not be resized or
                                // reallocated.
#define FADF_BSTR       0x0100  // An array of BSTRs.
#define FADF_UNKNOWN    0x0200  // An array of IUnknown*.
#define FADF_DISPATCH   0x0400  // An array of IDispatch*.
#define FADF_VARIANT    0x0800  // An array of VARIANTs.
#define FADF_RESERVED   0xF0E8  // Bits reserved for future use.
```

SAFEARRAYBOUND Structure

Represents the bounds of one dimension of the array. The lower bound of the dimension is represented by lLbound, and cElements represents the number of elements in the dimension. The structure is defined as follows:

```
typedef struct tagSAFEARRAYBOUND
{
    unsigned long cElements;
    long lLbound;
} SAFEARRAYBOUND;
```

SafeArrayAccessData

> **HRESULT SafeArrayAccessData(**
> **SAFEARRAY FAR*** *psa,*
> **void HUGEP* FAR*** *ppvData*
> **);**

Increments the lock count of an array, and retrieves a pointer to the array data.

Parameters

psa

Pointer to an array descriptor created by **SafeArrayCreate**.

ppvData

On exit, pointer to a pointer to the array data. Arrays may be larger than 64K, so very large pointers should be used only in Windows version 3.1 or later.

Return Value

The return value obtained from the returned HRESULT is one of the following.

Return value	Meaning
S_OK	Success.
E_INVALIDARG	The argument *psa* was not a valid safe array descriptor.
E_UNEXPECTED	The array could not be locked.

Example

The following example sorts a safe array of one dimension that contains BSTRs by accessing the array elements directly. This approach is faster than using **SafeArrayGetElement** and **SafeArrayPutElement**.

```
long i, j, min;
BSTR bstrTemp;
BSTR HUGEP *pbstr;
HRESULT hr;
// Get a pointer to the elements of the array.

hr = SafeArrayAccessData(psa, (void HUGEP* FAR*)&pbstr);
if (FAILED(hr))
goto error;

// Bubble sort.

cElements = lUBound-lLBound+1;
for (i = 0; i < cElements-1; i++)
{
    min = i;
    for (j = i+1; j < cElements; j++)
    {
        if (wcscmp(pbstr[j], pbstr[min]) < 0)
            min = j;
    }

    // Swap array[min] and array[i].
    bstrTemp = pbstr[min];
    pbstr[min] = pbstr[i];
    pbstr[i] = bstrTemp;

}

SafeArrayUnaccessData(psa);
```

SafeArrayAllocData

HRESULT SafeArrayAllocData(
SAFEARRAY FAR* *psa*
);

Allocates memory for a safe array, based on a descriptor created with
SafeArrayAllocDescriptor.

Parameter

psa
    Pointer to an array descriptor created by **SafeArrayAllocDescriptor.**

Return Value

The return value obtained from the returned HRESULT is one of the following.

Return value	Meaning
S_OK	Success.
E_INVALIDARG	The argument *psa* was not a valid safe array descriptor.
E_UNEXPECTED	The array could not be locked.

Example

The following example creates a safe array using the **SafeArrayAllocDescriptor** and
SafeArrayAllocData functions.

```
SAFEARRAY FAR* FAR*ppsa;
unsigned int ndim = 2;
HRESULT hresult = SafeArrayAllocDescriptor(ndim, ppsa);
if( FAILED(hresult))
    return ERR_OutOfMemory;
(*ppsa)->rgsabound[ 0 ].lLbound = 0;
(*ppsa)->rgsabound[ 0 ].cElements = 5;
(*ppsa)->rgsabound[ 1 ].lLbound = 1;
(*ppsa)->rgsabound[ 1 ].cElements = 4;
hresult = SafeArrayAllocData(*ppsa);
if( FAILED(hresult))
{
    SafeArrayDestroyDescriptor(*ppsa)
    return ERR_OutOfMemory;
}
```

See Also

SafeArrayDestroyData, SafeArrayDestroyDescriptor

SafeArrayAllocDescriptor

HRESULT SafeArrayAllocDescriptor(
unsigned int *cDims,*
SAFEARRAY FAR* FAR* *ppsaOut*

);

Allocates memory for a safe array descriptor.

Parameters

cDims
> The number of dimensions of the array.

ppsaOut
> Pointer to a location in which to store the created array descriptor.

Return Value

The return value obtained from the returned HRESULT is one of the following.

Return value	Meaning
S_OK	Success.
E_INVALIDARG	The argument *psa* was not a valid safe array descriptor.
E_UNEXPECTED	The array could not be locked.

Comments

This function allows the creation of safe arrays that contain elements with data types other than those provided by **SafeArrayCreate**. After creating an array descriptor using **SafeArrayAllocDescriptor**, set the element size in the array descriptor, an call **SafeArrayAllocData** to allocate memory for the array elements.

Example

The following example creates a safe array using the **SafeArrayAllocDescriptor** and **SafeArrayAllocData** functions.

```
SAFEARRAY FAR* FAR*ppsa;
unsigned int ndim = 2;
HRESULT hresult = SafeArrayAllocDescriptor( ndim, ppsa );
if( FAILED( hresult ) )
    return ERR_OutOfMemory;
(*ppsa)->rgsabound[ 0 ].lLbound = 0;
(*ppsa)->rgsabound[ 0 ].cElements = 5;
(*ppsa)->rgsabound[ 1 ].lLbound = 1;
(*ppsa)->rgsabound[ 1 ].cElements = 4;
hresult = SafeArrayAllocData( *ppsa );
if( FAILED( hresult ) )
{
    SafeArrayDestroyDescriptor( *ppsa )
    return ERR_OutOfMemory;
}
```

See Also   **SafeArrayAllocData, SafeArrayDestroyData, SafeArrayDestroyDescriptor**

SafeArrayCopy

HRESULT SafeArrayCopy(
SAFEARRAY FAR* *psa,*
SAFEARRAY FAR* FAR* *ppsaOut*
);

Creates a copy of an existing safe array.

Parameters   *psa*
   Pointer to an array descriptor created by **SafeArrayCreate.**

ppsaOut
   Pointer to a location in which to return the new array descriptor.

Return Value   The return value obtained from the returned HRESULT is one of the following.

Return value	Meaning
S_OK	Success.
E_INVALIDARG	The argument *psa* was not a valid safe array descriptor.
E_OUTOFMEMORY	Insufficient memory to create the copy.

Comments   **SafeArrayCopy** calls the string or variant manipulation functions if the array to copy contains either of these data types. If the array being copied contains object references, the reference counts for the objects are incremented.

See Also   **SysAllocStringLen, VariantCopy, VariantCopyInd**

SafeArrayCopyData

HRESULT SafeArrayCopyData(
SAFEARRAY FAR* *psaSource,*
SAFEARRAY FAR* FAR* *psaTarget*
);

Copies the source array to the target array after releasing any resources in the target array. This is similar to **SafeArrayCopy,** except that the target array has to be set up by the caller. The target is not allocated or reallocated.

Parameters

psaSource
    The safe array from which to be copied.

psaTarget
    On exit, the array referred to by *psaTarget* contains a copy of the data in *psaSource.*

Return Value

The return value obtained from the returned HRESULT is one of the following.

Return value	Meaning
S_OK	Success.
E_INVALIDARG	The argument *psa* was not a valid safearray descriptor.
E_OUTOFMEMORY	Insufficient memory to create the copy.

Comments

Visual Basic for Applications (VBA) and Automation use the same set of rules with cases in which the size or types of source and destination arrays do not match. The rules of Visual Basic are described in the following comments.

Array Assignment

In general, VBA5.0 supports array assignment.

```
Dim lhs(1 To 10) As Integer
Dim rhs(1 To 10) As Integer

lhs = rhs
```

When the number of dimensions, the size of those dimensions, and the element types match, data types are differentiated based on the following factors:

- **Fixed-size, left side.** The left side is fixed if the type of the expression on the left side is a fixed-size array. For example, the following statement is a declaration of a fixed-size array.

  ```
  Dim x (1 To 10) As Integer
  ```

- **Matching number of dimensions.** The number of dimensions of the left side may or may not match the number of dimensions of the array on the right side.

- **Dimensions match.** The dimensions match if, for each dimension, the number of elements match. The dimensions can match even if the declarations are slightly different, such as when one array is zero-based and another is one-based, but they have the same number of elements.

The following table shows what happens when the number of dimensions, size of the dimension, and element types do not match:

Fixed-size, left side	Number of dimensions	Dimensions match	What happens
No	Yes or No	Yes or No	Success. If necessary, the left side is resized to the size of the right side.
Yes	No		Failure.
Yes	Yes	No	Treated in same manner as fixed-length strings.
			If the right side has more elements than the left side, the assignment succeeds and the extra elements have no effect. If the left side has more elements than the right side, the assignment succeeds and the unaffected elements of the left side are zero-, null-, or empty-filled, depending on the types of the elements.
Yes	Yes	Yes	Success.

See Also   **SysAllocStringLen, VariantCopy, VariantCopyInd**

SafeArrayCreate

      SAFEARRAY * SafeArrayCreate(
      VARTYPE *vt***,**

      unsigned int *cDims***,**

      SAFEARRRAYBOUND FAR* *rgsabound*

      );

Creates a new array descriptor, allocates and initializes the data for the array, and returns a pointer to the new array descriptor.

Parameters   *vt*

      The base type of the array (the VARTYPE of each element of the array). The VARTYPE is restricted to a subset of the variant types. Neither the VT_ARRAY nor the VT_BYREF flag can be set. VT_EMPTY and VT_NULL are not valid base types for the array. All other types are legal.

cDims

> Number of dimensions in the array. The number cannot be changed after the array is created.

rgsabound

> Pointer to a vector of bounds (one for each dimension) to allocate for the array.

Return Value   Points to the array descriptor, or Null if the array could not be created.

Example

```
HRESULT PASCAL __export CPoly::EnumPoints(IEnumVARIANT FAR* FAR* ppenum)
{
    unsigned int i;
    HRESULT hresult;
    VARIANT var;
    SAFEARRAY FAR* psa;
    CEnumPoint FAR* penum;
    POINTLINK FAR* ppointlink;
    SAFEARRAYBOUND rgsabound[1];
    rgsabound[0].lLbound = 0;
    rgsabound[0].cElements = m_cPoints;
    psa = SafeArrayCreate(VT_VARIANT, 1, rgsabound);
    if(psa == NULL){hresult = ReportResult(0, E_OUTOFMEMORY, 0, 0);
        goto LError0}

    // Code omitted here for brevity.

LError0::;
    return hresult;
}
```

SafeArrayCreateVector

> **SAFEARRAY * SafeArrayCreateVector(**
> **VARTYPE** *vt,*
>
> **long** *lLbound,*
>
> **unsigned int** *cElements*
>
> **);**

Creates a one-dimensional array whose lower bound is always zero. A safe array created with **SafeArrayCreateVector** is a fixed size, so the constant FADF_FIXEDSIZE is always set.

Parameters

vt

The base type of the array (the VARTYPE of each element of the array). The VARTYPE is restricted to a subset of the variant types. Neither the VT_ARRAY nor the VT_BYREF flag can be set. VT_EMPTY and VT_NULL are not valid base types for the array. All other types are legal.

lLbound

The lower bound for the array. Can be negative.

cElements

The number of elements in the array.

Return Value

Points to the array descriptor, or Null if the array could not be created.

Comments

SafeArrayCreateVector allocates a single block of memory containing a SAFEARRAY structure for a single-dimension array (24 bytes), immediately followed by the array data. All of the existing safe array functions work correctly for safe arrays that are allocated with **SafeArrayCreateVector**.

A **SafeArrayCreateVector** is allocated as a single block of memory. Both the **SafeArray** descriptor and the array data block are allocated contiguously in one allocation, which speeds up array allocation. However, a user can allocate the descriptor and data area separately using the **SafeArrayAllocDescriptor** and **SafeArrayAllocData** calls.

SafeArrayDestroy

HRESULT SafeArrayDestroy(
SAFEARRAY FAR* *psa*

);

Destroys an existing array descriptor and all of the data in the array. If objects are stored in the array, **Release** is called on each object in the array.

Parameter

psa

Pointer to an array descriptor created by **SafeArrayCreate**.

Return Value

The return value obtained from the returned HRESULT is one of the following.

Return value	Meaning
S_OK	Success.
DISP_E_ARRAYISLOCKED	The array is currently locked.
E_INVALIDARG	The item pointed to by *psa* is not a safe array descriptor.

Example

```
STDMETHODIMP_(ULONG) CEnumPoint::Release()
{
    if(--m_refs == 0)
    {
        if(m_psa != NULL)
        SafeArrayDestroy(m_psa);
        delete this;
        return 0;
    }
    return m_refs;
}
```

SafeArrayDestroyData

HRESULT SafeArrayDestroyData(
SAFEARRAY FAR* *psa*
);

Destroys all the data in a safe array.

Parameter

psa
  Pointer to an array descriptor.

Return Value

The return value obtained from the returned HRESULT is one of the following.

Return value	Meaning
S_OK	Success.
DISP_E_ARRAYISLOCKED	The array is currently locked.
E_INVALIDARG	The item pointed to by *psa* is not a safe array descriptor.

Comments

This function is typically used when freeing safe arrays that contain elements with data types other than variants. If objects are stored in the array, **Release** is called on each object in the array.

See Also

SafeArrayAllocData, SafeArrayAllocDescriptor, SafeArrayDestroyDescriptor

SafeArrayDestroyDescriptor

HRESULT SafeArrayDestroyDescriptor(
SAFEARRAY FAR* *psa*
);

Destroys a descriptor of a safe array.

Parameter

psa
Pointer to a safe array descriptor.

Return Value

The return value obtained from the returned HRESULT is one of the following.

Return value	Meaning
S_OK	Success.
DISP_E_ARRAYISLOCKED	The array is currently locked.
E_INVALIDARG	The item pointed to by *psa* is not a safe array descriptor.

Comments

This function is typically used to destroy the descriptor of a safe array that contains elements with data types other than variants. Destroying the array descriptor does not destroy the elements in the array. Before destroying the array descriptor, call **SafeArrayDestroyData** to free the elements.

See Also

SafeArrayAllocData, **SafeArrayAllocDescriptor**, **SafeArrayDestroyData**

SafeArrayGetDim

UINT SafeArrayGetDim(
SAFEARRAY FAR* *psa*
);

Returns the number of dimensions in the array.

Parameter

psa
Pointer to an array descriptor created by **SafeArrayCreate**.

Return Value

Returns the number of dimensions in the array.

Example

```
HRESULT
CEnumPoint::Create(SAFEARRAY FAR* psa, CEnumPoint FAR* FAR* ppenum)
{
    long lBound;
    HRESULT hresult;
    CEnumPoint FAR* penum;

    // Verify that the SafeArray is the proper shape.

    if(SafeArrayGetDim(psa) != 1)
        return ReportResult(0, E_INVALIDARG, 0, 0);

    // Code omitted here for brevity.

}
```

SafeArrayGetElement

HRESULT SafeArrayGetElement(
SAFEARRAY FAR* *psa,*

long FAR* *rgIndices,*

void FAR* *pv*

);

Retrieves a single element of the array.

Parameters

psa
Pointer to an array descriptor created by **SafeArrayCreate**.

rgIndices
Pointer to a vector of indexes for each dimension of the array. The right-most (least significant) dimension is *rgIndices*[0]. The left-most dimension is stored at *rgIndices*[*psa->cDims* – 1].

pv
Pointer to the location to place the element of the array.

Comments

This function calls **SafeArrayLock** and **SafeArrayUnlock** automatically, before and after retrieving the element. The caller must provide a storage area of the correct size to receive the data. If the data element is a string, object, or variant, the function copies the element in the correct way.

Return Value   The return value obtained from the returned HRESULT is one of the following.

Return value	Meaning
S_OK	Success.
DISP_E_BADINDEX	The specified index is invalid.
E_INVALIDARG	One of the arguments is invalid.

Example

E_OUTOFMEMORY   Memory could not be allocated for the element.

```
STDMETHODIMP CEnumPoint::Next(
    ULONG celt,
    VARIANT FAR rgvar[],
    ULONG FAR* pceltFetched)
{
    unsigned int i;
    long ix;
    HRESULT hresult;

    for(i = 0; i < celt; ++i)
        VariantInit(&rgvar[i]);

    for(i = 0; i < celt; ++i)
    {
        if(m_iCurrent == m_celts)
        {
            hresult = ReportResult(0, S_FALSE, 0, 0);
                goto LDone;
        }

        ix = m_iCurrent++;
        hresult = SafeArrayGetElement(m_psa, &ix, &rgvar[i]);
        if(FAILED(hresult))
            goto LError0;
    }
    hresult = NOERROR;

LDone:;
    *pceltFetched = i;
    return hresult;

LError0:;
    for(i = 0; i < celt; ++i)
        VariantClear(&rgvar[i]);
    return hresult;
}
```

SafeArrayGetElemsize

UINT SafeArrayGetElemsize(
SAFEARRAY FAR* *psa*
);

Parameter

psa
    Pointer to an array descriptor created by **SafeArrayCreate**.

Return Value

Returns the size (in bytes) of the elements of a safe array.

SafeArrayGetLBound

HRESULT SafeArrayGetLBound(
SAFEARRAY FAR* *psa,*
unsigned int *nDim,*
long FAR* *plLbound*
);

Returns the lower bound for any dimension of a safe array.

Parameters

psa
    Pointer to an array descriptor created by **SafeArrayCreate**.

nDim
    The array dimension for which to get the lower bound.

plLbound
    Pointer to the location to return the lower bound.

Return Value

The return value obtained from the returned HRESULT is one of the following.

Return value	Meaning
S_OK	Success.
DISP_E_BADINDEX	The specified index is out of bounds.
E_INVALIDARG	One of the arguments is invalid.

Example
```
HRESULT
CEnumPoint::Create(SAFEARRAY FAR* psa, CEnumPoint FAR* FAR* ppenum)
{
    long lBound;
    HRESULT hresult;
    CEnumPoint FAR* penum;

    // Verify that the SafeArray is the proper shape.

    hresult = SafeArrayGetLBound(psa, 1, &lBound);
    if(FAILED(hresult))
        return hresult;

    // Code omitted here for brevity.

}
```

SafeArrayGetUBound

HRESULT SafeArrayGetUBound(
SAFEARRAY FAR* *psa,*

unsigned int *nDim,*

long FAR* *plUbound*

);

Returns the upper bound for any dimension of a safe array.

Parameters

psa
> Pointer to an array descriptor created by **SafeArrayCreate**.

nDim
> The array dimension for which to get the upper bound.

plUbound
> Pointer to the location to return the upper bound.

Return Value

The return value obtained from the returned HRESULT is one of the following.

Return value	Meaning
S_OK	Success.
DISP_E_BADINDEX	The specified index is out of bounds.
E_INVALIDARG	One of the arguments is invalid.

Example

```
HRESULT
CEnumPoint::Create(SAFEARRAY FAR* psa, CEnumPoint FAR* FAR* ppenum)
{
    long lBound;
    HRESULT hresult;
    CEnumPoint FAR* penum;

    // Verify that the SafeArray is the proper shape.

    hresult = SafeArrayGetUBound(psa, 1, &lBound);
    if(FAILED(hresult))
        goto LError0;

    // Code omitted here for brevity.

LError0:;
    penum->Release();

    return hresult;
}
```

SafeArrayLock

HRESULT SafeArrayLock(
SAFEARRAY FAR* *psa*
);

Increments the lock count of an array, and places a pointer to the array data in *pvData* of the array descriptor.

Parameter

psa
  Pointer to an array descriptor created by **SafeArrayCreate**.

Return Value

The return value obtained from the returned HRESULT is one of the following.

Return value	Meaning
S_OK	Success.
E_INVALIDARG	The argument *psa* was not a valid safe array descriptor.
E_UNEXPECTED	The array could not be locked.

Comments   The pointer in the array descriptor is valid until **SafeArrayUnlock** is called. Calls to **SafeArrayLock** can be nested. An equal number of calls to **SafeArrayUnlock** are required.

An array cannot be deleted while it is locked.

SafeArrayPtrOfIndex

HRESULT SafeArrayPtrOfIndex(
SAFEARRAY FAR* *psa,*
long FAR* *rgIndices,*
void HUGEP* FAR* *ppvData*
);

Returns a pointer to an array element.

Parameters   *psa*
Pointer to an array descriptor created by **SafeArrayCreate**.

rgIndices
An array of index values that identify an element of the array. All indexes for the element must be specified.

ppvData
On return, pointer to the element identified by the values in *rgIndices*.

Return Value   The return value obtained from the returned HRESULT is one of the following.

Return value	Meaning
S_OK	Success.
E_INVALIDARG	The argument *psa* was not a valid safe array descriptor.
DISP_E_BADINDEX	The specified index was invalid.

Comments   The array should be locked before **SafeArrayPtrOfIndex** is called. Failing to lock the array can cause unpredictable results.

SafeArrayPutElement

HRESULT SafeArrayPutElement(
SAFEARRAY FAR* *psa,*

long FAR* *rgIndices,*

void FAR* *pv*

);

Assigns a single element to the array.

Parameters

psa
Pointer to an array descriptor created by **SafeArrayCreate**.

rgIndices
Pointer to a vector of indexes for each dimension of the array. The right-most (least significant) dimension is *rgIndices*[0]. The left-most dimension is stored at *rgIndices[psa->cDims – 1]*.

pv
Pointer to the data to assign to the array. The variant types VT_DISPATCH, VT_UNKNOWN, and VT_BSTR are pointers, and do not require another level of indirection.

Return Value

The return value obtained from the returned HRESULT is one of the following.

Return value	Meaning
S_OK	Success.
DISP_E_BADINDEX	The specified index was invalid.
E_INVALIDARG	One of the arguments is invalid.
E_OUTOFMEMORY	Memory could not be allocated for the element.

Comments

This function automatically calls **SafeArrayLock** and **SafeArrayUnlock** before and after assigning the element. If the data element is a string, object, or variant, the function copies it correctly. If the existing element is a string, object, or variant, it is cleared correctly.

Note Multiple locks can be on an array. Elements can be put into an array while the array is locked by other operations.

Example

```
HRESULT PASCAL __export CPoly::EnumPoints(IEnumVARIANT FAR* FAR* ppenum)
{
    unsigned int i;
    HRESULT hresult;
    VARIANT var;
    SAFEARRAY FAR* psa;
    CEnumPoint FAR* penum;
    POINTLINK FAR* ppointlink;
    SAFEARRAYBOUND rgsabound[1];
    rgsabound[0].lLbound = 0;
    rgsabound[0].cElements = m_cPoints;

    psa = SafeArrayCreate(VT_VARIANT, 1, rgsabound);
    if(psa == NULL)
    {
        hresult = ResultFromScode(E_OUTOFMEMORY);
        goto LError0;
    }

    // Code omitted here for brevity.

        V_VT(&var) = VT_DISPATCH;
        hresult = ppointlink->ppoint->QueryInterface(
        IID_IDispatch, (void FAR* FAR*)&V_DISPATCH(&var));
        if(hresult != NOERROR)
            goto LError1;

        ix[0] = i;
        SafeArrayPutElement(psa, ix, &var);

        ppointlink = ppointlink->next;
    }

    hresult = CEnumPoint::Create(psa, &penum);
    if(hresult != NOERROR)
        goto LError1;
    *ppenum = penum;
    return NOERROR;

LError1:;
    SafeArrayDestroy(psa);

LError0:;
    return hresult;
}
```

SafeArrayRedim

HRESULT SafeArrayRedim(
SAFEARRAY FAR* *psa,*
SAFEARRAYBOUND FAR* *psaboundNew*
);

Changes the right-most (least significant) bound of a safe array.

Parameters

psa
Pointer to an array descriptor.

psaboundNew
Pointer to a new safe array bound structure that contains the new array boundary. You can change only the least significant dimension of an array.

Return Value

The return value obtained from the returned HRESULT is one of the following.

Return value	Meaning
S_OK	Success.
DISP_E_ARRAYISLOCKED	The array is currently locked.
E_INVALIDARG	The item pointed to by *psa* is not a safe array descriptor.

Comments

If you reduce the bound of an array, **SafeArrayRedim** deallocates the array elements outside the new array boundary. If the bound of an array is increased, **SafeArrayRedim** allocates and initializes the new array elements. The data is preserved for elements that exist in both the old and new array.

SafeArrayUnaccessData

HRESULT SafeArrayUnaccessData(
SAFEARRAY FAR* *psa*
);

Decrements the lock count of an array, and invalidates the pointer retrieved by **SafeArrayAccessData**.

Parameter

psa
Pointer to an array descriptor created by **SafeArrayCreate**.

Return Value   The return value obtained from the returned HRESULT is one of the following.

Return value	Meaning
S_OK	Success.
E_INVALIDARG	The argument *psa* was not a valid safe array descriptor.
E_UNEXPECTED	The array could not be unlocked.

SafeArrayUnlock

HRESULT SafeArrayUnlock(
SAFEARRAY FAR* *psa*
);

Decrements the lock count of an array so it can be freed or resized.

Parameter   *psa*
                        Pointer to an array descriptor created by **SafeArrayCreate**.

Return Value   The return value obtained from the returned HRESULT is one of the following.

Return value	Meaning
S_OK	Success.
E_INVALIDARG	The argument *psa* was not a valid safe array descriptor.
E_UNEXPECTED	The array could not be unlocked.

Comments   This function is called after access to the data in an array is finished.

String Manipulation Functions

To handle strings that are allocated by one component and freed by another, Automation defines a special set of functions. These functions use the following data type:

```
typedef OLECHAR FAR* BSTR;
```

These strings are zero-terminated, and in most cases they can be treated just like OLECHAR* strings. However, you can query a BSTR for its length rather than scan it, so it can contain embedded null characters. The length is stored as an integer at the memory location preceding the data in the string. Instead of reading this location directly, applications should use the string manipulation functions to access the length of a BSTR.

In situations where a BSTR will not be translated from ANSI to Unicode, or vice versa, you can use BSTRs to pass binary data. For example, if code will run only on 16-bit systems and interact only with other 16-bit systems, you can use BSTRs. The preferred method of passing binary data is to use a SAFEARRAY of VT_UI1.

In 32-bit OLE, BSTRs use Unicode like all other strings in 32-bit OLE. In 16-bit OLE, BSTRs use ANSI. Win32 provides **MultiByteToWideChar** and **WideCharToMultiByte** to convert ANSI strings to Unicode, and Unicode strings to ANSI. Automation caches the space allocated for BSTRs. This speeds up the **SysAllocString/SysFreeString** sequence. However, this may also cause **IMallocSpy** to assign leaks to the wrong memory user because it is not aware of the caching done by Automation.

For example, if the application allocates a BSTR and frees it, the free block of memory is put into the BSTR cache by Automation. If the application then allocates another BSTR, it can get the free block from the cache. If the second BSTR allocation is not freed, **IMallocSpy** will attribute the leak to the first allocation of the BSTR. You can determine the correct source of the leak (the second allocation) by disabling the BSTR caching using the debug version of Oleaut32.dll, and by setting the environment variable OANOCACHE=1 before running the application. A null pointer is a valid value for a BSTR variable. By convention, it is always treated the same as a pointer to a BSTR that contains zero characters. Also by convention, calls to functions that take a BSTR reference parameter must pass either a null pointer, or a pointer to an allocated BSTR. If the implementation of a function that takes a BSTR reference parameter assigns a new BSTR to the parameter, it must free the previously referenced BSTR.

SysAllocString

BSTR SysAllocString(
   OLECHAR FAR* *sz*
   );

Allocates a new string and copies the passed string into it. Returns Null if there is insufficient memory, and if Null, Null is passed in.

Parameter   *sz*
          A zero-terminated string to copy. The *sz* parameter must be a Unicode string in 32-bit applications, and an ANSI string in 16-bit applications.

Return Value   If successful, points to a BSTR containing the string. If insufficient memory exists or *sz* was Null, returns Null.

Comments   You can free strings created with **SysAllocString** using **SysFreeString**.

Example
```
inline void CStatBar::SetText(OLECHAR FAR* sz)
{
    SysFreeString(m_bstrMsg);
    m_bstrMsg = SysAllocString(sz);
}
```

SysAllocStringByteLen

BSTR SysAllocStringByteLen(
char FAR* *psz,*

unsigned int *len*

);

Takes an ANSI string as input, and returns a BSTR that contains an ANSI string. Does not perform any ANSI-to-Unicode translation.

Parameters   *psz*

A zero-terminated string to copy, or Null to keep the string uninitialized.

len

Number of bytes to copy from *psz*. A null character is placed afterwards, allocating a total of *len*+1 bytes.

Allocates a new string of *len* bytes, copies *len* bytes from the passed string into it, and then appends a null character. Valid only for 32-bit systems.

Return Value   Points to a copy of the string, or Null if insufficient memory exists.

Comments   This function is provided to create BSTRs that contain binary data. You can use this type of BSTR only in situations where it will not be translated from ANSI to Unicode, or vice versa.

For example, do not use these BSTRs between a 16-bit and a 32-bit application running on a 32-bit Windows system. The OLE 16-bit to 32-bit (and 32-bit to 16-bit) interoperability layer will translate the BSTR and corrupt the binary data. The preferred method of passing binary data is to use a SAFEARRAY of VT_UI1, which will not be translated by OLE.

If *psz* is Null, a string of the requested length is allocated, but not initialized. The string *psz* can contain embedded null characters, and does not need to end with a Null. Free the returned string later with **SysFreeString**.

SysAllocStringLen

BSTR SysAllocStringLen(
OLECHAR FAR* *pch***,**

unsigned int *cch*

);

Allocates a new string, copies *cch* characters from the passed string into it, and then appends a null character.

Parameters

pch
A pointer to *cch* characters to copy, or Null to keep the string uninitialized.

cch
Number of characters to copy from *pch*. A null character is placed afterwards, allocating a total of *cch*+1 characters.

Return Value
Points to a copy of the string, or Null if insufficient memory exists.

Comments
If *pch* is Null, a string of the requested length is allocated, but not initialized. The *pch* string can contain embedded null characters and does not need to end with a Null. Free the returned string later with **SysFreeString**.

SysFreeString

void SysFreeString(
BSTR *bstr*

);

Frees a string allocated previously by **SysAllocString**, **SysAllocStringByteLen**, **SysReAllocString**, **SysAllocStringLen**, or **SysReAllocStringLen**.

Parameter

bstr
A BSTR allocated previously, or Null. If Null, the function simply returns.

Return Value
None.

Example

```
CStatBar::~CStatBar()
{
    SysFreeString(m_bstrMsg);
}
```

SysReAllocString

INT SysReAllocString(
BSTR FAR* *pbstr,*
OLECHAR FAR* *sz*
);

Allocates a new BSTR and copies the passed string into it, then frees the BSTR referenced by *pbstr,* and finally resets *pbstr* to point to the new BSTR.

Parameters   *pbstr*
Points to a variable containing a BSTR.

sz
A zero-terminated string to copy.

Return Value   Returns False if insufficient memory exists.

SysReAllocStringLen

INT SysReAllocStringLen(
BSTR FAR* *pbstr,*
OLECHAR FAR* *pch,*
unsigned int *cch*
);

Creates a new BSTR containing a specified number of characters from an old BSTR, and frees the old BSTR.

Parameters   *pbstr*
Pointer to a variable containing a BSTR.

pch
Pointer to *cch* characters to copy, or Null to keep the string uninitialized.

cch
Number of characters to copy from *pch.* A null character is placed afterward, allocating a total of *cch*+1 characters.

Return Value   Returns True if the string is reallocated successfully, or False if insufficient memory exists.

Comments   Allocates a new string, copies *cch* characters from the passed string into it, and then appends a null character. Frees the BSTR referenced currently by *pbstr*, and resets *pbstr* to point to the new BSTR. If *pch* is Null, a string of length *cch* is allocated but not initialized.

The *pch* string can contain embedded null characters and does not need to end with a Null.

SysStringByteLen

UINT SysStringByteLen(
BSTR *bstr*
);

Returns the length (in bytes) of a BSTR. Valid for 32-bit systems only.

Parameter   *bstr*
A BSTR allocated previously. It cannot be Null.

Return Value   The number of bytes in *bstr*, not including a terminating null character.

Comments   The returned value may be different from **fstrlen**(*bstr*) if the BSTR was allocated with **Sys[Re]AllocStringLen** or **SysAllocStringByteLen**, and the passed-in characters included a null character in the first *len* characters. For a BSTR allocated with **Sys[Re]AllocStringLen** or **SysAllocStringByteLen**, this function always returns the number of bytes specified in the *len* parameter at allocation time.

Example
```
// Display the status message.

TextOut(
    hdc,
    rcMsg.left + (m_dxFont / 2),
    rcMsg.top + ((rcMsg.bottom - rcMsg.top - m_dyFont) / 2),
    m_bstrMsg, SysStringByteLen(m_bstrMsg));
```

SysStringLen

UINT SysStringLen(
BSTR *bstr*
);

Returns the length of a BSTR.

Parameter

bstr
A BSTR allocated previously. Cannot be Null.

Return Value

The number of characters in *bstr*, not including a terminating null character.

Comments

The returned value may be different from **_fstrlen**(*bstr*) if the BSTR was allocated with **Sys[Re]AllocStringLen** or **SysAllocStringByteLen**, and the passed-in characters included a null character in the first *cch* characters. For a BSTR allocated with **Sys[Re]AllocStringLen** or **SysAllocStringByteLen**, this function always returns the number of characters specified in the *cch* parameter at allocation time.

Example

```
// Display the status message.

TextOut(
    hdc,
    rcMsg.left + (m_dxFont / 2),
    rcMsg.top + ((rcMsg.bottom - rcMsg.top - m_dyFont) / 2),
    m_bstrMsg, SysStringLen(m_bstrMsg));
```

Variant Manipulation API Functions

These functions are provided to allow applications to manipulate VARIANTARG variables. Applications that implement **IDispatch** should test each VARIANTARG for all permitted types by attempting to coerce the variant to each type using **VariantChangeType** or **VariantChangeTypeEx**. If objects are allowed, the application should always test for object types before other types. If an object type is expected, the application must use **IUnknown::QueryInterface** to test whether the object is the desired type.

Although applications can access and interpret the VARIANTARGs without these functions, using them ensures uniform conversion and coercion rules for all implementors of **IDispatch**. For example, these functions automatically coerce numeric arguments to strings, and vice versa, when necessary.

Because variants can contain strings, references to scalars, objects, and arrays, all data ownership rules must be followed. All variant manipulation functions should conform to the following rules:

1. Before use, all VARIANTARGs must be initialized by **VariantInit**.

2. For the types VT_UI1, VT_I2, VT_I4, VT_R4, VT_R8, VT_BOOL, VT_ERROR, VT_CY, and VT_DATE, data is stored within the VARIANT structure. Any pointers to the data become invalid when the type of the variant is changed.

3. For VT_BYREF | any type, the memory pointed to by the variant is owned and freed by the caller of the function.

4. For VT_BSTR, there is only one owner for the string. All strings in variants must be allocated with the **SysAllocString** function. When releasing or changing the type of a variant with the VT_BSTR type, **SysFreeString** is called on the contained string.

5. For VT_ARRAY | any type, the rule is analogous to the rule for VT_BSTR. All arrays in variants must be allocated with **SafeArrayCreate**. When releasing or changing the type of a variant with the VT_ARRAY flag set, **SafeArrayDestroy** is called.

6. For VT_DISPATCH and VT_UNKNOWN, the objects that are pointed to have reference counts that are incremented when they are placed in a variant. When releasing or changing the type of the variant, **Release** is called on the object that is pointed to.

VariantChangeType

HRESULT VariantChangeType(
VARIANTARG FAR* *pvargDest,*
VARIANTARG FAR* *pvarSrc,*
unsigned short *wFlags,*
VARTYPE *vt*
);

Converts a variant from one type to another.

Parameters   *pvargDest*
Pointer to the VARIANTARG to receive the coerced type. If this is the same as *pvarSrc*, the variant will be converted in place.

pvarSrc

   Pointer to the source VARIANTARG to be coerced.

wFlags

   Flags that control the coercion. The only defined flag is
   VARIANT_NOVALUEPROP, which prevents the function from attempting to
   coerce an object to a fundamental type by getting the **Value** property. Applications
   should set this flag only if necessary, because it makes their behavior inconsistent
   with other applications.

vt

   The type to coerce to. If the return code is S_OK, the *vt* field of the **pvargDest* is
   always the same as this value.

Return Value

The return value obtained from the returned HRESULT is one of the following.

Return value	Meaning
S_OK	Success.
DISP_E_BADVARTYPE	The variant type *vt* is not a valid type of variant.
DISP_E_OVERFLOW	The data pointed to by *pvarSrc* does not fit in the destination type.
DISP_E_TYPEMISMATCH	The argument could not be coerced to the specified type.
E_INVALIDARG	One of the arguments is invalid.
E_OUTOFMEMORY	Memory could not be allocated for the conversion.

Comments

The **VariantChangeType** function handles coercions between the fundamental types
(including numeric-to-string and string-to-numeric coercions). A variant that has
VT_BYREF set is coerced to a value by obtaining the referenced value. An object is
coerced to a value by invoking the object's **Value** property (DISPID_VALUE).

Typically, the implementor of **IDispatch::Invoke** determines which member is being
accessed, and then calls **VariantChangeType** to get the value of one or more
arguments. For example, if the **IDispatch** call specifies a **SetTitle** member that takes
one string argument, the implementor would call **VariantChangeType** to attempt to
coerce the argument to VT_BSTR. If **VariantChangeType** does not return an error,
the argument could then be obtained directly from the *bstrVal* field of the
VARIANTARG. If **VariantChangeType** returns DISP_E_TYPEMISMATCH, the
implementor would set **puArgErr* to 0 (indicating the argument in error) and return
DISP_E_TYPEMISMATCH from **IDispatch::Invoke**.

Arrays of one type cannot be converted to arrays of another type with this function.

Note The type of a VARIANTARG should not be changed in the *rgvarg* array in
place.

See Also   VariantChangeTypeEx

VariantChangeTypeEx

> **HRESULT VariantChangeTypeEx(**
> **VARIANTARG FAR*** *pvargDest,*
> **VARIANTARG FAR*** *pvarSrc,*
> **LCID** *lcid,*
> **unsigned short** *wFlags,*
> **VARTYPE** *vt*
> **);**

Converts a variant from one type to another, using a LCID.

Parameters   *pvargDest*

Pointer to the VARIANTARG to receive the coerced type. If this is the same as *pvarSrc*, the variant will be converted in place.

pvarSrc

Pointer to the source VARIANTARG to be coerced.

lcid

The LCID for the variant to coerce. The LCID is useful when the type of the source or destination VARIANTARG is VT_BSTR, VT_DISPATCH, or VT_DATE.

wFlags

Flags that control the coercion. The only defined flag is VARIANT_NOVALUEPROP, which prevents the function from attempting to coerce an object to a fundamental type by getting its **Value** property. Applications should set this flag only if necessary, because it makes their behavior inconsistent with other applications.

vt

The type to coerce to. If the return code is S_OK, the *vt* field of the **pvargDest* is guaranteed to be equal to this value.

Return Value   The return value obtained from the returned HRESULT is one of the following.

Return value	Meaning
S_OK	Success.
DISP_E_BADVARTYPE	The variant type *vt* is not a valid type of variant.
DISP_E_OVERFLOW	The data pointed to by *pvarSrc* does not fit in the destination type.
DISP_E_TYPEMISMATCH	The argument could not be coerced to the specified type.
E_INVALIDARG	One of the arguments is invalid.
E_OUTOFMEMORY	Memory could not be allocated for the conversion.

Comments   The **VariantChangeTypeEx** function handles coercions between the fundamental types (including numeric-to-string and string-to-numeric coercions). To change a type with the VT_BYREF flag set to one without VT_BYREF, change the referenced value to **VariantChangeTypeEx**. To coerce objects to fundamental types, obtain the value of the **Value** property.

Typically, the implementor of **IDispatch::Invoke** determines which member is being accessed, and then calls **VariantChangeType** to get the value of one or more arguments. For example, if the **IDispatch** call specifies a **SetTitle** member that takes one string argument, the implementor would call **VariantChangeTypeEx** to attempt to coerce the argument to VT_BSTR.

If **VariantChangeTypeEx** does not return an error, the argument could then be obtained directly from the *bstrVal* field of the VARIANTARG. If **VariantChangeTypeEx** returns DISP_E_TYPEMISMATCH, the implementor would set **puArgErr* to 0 (indicating the argument in error) and return DISP_E_TYPEMISMATCH from **IDispatch::Invoke**.

Arrays of one type cannot be converted to arrays of another type with this function.

Note The type of a VARIANTARG should not be changed in the *rgvarg* array in place.

See Also   **VariantChangeType**

VariantClear

HRESULT VariantClear(
VARIANTARG FAR* *pvarg*
);

Clears a variant.

Parameter

pvarg
Pointer to the VARIANTARG to clear.

Return Value

The return value obtained from the returned HRESULT is one of the following.

Return value	Meaning
S_OK	Success.
DISP_E_ARRAYISLOCKED	The variant contains an array that is locked.
DISP_E_BADVARTYPE	The variant type *pvarg* is not a valid type of variant.
E_INVALIDARG	One of the arguments is invalid.

Comments

Use this function to clear variables of type VARIANTARG (or VARIANT) before the memory containing the VARIANTARG is freed (as when a local variable goes out of scope).

The function clears a VARIANTARG by setting the *vt* field to VT_EMPTY and the *wReserved* field to 0. The current contents of the VARIANTARG are released first. If the *vt* field is VT_BSTR, the string is freed. If the *vt* field is VT_DISPATCH, the object is released. If the *vt* field has the VT_ARRAY bit set, the array is freed.

In certain cases, it may be preferable to clear a variant in code without calling **VariantClear**. For example, you can change the type of a VT_I4 variant to another type without calling this function. However, you must call **VariantClear** if a VT_type is received but cannot be handled. Using **VariantClear** in these cases ensures that code will continue to work if Automation adds new variant types in the future.

Example

```
for(i = 0; i < celt; ++i)
    VariantClear(&rgvar[i]);
```

VariantCopy

HRESULT VariantCopy(
VARIANTARG FAR* *pvargDest*,
VARIANTARG FAR* *pvargSrc*
);

Frees the destination variant and makes a copy of the source variant.

Parameters

pvargDest
    Pointer to the VARIANTARG to receive the copy.

pvargSrc
    Pointer to the VARIANTARG to be copied.

Return Value

The return value obtained from the returned HRESULT is one of the following.

Return value	Meaning
S_OK	Success.
DISP_E_ARRAYISLOCKED	The variant contains an array that is locked.
DISP_E_BADVARTYPE	The source and destination have an invalid variant type (usually uninitialized).
E_OUTOFMEMORY	Memory could not be allocated for the copy.
E_INVALIDARG	One of the arguments is invalid.

Comments

First, free any memory that is owned by *pvargDest*, such as **VariantClear** (*pvargDest* must point to a valid initialized variant, and not simply to an uninitialized memory location). Then *pvargDest* receives an exact copy of the contents of *pvargSrc*.

If *pvargSrc* is a VT_BSTR, a copy of the string is made. If *pvargSrc* is a VT_ARRAY, the entire array is copied. If *pvargSrc* is a VT_DISPATCH or VT_UNKNOWN, **AddRef** is called to increment the object's reference count.

VariantCopyInd

HRESULT VariantCopyInd(
VARIANT FAR* *pvarDest*,
VARIANTARG FAR* *pvargSrc*
);

Frees the destination variant and makes a copy of the source VARIANTARG, performing the necessary indirection if the source is specified to be VT_BYREF.

Parameters

pvarDest
Pointer to the VARIANTARG that will receive the copy.

pvargSrc
Pointer to the VARIANTARG that will be copied.

Return Value

The return value obtained from the returned HRESULT is one of the following.

Return value	Meaning
S_OK	Success.
DISP_E_ARRAYISLOCKED	The variant contains an array that is locked.
DISP_E_BADVARTYPE	The source and destination have an invalid variant type (usually uninitialized).
E_OUTOFMEMORY	Memory could not be allocated for the copy.
E_INVALIDARG	The argument *pvargSrc* was VT_ARRAY.

Comments

This function is useful when a copy of a variant is needed, and to guarantee that it is not VT_BYREF, such as when handling arguments in an implementation of **IDispatch::Invoke**.

For example, if the source is a (VT_BYREF | VT_I2), the destination will be a BYVAL | VT_I2. The same is true for all legal VT_BYREF combinations, including VT_VARIANT.

If *pvargSrc* is (VT_BYREF | VT_VARIANT), and the contained variant is VT_BYREF, the contained variant is also dereferenced.

This function frees any existing contents of *pvarDest*.

VariantInit

> **void VariantInit(**
> **VARIANTARG FAR*** *pvarg*
> **);**

Initializes a variant.

Parameter

pvarg
   Pointer to the VARIANTARG that will be initialized.

Comments

The **VariantInit** function initializes the VARIANTARG by setting the *vt* field to VT_EMPTY. Unlike **VariantClear**, this function does not interpret the current contents of the VARIANTARG. Use **VariantInit** to initialize new local variables of type VARIANTARG (or VARIANT).

Example

```
for(i = 0; i < celt; ++i)
    VariantInit(&rgvar[i]);
```

Data Type Conversion APIs

The files Oleaut32.dll (for 32-bit systems) and Ole2disp.dll (for 16-bit systems) provide the following low-level functions for converting variant data types. Higher-level variant manipulation functions (such as **VariantChangeType**) use these functions, but they can also be called directly.

Convert to type	From type	Function
unsigned char	**unsigned char**	None
	short	**VarUI1FromI2**(*sIn, pbOut*)
	long	**VarUI1FromI4**(*lIn, pbOut*)
	float	**VarUI1FromR4**(*fltIn, pbOut*)
	double	**VarUI1FromR8**(*dblIn, pbOut*)
	CURRENCY	**VarUI1FromCy**(*cyIn, pbOut*)
	DATE	**VarUI1FromDate**(*dateIn, pbOut*)
	OLECHAR FAR*	**VarUI1FromStr**(*strIn, lcid, dwFlags, pbOut*)
	IDispatch FAR*	**VarUI1FromDisp**(*pdispIn, lcid, pbOut*)
	BOOL	**VarUI1FromBool**(*boolIn, pbOut*)

Convert to type	From type	Function
short	unsigned char	**VarI2FromUI1**(*bIn, psOut*)
	short	None
	long	**VarI2FromI4**(*lIn, psOut*)
	float	**VarI2FromR4**(*fltIn, psOut*)
	double	**VarI2FromR8**(*dblIn, psOut*)
	CURRENCY	**VarI2FromCy**(*cyIn, psOut*)
	DATE	**VarI2FromDate**(*dateIn, psOut*)
	OLECHAR FAR*	**VarI2FromStr**(*strIn, lcid, dwFlags, psOut*)
	IDispatch FAR*	**VarI2FromDisp**(*pdispIn, lcid, psOut*)
	BOOL	**VarI2FromBool**(*boolIn, psOut*)
long	unsigned char	**VarI4FromUI1**(*bIn, plOut*)
	short	**VarI4FromI2**(*sIn, plOut*)
	long	None
	float	**VarI4FromR4**(*fltIn, plOut*)
	double	**VarI4FromR8**(*dblIn, plOut*)
	CURRENCY	**VarI4FromCy**(*cyIn, plOut*)
	DATE	**VarI4FromDate**(*dateIn, plOut*)
	OLECHAR FAR*	**VarI4FromStr**(*strIn, lcid, dwFlags, plOut*)
	IDispatch FAR*	**VarI4FromDisp**(*pdispIn, lcid, plOut*)
	BOOL	**VarI4FromBool**(*boolIn, plOut*)
float	unsigned char	**VarR4FromUI1**(*bIn, pfltOut*)
	short	**VarR4FromI2**(*sIn, pfltOut*)
	long	**VarR4FromI4**(*lIn, pfltOut*)
	float	None
	double	**VarR4FromR8**(*dblIn, pfltOut*)
	CURRENCY	**VarR4FromCy**(*cyIn, pfltOut*)
	DATE	**VarR4FromDate**(*dateIn, pfltOut*)
	OLECHAR FAR*	**VarR4FromStr**(*strIn, lcid, dwFlags, pfltOut*)
	IDispatch FAR*	**VarR4FromDisp**(*pdispIn, lcid, pfltOut*)
	BOOL	**VarR4FromBool**(*boolIn, pfltOut*)

Convert to type	From type	Function
double	unsigned char	**VarR8FromUI1**(*bIn*, *pdblOut*)
	short	**VarR8FromI2**(*sIn*, *pdblOut*)
	long	**VarR8FromI4**(*lIn*, *pdblOut*)
	float	**VarR8FromR4**(*fltIn*, *pdblOut*)
	double	None
	CURRENCY	**VarR8FromCy**(*cyIn*, *pdblOut*)
	DATE	**VarR8FromDate**(*dateIn*, *pdblOut*)
	OLECHAR FAR*	**VarR8FromStr**(*strIn*, *lcid*, *dwFlags*, *pdblOut*)
	IDispatch FAR*	**VarR8FromDisp**(*pdispIn*, *lcid*, *pdblOut*)
	BOOL	**VarR8FromBool**(*boolIn*, *pdblOut*)
DATE	unsigned char	**VarDateFromUI1**(*bIn*, *pdateOut*)
	short	**VarDateFromI2**(*sIn*, *pdateOut*)
	long	**VarDateFromI4**(*lIn*, *pdateOut*)
	float	**VarDateFromR4**(*fltIn*, *pdateOut*)
	double	**VarDateFromR8**(*dblIn*, *pdateOut*)
	CURRENCY	**VarDateFromCy**(*cyIn*, *pdateOut*)
	DATE	None
	OLECHAR FAR*	**VarDateFromStr**(*strIn*, *lcid*, *dwFlags*, *pdateOut*)
	IDispatch FAR*	**VarDateFromDisp**(*pdispIn*, *lcid*, *pdateOut*)
	BOOL	**VarDateFromBool**(*boolIn*, *pdateOut*)
CURRENCY	unsigned char	**VarCyFromUI1**(*bIn*, *pcyOut*)
	short	**VarCyFromI2**(*sIn*, *pcyOut*)
	long	**VarCyFromI4**(*lIn*, *pcyOut*)
	float	**VarCyFromR4**(*fltIn*, *pcyOut*)
	double	**VarCyFromR8**(*dblIn*, *pcyOut*)
	CURRENCY	None
	DATE	**VarCyFromDate**(*dateIn*, *pcyOut*)
	OLECHAR FAR*	**VarCyFromStr**(*strIn*, *lcid*, *dwFlags*, *pcyOut*)
	IDispatch FAR*	**VarCyFromDisp**(*pdispIn*, *lcid*, *pcyOut*)

Convert to type	From type	Function
CURRENCY	BOOL	**VarCyFromBool**(*boolIn*, *pcyOut*)
BSTR	unsigned char	**VarBstrFromUI1**(*bVal*, *lcid*, *dwFlags*, *pbstrOut*)
	short	**VarBstrFromI2**(*iVal*, *lcid*, *dwFlags*, *pbstrOut*)
	long	**VarBstrFromI4**(*lIn*, *lcid*, *dwFlags*, *pbstrOut*)
	float	**VarBstrFromR4**(*fltIn*, *lcid*, *dwFlags*, *pbstrOut*)
	double	**VarBstrFromR8**(*dblIn*, *lcid*, *dwFlags*, *pbstrOut*)
	CURRENCY	**VarBstrFromCy**(*cyIn*, *lcid*, *dwFlags*, *pbstrOut*)
	DATE	**VarBstrFromDate**(*dateIn*, *lcid*, *dwFlags*, *pbstrOut*)
	OLECHAR FAR*	None
	IDispatch FAR*	**VarBstrFromDisp**(*pdispIn*, *lcid*, *dwFlags*, *pbstrOut*)
	BOOL	**VarBstrFromBool**(*boolIn*, *lcid*, *dwFlags*, *pbstrOut*)
BOOL	unsigned char	**VarBoolFromUI1**(*bIn*, *pboolOut*)
	short	**VarBoolFromI2**(*sIn*, *pboolOut*)
	long	**VarBoolFromI4**(*lIn*, *pboolOut*)
	float	**VarBoolFromR4**(*fltIn*, *pboolOut*)
	double	**VarBoolFromR8**(*dblIn*, *pboolOut*)
	CURRENCY	**VarBoolFromCy**(*cyIn*, *pboolOut*)
	DATE	**VarBoolFromDate**(*dateIn*, *pboolOut*)
	OLECHAR FAR*	**VarBoolFromStr**(*strIn*, *lcid*, *dwFlags*, *pboolOut*)
	IDispatch FAR*	**VarBoolFromDisp**(*pdispIn*, *lcid*, *pboolOut*)
	BOOL	None

Parameters
bIn, sIn, lIn, fltIn, dblIn, cyIn, dateIn, strIn, pdispIn, boolIn

The value to coerce. These parameters have the following data types:

Parameter	Data type
bIn	**unsigned char**
sIn	**short**
lIn	**long**
fltIn	**float**
dblIn	**double**
cyIn	**CURRENCY**
dateIn	**DATE**
strIn	**OLECHAR FAR***
pdispIn	**IDispatch FAR***
boolIn	**BOOL**

lcid

For conversions from string and VT_DISPATCH input, the LCID to use for the conversion. For a list of LCIDs, see "Supporting Multiple National Languages" in Chapter 2, "Exposing Automation Objects."

dwFlags

One or more of the following flags:

Flag	Description
LOCALE_NOUSEROVERRIDE	Uses the system default locale settings, rather than custom locale settings.
VAR_TIMEVALUEONLY	Omits the date portion of a VT_DATE and returns only the time. Applies to conversions to or from dates.
VAR_DATEVALUEONLY	Omits the time portion of a VT_DATE and returns only the time. Applies to conversions to or from dates.

pbOut, psOut, plOut, pfltOut, pdblOut, pcyOut, pstrOut, pdispOut, pboolOut

A pointer to the coerced value. These parameters have the following data types:

Parameter	Data type
pbOut	**unsigned char**
psOut	**short**
plOut	**long**
pfltOut	**float**

Parameter	Data type
pdblOut	**double**
pcyOut	**CURRENCY**
pdateOut	**DATE**
pstrOut	**OLECHAR FAR***
pdispOut	**IDispatch FAR***
pboolOut	**BOOL**

Return Value

The return value obtained from the returned HRESULT is one of the following.

Return value	Meaning
S_OK	Success.
DISP_E_BADVARTYPE	The input parameter is not a valid type of variant.
DISP_E_OVERFLOW	The data pointed to by the output parameter does not fit in the destination type.
DISP_E_TYPEMISMATCH	The argument could not be coerced to the specified type.
E_INVALIDARG	One of the arguments is invalid.
E_OUTOFMEMORY	Memory could not be allocated for the conversion.

BSTR and Vector Conversion Functions

Automation supports conversion between an array of bytes and a BSTR through the two low-level conversion functions **VectorFromBstr** and **BstrFromVector**, and by performing the appropriate conversions in **VariantChangeType, ITypeInfo::Invoke, DispInvoke,** and other relevant locations.

BSTRs are wide, double-byte (Unicode) strings on 32-bit Windows platforms, and narrow, single-byte strings on the Apple PowerMac. These functions do not perform any special string handling. They simply move bytes from one location to another, so the width of strings does not affect these API functions.

VectorFromBstr

HRESULT VectorFromBstr(
BSTR *bstr*,
SAFEARRAY FAR* FAR* *ppsa*
);

Returns a vector, assigning each character in the BSTR to an element of the vector.

Parameters   *bstr*
                         The BSTR to be converted to a vector.

                      ppsa
                         On exit, *ppsa* points to a one-dimensional safe array containing the characters in
                         the BSTR.

Return Value   The return value obtained from the returned HRESULT is one of the following.

Return value	Meaning
S_OK	Success.
E_OUTOFMEMORY	Out of memory.
E_INVALIDARG	BSTR is Null.

BstrFromVector

HRESULT BstrFromVector(
SAFEARRAY FAR* *psa*,
BSTR FAR* *pbstr*
);

Returns a BSTR, assigning each element of the vector to a character in the BSTR.

Parameters   *psa*
                         The vector to be converted to a BSTR.

                      pbstr
                         On exit, *pbstr* points to a BSTR, each character of which is assigned to an element
                         from the vector.

Return Value   The return value obtained from the returned HRESULT is one of the following.

Return value	Meaning
S_OK	Success.
E_OUTOFMEMORY	Out of memory.
E_INVALIDARG	The argument *psa* is Null.
DISP_E_TYPEMISMATCH	The argument *psa* is not a vector (not an array of bytes).

Numeric Parsing Functions

Automation supports string parsing through two low-level API functions. **VarParseNumFromStr** parses a string and provides a type-independent representation of the number it represents. **VarNumFromParseNum** converts the type-independent result to a number. String information is passed using the NUMPARSE structure.

VarParseNumFromStr

HRESULT VarParseNumFromStr(
[in] **OLECHAR*** *strIn*,
[in] **LCID** *lcid*,
[in] **unsigned long** *dwFlags*,
[in] **NUMPARSE** **pnumprs*,
[out] **unsigned char** **rgbDig*
);

Parses a string, and creates a type-independent description of the number it represents.

The **VarParseNumFromStr** function fills in the *dwOutFlags* element with each corresponding feature that was actually found in the string. This allows the caller to make decisions about what numeric type to use for the number, based on the format in which it was entered. For example, one application might want to use the CURRENCY data type if the currency symbol is used, and others may want to force a floating point type if an exponent was used.

Parameters

strIn
Input string to be converted to a number.

lcid
Locale identifier

pnumprs
Parsed results.

dwFlags
Allows the caller to control parsing, therefore defining the acceptable syntax of a number. If this field is set to zero, the input string must contain nothing but decimal digits. Setting each defined flag bit enables parsing of that syntactic feature. Standard Automation parsing (for example, as used by **VarI2FromStr**) has all flags set (NUMPRS_STD).

RgbDig
The *rgbDig* array is filled in with the values for the digits in the range 0–7, 0–9, or 0–15, depending on whether the number is octal, decimal, or hexadecimal. All leading zeros have been stripped off. For decimal numbers, trailing zeros are also stripped off, unless the number is zero, in which case a single zero digit will be present.

Return Value

The return value obtained from the returned HRESULT is one of the following.

Return value	Meaning
S_OK	Success.
E_OUTOFMEMORY	Internal memory allocation failed. (Used for DBCS only to create a copy with all wide characters mapped narrow.)
DISP_E_TYPEMISMATCH	There is no valid number in the string, or there is no closing parenthesis to match an opening one. In the former case, *cDig* and *cchUsed* in the NUMPARSE structure will be zero. In the latter, the NUMPARSE structure and digit array are fully updated, as if the closing parenthesis was present.
DISP_E_OVERFLOW	For hexadecimal and octal digits, there are more digits than will fit into the array. For decimal, the exponent exceeds the maximum possible. In both cases, the NUMPARSE structure and digit array are fully updated (for decimal, the *cchUsed* field excludes the entire exponent).

VarNumFromParseNum

HRESULT VarNumFromParseNum(
[in] **NUMPARSE** *pnumprs,*
[in] **unsigned char** *rgbDig,*
[in] **unsigned long** *dwVtBits,*
[out] **VARIANT** *pvar*
);

Once the number is parsed, the caller can call **VarNumFromParseNum** to convert the parse results to a number. The NUMPARSE structure and digit array can be passed in unchanged from the **VarParseNumFromStr** call or you can fill in the parameters from any source. This function will choose the smallest type allowed that can hold the result value with as little precision loss as possible. The result variant is an [out] parameter, so its contents are not freed before storing the result.

Parameters

pnumprs
Parsed results. *cDig* = size of *rgbDic*

rgbDig
Contains the values of the digits. The *cDig* field of NUMPARSE contains the number of digits.

dwVtBits
Contains one bit set for each type that is acceptable as a return value (in many cases, just one bit).

VarNumFromParseNum flags that indicate acceptable result types:

```
VTBIT_I1
VTBIT_UI1
VTBIT_I2
VTBIT_UI2
VTBIT_I4
VTBIT_UI4
VTBIT_R4
VTBIT_R8
VTBIT_CY
VTBIT_DECIMAL
```

pvar
Pointer to the result variant.

Return Value   The return value obtained from the returned HRESULT is one of the following.

Return value	Meaning
S_OK	Success.
E_OUTOFMEMORY	Out of memory.
DISP_E_OVERFLOW	The number is too large to be represented in an allowed type. There is no error if precision is lost in the conversion.

For rounding decimal numbers, the digit array must be at least one digit longer than the maximum required for data types. The maximum number of digits required for the DECIMAL data type is 29, so the digit array must have room for 30 digits. There must also be enough digits to accept the number in octal, if that parsing options is selected. (Hexadecimal and octal numbers are limited by **VarNumFromParseNum** to the magnitude of an **unsigned long** [32 bits], so they need 11 octal digits.)

NUMPARSE Structure

Flags used by both *dwInFlags* and *dwOutFlags*:

```
NUMPRS_LEADING_WHITE
NUMPRS_TRAILING_WHITE
NUMPRS_LEADING_PLUS
NUMPRS_TRAILING_PLUS
NUMPRS_LEADING_MINUS
NUMPRS_TRAILING_MINUS
NUMPRS_HEX_OCT
NUMPRS_PARENS
NUMPRS_DECIMAL
NUMPRS_THOUSANDS
NUMPRS_CURRENCY
NUMPRS_EXPONENT
NUMPRS_USE_ALL
NUMPRS_STD
```

Flags used by *dwOutFlags* only:

```
NUMPRS_NEG
NUMPRS_INEXACT
```

The caller of **VarParseNumFromStr** must initialize two elements of the passed-in NUMPARSE structure:

```
typedef struct {
    int cDig;
    unsigned long    dwInFlags;
    unsigned long    dwOutFlags;
    int cchUsed;
    int nBaseShift;
    int nPwr10;
} NUMPARSE;
```

The *cDig* element is set to the size of the *rgbDig* array, and *dwInFlags* is set to parsing options. All other elements may be uninitialized and are set by the function, except on error, as described in the following paragraphs. The *cDig* element is also modified by the function to reflect the actual number of digits written to the *rgbDig* array.

The *cchUsed* element of the NUMPARSE structure is filled in with the number of characters (from the beginning of the string) that were successfully parsed. This allows the caller to determine if the entire string was part of the number (as required by functions such as **VarI2FromStr**), or where to continue parsing the string.

The *nBaseShift* element gives the number of bits per digit (3 or 4 for octal and hexadecimal numbers, and zero for decimal).

The following apply only to decimal numbers:

- *nPwr10* sets the decimal point position by giving the power of 10 of the least significant digit.
- If the number is negative, NUMPRS_NEG will be set in *dwOutFlags*.
- If there are more non-zero decimal digits than will fit into the digit array, the NUMPRS_INEXACT flag will be set.

Date and Time Conversion Functions

The following functions are provided by Oleauto32.dll (for 32-bit systems) and Ole2disp.dll (for 16-bit systems) to convert between dates and times stored in MS-DOS format and the variant representation.

VarDateFromUdate

HRESULT VarDateFromUdate(
[in] **UDATE** **pudateIn,*
[in] **unsigned long** **dwFlags,*
[out] **DATE** **pdateOut*
);

Packs a date.

Parameters

pudateIn
    Unpacked date.

dwFlags
    Returns VAR_VALIDDATE on valid date.

pdateOut
    Packed date

Return Value

The return value obtained from the returned HRESULT is one of the following.

Return value	Meaning
S_OK	Success.
E_OUTOFMEMORY	Out of memory.

Comments

The UDATE structure is used with **VarDateFromUdate** and **VarUdateFromDate**.
It represents an "unpacked" date.

```
typedef struct
{
    SYSTEMTIME st;
    USHORT   wDayOfYear;
} UDATE;
```

VarUdateFromDate

HRESULT VarUdateFromDate(
[in] **DATE** *dateIn,*
[in] **unsigned long** *dwFlags,*
[out] **UDATE** *pudateOut*
);

Unpacks a date.

Parameters

dateIns
Unpacked date.

dwFlags
Set for alternative calendars such as Hijri, Polish and Russian.

pudateOut
Packed date.

Return Value

The return value obtained from the returned HRESULT is one of the following.

Return value	Meaning
S_OK	Success.
E_OUTOFMEMORY	Out of memory.

Comments

The UDATE structure is used with **VarDateFromUdate** and **VarUdateFromDate**. It represents an "unpacked" date.

```
typedef struct
{
    SYSTEMTIME st;
    USHORT  wDayOfYear;
} UDATE;
```

DosDateTimeToVariantTime

INT DosDateTimeToVariantTime(
unsigned short *wDosDate*,

unsigned short *wDosTime*,

double FAR* *pvtime*

);

Converts the MS-DOS representation of time to the date and time representation stored in a variant.

Parameters

wDosDate
The MS-DOS date to convert.

wDosTime
The MS-DOS time to convert.

pvtime
Pointer to the location to store the converted time.

Return Value

The return value obtained from the returned INT is one of the following.

Result	Meaning
True	Success.
False	Failure.

Comments

MS-DOS records file dates and times as packed 16-bit values. An MS-DOS date has the following format.

Bits	Contents
0–4	Day of the month (1–31).
5–8	Month (1 = January, 2 = February, and so on).
9–15	Year offset from 1980 (add 1980 to get the actual year).

An MS-DOS time has the following format.

Bits	Contents
0–4	Second divided by 2.
5–10	Minute (0–59).
11–15	Hour (0–23 on a 24-hour clock).

VariantTimeToDosDateTime

INT VariantTimeToDosDateTime(
double *vtime*,
unsigned short FAR* *pwDosDate*,
unsigned short FAR* *pwDosTime*
);

Converts the variant representation of a date and time to MS-DOS date and time values.

Parameters

vtime
    The variant time to convert.

pwDosDate
    Pointer to the location to store the converted MS-DOS date.

pwDosTime
    Pointer to the location to store the converted MS-DOS time.

Return Value

The return value obtained from the returned INT is one of the following.

Result	Meaning
True	Success.
False	Failure.

Comments

A variant time is stored as an 8-byte real value (**double**), representing a date between January 1, 1753 and December 31, 2078, inclusive. The value 2.0 represents January 1, 1900; 3.0 represents January 2, 1900, and so on. Adding 1 to the value increments the date by a day. The fractional part of the value represents the time of day. Therefore, 2.5 represents noon on January 1, 1900; 3.25 represents 6:00 A.M. on January 2, 1900, and so on. Negative numbers represent the dates prior to December 30, 1899.

For a description of the MS-DOS date and time formats, see **DosDateTimeToVariantTime**.

VariantTimeToSystemTime

INT VariantTimeToSystemTime(
double *vtime,*
LPSYSTEMTIME *lpSystemTime*
);

Converts the variant representation of time-to-system time values.

Parameters

vtime
The variant time that will be converted.

lpSystemTime
Pointer to the location where the converted time will be stored.

Return Value

The return value obtained from the returned INT is one of the following.

Result	Meaning
True	Success.
False	Failure.

Comments

A variant time is stored as an 8-byte real value (**double**), representing a date between January 1, 1753 and December 31, 2078, inclusive. The value 2.0 represents January 1, 1900; 3.0 represents January 2, 1900, and so on. Adding 1 to the value increments the date by a day. The fractional part of the value represents the time of day. Therefore, 2.5 represents noon on January 1, 1900; 3.25 represents 6:00 A.M. on January 2, 1900, and so on. Negative numbers represent the dates prior to December 30, 1899.

Using the SYSTEMTIME structure is useful because:

- It spans all time/date periods. MS-DOS date/time is limited to representing only those dates between 1/1/1980 and 12/31/2107.

- The date/time elements are all easily accessible without needing to do any bit decoding.

- The National Language Support data and time formatting functions **GetDateFormat** and **GetTimeFormat** take a SYSTEMTIME value as input.

- It is the default Win32 time and date data format supported by Windows NT and Windows 95.

SystemTimeToVariantTime

INT SystemTimeToVariantTime(
  SYSTEMTIME *lpSystemTime*

  double **pvtime*

  );

Converts the variant representation of time-to-system-time values.

Parameters

lpSystemTime
  The system time.

pvtime
  Returned variant time.

Return Value

The return value obtained from the returned INT is one of the following.

Result	Meaning
True	Success.
False	Failure.

Comments

A variant time is stored as an 8-byte real value (**double**), representing a date between January 1, 1753 and December 31, 2078, inclusive. The value 2.0 represents January 1, 1900; 3.0 represents January 2, 1900, and so on. Adding 1 to the value increments the date by a day. The fractional part of the value represents the time of day. Therefore, 2.5 represents noon on January 1, 1900; 3.25 represents 6:00 A.M. on January 2, 1900, and so on. Negative numbers represent the dates prior to December 30, 1899.

The SYSTEMTIME structure is useful for the following reasons:

- It spans all time/date periods. MS-DOS date/time is limited to representing only those dates between 1/1/1980 and 12/31/2107.

- The date/time elements are all easily accessible without needing to do any bit decoding.

- The National Data Support data and time formatting functions **GetDateFormat** and **GetTimeFormat** take a SYSTEMTIME value as input. For more information, see the *Win32 Programmer's Reference* in the Win32 SDK.

- It is the default Win32 time/date data format supported by Windows NT and Windows 95.

GetAltMonthNames

HRESULT GetAltMonthNames(
LCID *lcid,*
OLECHAR FAR* *prgp*
);

Retrieves the secondary (*altername*) month names.

Parameters

lcid
The variant time that will be converted.

prgp
Pointer to the location where the converted time will be stored.

Return Value

The return value obtained from the returned HRESULT is one of the following.

Result	Meaning
True	Success.
False	Failure.

Comments

Useful for Hijri, Polish and Russian alternate month names.

Type Libraries and the Object Description Language

When you expose ActiveX objects, it allows interoperability with the programs of other vendors. For vendors to use these objects, they must have access to the characteristics of the objects (properties and methods). To make this information available developers must:

- Publish object and type definitions (for example, as printed documentation).

- Code objects into a compiled .c or .cpp file so they can be accessed using **IDispatch::GetTypeInfo** or implementations of the **ITypeInfo** and **ITypeLib** interfaces.

- Use the Microsoft Interface Definition Language (MIDL) compiler or the MkTypLib utility to create a type library that contains the objects, and then make the type library available.

The MIDL compiler and the MkTypLib utility both compile scripts that are written in the Object Description Language (ODL). Microsoft has expanded the Interface Definition Language (IDL) to contain the complete ODL syntax. You should use the MIDL compiler in preference to MkTypLib, since MkTypLib is being phased out and will no longer be supported.

For more information about the MIDL compiler, refer to the *MIDL Programmer's Guide and Reference* in the Win32 Software Development Kit (SDK).

The following descriptions and references are contained in this chapter:

- Contents of a type library
- Using MIDL and MkTypLib
- Differences between MIDL and MkTypLib
- MkTypLib type library creation
- ODL file syntax
- ODL reference

Contents of a Type Library

Type libraries are compound document files (.tlb files) that include information about types and objects exposed by an ActiveX application. A type library can contain any of the following:

- Information about data types, such as aliases, enumerations, structures, or unions.
- Descriptions of one or more objects, such as a module, interface, **IDispatch** interface (dispinterface), or component object class (coclass). Each of these descriptions is commonly referred to as a *typeinfo*.
- References to type descriptions from other type libraries.

By including the type library with a product, the information about the objects in the library can be made available to the users of the applications and programming tools. Type libraries can be shipped in any of the following forms:

- A resource in a dynamic-link library (DLL). This resource should have the type TypeLib and an integer identifier. It must be declared in the resource (.rc) file as follows:

```
1 typelib mylib1.tlb
2 typelib mylib2.tlb
```

  There can be multiple type library resources in a DLL. Application developers should use the resource compiler to add the .tlb file to their own DLL. A DLL with one or more type library resources typically has the file extension .olb (object library).

- A resource in an .exe file. The file can contain multiple type libraries.
- A stand-alone binary file. The .tlb (type library) file output by the MkTypLib utility is a binary file.

Object browsers, compilers, and similar tools access type libraries through the interfaces **ITypeLib**, **ITypeLib2**, **ITypeInfo**, **ITypeInfo2** and **ITypeComp**. Type library tools (such as MkTypLib) can be created using the interfaces **ICreateTypeLib**, **ICreateTypeLib2**, **ICreateTypeInfo** and **ICreateTypeInfo2**.

Using MIDL and MkTypLib

Files parsed by MkTypLib are .odl files. Files parsed by MIDL are referred to as .idl files, although they can contain the same syntax elements as .odl files. The MIDL compiler and the MkTypLib utility both compile scripts written in ODL. However, MkTypLib is obsolete and you should use the MIDL compiler instead. The following sections describe the differences and special considerations for using MkTypLib and MIDL to create type libraries.

Adding ODL to an IDL Definition

The .odl files provide object definitions that are added to the type descriptions in a type library. The MkTypLib utility parses files written in ODL syntax, generates the type libraries, and optionally creates C++ header files that contain the same definitions.

The top-level element of ODL syntax is the **library** statement (or library block). Every other ODL statement (with the exception of the attributes that can be applied to the **library** statement) must be defined in the library block.

The MIDL compiler generates a type library when it sees a **library** statement in the same way that MkTypLib does. The statements found in the library block follow essentially the same syntax as earlier versions of ODL.

ODL attributes can be applied to an element both inside and outside of the library block. Outside the block, they typically do nothing, unless the element is referenced from within the block by using it as a base type, inheriting from it, or referencing it on a line such as this:

```
library a
{
    interface [xyz]];
    struct bar;
    ...
}
```

If an element defined outside of the block is referenced in the block, its definition is put into the generated type library.

Anything outside of the library block is an .idl file, and the MIDL compiler processes it as usual. Typically, this means generating proxy stubs for it.

Differences Between MIDL and MkTypLib

There are a few key areas in which the MIDL compiler differs from the MkTypLib utility. Most of these differences arise because MIDL is more C-syntax oriented than MkTypLib. All of the differences described here, with the exception of floating point constants and the **enum** scope, can be resolved by using the **/mktyplib203** MIDL compiler option (see "The /mktyplib203 Option" later in this chapter). This switch forces MIDL to behave like MkTypLib.exe, version 2.03, the last release of MkTypLib.exe.

In general, you will want to use the MIDL syntax in your .idl files. However, the **/mktyplib203** option is useful if you need to compile an existing .odl file, or otherwise maintain compatibility with MkTypLib.

Typedef Syntax for Complex Data Types

In MkTypLib, both of the following definitions generate a TKIND_RECORD for "bar" in the type library. The tag "foo" is optional and, if used, will not show up in the type library.

```
typedef struct foo { ... } bar;
typedef struct { ... } bar;
```

In MIDL, the first definition will generate a TKIND_RECORD for "foo" and a TKIND_ALIAS for "bar" (defining "bar" as an alias for "foo"). For the second definition, MIDL will generate a TKIND_RECORD for a mangled name internal to MIDL that is not meaningful to the user and a TKIND_ALIAS for "bar." This has potential implications for type library browsers that simply show the name of a record in its user interface. If you expect a TKIND_RECORD to have a real name, there is a potential for unrecognizable names to appear in the user interface. This behavior also applies to **union** and **enum** definitions, with the MIDL compiler generating TKIND_UNIONs and TKIND_ENUMs, respectively.

MIDL also allows C-style **struct**, **union**, and **enum** definitions. For example, the following definition is legal in MIDL:

```
struct foo { ... };
typedef struct foo bar;
```

MkTypLib and Boolean Data Types

In MkTypLib, the **boolean** base type and the MkTypLib data type BOOL equate to VT_BOOL, which maps to VARIANT_BOOL, and which is defined as a **short**. In MIDL, the **boolean** base type is equivalent to VT_UI1, which is defined as an **unsigned char**, and the BOOL data type is defined as a **long**. This leads to difficulties if you mix IDL syntax and ODL syntax in the same file while still trying to maintain compatibility with MkTypLib. Because the data types are different sizes, the marshaling code will not match what is described in the type information. If you want a VT_BOOL in your type library, you should use the VARIANT_BOOL data type.

GUID Definitions in Header Files

When using the MkTypLib utility, GUIDs are defined in the header file with a macro that can be conditionally compiled to generate either a GUID predefinition or an instantiated GUID. MIDL normally puts GUID predefinitions in its generated header files and only puts GUID instantiations in the file generated by the **/iid** switch.

Scope of Symbols in an enum Declaration

In MkTypLib the scope of symbols in an enum is local. In MIDL, the scope of symbols in an enum is global with MIDL, as it is in C. For example, the following code will compile in MkTypLib, but will generate a duplicate name error in MIDL:

```
typedef struct { ... } a;
enum {a=1, b=2, c=3};
```

Support for ODL Base Types

There are a number of base types supported by MkTypLib that are not directly supported by MIDL. The MIDL function gets its definitions for these base types by automatically importing oleauto.idl, and oleidl.idl whenever it encounters a library statement. This means that oleauto.idl, oaidl.idl, and oleidl.idl (along with the imported unknwn.idl and wtypes.idl files) must be somewhere in the user's INCLUDE path. The OLE and Automation DLLs must also be in the system if the user compiles an .idl file that contains a library statement.

The /mktyplib203 Option

The MIDL compiler behaves differently from the MkTypLib utility. The **/mktyplib203** option removes most of these differences and makes MIDL act like MkTypLib, version 2.03.

For example, BOOL (a MkTypLib base type) is defined differently in MIDL than it is in MkTypLib. MkTypLib treats BOOL as a VARIANT_BOOL. However, BOOL is defined in the file Wtypes.idl as a long data type. If a VARIANT_BOOL is to be placed in the type library, it has to explicitly use VARIANT_BOOL in the .idl/.odl file. If BOOL is used when VARIANT_BOOL is meant to be used, then the **/mktyplib203** option should also be used.

MIDL normally puts globally unique identifier (GUID) predefinitions in its generated header files, and only puts GUID instantiations in the file generated by the **/iid** option. With the **/mktyplib203** option, MIDL defines GUIDs in the header files in the way that MkTypLib does. They are defined with a macro that can be compiled conditionally to generate either a predefined or an instantiated GUID.

With the **/mktyplib203** option enabled, it is invalid to put any statements outside of the library block. A pure ODL syntax must be used; it cannot be mixed and matched in this mode.

MkTypLib is used to require **struct, union,** and **enum** to be defined as part of type definitions. For example:

```
typedef struct foo { int i; } bar;
```

In this statement, MkTypLib generates a TKIND_RECORD named "bar." Because the "foo" was not recorded anywhere in the type library, it can be omitted.

MIDL allows normal C definitions of **structure, union,** and **enum**:

```
struct foo {int i;};
    typedef struct foo bar;
```

–Or–

```
    typedef struct foo {int i;} bar;
```

This statement generates a TKIND_RECORD named "foo" and (if the type definition is public) a TKIND_ALIAS named "bar." The "foo" can still be omitted, in which case MIDL generates a name for it.

When the **/mktyplib203** option is enabled, the original MkTypLib type definition syntax is required for structures, unions, and enumerators. The behavior is the same as under MkTypLib (that is, "foo" is not included in the type library).

Note   MkTypLib permits some scoping errors, such as giving enumerators their own scope. These errors are fixed by MIDL, and cannot be reintroduced, even with the **/mktyplib203** switch. Even though the **/mktyplib203** switch enables MIDL to compile most earlier .odl files, there can be a few exceptions. These are cases where the .odl files were already broken, and MkTypLib did not catch the errors.

MkTypLib: Type Library Creation Tool

MkTypLib processes scripts written in ODL, producing a type library and an optional C or C++ header file.

MkTypLib uses the **ICreateTypeLib** and **ICreateTypeInfo** interfaces to create type libraries. Type libraries can then be accessed by tools, such as type browsers and compilers that use the **ITypeLib** and **ITypeInfo** interfaces, as shown in the following figure.

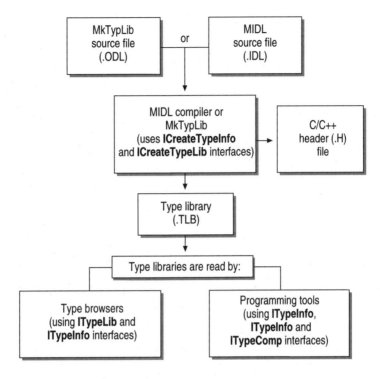

Invoking MkTypLib

To invoke MkTypLib, enter the following command line:

MkTypLib [*options*] *ODLfile*

MkTypLib creates a type library (.tlb) file based on the object description script in the file specified by *ODLfile*. It can optionally produce a header (.h) file, which is a stripped version of the input file. This file is included in C or C++ programs that want to access the types defined in the input file. In the header file, MkTypLib inserts DEFINE_GUID macros for each element defined in the type library (such as interface, dispinterface, and so on).

There can be a series of options, each prefixed with a hyphen (-) or a slash (/), as follows:

Option	Description
/? or **/help**	Displays command line Help. In this case, *ODLfile* does not need to be specified.
/align:*alignment*	Sets the default alignment for types in the library. An *alignment* value of 1 indicates natural alignment; *n* indicates alignment on byte *n*.
/cpp_cmd *cpppath*	Specifies *cpppath* as the command to run the C preprocessor. By default, MkTypLib invokes CL.

Option	Description
/cpp_opt "*options*"	Specifies options for the C preprocessor. The default is **/C /E /D__MkTypLib__**.
/D *define*[=*value*]	Defines the name *define* for the C preprocessor. The *value* is its optional value. No space is allowed between the equal sign (=) and the value.
/h *filename*	Specifies *filename* as the name for a stripped version of the input file. This file can be used as a C or C++ header file.
/I *includedir*	Specifies *includedir* as the directory where include files are located for the C preprocessor.
/nocpp	Suppresses invocation of the C preprocessor.
/nologo	Disables the display of the copyright banner.
/o *outputfile*	Redirects output (for example, error messages) to the specified *outputfile*.
/tlb *filename*	Specifies *filename* as the name of the output .tlb file. If not specified, it will be the same name as the *ODLfile*, with the extension .tlb.
/win16 /win32 /mac /mips /alpha /ppc /ppc32	Specifies the output type library to be produced. The default is the current operating system.
/w0	Disables warnings.

Although MkTypLib offers minimal error reporting, error messages include accurate line number and column number information that can be used with text editors to locate the source of errors.

MkTypLib spawns the C preprocessor. The symbol **__MKTYPLIB__** is predefined for the preprocessor.

ODL File Syntax

The general syntax for an .odl file is as follows:

[*attributes*] **library** *libname* {*definitions*};
The *attributes* associate characteristics with the library, such as its Help file and universally unique identifier (UUID). Attributes must be enclosed in square brackets.

The *definitions* consist of the descriptions of the imported libraries, data types, modules, interfaces, dispinterfaces, and coclasses that are part of the type library. Braces ({ }) must surround the definitions.

The following table summarizes the elements that can appear in *definitions*. Each element is described in more detail later in this chapter, in the section "ODL Reference."

Purpose	Library element	Description
Allows references to other type libraries.	**importlib** (*lib1*)	Specifies an external type library that contains definitions that are referenced in this type library.
Declares data types used by the objects in this type library.	**typedef** [*attributes*] *aliasname*	An alias declared using C syntax. Must have at least one *attribute* to be included in the type library.
	typedef [*attributes*] **enum**	An enumeration declared using the C keywords **typedef** and **enum**.
	typedef [*attributes*] **struct**	A structure declared using the C keywords **typedef** and **struct**.
	typedef [*attributes*] **union**	A union declared using the C keywords **typedef** and **union**.
Describes functions that enable querying the DLL.	[*attributes*] **module**	Constants and general data functions whose actions are not restricted to any specified class of objects.
Describes interfaces.	[*attributes*] **dispinterface**	An interface describing the methods and properties for an object that must be accessed through **IDispatch::Invoke**.
	[*attributes*] **interface**	An interface describing the methods and properties for an object that can be accessed either through **IDispatch::Invoke** or through VTBL entries.
Describes OLE classes.	[*attributes*] **coclass**	Specifies a top-level object with all of its interfaces and dispinterfaces.

In the library description, modules, interfaces, dispinterfaces, and coclasses follow the same general syntax:

[*attributes*] *elementname typename*
{
    memberdescriptions
}

The *attributes* set characteristics for the element. The *elementname* is a keyword that indicates the kind of item (module, interface, dispinterface, or coclass), and the *typename* defines the name of the item. The *memberdescriptions* define the members (constants, functions, properties, and methods) of each element.

Aliases, enumerations, unions, and structures have the following syntax:

typedef [*typeattributes*] *typekind typename*
{
     memberdescriptions
}

For these types, the attributes follow the **typedef** keyword, and the *typekind* indicates the data type (**enum**, **union**, or **struct**). For details, see "Attribute Descriptions" later in this chapter.

Note   The square brackets ([ ])and braces ({ }) in these descriptions are part of the syntax, and are not descriptive symbols. The semicolon after the closing brace (}) that terminates the library definition (and all other type definitions) is optional.

ODL File Example

The following example shows the .odl file for the Lines sample file, extracted from Lines.odl:

```
[
    uuid(3C591B20-1F13-101B-B826-00DD01103DE1),        // LIBID_Lines.
    helpstring("Lines 1.0 Type Library"),
    lcid(0x09),
    version(1.0)
]
library Lines
{
    importlib("stdole.tlb");
    #define DISPID_NEWENUM -4

    [
        uuid(3C591B25-1F13-101B-B826-00DD01103DE1),  // IID_Ipoint.
        helpstring("Point object."),
        oleautomation,
        dual
    ]
    interface IPoint : IDispatch
    {
        [propget, helpstring("Returns and sets x coordinate.")]
        HRESULT x([out, retval] int* retval);
        [propput, helpstring("Returns and sets x coordinate.")]
        HRESULT x([in] int Value);

        [propget, helpstring("Returns and sets y coordinate.")]
        HRESULT y([out, retval] int* retval);
        [propput, helpstring("Returns and sets y coordinate.")]
        HRESULT y([in] int Value);
    }
```

```
// Additional interfaces omitted for brevity.

    [
        uuid(3C591B27-1F13-101B-B826-00DD01103DE1),        // IID_Ipoints.
        helpstring("Points collection."),
        oleautomation,
        dual
    ]
    interface IPoints : IDispatch
    {
        [propget, helpstring("Returns number of points in collection.")]
        HRESULT Count([out, retval] long* retval);

        [propget, id(0),
        helpstring("Given an index, returns a point in the
collection.")]
        HRESULT Item([in] long Index, [out, retval] IPoint** retval);

        [propget, restricted, id(DISPID_NEWENUM)]    // Must be propget.
        HRESULT _NewEnum([out, retval] IUnknown** retval);
    }

// Additional interface omitted for brevity.

    [
        uuid(3C591B22-1F13-101B-B826-00DD01103DE1), // IID_Iapplication.
        helpstring("Application object."),
        oleautomation,
        dual
    ]
    interface IApplication : IDispatch
    {
        [propget, helpstring("Returns the application of the object.")]
        HRESULT Application([out, retval] IApplication** retval);

        [propget,
        helpstring("Returns the full name of the application.")]
        HRESULT FullName([out, retval] BSTR* retval);
        [propget, id(0),
        helpstring("Returns the name of the application.")]
        HRESULT Name([out, retval] BSTR* retval);

        [propget, helpstring("Returns the parent of the object.")]
        HRESULT Parent([out, retval] IApplication** retval);
```

```
        [propput]
        HRESULT Visible([in] boolean VisibleFlag);
        [propget, helpstring
        ("Sets or returns whether the main window is visible.")]
        HRESULT Visible([out, retval] boolean* retval);

        [helpstring("Exits the application.")]
        HRESULT Quit();

// Additional methods omitted for brevity.

        [helpstring("Creates new Point object initialized to (0,0).")]
        HRESULT CreatePoint([out, retval] IPoint** retval);
    }

    [
        uuid(3C591B21-1F13-101B-B826-00DD01103DE1),  // CLSID_Lines.
        helpstring("Lines Class"),
        appobject
    ]
    coclass Lines
    {
        [default] interface IApplication;
            interface IDispatch;
    }
}
```

The example describes a library named Lines that imports the standard OLE library Stdole.tlb. The **#define** directive defines the constant DISPID_NEWENUM, which is needed for the **_NewEnum** property of the IPoints collection.

The example shows declarations for three interfaces in the library: IPoint, IPoints, and IApplication. Because all three are dual interfaces, their members can be invoked through **IDispatch** or directly through virtual function tables (VTBLs). In addition, all of their members return HRESULT values and pass their return values as **retval** parameters. Therefore, they can support the **IErrorInfo** interface, through which they can return detailed error information in whatever way they are invoked.

The IPoint interface has two properties, X and Y, and two pairs of accessor functions to get and set the properties.

The IPoint interface is a collection of points. It supports three read-only properties, each of which has a single accessor function. The **Count** and **Item** properties return the number of points and the value of a single point, respectively. The **_NewEnum** property, required for collection objects, returns an enumerator object for the collection. This property has the **restricted** attribute, indicating that it should not be invoked from a macro language.

The **IApplication** interface describes the application object. It supports the properties **Application, FullName, Name, Parent, Visible,** and **Pane.** It supports the methods **Quit, CreateLine,** and **CreatePoint.**

Finally, the script defines a coclass named Lines. The **appobject** attribute makes the members of the coclass (**IApplication** and **IDispatch**) globally accessible in the type library. **IApplication** is defined as the **default** member, indicating that it is the programmability interface intended for use by macro languages.

Source File Contents

The following sections describe the proper format for comments, constants, identifiers, and other syntactic items in an .odl file.

Array Definitions

MkTypLib accepts both fixed-size arrays and arrays declared as SAFEARRAY.

Use a C-style syntax for a fixed size array:

type arrname[*size*]**;**

To describe a SAFEARRAY, use the following syntax:

SAFEARRAY (*elementtype*) **arrayname*

A function returning a SAFEARRAY has the following syntax:

SAFEARRAY (*elementtype*) *myfunction*(*parameterlist*)**;**

Comments

To include comments in an .odl file, use a C-style syntax in either block form (/*...*/) or single-line form (//). MkTypLib ignores the comments, and does not preserve them in the header (.h) file.

Constants

A constant can be either numeric or a string, depending on the attribute.

Numeric

Numeric input is usually an integer (in either decimal or in hexadecimal, using the standard 0x format), but can also be a single character constant (for example, \0).

String

A string is delimited by double quotation marks (") and cannot span multiple lines. The backslash character (\) acts as an escape character. The backslash character followed by any character (even another backslash) prevents the second character from being interpreted with any special meaning. The backslash is not included in the text.

For example, to include a double quotation mark (") in the text without causing it to be interpreted as the closing delimiter, it should be preceded with a backslash (\"). Similarly, a double backslash (\\) should be used to put a backslash into the text. Some examples of valid strings are:

```
"commandName"
"This string contains a \"quote\"."
"Here's a pathname: c:\\bin\\binp"
```

A string can be up to 255 characters long.

File Names

A file name is a string that represents either a full or partial path. Automation expects to find files in directories that are referenced by the type library registration entries, so partial path names are typically used. For more information about registration, refer to Chapter 2, "Exposing ActiveX objects."

Forward Declarations

Forward declarations permit forward references to types. Forward references have the following form:

```
typedef struct mydata;
interface aninterface;
dispinterface fordispatch;
coclass pococlass;
```

Globally Unique Identifier (GUID)

A universally unique identifier (UUID) is a globally unique identifier (GUID). This number is created by running the Guidgen.exe command line program. Guidgen.exe never produces the same number twice, no matter how many times it is run or how many different machines it runs on. Every entity that needs to be uniquely identified (such as an interface) has a GUID.

Identifiers

Identifiers can be up to 255 characters long, and must conform to C-style syntax. MkTypLib is case sensitive, but it generates type libraries that are case insensitive. It is therefore possible to define a user-defined type whose name differs from that of a built-in type only by case. User-defined type names (and member names) that differ only in case refer to the same type or member. Except for property accessor functions, it is invalid for two members of a type to have the same name, regardless of case.

Intrinsic Data Types

The following data types are recognized by MkTypLib:

Type	Description
boolean	Data item that can have the value **True** or **False**. The size maps to VARIANT_BOOL.
char	8-bit signed data item.
double	64-bit IEEE floating-point number.
int	Signed integer, whose size is system dependent.
float	32-bit IEEE floating point number.
long	32-bit signed integer.
short	16-bit signed integer.
wchar_t	Unicode character accepted only for 32-bit type libraries.
BSTR	Length-prefixed string, as described in Chapter 5, "Dispatch Interface and API Functions."
CURRENCY	8-byte, fixed-point number.
DATE	64-bit floating-point fractional number of days since December 30, 1899.
DECIMAL	96-bit unsigned binary integer scaled by a variable power of 10. Provides a size and scale for a number (as in coordinates).
SCODE	Built-in error type that corresponds to VT_ERROR. An SCODE (used in 16-bit systems only) does not contain the additional error information provided by HRESULT.
VARIANT	One of the variant data types as described in Chapter 5, "Dispatch Interface and API Functions."
IDispatch *	Pointer to the **IDispatch** interface.
IUnknown *	Pointer to the **IUnknown** interface. (Any OLE interface can be represented by its **IUnknown** interface.)

Type	Description
SAFEARRAY(TypeName)	**TypeName** is any of the above types. Array of these types.
TypeName*	**TypeName** is any of the above types. Pointer to a type.
void	Allowed only as return type for a function, or in a function parameter list to indicate no arguments.
HRESULT	Return type used for reporting error information in interfaces, as described in *OLE Programmer's Reference*.
LPWSTR	Unicode string accepted only for 32-bit type libraries.
LPSTR	Zero-terminated string.

Not all of the above types can be marshaled by Automation to another process or thread. The list of types that can be marshaled are called Automation compatible types, and are listed under the **oleautomation** attribute description.

The keyword **unsigned** can be specified before **int, char, short,** and **long**.

String Definitions

Strings can be declared using the LPSTR data type, which indicates a zero-terminated string, and with the BSTR data type, which indicates a length-prefixed string (as defined in Chapter 5, "Dispatch Interface and API Functions"). In 32-bit type libraries, Unicode strings can be defined with the LPWSTR data type.

ODL Reference

This section provides reference material on the attributes, statements, and directives that are part of the ODL.

Attribute Descriptions

The following sections describe the ODL attributes and the types of objects that they apply to, along with the equivalent flags set in the object's type information.

appobject

Description	Identifies the Application object.
Allowed on	Coclass.
Comments	Indicates that the members of the class can be accessed without qualification when accessing this type library.
Flags	TYPEFLAG_FAPPOBJECT

aggregatable

Description	Indicates that the class supports aggregation.
Allowed on	Coclass.
Comments	Indicates that the members of the class can be aggregated.
Flags	TYPEFLAG_FAGGREGATABLE
Example	

```
[    uuid(1e196b20-1f3c-1069-996b-00dd010fe676),
     aggregatable
]
coclass Form
{
     [default] interface IForm;
     [default, source] interface IFormEvents;
}
```

bindable

Description	Indicates that the property supports data binding.
Allowed on	Property.
Comments	Refers to the property as a whole, so it must be specified wherever the property is defined. The attribute should be specified on both the property get description and the property set description.
Flags	FUNCFLAG_FBINDABLE VARFLAG_FBINDABLE

control

Description   Indicates that the item represents a control from which a container site will derive additional type libraries or coclasses.

Allowed on   Type libraries, coclasses

Comments   This attribute allows type libraries that describe controls to be marked so that they are not displayed in type browsers intended for nonvisual objects.

Flags   TYPEFLAG_FCONTROL
LIBFLAG_FCONTROL

custom(*guid*, *value*)

Description   Indicates a custom attribute (one not defined by Automation). This feature enables the independent definition and use of attributes.

Parameters   *guid*
    The standard GUID form.

value
    A value that can be put into a variant. See also the **Const** directive.

Allowed on   Library, typeinfo, typlib, variable, function, parameter.

Not allowed on   A member of a coclass (IMPLTYPE).

Representation   Can be retrieved using:

ITypeLib2::GetCustData
ITypeInfo2::GetCustData
ITypeInfo2::GetAllCustData
ITypeInfo2::GetFuncCustData
ITypeInfo2::GetAllFuncCustData
ITypeInfo2::GetVarCustData
ITypeInfo2::GetAllVarCustData
ITypeInfo2::GetParamCustData
ITypeInfo2::GetAllParamCustData
ITypeInfo2::GetImplTypeCustData
ITypeInfo2::GetAllImplTypeCustData

Example   The following example shows how to add a string-valued attribute that gives the ProgID for a class:

```
[
    custom(GUID_PROGID, "DAO.Dynaset")
]
coclass Dynaset
{
    [default] interface Dynaset;
    [default, source] interface IDynasetEvents;
}
```

default

Description   Indicates that the interface or dispinterface represents the default programmability interface. Intended for use by macro languages.

Allowed on   Coclass member.

Comments   A coclass can have two **default** members at most. One represents the source interface or dispinterface, and the other represents the sink interface or dispinterface. If the **default** attribute is not specified for any member of the coclass or cotype, the first source and sink members that do not have the **restricted** attribute will be treated as the defaults.

Flags   IMPLTYPEFLAG_FDEFAULT

defaultbind

Description   Indicates the single, bindable property that best represents the object.

Allowed on   Property.

Comments   Properties that have the **defaultbind** attribute must also have the **bindable** attribute. The **defaultbind** attribute cannot be specified on more than one property in a dispinterface.

This attribute is used by containers that have a user model that involves binding to an object rather than binding to a property of an object. An object can support data binding and not have this attribute.

Flags   FUNCFLAG_FDEFAULTBIND
VARFLAG_FDEFAULTBIND

defaultcollelem

Description

Allows for optimization of code.

Allowed on

Property, members in dispinterfaces and interfaces.

Comments

In Visual Basic for Applications (VBA5.0), "MyForm!bar" is normally syntactic shorthand for foo.defaultprop("bar"). Because such a call is significantly slower than accessing a data member of foo directly, an optimization has been added in which the compiler looks for a member named "bar" on the type of MyForm. If such a member is found and flagged as an accessor function for an element of the default collection, a call is generated to that member function. To allow vendors to produce object servers that will be optimized in this way, the member flag should be documented.

Because this optimization searches the type of item that precedes the "!", it will optimize calls of the form MyForm!bar only if MyForm has a member named "bar," and it will optimize MyForm.Controls!bar only if the return type of Controls has a member named bar. Even though MyForm!bar and MyForm.Controls!bar both would normally generate the same calls to the object server, optimizing these two forms requires that the object server add the bar method in both places.

Use of [**defaultcollitem**] must be consistent for a property. For example, if it is present on a **Get**, it must also be present on a **Put**.

Flags

FUNCFLAG_FDEFAULTCOLLELEM
VARFLAG_FDEFAULTCOLLELEM

Example

A form has a button on it named Button1. User code can access the button using property syntax or ! syntax, as shown below.

```
Sub Test()
    Dim f As Form1
    Dim b1 As Button
    Dim b2 As Button

    Set f = Form1

    Set b1 = f.Button1      ' Property syntax
    Set b = f!Button1       ' ! syntax
End Sub
```

To use the property syntax and the ! syntax properly, see the form in the type information below.

```
[   odl,
    dual,
    uuid(1e196b20-1f3c-1096-996b-00dd010ef676),
    helpstring("This is IForm"),
    restricted
]
```

```
interface IForm1: IForm
{
    [propget, defaultcollelem]
    HRESULT Button1([out, retval] Button *Value);
}
```

defaultvalue(*value*)

Description

Enables specification of a default value for a typed optional parameter.

Allowed on

Parameter.

Comments

The expression *value* resolves to a constant that can be described in a variant. The ODL already allows some expression forms, as when a constant is declared in a module. The same expressions are supported without modification.

The following example shows some legal parameter descriptions:

```
interface IMyInterface
{
    void Ex1([defaultvalue(44)] LONG    i);
    void Ex2([defaultvalue(44)] SHORT   i);
    void Ex3([defaultvalue("Hello")] BSTR · i);
}
```

The following rules apply:

1. It is invalid to specify a default value for a parameter whose type is a safe array. It is invalid to specify a default value for any type that cannot go in a variant, including structures and arrays.

2. Parameters can be mixed. Optional parameters and default value parameters must follow mandatory parameters.

3. The default value can be any constant that is represented by a VARIANT data type.

Flags

None.

Example

```
interface QueryDef
{

// Type is now known to be a LONG type (good for browser in VBA and
// for a C/C++ programmer) and also has a default value of
// dbOpenTable (constant).
```

```
HRESULT OpenRecordset(  [in, defaultvalue(dbOpenTable)]
    LONG Type,

    [out,retval]
Recordset **pprst);
}
```

defaultvtbl

Description

Enables an object to have two different source interfaces.

Allowed on

A member of a coclass.

Comments

The **default** interface is an interface or dispinterface that is the default source interface. If the interface is a:

- **dual** interface, sinks receive events through **IDispatch**.
- **VTBL** interface, event sinks receive events through VTBL.
- **dispinterface,** sinks receive events through **IDispatch**.
- **defaultvtable,** a default VTBL interface, which cannot be a dispinterface—it must be a dual, VTBL, or interface. If the interface is a dual interface, then sinks receive events through the VTBL.

An object can have both a default source and a default VTBL source interface with the same interface identifier (IID or GUID). In this case, a sink should advise using IID_IDISPATCH to receive dispatch events, and use the specific interface identifier to receive VTBL events.

For normal (non-source) interfaces, an object can support a single interface that satisfies consumers who want to use **IDispatch** access as well as VTBL access (a dual interface). Because of the way source interfaces work, it is not possible to use dual interface for source interfaces. The object with the source interface is in control of whether calls are made through **IDispatch** or through the VTBL. The sink does not provide any information about how it wants to receive the events. The only action that object-sourcing events can take would be to use the least common denominator, the **IDispatch** interface. This effectively reduces a dual interface to a dispatch interface with regard to sourcing events.

Interface	Flag it translates into
default	IMPLTYPEFLAG_FDEFAULT
default, source	IMPLTYPEFLAG_FDEFAULT
	IMPLTYPEFLAG_FSOURCE
defaultvtable, source	IMPLTYPEFLAG_FDEFAULT
	IMPLTYPEFLAG_FDEFAULTVTABLE
	IMPLTYPEFLAG_FSOURCE

Flags

IMPLTYPEFLAG_FDEFAULTVTABLE. (If this flag is set, then
IMPLTYPEFLAG_FSOURCE is also set.)

Example

```
[   odl,
    dual,
    uuid(1e196b20-1f3c-1069-996b-00dd010ef676),
    restricted
]
interface IForm: IDispatch
{
    [propget]
    HRESULT Backcolor([out, retval] long *Value);

    [propput]
    HRESULT Backcolor([in] long Value);


    [propget]
    HRESULT Name([out, retval] BSTR *Value);

    [propput]
    HRESULT Name([in] BSTR Value);
}
 [   odl,
    dual,
    uuid(1e196b20-1f3c-1069-996b-00dd010ef767),
    restricted
]
interface IFormEvents: IDispatch
{
    HRESULT Click();
    HRESULT Resize();
}

[uuid(1e196b20-1f3c-1069-996b-00dd010fe676)]
coclass Form
{
    [default] interface IForm;
    [default, source] interface IFormEvents;
    [defaultvtable, source] interface IFormEvents;
}
```

displaybind

Description   Indicates that a property should be displayed as bindable to the user.

Allowed on   Property.

Comments   Properties that have the **displaybind** attribute must also have the **bindable** attribute. An object can support data binding and not have this attribute.

Flags   FUNCFLAG_FDISPLAYBIND
VARFLAG_FDISPLAYBIND

dllname(*str*)

Description   Defines the name of the DLL that contains the entry points for a module.

Allowed on   Module (required).

Comments   The *str* argument gives the file name of the DLL.

dual

Description   Identifies an interface that exposes properties and methods through **IDispatch** and directly through the VTBL.

Allowed on   Interface.

Comments   The interface must be compatible with Automation and derive from **IDispatch**. Not allowed on dispinterfaces.

The **dual** attribute creates an interface that is both a **Dispatch** interface and a Component Object Model (COM) interface. The first seven entries of the VTBL for a dual interface are the seven members of **IDispatch**, and the remaining entries are COM entries for direct access to members of the dual interface. All of the parameters and return types specified for members of a dual interface must be compatible with Automation types.

All members of a dual interface must pass an HRESULT as the function's return value. Members that need to return other values should specify the last parameter as [**retval, out**] indicating an output parameter that returns the value of the function. In addition, members that need to support multiple locales should pass an *lcid* parameter.

A dual interface provides for both the speed of direct VTBL binding and the flexibility of **IDispatch** binding. For this reason, dual interfaces are recommended whenever possible.

Note If an application accesses object data by casting the THIS pointer in the interface call, the VTBL pointers in the object should be checked against the VTBL pointers to ensure that they are connected to the appropriate proxy.

Specifying dual on an interface implies that the interface is compatible with Automation, and therefore causes both the TYPEFLAG_FDUAL and TYPEFLAG_FOLEAUTOMATION flags to be set.

Flags

TYPEFLAG_FDUAL
TYPEFLAG_FOLEAUTOMATION

---

entry(*entryid*)

Description   Identifies the entry point in the DLL.

Allowed on   Functions in a module (required).

Comments   If *entryid* is a string, this is a named entry point. If *entryid* is a number, the entry point is defined by an ordinal. This attribute provides a way to obtain the address of a function in a module.

---

helpcontext(*numctxt*)

Description   Sets the context in the Help file.

Allowed on   Library, interface, dispinterface, struct, enum, union, module, typedef, method, struct member, enum value, property, coclass, const.

Comments   Retrieved by the 'GetDocumentation' functions in the **ITypeLib** and **ITypeInfo** interfaces. The *numctxt* is a 32-bit Help context identifier in the Help file.

helpfile(*filename*)

Description   Sets the name of the Help file.

Allowed on   Library.

Comments   Retrieved through the **GetDocumentation** functions in the **ITypeLib** and **ITypeInfo** interfaces.

All types in a library share the same Help file.

helpstring(*string*)

Description   Sets the Help string.

Allowed on   **Library**, **interface**, **dispinterface**, **struct**, **enum**, **union**, **module**, **typedef**, **method**, structure member, enum value, property, coclass, const.

Comments   Retrieved through the **GetDocumentation** functions in the **ITypeLib** and **ITypeInfo** interfaces.

helpstringcontext(*contextid*)

Description   Sets the string context in the Help file.

Allowed on   Type library, type information (TypeInfo), function, and variable level.

Comments   Retrieved by the **GetDocumentation2** functions in the **ITypeLib2** and **ITypeInfo2** interfaces. The *contextid* is a 32-bit Help context identifier in the Help file.

helpstringdll(*dllname*)

Description   Sets the name of the DLL to use to perform the document string lookup (localization).

Allowed on   Type library.

Comments   Retrieved through the **GetDocumentation2** functions in the **ITypeLib2** and **ITypeInfo2** interfaces.

hidden

Description

Indicates that the item exists, but should not be displayed in a user-oriented browser.

Allowed on

Property, method, coclass, dispinterface, interface, library.

Comments

This attribute allows members to be removed from an interface by shielding them from further use, while maintaining compatibility with existing code.

When specified for a library, the attribute prevents the entire library from being displayed. It is intended for use by controls. Hosts need to create a new type library that wraps the control with extended properties.

Flags

VARFLAG_FHIDDEN
FUNCFLAG_FHIDDEN
TYPEFLAG_FHIDDEN

id(*num*)

Description

Identifies the DISPID of the member.

Allowed on

Method or property in an interface or dispinterface.

Comments

The *num* is a 32-bit integral value in the following format:

Bits	Value
0–15	Offset. Any value is permissible.
16–21	The nesting level of this type information in the inheritance hierarchy. For example:
	`interface mydisp : IDispatch`
	The nesting level of **IUnknown** is 0, **IDispatch** is 1, and MyDisp is 2.
22–25	Reserved. Must be zero.
26–28	Dispatch identifier (DISPID) value.
29	True if this is the member identifier for a FuncDesc; otherwise False.
30–31	Must be 01.

Negative identifiers are reserved for use by Automation.

immediatebind

Description   Allows individual bindable properties on a form to specify this behavior. When this bit is set, all changes will be notified.

Comments   Allows controls to differentiate two different types of bindable properties. One type of bindable property needs to notify every change to the database (for example, with a check box control where every change needs to be sent through to the underlying database, even though the control has not lost the focus). However, controls such as a list box need to have the change of a property communicated to the database when the control loses focus, because the user may have changed the selection with the arrow keys before finding the desired setting. If the change notification was sent to the database every time the user pressed an arrow key, it would give an unacceptable performance.

The **bindable** and **requestedit** attribute bits need to be set for this new bit to have an effect.

Flags   VARFLAG_FIMMEDIATEBIND
FUNCFLAG_FIMMEDIATEBIND

in

Description   Specifies an input parameter.

Allowed on   Parameter.

Comments   The parameter can be a pointer (such as **char***) but the value it refers to is not returned.

lcid

Description   Indicates that the parameter is a locale ID (LCID).

Allowed on   Parameter in a member of an interface.

Comments   Only one parameter can have this attribute. The parameter must have the *in* attribute and not the **out** attribute, and its type must be **long**. The **lcid** attribute is not allowed on dispinterfaces.

The **lcid** attribute allows members in the VTBL to receive an LCID at the time of invocation. By convention, the **lcid** parameter is the last parameter not to have the **retval** attribute. If the member specifies *propertyput* or *propertyputref*, the **lcid** parameter must precede the parameter that represents the right side of the property assignment.

ITypeInfo::Invoke passes the LCID of the type information into the **lcid** parameter. Parameters with this attribute are not displayed in user-oriented browsers.

---

lcid(*numid*)

Description	This attribute identifies the locale for a type library.
Allowed on	Library.
Comments	The *numid* is a 32-bit LCID, as used in Win32 National Language Support. The LCID is typically entered in hexadecimal format.

---

licensed

Description	Indicates that the class is licensed.
Allowed on	Coclass.
Flags	TYPEFLAG_FLICENSED

---

nonbrowsable

Description	Indicates that the property appears in an object browser (which does not show property values), but does not appear in a properties browser (which does show property values).
Allowed on	Property.
Flags	VARFLAG_FNONBROWSABLE FUNCFLAG_FNONBROWSABLE

noncreatable

Description

Indicates that the class does not support creation at the top level (for example, through **ITypeInfo::CreateInstance** or **CoCreateInstance**). An object of such a class is usually obtained through a method call on another object.

Allowed on

Coclass.

Example

```
[
    uuid(1e196b20-1fc3-1069-996b-00dd010ef671),
    helpstring("This is Dynaset"),
    noncreatable
]
coclass Dynaset
{
    [default] interface IDynaset;
    [default, source] interface IDynasetEvents;
}
```

Flags

TYPEFLAG_FCANCREATE

nonextensible

Description

Indicates that the **IDispatch** implementation includes only the properties and methods listed in the interface description.

Allowed on

Dispinterface, interface.

Comments

The interface must have the **dual** attribute.

By default, Automation assumes that interfaces can add members at run time, meaning that it assumes the interfaces are extensible.

Flags

TYPEFLAG_FNONEXTENSIBLE

odl

Description

Identifies an interface as an Object Description Language (ODL) interface.

Allowed on

Interface (required).

Comments

This attribute must appear on all interfaces.

oleautomation

Description

The **oleautomation** attribute indicates that an interface is compatible with Automation.

Allowed on

Interface.

Comments

Not allowed on dispinterfaces.

The parameters and return types specified for its members must be compatible with Automation, as listed in the following table:

Type	Description
boolean	Data item that can have the value **True** or **False**. The size corresponds to VARIANT_BOOL. Use VT_TRUE, VT_FALSE.
unsigned char	8-bit unsigned data item.
double	64-bit IEEE floating-point number.
float	32-bit IEEE floating-point number.
int	Signed integer, whose size is system dependent.
long	32-bit signed integer.
short	16-bit signed integer.
BSTR	Length-prefixed string, as described in Chapter 5, "Dispatch Interface and API Functions."
CURRENCY	8-byte, fixed-point number.
DATE	64-bit, floating-point fractional number of days since December 30, 1899.
SCODE	For 16-bit systems - Built-in error type that corresponds to VT_ERROR.
Typedef enum *myenum*	Signed integer, whose size is system dependent.
Interface IDispatch *	Pointer to the **IDispatch** interface (VT_DISPATCH).
Interface IUnknown *	Pointer to an interface that does not derive from **IDispatch** (VT_UNKNOWN). (Any OLE interface can be represented by its **IUnknown** interface.)
dispinterface *Typename* *	Pointer to an interface derived from **IDispatch** (VT_DISPATCH).
Coclass *Typename* *	Pointer to a coclass name (VT_UNKNOWN).
[oleautomation] interface *Typename* *	Pointer to an interface that derives from **IDispatch**.

Type	Description
SAFEARRAY(*TypeName*)	*TypeName* is any of the above types. Array of these types.
TypeName*	*TypeName* is any of the above types. Pointer to a type.
Decimal	96-bit unsigned binary integer scaled by a variable power of 10. A decimal data type that provides a size and scale for a number (as in coordinates).

A parameter is compatible with Automation if its type is compatible with an Automation type, a pointer to an Automation type, or a SAFEARRAY of an Automation type.

A return type is compatible with Automation if its type is an HRESULT or is **void**. Methods in Automation must return either HRESULT or **void**.

A member is compatible with Automation if its return type and all of its parameters are compatible with Automation.

An interface is compatible with Automation if it derives from **IDispatch** or **IUnknown,** if it has the **oleautomation** attribute, or if all of its VTBL entries are compatible with Automation. For 32-bit systems, the calling convention for all methods in the interface must be STDCALL. For 16-bit systems, all methods must have the CDECL calling convention. Every dispinterface is compatible with Automation.

Flags   TYPEFLAG_FOLEAUTOMATION

---

optional

Description   Specifies an optional parameter.

Allowed on   Parameter.

Comments   Valid only if the parameter is of type VARIANT or VARIANT*. All subsequent parameters of the function must also be **optional**.

---

out

Description   Specifies an output parameter.

Allowed on   Parameter.

Comments   The parameter must be a pointer to memory that will receive a result.

propget

Description	Specifies a property-accessor function.
Allowed on	Functions, methods in interfaces, dispinterfaces.
Comments	The property must have the same name as the function. At most, one of **propget, propput,** and **propputref** can be specified for a function.
Flags	INVOKE_PROPERTYGET

propput

Description	Specifies a property-setting function.
Allowed on	Functions, methods in interfaces, dispinterfaces.
Comments	The property must have the same name as the function. Only one **propget, propput,** and **propputref** can be specified.
Flags	INVOKE_PROPERTYPUT

propputref

Description	Specifies a property-setting function that uses a reference instead of a value.
Allowed on	Functions, methods in interfaces, dispinterfaces.
Comments	The property must have the same name as the function. Only one **propget, propput,** and **propputref** can be specified.
Flags	INVOKE_PROPERTYPUTREF

public

Description	Includes an alias declared with the **typedef** keyword in the type library.
Allowed on	Alias declared with **typedef.**
Comments	By default, an alias that is declared with **typedef,** and has no other attributes, is treated as a **#define**, and is not included in the type library. Using the **public** attribute ensures that the alias becomes part of the type library.

readonly

Description	Prohibits assignment to a variable.
Allowed on	Variable.
Flags	VARFLAG_FREADONLY

replaceable

Description	Tags an interface as having default behaviors.
Allowed on	Methods and properties of dispinterfaces and interfaces.
Comments	The object supports **IConnectionPointWithDefault**.
Flags	TYPEFLAG_FREPLACEABLE
	FUNCFLAG_FREPLACEABLE
	VARFLAG_FREPLACEABLE

requestedit

Description	Indicates that the property supports the **OnRequestEdit** notification.
Allowed on	Property.
Comments	The property supports the **OnRequestEdit** notification, raised by a property before it is edited. An object can support data binding and not have this attribute.
Flags	FUNCFLAG_FREQUESTEDIT
	VARFLAG_FREQUESTEDIT

restricted

Description	Prevents the item from being used by a macro programmer.
Allowed on	Type library, type information, coclass member, or member of a module or interface.
Comments	This attribute is allowed on a member of a coclass, independent of whether the member is a dispinterface or interface, and independent of whether the member is a sink or source. A member of a coclass cannot have both the **restricted** and **default** attributes.

Flags

IMPLTYPEFLAG_FRESTRICTED
FUNCFLAG_FRESTRICTED
TYPEFLAG_FRESTRICTED
VARFLAG_FRESTRICTED

Example

```
[   odl,
      dual,
      uuid(1e196b20-1f3c-1069-996b-00dd010ef676),
      helpstring("This is IForm"),
      restricted
]
interface IForm: IDispatch
{
    [propget]
    HRESULT Backcolor([out, retval] long *Value);

    [propput]
    HRESULT Backcolor([in] long Value);
}

[   odl,
      dual,
      uuid(1e196b20-1f3c-1069-996b-00dd010ef767),
      helpstring("This is IFormEVents"),
      restricted
]
interface IFormEvents: IDispatch
{
    HRESULT Click();
}

[   uuid(1e196b20-1f3c-1069-996b-00dd010fe676),
      helpstring("This is Form")
]
coclass Form
{
    [default] interface IForm;
    [default, source] interface IFormEvents;
}
```

retval

Description   Designates the parameter that receives the return value of the member.

Allowed on   Parameters of interface members that describe methods or get properties.

Comments   This attribute can be used only on the last parameter of the member. The parameter must have the **out** attribute and must be a pointer type.

Parameters with this attribute are not displayed in user-oriented browsers.

Flags   IDLFLAG_FRETVAL

source

Description   Indicates that a member is a source of events.

Allowed on   Member of a coclass, property, or method.

Comments   For a member of a coclass, this attribute indicates that the member is called rather than implemented.

On a property or method, this attribute indicates that the member returns an object or VARIANT that is a source of events. The object implements the interface **IConnectionPointContainer**.

Flags   IMPLTYPEFLAG_FSOURCE
VARFLAG_SOURCE
FUNCFLAG_SOURCE

string

Description   Specifies a string.

Allowed on   Structure, member, parameter, property.

Comments   Included only for compatibility with the Interface Definition Language (IDL). Use LPSTR for a zero-terminated string.

uidefault

Description

Indicates that the type information member is the default member for display in the user interface.

Allowed on

A member of an interface or dispinterface.

Comments

This attribute is used to mark an event as the default (the first one created) or a property as the default (the one to select first in the properties browser).

For example, Visual Basic uses this attribute in the following ways:

- When an object is double-clicked at design time, Visual Basic jumps to the event in the default source interface that is marked as [**uidefault**]. If there is no such member, then Visual Basic displays the first one listed in the default source interface.

- When an object is selected at design time, by default, the Properties window in Visual Basic displays the property in the default interface that is marked as [**uidefault**]. If there is no such member, then Visual Basic displays the first one listed in the default interface.

Flags

FUNCFLAG_FUIDEFAULT
VARFLAG_FUIDEFAULT

Example

```
[   odl,
    dual,
    uuid(1e196b20-1f3c-1069-996b-00dd010ef676),
    restricted
]
interface IForm: IDispatch
{
    [propget]
    HRESULT Backcolor([out, retval] long *Value);

    [propput]
    HRESULT Backcolor([in] long Value);

    [propget, uidefault]
    HRESULT Name([out, retval] BSTR *Value);

    [propput, uidefault]
    HRESULT Name([in] BSTR Value);
}
```

```
[   odl,
    dual,
    uuid(1e196b20-1f3c-1069-996b-00dd010ef767),
    restricted
]
interface IFormEvents: IDispatch
{
   [uidefault]
   HRESULT Click();

   HRESULT Resize();
}

[uuid(1e196b20-1f3c-1069-996b-00dd010fe676)]
coclass Form
{
    [default] interface IForm;
    [default, source] interface IFormEvents;
}
```

usesgetlasterror

Description

Tells the caller that, if there is an error when calling that function, the caller can then call **GetLastError** to retrieve the error code.

Allowed on

Member of a module

Comments

The **usesgetlasterror** attribute can be set on a module entry point, if that entry point uses the Win32 function **SetLastError** to return error codes. The attribute tells the caller that, if there is an error when calling that function, the caller can then call GetLastError to retrieve the error code.

Example

```
[dllname("MyOwn.dll")] module MyModule
{
    [entry("One"), usesgetlasterror, bindable, requestedit,
  propputref, defaultbind]
        void Func1 ([in]IUnknown * iParam1, [out] long * Param2);
    [entry("TwentyOne"), usesgetlasterror, hidden, vararg]
        SAFEARRAY (int) Func2 ([in, out] SAFEARRAY (variant) *varP);

// Code omitted for brevity.

};
```

uuid(*uuidval*)

Description   Specifies the universally unique ID (UUID) of the item.

Allowed on   Required for library, dispinterface, interface, and coclass. Optional for struct, enum, union, module, and typedef.

Comments   The *uuidval* is a 16-byte value using hexadecimal digits in the following format: `12345678-1234-1234-1234-123456789ABC`. This value is returned in the **TypeAttr** structure retrieved by **ITypeInfo::GetTypeAttr.**

vararg

Description   Indicates a variable number of arguments.

Allowed on   Function.

Comments   Indicates that the last parameter is a safe array of VARIANT type, which contains all of the remaining parameters.

version(*versionval*)

Description   Specifies a version number.

Allowed on   Library, struct, module, dispinterface, interface, coclass, enum, union.

Comments   The argument *versionval* is a real number in the format *n.m*, where *n* is a major version number and *m* is a minor version number.

ODL Statements and Directives

The following sections describe the statements and directives that make up the Object Description Language (ODL).

---

coclass

This statement describes the globally unique ID (GUID) and the supported interfaces for a Component Object Model (COM).

Syntax

[*attributes*]
coclass *classname*
{
    [*attributes2*] [**interface** I **dispinterface**] *interfacename*;
...};

Syntax Elements

attributes

The **uuid** attribute is required on a coclass. This is the same **uuid** that is registered as a CLSID in the system registration database. The **helpstring, helpcontext, licensed, version, control, hidden**, and **appobject** attributes are accepted, but not required, before a coclass definition. For more information about the attributes accepted before a coclass definition, see "Attribute Descriptions" earlier in this chapter. The **appobject** attribute makes the functions and properties of the coclass globally available in the type library.

classname

Name by which the common object is known in the type library.

attributes2

Optional attributes for the interface or dispinterface. The **source, default,** and **restricted** attributes are accepted on an interface or dispinterface in a coclass.

interfacename

Either an interface declared with the **interface** keyword, or a dispinterface declared with the **dispinterface** keyword.

Comments

The Component Object Model defines a class as an implementation that allows **QueryInterface** between a set of interfaces.

Example

```
[ uuid(BFB73347-822A-1068-8849-00DD011087E8), version(1.0),
helpstring("A class"), helpcontext(2481), appobject]
coclass myapp
{
    [source] interface IMydocfuncs;
    dispinterface DMydocfuncs;
};

[uuid 00000000-0000-0000-0000-123456789019]
coclass foo
{
    [restricted] interface bar;
    interface bar;
}
```

dispinterface

This statement defines a set of properties and methods on which **IDispatch::Invoke** can be called. A dispinterface can be defined by explicitly listing the set of supported methods and properties (Syntax 1) or by listing a single interface (Syntax 2).

Syntax 1

[*attributes*]
dispinterface *intfname*
{
    properties:
        proplist
    methods:
        methlist
};

Syntax 2

[*attributes*]
dispinterface *intfname*
{
    interface *interfacename*
};

Syntax Elements

attributes

The **helpstring, helpcontext, hidden, uuid,** and **version** attributes are accepted before **dispinterface**. For more information about the attributes accepted before a **dispinterface** definition, see "Attribute Descriptions" earlier in this chapter. Attributes (including the brackets) can be omitted, except for the **uuid** attribute, which is required.

intfname

The name by which the dispinterface is known in the type library. This name must be unique within the type library.

interfacename

(Syntax 2) The name of the interface to declare as an **IDispatch** interface.

proplist

(Syntax 1) An optional list of properties supported by the object, declared in the form of variables. This is the short form for declaring the property functions in the methods list. See the comments section for details.

methlist

(Syntax 1) A list comprising a function prototype for each method and property in the dispinterface. Any number of function definitions can appear in *methlist*. A function in *methlist* has the following form:

[*attributes*] *returntype methname*(*params*);

The following attributes are accepted on a method in a dispinterface: **helpstring, helpcontext, string** (for compatibility with the Interface Definition Language), **bindable, defaultbind, displaybind, propget, propput, propputref,** and **vararg**. If **vararg** is specified, the last parameter must be a safe array of VARIANT type.

The parameter list is a comma-delimited list, each element of which has the following form:

[*attributes*] *type paramname*

The *type* can be any declared or built-in type, or a pointer to any type. Attributes on parameters are **in, out, optional,** and **string**.

If **optional** is specified, it must only be specified on the right-most parameters, and the types of those parameters must be VARIANT.

Comments

Method functions are specified exactly as described in the "module statement" except that the **entry** attribute is not allowed.

Note Stdole2.tlb (Stdole.tlb on 16-bit systems) must be imported, because a dispinterface inherits from **IDispatch**.

Properties can be declared either in the properties or methods lists. Declaring properties in the properties list does not indicate the type of access the property supports (**get, put,** or **putref**). Specify the **readonly** attribute for properties that do not support **put** or **putref**. If the property functions are declared in the methods list, functions for one property will all have the same ID.

Using Syntax 1, the *properties:* and *methods:* tags are required. The **id** attribute is also required on each member. For example:

```
properties:
    [id(0)] int Value;   // Default property.
methods:
    [id(1)] void Show();
```

Unlike interface members, dispinterface members cannot use the **retval** attribute to return a value in addition to an HRESULT error code. The **lcid** attribute is also invalid for dispinterfaces because **IDispatch::Invoke** passes a locale ID (LCID). However, it is possible to declare an interface again that uses these attributes.

Using Syntax 2, interfaces that support **IDispatch** and are declared earlier in an Object Definition Language (ODL) script can be redeclared as **IDispatch** interfaces as follows:

```
dispinterface helloPro
{
    interface hello;
};
```

This example declares all of the members of the Hello sample and all of the members that it inherits to support **IDispatch**. In this case, if Hello was declared earlier with **lcid** and **retval** members that returned HRESULTs, MkTypLib would remove each **lcid** parameter and HRESULT return type, and instead mark the return type as that of the **retval** parameter.

The properties and methods of a dispinterface are not part of the VTBL of the dispinterface. Consequently, **CreateStdDispatch** and **DispInvoke** cannot be used to implement **IDispatch::Invoke**. The dispinterface is used when an application needs to expose existing non-VTBL functions through Automation. These applications can implement **IDispatch::Invoke** by examining the *dispidMember* parameter and directly calling the corresponding function.

Example

```
[uuid(BFB73347-822A-1068-8849-00DD011087E8), version(1.0),
helpstring("Useful help string."), helpcontext(2480)]
dispinterface MyDispatchObject
{
    properties:
        [id(1)] int x;          // An integer property named x.
        [id(2)] BSTR y;         // A string property named y.
    methods:
        [id(3)] void show();    // No arguments, no result.
        [id(11)] int computeit(int inarg, double *outarg);
}

[uuid 00000000-0000-0000-0000-123456789012]
dispinterface MyObject
{
    properties:
    methods:
        [id(1), propget, bindable, defaultbind, displaybind]
        long x();

        [id(1), propput, bindable, defaultbind, displaybind]
        void x(long rhs);
}
```

enum

This statement defines a C-style enumerated type.

Syntax

typedef [*attributes*] **enum** [*tag*]
{
    enumlist
} *enumname*;

Syntax Elements

attributes

    The **helpstring, helpcontext, hidden,** and **uuid** attributes are accepted before an **enum** statement. The **helpstring** and **helpcontext** attributes are accepted on an enumeration element. For more information about the attributes accepted before an enumeration definition, see "Attribute Descriptions" earlier in this chapter. Attributes (including the brackets) can be omitted. If *uuid* is omitted, the enumeration is not uniquely specified in the system.

tag

    An optional tag, as with a C **enum**.

enumlist

    List of enumerated elements.

enumname

    Name by which the enumeration is known in the type library.

Comments

The **enum** keyword must be preceded by **typedef**. The enumeration description must precede other references to the enumeration in the library. If **value** is not specified for enumerators, the numbering progresses, as with enumerations in C. The type of the **enum** element is **int,** the system default integer, which depends on the target type library specification.

Examples

```
typedef [uuid(DEADF00D-C0DE-B1FF-F001-A100FF001ED),
        helpstring("Farm Animals are friendly"), helpcontext(234)]
enum
{
    [helpstring("Moo")] cows = 1,
    pigs = 2
} ANIMALS;
```

importlib

This directive makes types that have already been compiled into another type library available to the library currently being created. All **importlib** directives must precede the other type descriptions in the library.

Syntax

importlib(*filename*);

Syntax Element

filename
    The location of the type library file when MkTypLib is executed.

Comments

The **importlib** directive makes any type defined in the imported library accessible from within the library being compiled. Ambiguity is resolved as the current library is searched for the type. If the type cannot be found, MkTypLib searches the imported library that is lexically first, and then the next, and so on. To import a type name in code, the name should be entered as *libname.typename,* where *libname* is the library name as it appeared in the **library** statement when the library was compiled.

The imported type library should be distributed with the library being compiled.

Example

The following example imports the libraries Stdole.tlb and Mydisp.tlb:

```
library BrowseHelper
{
    importlib("stdole.tlb");
    importlib("mydisp.tlb");

// Additional text omitted.
}
```

interface

This statement defines an interface, which is a set of function definitions. An interface can inherit from any base interface.

Syntax

[*attributes*]
interface *interfacename* [*:baseinterface*]
{
    functionlist
}

Syntax Elements   *attributes*

The attributes **dual, helpstring, helpcontext, hidden, odl, oleautomation, uuid,** and **version** are accepted before **interface**. If the interface is a member of a coclass, the attributes **source, default,** and **restricted** are also accepted. For more information about the attributes that can be accepted before an **interface** definition, refer to the section "Attribute Descriptions" earlier in this chapter.

The attributes **odl** and **uuid** are required on all **interface** declarations.

interfacename
The name by which the interface is known in the type library.

baseinterface
The name of the interface that is the base class for this interface.

functionlist
List of function prototypes for each function in the interface. Any number of function definitions can appear in the function list. A function in the function list has the following form:

[*attributes*] *returntype* [*calling convention*] *funcname*(*params*);

The following attributes are accepted on a function in an interface: **helpstring, helpcontext, string, propget, propput, propputref, bindable, defaultbind, displaybind,** and **vararg.** If **vararg** is specified, the last parameter must be a safe array of VARIANT type. The optional calling convention can be **__pascal/_pascal/pascal, __cdecl/_cdecl/cdecl,** or **__stdcall/_stdcall/stdcall.** The calling convention specification can include up to two leading underscores.

The parameter list is a comma-delimited list, as follows:

[*attributes*] *type paramname*

The *type* can be any previously declared type, built-in type, a pointer to any type, or a pointer to a built-in type. Attributes on parameters are **in, out, optional,** and **string.**

If **optional** is used, it must be specified only on the right-most parameters, and the types of those parameters must be VARIANT.

Comments   Because the functions described by the **interface** statement are in the VTBL, **DispInvoke** and **CreateStdDispatch** can be used to provide an implementation of **IDispatch::Invoke.** For this reason, **interface** is more commonly used than **dispinterface** to describe the properties and methods of an object.

Functions in interfaces are the same as described in the "module" statement except that the **entry**attribute is not allowed.

Members of interfaces that need to raise exceptions should return an HRESULT and specify a **retval** parameter for the actual return value. The **retval** parameter is always the last parameter in the list.

Examples The following example defines an interface named Hello with two member functions, **HelloProc** and **Shutdown**:

```
[uuid(BFB73347-822A-1068-8849-00DD011087E8), version(1.0)]
interface hello : IUnknown
{
void HelloProc([in, string] unsigned char * pszString);
void Shutdown(void);
};
```

The next example defines a dual interface named **IMyInt**, which has a pair of accessor functions for the **MyMessage** property, and a method that returns a string.

```
[dual]
interface IMyInt : IDispatch
{
    // A property that is a string.

    [propget] HRESULT MyMessage([in, lcid] LCID lcid,
                                [out, retval] BSTR *pbstrRetVal);
    [propput] HRESULT MyMessage([in] BSTR rhs, [in, lcid] DWORD lcid);

    // A method returning a string.

    HRESULT SayMessage([in] long NumTimes,
                       [in, lcid] DWORD lcid,
                       [out, retval] BSTR *pbstrRetVal);
}
```

The members of this interface return error information and function return values through the HRESULT values and **retval** parameters, respectively. Tools that access the members can return the HRESULT to their users, or can simply expose the **retval** parameter as the return value, and handle the HRESULT transparently.

A dual interface must derive from **IDispatch**.

library

This statement describes a type library. This description contains all of the information in a MkTypLib input file (ODL).

Syntax

[*attributes*] **library** *libname*
{
    definitions
};

Syntax Elements

attributes
> The **helpstring, helpcontext, lcid, restricted, hidden, control**, and **uuid** attributes are accepted before a **library** statement. For more information about the attributes accepted before a **library** definition, see "Attribute Descriptions" earlier in this chapter. The **uuid** attribute is required.

libname
> The name by which the type library is known.

definitions
> Descriptions of any imported libraries, data types, modules, interfaces, dispinterfaces, and coclasses relevant to the object being exposed.

Comments

The **library** statement must precede any other type definitions.

Example

```
[
    uuid(F37C8060-4AD5-101B-B826-00DD01103DE1), // LIBID_Hello.
    helpstring("Hello 2.0 Type Library"),
    lcid(0x0409),
    version(2.0)
]
library Hello
{
    importlib("stdole.tlb");
    [
        uuid(F37C8062-4AD5-101B-B826-00DD01103DE1), // IID_Ihello.
        helpstring("Application object for the Hello application."),
        oleautomation,
        dual
    ]
    interface IHello : IDispatch
    {
        [propget, helpstring("Returns the application of the object.")]
        HRESULT Application([in, lcid] long localeID,
            [out, retval] IHello** retval)
    }
}
```

module

This statement defines a group of functions, typically a set of DLL entry points.

Syntax

[*attributes*]
module *modulename*
{
  elementlist
};

Syntax Elements

attributes

The attributes **uuid, version, helpstring, helpcontext, hidden,** and **dllname** are accepted before a **module** statement. For more information about the attributes that can be accepted before a module definition, see "Attribute Descriptions" earlier in this chapter. The **dllname** attribute is required. If **uuid** is omitted, the module is not uniquely specified in the system.

modulename

The name of the module.

elementlist

List of constant definitions and function prototypes for each function in the DLL. Any number of function definitions can appear in the function list. A function in the function list has the following form:

[*attributes*] *returntype* [*calling convention*] *funcname(params)*;
[*attributes*] **const** *constname* = *constval*;

Only the attributes **helpstring** and **helpcontext** are accepted for a **const**.

The following attributes are accepted on a function in a module: **helpstring, helpcontext, string, entry, propget, propput, propputref, vararg.** If **vararg** is specified, the last parameter must be a safe array of VARIANT type.

The optional *calling convention* can be one of **__pascal/_pascal/pascal, __cdecl/_cdecl/cdecl,** or **__stdcall/_stdcall/stdcall.** The calling convention can include up to two leading underscores.

The parameter list is a comma-delimited list.

[*attributes*] *type paramname*

The *type* can be any previously declared type or built-in type, a pointer to any type, or a pointer to a built-in type. Attributes on parameters are **in, out,** and **optional.**

If **optional** is specified, it must only be specified on the right-most parameters, and the types of those parameters must be VARIANT.

Comments

The header file (.h) output for modules is a series of function prototypes. The **module** keyword and surrounding brackets are stripped from the header file output, but a comment (// **module** *modulename*) is inserted before the prototypes. The keyword **extern** is inserted before the declarations.

Example

```
[uuid(D00BED00-CEDE-B1FF-F001-A100FF001ED),
    helpstring("This is not GDI.EXE"), helpcontext(190),
    dllname("MATH.DLL")]
module somemodule{
    [helpstring("Color for the frame")] unsigned long const COLOR_FRAME
        = 0xH80000006;
    [helpstring("Not a rectangle but a square"), entry(1)] pascal double
square([in] double x);
};
```

struct

This statement defines a C-style structure.

Syntax

typedef [*attributes*]
struct [*tag*]
{
   memberlist
} *structname*;

Syntax Elements

attributes

The attributes **helpstring, helpcontext, uuid, hidden**, and **version** are accepted before a **struct** statement. The attributes **helpstring, helpcontext,** and **string** are accepted on a structure member. For more information about the attributes accepted before a structure definition, see "Attribute Descriptions" earlier in this chapter. Attributes (including the brackets) can be omitted. If **uuid** is omitted, the structure is not specified uniquely in the system.

tag

An optional tag, as with a C **struct**.

memberlist

List of structure members defined with C syntax.

structname

Name by which the structure is known in the type library.

Comments
The **struct** keyword must be preceded with a **typedef**. The structure description must precede other references to the structure in the library. Members of a **struct** can be of any built-in type, or any type defined lexically as a **typedef** before the **struct**. For a description of how strings and arrays can be entered, see the sections "String Definitions" and "Array Definitions" earlier in this chapter.

Example
```
typedef [uuid(BFB7334B-822A-1068-8849-00DD011087E8),
    helpstring("A task"), helpcontext(1019)]
struct
{
    DATE startdate;
    DATE enddate;
    BSTR ownername;
    SAFEARRAY (int) subtasks;
    int A_C_array[10];
} TASKS;
```

typedef

This statement creates an alias for a type.

Syntax
typedef [*attributes*] *basetype aliasname*;

Syntax Elements
attributes
Any attribute specifications must follow the **typedef** keyword. If no attributes and no other type (for example, **enum, struct**, or **union**) are specified, the alias is treated as a **#define** and does not appear in the type library. If no other attribute is desired, **public** can be used to explicitly include the alias in the type library. The **helpstring, helpcontext**, and **uuid** attributes are accepted before a **typedef**. For more information, see "Attribute Descriptions" earlier in this chapter. If **uuid** is omitted, the **typedef** is not uniquely specified in the system.

basetype
The type for which the alias is defined.

aliasname
Name by which the type will be known in the type library.

Comments
The **typedef** keyword must also be used whenever a **struct** or **enum** is defined. The name recorded for the **enum** or **struct** is the **typedef** name, and not the tag for the enumeration. No attributes are required to make sure the alias appears in the type library.

Enumerations, structures, and unions must be defined with the **typedef** keyword. The attributes for a type defined with **typedef** are enclosed in brackets following the **typedef** keyword. If a simple alias **typedef** has no attributes, it is treated like a **#define**, and the *aliasname* does not appear in the library. Any attribute (**public** can be used if no others are desired) specified between the **typedef** keyword and the rest of a simple alias definition causes the alias to appear explicitly in the type library. The attributes typically include such items as a Help string and Help context.

Examples

```
typedef [public]  long DWORD:
```

This example creates a type description for an alias type with the name DWORD.

```
typedef enum
{
        TYPE_FUNCTION = 0,
        TYPE_PROPERTY = 1,
        TYPE_CONSTANT = 2,
        TYPE_PARAMETER = 3
} OBJTYPE;
```

The second example creates a type description for an enumeration named OBJTYPE, which has four enumerator values.

---

union

This statement defines a C-style union.

Syntax

typedef [*attributes*] **union** [*tag*]
{
    memberlist
} *unionname*;

Syntax Elements

attributes

The attributes **helpstring, helpcontext, uuid, hidden,** and **version** are accepted before a **union**. The **helpstring, helpcontext,** and **string** attributes are accepted on a **union** member. For more information about the attributes accepted before a union definition, see "Attribute Descriptions" earlier in this chapter. Attributes (including the square brackets) can be omitted. If **uuid** is omitted, the union is not uniquely specified in the system.

tag

An optional tag, as with a C **union**.

memberlist

List of **union** members defined with C syntax.

unionname

Name by which the **union** is known in the type library.

Comments   The **union** keyword must be preceded with a **typedef**. The **union** description must precede other references to the structure in the library. Members of a **union** can be of any built-in type, or any type defined lexically as a **typedef** before the **union**. For a description of how strings and arrays can be entered, see the sections "String Definitions" and "Array Definitions" earlier in this chapter.

Example
```
[uuid(BFB7334C-822A-1068-8849-00DD011087E8), helpstring("A task"),
helpcontext(1019)]
typedef union
{
    COLOR polycolor;
    int cVertices;
    boolean filled;
    SAFEARRAY (int) subtasks;
} UNIONSHOP;
```

Type Description Interfaces

Type description interfaces provide a way to read and bind to the descriptions of objects in a type library. These descriptions are used by ActiveX clients when they browse, create, and manipulate ActiveX (Automation) objects.

The type description interfaces described in this chapter include:

- **ITypeLib**—Retrieves information about a type library.
- **ITypeLib2**— Allows **ITypeLib** to cast to an **ITypeLib2** in performance-sensitive cases.
- **ITypeInfo**—Reads the type information within the type library.
- **ITypeInfo2**—Allows **ITypeInfo** to cast to an **ITypeInfo2** in performance-sensitive cases.
- **ITypeComp**—Creates compilers that use type information.

This chapter also describes functions for loading, registering, and querying type libraries.

Overview of Type Description Interfaces

A type library is a container for type descriptions of one or more objects, and is accessed through the **ITypeLib** interface. The **ITypeLib** interface provides access to information about the type description in a type library. The descriptions of individual objects are accessed through the **ITypeInfo** interface.

In addition, there are two new interfaces for Automation:

ITypeInfo2::ITypeInfo
ITypeLib2::ITypeLib

Because they inherit from **ITypeInfo** and **ITypeLib,** an **ITypeInfo** can be cast to an **ITypeInfo2** instead of using the calls **QueryInterface** and **Release**.

By adding the new methods described in the following section, **QueryInterface** can be called to **ITypeInfo2** and **ITypeLib2** in the same way as **ITypeInfo** and **ITypeLib**.

The following table describes the member functions of each of the type description interfaces:

Interface	Member function	Purpose
ITypeLib	**FindName**	Finds occurrences of a type description in a type library.
	GetDocumentation	Retrieves the library's documentation string, name of the complete Help file name and path, and the context identifier for the library Help topic.
	GetLibAttr	Retrieves the structure containing the library's attributes.
	GetTypeComp	Retrieves a pointer to the **ITypeComp** for a type library. This enables a client compiler to bind to the library's types, variables, constants, and global functions.
	GetTypeInfo	Retrieves the specified type description in the library.
	GetTypeInfoCount	Retrieves the number of type descriptions in the library.
	GetTypeInfoOfGuid	Retrieves the type description corresponding to the specified globally unique identifier (GUID).
	GetTypeInfoType	Retrieves the type of a type description.
	IsName	Indicates whether a passed-in string contains the name of a type, or a member described in the library.
	ReleaseTLibAttr	Releases TLIBATTR, originally obtained from **ITypeLib::GetLibAttr**.

Interface	Member function	Purpose
ITypeLib2	GetCustData	Gets custom data.
	GetDocumentation2	Retrieves the library's documentation string and Help related information.
	GetLibStatistics	Returns statistics about a type library that are required for efficient sizing of hash tables.
	GetAllCustData	Gets all custom data items for the library.
ITypeInfo	AddressOfMember	Retrieves the addresses of static functions or variables, such as those defined in a dynamic-link library (DLL).
	CreateInstance	Creates a new instance of a type that describes a component object class (coclass).
	GetContainingTypeLib	Retrieves both the type library that contains a specific type description and the index of the type description within the type library.
	GetDllEntry	Retrieves a description or specification of an entry point for a function in DLL.
	GetDocumentation	Retrieves the documentation string, name of the complete Help file name and path, and the context identifier for the Help topic for a specified type description.
	GetFuncDesc	Retrieves the FUNCDESC structure that contains information about a specified function.
	GetIDsOfNames	Maps between member names and member identifiers, and parameter names and parameter identifiers.
	GetImplTypeFlags	Retrieves the IMPLTYPE flags for an interface.
	GetMops	Retrieves marshaling information.
	GetNames	Retrieves the variable with the specified member identifier, or the name of the function and parameter names corresponding to the specified function identifier.

Interface	Member function	Purpose
	GetRefTypeInfo	Retrieves the type descriptions referenced by a given type description.
	GetRefTypeOfImplType	Retrieves the type description of implemented interface types for a coclass or an inherited interface.
	GetTypeAttr	Retrieves a TYPEATTR structure that contains the attributes of the type description.
	GetTypeComp	Retrieves the **ITypeComp** interface for the type description, which enables a client compiler to bind to the type description's members.
	GetVarDesc	Retrieves a VARDESC structure that describes the specified variable.
	Invoke	Invokes a method or accesses a property of an object that implements the interface described by the type description.
	ReleaseFuncDesc	Releases a FUNCDESC previously returned by **GetFuncDesc**.
	ReleaseTypeAttr	Releases a TYPEATTR previously returned by **GetTypeAttr**.
	ReleaseVarDesc	Releases a VARDESC previously returned by **GetVarDesc**.
ITypeInfo2	GetTypeKind	Returns the TYPEKIND enumeration quickly, without doing any allocations.
	GetTypeFlags	Returns the TYPEFLAGS quickly, without doing any allocations.
	GetFuncIndexOfMemId	Binds to a specific member based on a known dispatch identifier (DISPID)
	GetVarIndexOfMemId	Binds to a specific member based on a known DISPID.
	GetCustData	Gets the custom data.
	GetAllCustData	Gets all custom data items for the library.
	GetFuncCustData	Gets the custom data from the specified function.
	GetAllFuncCustData	Gets all of the custom data from the specified function.

Interface	Member function	Purpose
	GetParamCustData	Gets the specified custom data parameter.
	GetAllParamCustData	Gets all of the custom data for the specified parameter.
	GetVarCustData	Gets the variable for the custom data.
	GetAllVarCustData	Gets all of the custom data for the specified variable.
	GetImplTypeCustData	Gets the implementation type of the custom data.
	GetAllImplTypeCustData	Gets all of the custom data for the specified implementation type.
	GetDocumentation2	Retrieves the documentation string and other Help related information.
ITypeComp	Bind	Maps a name to a member of a type, or binds global variables and functions contained in a type library.
	BindType	Binds to the type descriptions contained within a type library.

ITypeLib Interface

The data that describes a set of objects is stored in a type library. A type library can be a stand-alone binary file (.tlb), a resource in a dynamic-link library or executable file (.dll or .exe), or part of a compound document file.

Implemented by	Used by	Header file name
Oleaut32.dll (32-bit systems) Typelib.dll (16-bit systems)	Tools that need to access the descriptions of objects contained in type libraries.	Oleauto.h Dispatch.h

The system registry contains a list of all the installed type libraries. Type library organization is illustrated in the following figure:

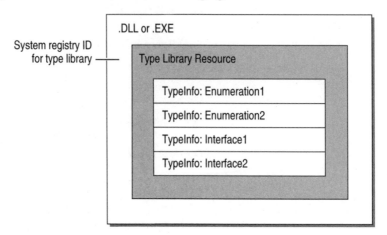

The **ITypeLib** interface provides methods for accessing a library of type descriptions. This interface supports the following:

- Generalized containment for type information. **ITypeLib** allows iteration over the type descriptions contained in the library.

- Global functions and data. A type library can contain descriptions of a set of modules, each of which is the equivalent of a C or C++ source file that exports data and functions. The type library supports compiling references to the exported data and functions.

- General information, including a user-readable name for the library and help for the library as a whole.

ITypeLib::FindName

HRESULT FindName(
OLECHAR FAR* *szNameBuf*,
unsigned long *lHashVal*,
ITypeInfo FAR* FAR* *ppTInfo*,
MEMBERID FAR* *rgMemId*,
unsigned int FAR* *pcFound*
);

Finds occurrences of a type description in a type library. This may be used to quickly verify that a name exists in a type library.

Parameters

szNameBuf
> The name to search for.

lHashVal
> A hash value to speed up the search, computed by the **LHashValOfNameSys** function. If *lHashVal* = 0, a value is computed.

ppTInfo
> On return, an array of pointers to the type descriptions that contain the name specified in *szNameBuf*. Cannot be Null.

rgMemId
> An array of the MEMBERIDs of the found items; *rgMemId*[*i*] is the MEMBERID that indexes into the type description specified by *ppTInfo*[*i*]. Cannot be Null.

pcFound
> On entry, indicates how many instances to look for. For example, **pcFound* = 1 can be called to find the first occurrence. The search stops when one is found.

> On exit, indicates the number of instances that were found. If the *in* and *out* values of **pcFound* are identical, there may be more type descriptions that contain the name.

Return Value

The return value obtained from the returned HRESULT is one of the following:

Return value	Meaning
S_OK	Success.
E_OUTOFMEMORY	Out of memory.
E_INVALIDARG	One or more of the arguments is invalid.
TYPE_E_IOERROR	The function could not write to the file.
TYPE_E_INVDATAREAD	The function could not read from the file.
TYPE_E_UNSUPFORMAT	The type library has an older format.
TYPE_E_INVALIDSTATE	The type library could not be opened.
TYPE_E_CANTLOADLIBRARY	The library or .dll file could not be loaded.
TYPE_E_ELEMENTNOTFOUND	The element was not found.

Comments

Passing **pcFound* = *n* indicates that there is enough room in the *ppTInfo* and *rgMemId* arrays for *n* (*ptinfo*, *memid*) pairs. The function returns MEMBERID_NIL in *rgMemId*[*i*], if the name in *szNameBuf* is the name of the type information in *ppTInfo*[*i*].

ITypeLib::GetDocumentation

HRESULT GetDocumentation(
int *index*,
BSTR FAR* *pBstrName*,
BSTR FAR* *pBstrDocString*,
unsigned long FAR* *pdwHelpContext*,
BSTR FAR* *pBstrHelpFile*
);

Retrieves the library's documentation string, the complete Help file name and path, and the context identifier for the library Help topic in the Help file.

Parameters

index

Index of the type description whose documentation is to be returned. I If *index* is–1, then the documentation for the library itself is returned.

pBstrName

Returns a BSTR that contains the name of the specified item. If the caller does not need the item name, then *pBstrName* can be Null.

pBstrDocString

Returns a BSTR that contains the documentation string for the specified item. If the caller does not need the documentation string, then *pBstrDocString* can be Null.

pdwHelpContext

Returns the Help context identifier (ID) associated with the specified item. If the caller does not need the Help context ID, then *pdwHelpContext* can be Null.

pBstrHelpFile

Returns a BSTR that contains the fully qualified name of the Help file. If the caller does not need the Help file name, then *pBstrHelpFile* can be Null.

Return Value

The return value obtained from the returned HRESULT is one of the following:

Return value	Meaning
S_OK	Success.
STG_E_INSUFFICIENTMEMORY	Out of memory.
E_INVALIDARG	One or more of the arguments is invalid.
TYPE_E_IOERROR	The function could not write to the file.

Return value	Meaning
TYPE_E_INVDATAREAD	The function could not read from the file.
TYPE_E_UNSUPFORMAT	The type library has an older format.
TYPE_E_INVALIDSTATE	The type library could not be opened.
TYPE_E_ELEMENTNOTFOUND	The element was not found.

Comments

The caller should free the BSTR parameters *pBstrName*, *pBstrDocString*, and *pBstrHelpFile*.

Example

```
for (i = 0; i < utypeinfoCount; i++)
{
    CHECKRESULT(ptlib->GetDocumentation(i, &bstrName, NULL, NULL,
NULL));
    .
    .
    .
    SysFreeString(bstrName);
}
```

ITypeLib::GetLibAttr

HRESULT GetLibAttr(
TLIBATTR FAR* FAR* *ppTLibAttrr*
);

Retrieves the structure that contains the library's attributes.

Parameter

ppTLibAttrr
Pointer to a structure that contains the library's attributes.

Return Value

The return value obtained from the returned HRESULT is one of the following:

Return value	Meaning
S_OK	Success.
E_OUTOFMEMORY	Out of memory.
E_INVALIDARG	One or more of the arguments is invalid.
TYPE_E_IOERROR	The function could not write to the file.
TYPE_E_INVDATAREAD	The function could not read from the file.
TYPE_E_UNSUPFORMAT	The type library has an unsupported format.
TYPE_E_INVALIDSTATE	The type library could not be opened.

Comments   Use **ITypeLib::ReleaseTLibAttr** to free the memory occupied by the TLIBATTR
                  structure.

ITypeLib::GetTypeComp

HRESULT GetTypeComp(
ITypeComp FAR* FAR* *ppTComp*
);

Enables a client compiler to bind to a library's types, variables, constants, and global
functions.

Parameter   *ppTComp*
                  Points to a pointer to the **ITypeComp** instance for this **ITypeLib.** A client
                  compiler uses the methods in the ITypeComp interface to bind to types in
                  ITypeLib, as well as to the global functions, variables, and constants defined in
                  ITypeLib.

Return Value The return value obtained from the returned HRESULT is one of the following:

Return value	Meaning
S_OK	Success.
E_OUTOFMEMORY	Out of memory.
E_INVALIDARG	One or more of the arguments is invalid.
TYPE_E_IOERROR	The function could not read from the file.
TYPE_E_INVDATAREAD	Invalid data.
TYPE_E_UNSUPFORMAT	The type library has an older format.
TYPE_E_INVALIDSTATE	The type library could not be opened.
TYPE_E_WRONGTYPEKIND	Type mismatch.

Comments   The **Bind** function of the returned **TypeComp** binds to global functions, variables,
                  constants, enumerated values, and coclass members. The **Bind** function also binds the
                  names of the TYPEKIND enumerations of TKIND_MODULE, TKIND_ENUM, and
                  TKIND_COCLASS. These names shadow any global names defined within the type
                  information. The members of TKIND_ENUM, TKIND_MODULE, and
                  TKIND_COCLASS types marked as Application objects can be directly bound to
                  from **ITypeComp** without specifying the name of the module.

ITypeComp::Bind and ITypeComp::BindType accept only unqualified names. ITypeLib::GetTypeComp returns a pointer to the ITypeComp interface, which is then used to bind to global elements in the library. The names of some types (TKIND_ENUM, TKIND_MODULE, and TKIND_COCLASS) share the name space with variables, functions, constants, and enumerators.

If a member requires qualification to differentiate it from other items in the name space, GetTypeComp can be called successively for each qualifier in order to bind to the desired member. This allows programming language compilers to access members of modules, enumerations, and coclasses, even though the member can't be bound to with a qualified name.

ITypeLib::GetTypeInfo

HRESULT GetTypeInfo(
unsigned int *index*,
ITypeInfo FAR* FAR* *ppTInfo*
);

Retrieves the specified type description in the library.

Parameters   *index*
Index of the ITypeInfo interface to be returned.

ppTInfo
If successful, returns a pointer to the pointer to the ITypeInfo interface.

Return Value   The return value obtained from the returned HRESULT is one of the following:

Return value	Meaning
S_OK	Success.
TYPE_E_ELEMENTNOTFOUND	The *index* parameter is outside the range of 0 to GetTypeInfoCount –1.
E_OUTOFMEMORY	Out of memory.
E_INVALIDARG	One or more of the arguments is invalid.
TYPE_E_IOERROR	The function could not read from the file.
TYPE_E_INVDATAREAD	Invalid data.
TYPE_E_UNSUPFORMAT	The type library has an older format.
TYPE_E_REGISTRYACCESS	There was an error accessing the system registration database.
TYPE_E_INVALIDSTATE	The type library could not be opened.

Comments For dual interfaces, **ITypeLib::GetTypeInfo** returns only the TKIND_DISPATCH type information. To get the TKIND_INTERFACE type information, **ITypeInfo::GetRefTypeOfImplType** can be called on the TKIND_DISPATCH type information, passing an *index* of –1. Then, the returned type information handle can be passed to **ITypeInfo::GetRefTypeInfo**.

Example The following example gets the TKIND_INTERFACE type information for a dual interface.

```
ptlib->GetTypeInfo((unsigned int) dwIndex, &ptypeinfoDisp);
ptypeinfoDisp->GetRefTypeOfImplType(-1, &phreftype);
ptypeinfoDisp->GetRefTypeInfo(phreftype, &ptypeinfoInt);
```

ITypeLib::GetTypeInfoCount

HRESULT GetTypeInfoCount()

Parameters *None.*

Return Value The return value obtained from the returned HRESULT is one of the following:

Return value	Meaning
S_OK	Success.
E_NOTIMPL	Failure.

Comments Returns the number of type descriptions in the type library.

ITypeLib::GetTypeInfoOfGuid

HRESULT GetTypeInfoOfGuid(
REFGUID *guid,*
ITypeInfo FAR* FAR* *ppTinfo*
);

Retrieves the type description that corresponds to the specified GUID.

Parameters *guid*
  Pointer to the GUID of the type description.

ppTinfo
  Pointer to a pointer to the **ITypeInfo** interface.

Return Value   The return value obtained from the returned HRESULT is one of the following:

Return value	Meaning
S_OK	Success.
TYPE_E_ELEMENTNOTFOUND	No type description was found in the library with the specified GUID.
E_OUTOFMEMORY	Out of memory.
E_INVALIDARG	One or more of the arguments is invalid.
TYPE_E_IOERROR	The function could not write to the file.
TYPE_E_INVDATAREAD	The function could not read from the file.
TYPE_E_UNSUPFORMAT	The type library has an older format.
TYPE_E_REGISTRYACCESS	There was an error accessing the system registration database.
TYPE_E_INVALIDSTATE	The type library could not be opened.

ITypeLib::GetTypeInfoType

HRESULT GetTypeInfoType(
unsigned int *index,*
TYPEKIND FAR* *pTKind*
);

Retrieves the type of a type description.

Parameters   *index*
The index of the type description within the type library.

pTKind
A pointer to the TYPEKIND enumeration for the type description.

Return Value   The return value obtained from the returned HRESULT is one of the following:

Return value	Meaning
S_OK	Success.
TYPE_E_ELEMENTNOTFOUND	*Index* is outside the range of 0 to **GetTypeInfoCount** –1.

ITypeLib::IsName

HRESULT IsName(
OLECHAR FAR* *szNameBuf,*

unsigned long *lHashVal,*

BOOL *pfName*

);

Indicates whether a passed-in string contains the name of a type or member described in the library.

Parameter

szNameBuf
The string to test. If **IsName** is successful, *szNameBuf* is modified to match the case (capitalization) found in the type library.

lHashVal
The hash value of *szNameBuf*.

pfName
On return, set to True if *szNameBuf* was found in the type library; otherwise False.

Return Value

The return value obtained from the returned HRESULT is one of the following:

Return value	Meaning
S_OK	Success.
E_OUTOFMEMORY	Out of memory.
E_INVALIDARG	One or more of the arguments is invalid.
TYPE_E_IOERROR	The function could not read from the file.
TYPE_E_INVDATAREAD	Invalid data.
TYPE_E_UNSUPFORMAT	The type library has an older format.
TYPE_E_INVALIDSTATE	The type library could not be opened.

ITypeLib::ReleaseTLibAttr

HRESULT ReleaseTLibAttr(
TLIBATTR FAR* *pTLibAttr*
);

Releases the TLIBATTR originally obtained from **ITypeLib::GetLibAttr**.

Parameter   *pTLibAttr*
Pointer to the TLIBATTR to be freed.

Comments   Releases the specified TLIBATTR. This TLIBATTR was previously obtained with a call to **GetTypeLib::GetLibAttr**.

ITypeLib2 Interface

The **ITypeLib2** interface inherits from the **ITypeLib** interface. This allows **ITypeLib** to cast to an **ITypeLib2** in performance-sensitive cases, rather than perform extra **QueryInterface** and **Release** calls.

Example
```
DECLARE_INTERFACE_(ITypeLib2, ITypeLib)
{
BEGIN_INTERFACE
```

ITypeLib2::GetCustData

HRESULT GetCustData(
REFGUID *guid*,
VARIANT **pVarVal*
);

Retrieves the custom data.

Parameter   *guid*
GUID used to identify the data.

pVarVal
Where to put the retrieved data.

Return Value

The return value obtained from the returned HRESULT is one of the following:

Return value	Meaning
S_OK	Success.
E_OUTOFMEMORY	Out of memory.
E_INVALIDARG	One or more of the arguments is invalid.

ITypeLib2::GetDocumentation2

HRESULT GetDocumentation2(
[in] int *index,*
[in] LCID *lcid,*
[out] BSTR FAR* *pbstrHelpString,*
[out] unsigned long FAR* *pdwHelpStringContext,*
BSTR FAR* *pbstrHelpStringDll*
);

Retrieves the library's documentation string, the complete Help file name and path, the localization context to use, and the context ID for the library Help topic in the Help file.

Parameters

index
> Index of the type description whose documentation is to be returned; if *index* is −1, then the documentation for the library is returned.

lcid
> Locale identifier.

pbstrHelpString
> Returns a BSTR that contains the name of the specified item. If the caller does not need the item name, then *pbstrHelpString* can be Null.

pdwHelpStringContext
> Returns the Help localization context. If the caller does not need the Help context, then it can be Null.

pbstrHelpStringDll
> Returns a BSTR that contains the fully qualified name of the file containing the DLL used for Help file. If the caller does not need the file name, then it can be Null.

Return Value   The return value obtained from the returned HRESULT is one of the following:

Return value	Meaning
S_OK	Success.
STG_E_INSUFFICIENTMEMORY	Out of memory.
E_INVALIDARG	One or more of the arguments is invalid.
TYPE_E_IOERROR	The function could not write to the file.
TYPE_E_INVDATAREAD	The function could not read from the file.
TYPE_E_UNSUPFORMAT	The type library has an older format.
TYPE_E_INVALIDSTATE	The type library could not be opened.
TYPE_E_ELEMENTNOTFOUND	The element was not found.

Comments   Gets information at the type library level. The caller should free the BSTR parameters.

This function will call **_DLLGetDocumentation** in the specified DLL to retrieve the desired Help string, if there is a Help string context for this item. If no Help string context exists or an error occurs, then it will defer to the **GetDocumentation** method and return the associated documentation string.

ITypeLib2::GetLibStatistics

HRESULT GetLibStatistics(
unsigned long* *pcUniqueNames*,
unsigned long* *pcchUniqueNames*
);

Returns statistics about a type library that are required for efficient sizing of hash tables.

Parameter   *pcUniqueNames*
Returns a pointer to a count of unique names. If the caller does not need this information, set to NULL.

pcchUniqueNames
Returns a pointer to a change in the count of unique names.

Return Value	The return value obtained from the returned HRESULT is one of the following:

Return value	Meaning
S_OK	Success.
E_OUTOFMEMORY	Out of memory.
E_INVALIDARG	One or more of the arguments is invalid.

Example	`ITypeLib2::GetLibStatistics(DWORD *pcUniqueNames, DWORD * pcchUniqueNames)`

ITypeLib2::GetAllCustData

> **HRESULT**
> **CUSTDATA** *pCustData*
>);

Gets all custom data items for the library.

Parameter	*pCustData* Returns a pointer to CUSTDATA (that holds all custom data items).
Return Value	The return value obtained from the returned HRESULT is one of the following:

Return value	Meaning
S_OK	Success.
E_OUTOFMEMORY	Out of memory.
E_INVALIDARG	One or more of the arguments is invalid.

Comments	After the call, the caller needs to release memory used to hold the custom data item by calling **ClearCustData**.

ITypeInfo Interface

This section describes **ITypeInfo**, an interface typically used for reading information about objects. For example, an object browser tool can use **ITypeInfo** to extract information about the characteristics and capabilities of objects from type libraries.

Implemented by	Used by	Header file name
Oleaut32.dll (32-bit systems)	Tools that need to access the descriptions of objects contained in type libraries.	Oleauto.h
Typelib.dll (16-bit systems)		Dispatch.h

Type information interfaces are intended to describe the parts of the application that can be called by outside clients, rather than those that might be used internally to build an application.

The **ITypeInfo** interface provides access to the following:

- The set of function descriptions associated with the type. For interfaces, this contains the set of member functions in the interface.

- The set of data member descriptions associated with the type. For structures, this contains the set of fields of the type.

- The general attributes of the type, such as whether it describes a structure, an interface, and so on.

The type description of an **IDispatch** interface can be used to implement the interface. For more information, see the description of **CreateStdDispatch** in Chapter 5, "Dispatch Interface and API Functions."

An instance of **ITypeInfo** provides various information about the type of an object, and is used in different ways. A compiler can use an **ITypeInfo** to compile references to members of the type. A type interface browser can use it to find information about each member of the type. An **IDispatch** implementor can use it to provide automatic delegation of **IDispatch** calls to an interface.

Type Descriptions

The information associated with an object described by **ITypeInfo** can include a set of functions, a set of data members, and various type attributes. It is essentially the same as the information described by a C++ class declaration, which can be used to define both interfaces and structures, as well as any combination of functions and data members. In addition to interfaces and structure definitions, the **ITypeInfo** interface is used to describe other types, including enumerations and aliases. Because the interface to a C file or library is simply a set of functions and variable declarations, **ITypeInfo** can also be used to describe them.

Type information comprises individual type descriptions. Each type description must have one of the following forms:

Category	ODL keyword	Description
alias	**typedef**	An alias for another type.
enumeration	**enum**	An enumeration.
structure	**struct**	A structure.
union	**union**	A single data item that can have one of a specified group of types.
module	**module**	Data and functions not accessed through virtual function table (VTBL) entries.
IDispatch interface	**dispinterface**	**IDispatch** properties and methods accessed through **IDispatch::Invoke**.
OLE interface	**interface**	OLE member functions accessed through VTBL entries.
dual interface	**dual**	Supports either VTBL or **IDispatch**.
component object class	**coclass**	A component object class. Specifies an implementation of one or more OLE interfaces and one or more **IDispatch** interfaces.

Note   All bit flags that are not used specifically should be set to zero for future compatibility.

Alias

An alias has TypeKind = TKIND_ALIAS. An alias is an empty set of functions, an empty set of data members, and a type description (located in the TYPEATTR), which gives the actual type definition (**typedef**) of the alias.

Enumeration (Statement)

An enumeration (**enum**) has TypeKind = TKIND_ENUM. An enumeration is an empty set of functions and a set of constant data members.

Structure (Statement)

A structure (**struct**) description has TypeKind = TKIND_RECORD. A structure is an empty set of functions and a set of per-instance data members.

Union (Statement)

A **union** description has TypeKind = TKIND_UNION. A union is an empty set of functions and a set of per-instance data members, each of which has an instance offset of zero.

Module (Statement)

A **module** has TypeKind = TKIND_MODULE. A module is a set of static functions and a set of static data members.

IDispatch Interface

These include objects (TypeKind = TKIND_DISPATCH) that support the **IDispatch** interface with a specification of the dispatch data members (such as properties) and methods supported through the object's **Invoke** implementation. All members of the dispinterface should have different IDs, except for the accessor functions of properties.

OLE-Compatible Interface

An **interface** definition has TypeKind = TKIND_INTERFACE. An interface is a set of pure virtual functions and an empty set of data members. If a type description contains any virtual functions, then the pointer to the VTBL is the first 4 bytes of the instance.

The type information fully describes the member functions in the VTBL, including parameter names and types and function return types. It may inherit from no more than one other interface.

With interfaces and dispinterfaces, all members should have different names, except the accessor functions of properties. For property functions having the same name, the documentation string and Help context should be set for only one of the functions (because they define the same property conceptually).

Dual Interface

Dual interfaces (**dual**) have two different type descriptions for the same interface. The TKIND_INTERFACE type description describes the interface as a standard OLE Component Object Model (COM) interface. The TKIND_DISPATCH type description describes the interface as a standard dispatch interface. The *lcid* and *retval* parameters, and the HRESULT return types are removed, and the return type of the member is specified to be the same type as the *retval* parameter.

By default, the TYPEKIND enumeration for a dual interface is TKIND_DISPATCH. Tools that bind to interfaces should check the type flags for TYPEFLAG_FDUAL. If this flag is set, the TKIND_INTERFACE type description is available through a call to **ITypeInfo::GetRefTypeOfImplType** with an *index* of –1, followed by a call to **ITypeInfo::GetRefTypeInfo**.

Component Object Class

These coclass objects (TypeKind = TKIND_COCLASS) support a set of implemented interfaces, which can be of either TKIND_INTERFACE or TKIND_DISPATCH.

ITypeInfo::AddressOfMember

HRESULT AddressOfMember(
MEMBERID *memid,*
INVOKEKIND *invKind,*
VOID FAR* FAR* *ppv*
);

Retrieves the addresses of static functions or variables, such as those defined in a DLL.

Parameters

memid
Member ID of the static member whose address is to be retrieved. The member ID is defined by the DISPID.

invKind
Specifies whether the member is a property, and if so, what kind.

ppv
On return, points to a pointer to the static member.

Return Value
The return value obtained from the returned HRESULT is one of the following:

Return value	Meaning
S_OK	Success.
E_OUTOFMEMORY	Out of memory.
E_INVALIDARG	One or more of the arguments is invalid.
TYPE_E_IOERROR	The function could not read from the file.
TYPE_E_WRONGTYPEKIND	Type mismatch.
TYPE_E_INVDATAREAD	The function could not read from the file.
TYPE_E_UNSUPFORMAT	The type library has an older format.
TYPE_E_INVALIDSTATE	The type library could not be opened.
TYPE_E_ELEMENTNOTFOUND	The element was not found.
TYPE_E_DLLFUNCTIONNOTFOUND	The function could not be found in the DLL.
TYPE_E_CANTLOADLIBRARY	The type library or DLL could not be loaded.

Comments

The addresses are valid until the caller releases its reference to the type description. The *invKind* parameter can be ignored unless the address of a property function is being requested.

If the type description inherits from another type description, this function is recursive to the base type description, if necessary, to find the item with the requested member ID.

ITypeInfo::CreateInstance

HRESULT CreateInstance(
IUnknown FAR* *pUnkOuter,*
REFIID *riid,*
VOID FAR* FAR* *ppvObj*
);

Creates a new instance of a type that describes a component object class (coclass).

Parameters

pUnkOuter
A pointer to the controlling **IUnknown**. If Null, then a stand-alone instance is created. If valid, then an aggregate object is created.

riid
An ID for the interface that the caller will use to communicate with the resulting object.

ppvObj
On return, points to a pointer to an instance of the created object.

Return Value

The return value obtained from the returned HRESULT is one of the following:

Return value	Meaning
S_OK	Success.
E_OUTOFMEMORY	Out of memory.
TYPE_E_WRONGTYPEKIND	Type mismatch.
E_INVALIDARG	One or more of the arguments is invalid.
E_NOINTERFACE	OLE could not find an implementation of one or more required interfaces.
TYPE_E_UNSUPFORMAT	The type library has an older format.
TYPE_E_INVALIDSTATE	The type library could not be opened.
Other return codes	Additional errors may be returned from **GetActiveObject** or **CoCreateInstance**.

Comments   For types that describe a component object class (coclass), **CreateInstance** creates a new instance of the class. Normally, **CreateInstance** calls **CoCreateInstance** with the type description's GUID. For an Application object, it first calls **GetActiveObject**. If the application is active, **GetActiveObject** returns the active object; otherwise, if **GetActiveObject** fails, **CreateInstance** calls **CoCreateInstance**.

ITypeInfo::GetContainingTypeLib

HRESULT GetContainingTypeLib(
ITypeLib FAR* FAR* *ppTLib*,
unsigned int FAR* *pIndex*
);

Retrieves the containing type library and the index of the type description within that type library.

Parameters   *ppTLib*
On return, points to the containing type library.

pIndex
On return, points to the index of the type description within the containing type library.

Return Value   The return value obtained from the returned HRESULT is one of the following:

Return value	Meaning
S_OK	Success.
E_OUTOFMEMORY	Out of memory.
E_INVALIDARG	One or more of the arguments is invalid.
E_NOINTERFACE	OLE could not find an implementation of one or more required interfaces.
TYPE_E_IOERROR	The function could not write to the file.
TYPE_E_INVDATAREAD	The function could not read from the file.
TYPE_E_UNSUPFORMAT	The type library has an older format.
TYPE_E_INVALIDSTATE	The type library could not be opened.

ITypeInfo::GetDllEntry

HRESULT GetDllEntry(
MEMBERID *memid,*
INVOKEKIND *invKind,*
BSTR FAR* *pBstrDllName,*
BSTR FAR* *pBstrName,*
unsigned short FAR* *pwOrdinal*
);

Retrieves a description or specification of an entry point for a function in a DLL.

Parameters

memid
ID of the member function whose DLL entry description is to be returned.

invKind
Specifies the kind of member identified by *memid*. This is important for properties, because one *memid* can identify up to three separate functions.

pBstrDllName
If not Null, the function sets *pBstrDllName* to a BSTR that contains the name of the DLL.

pBstrName
If not Null, the function sets *lpbstrName* to a BSTR that contains the name of the entry point. If the entry point is specified by an ordinal, **lpbstrName* is set to Null.

pwOrdinal
If not Null, and if the function is defined by an ordinal, then *lpwOrdinal* is set to point to the ordinal.

Return Value

The return value obtained from the returned HRESULT is one of the following:

Return value	Meaning
S_OK	Success.
E_OUTOFMEMORY	Out of memory.
E_INVALIDARG	One or more of the arguments is invalid.
E_NOINTERFACE	OLE could not find an implementation of one or more required interfaces.

Return value	Meaning
TYPE_E_ELEMENTNOTFOUND	The element was not found.
TYPE_E_IOERROR	The function could not read from the file.
TYPE_E_INVDATAREAD	Invalid data.
TYPE_E_UNSUPFORMAT	The type library has an older format.
TYPE_E_INVALIDSTATE	The type library could not be opened.
TYPE_E_WRONGTYPEKIND	Type mismatch.

Comments

The caller passes in a member ID, which represents the member function whose entry description is desired. If the function has a DLL entry point, the name of the DLL that contains the function, as well as its name or ordinal identifier, are placed in the passed-in pointers allocated by the caller. If there is no DLL entry point for the function, an error is returned.

If the type description inherits from another type description, this function is recursive to the base type description, if necessary, to find the item with the requested member ID.

The caller should use **SysFreeString** to free the BSTRs referenced by *pBstrName* and *pBstrDllName*.

ITypeInfo::GetDocumentation

HRESULT GetDocumentation(
MEMBERID *memid,*
BSTR FAR* *pBstrName,*
BSTR FAR* *pBstrDocString,*
unsigned long FAR* *pdwHelpContext,*
BSTR FAR* *pBstrHelpFile*
);

Retrieves the documentation string, the complete Help file name and path, and the context ID for the Help topic for a specified type description.

Parameters

memid
    ID of the member whose documentation is to be returned.

pBstrName
    Pointer to a BSTR allocated by the callee into which the name of the specified item is placed. If the caller does not need the item name, *pBstrName* can be Null.

pBstrDocString
> Pointer to a BSTR into which the documentation string for the specified item is placed. If the caller does not need the documentation string, *pBstrDocString* can be Null.

pdwHelpContext
> Pointer to the Help context associated with the specified item. If the caller does not need the Help context, the *pdwHelpContext* can be Null.

pBstrHelpFile
> Pointer to a BSTR into which the fully qualified name of the Help file is placed. If the caller does not need the Help file name, *pBstrHelpFile* can be Null.

Return Value

The return value obtained from the returned HRESULT is one of the following:

Return value	Meaning
S_OK	Success.
E_OUTOFMEMORY	Out of memory.
E_INVALIDARG	One or more of the arguments is invalid.
TYPE_E_IOERROR	The function could not read from the file.
TYPE_E_ELEMENTNOTFOUND	The element was not found.
TYPE_E_INVDATAREAD	Invalid data.
TYPE_E_UNSUPFORMAT	The type library has an older format.
TYPE_E_INVALIDSTATE	The type library could not be opened.
TYPE_E_ELEMENTNOTFOUND	The element was not found.

Comments

The function **GetDocumentation** provides access to the documentation for the member specified by the *memid* parameter. If the passed-in *memid* is MEMBERID_NIL, then the documentation for the type description is returned.

If the type description inherits from another type description, this function is recursive to the base type description, if necessary, to find the item with the requested member ID.

The caller should use **SysFreeString** to free the BSTRs referenced by *pBstrName*, *pBstrDocString*, and *pBstrHelpFile*.

Example

```
CHECKRESULT(ptypeinfo->GetDocumentation(idMember, &bstrName, NULL, NULL,
    NULL));
    .
    .
    .
SysFreeString (bstrName);
```

ITypeInfo::GetFuncDesc

HRESULT GetFuncDesc(
unsigned int *index*,
FUNCDESC FAR* FAR* *ppFuncDesc*
);

Retrieves the FUNCDESC structure that contains information about a specified function.

Parameters

index
Index of the function whose description is to be returned. The *index* should be in the range of 0 to 1 less than the number of functions in this type.

ppFuncDesc
On return, points to a pointer to a FUNCDESC that describes the specified function.

Return Value

The return value obtained from the returned HRESULT is one of the following:

Return value	Meaning
S_OK	Success.
E_OUTOFMEMORY	Out of memory.
E_INVALIDARG	One or more of the arguments is invalid.
TYPE_E_IOERROR	The function could not read from the file.
TYPE_E_INVDATAREAD	Invalid data.
TYPE_E_UNSUPFORMAT	The type library has an older format.
TYPE_E_INVALIDSTATE	The type library could not be opened.

Comments

The function **GetFuncDesc** provides access to a FUNCDESC structure that describes the function with the specified *index*. The FUNCDESC should be freed with **ITypeInfo::ReleaseFuncDesc**. The number of functions in the type is one of the attributes contained in the TYPEATTR structure.

Example

```
CHECKRESULT(ptypeinfo->GetFuncDesc(i, &pfuncdesc));
idMember = pfuncdesc->elemdescFunc.ID;
CHECKRESULT(ptypeinfo->GetDocumentation(idMember, &bstrName, NULL, NULL,
NULL));
ptypeinfo->ReleaseFuncDesc(pfuncdesc);
```

ITypeInfo::GetIDsOfNames

HRESULT GetIDsOfNames(
OLECHAR FAR* FAR* *rgszNames***,**

unsigned int *cNames***,**

MEMBERID FAR* *pMemId*

);

Maps between member names and member IDs, and parameter names and parameter IDs.

Parameters

rgszNames
Passed-in pointer to an array of names to be mapped.

cNames
Count of the names to be mapped.

pMemId
Caller-allocated array in which name mappings are placed.

Return Value

The return value obtained from the returned HRESULT is one of the following:

Return value	Meaning
S_OK	Success.
STG_E_INSUFFICIENTMEMORY	Out of memory.
E_OUTOFMEMORY	Out of memory.
E_INVALIDARG	One or more of the arguments is invalid.
DISP_E_UNKNOWNNAME	One or more of the names could not be found.
DISP_E_UNKNOWNLCID	The locale identifier (LCID) could not be found in the OLE DLLs.
TYPE_E_IOERROR	The function could not write to the file.
TYPE_E_INVDATAREAD	The function could not read from the file.
TYPE_E_UNSUPFORMAT	The type library has an older format.
TYPE_E_INVALIDSTATE	The type library could not be opened.
TYPE_E_WRONGTYPEKIND	Type mismatch.

Comments
    The function **GetIDsOfNames** maps the name of a member (*rgszNames*[0]) and its parameters (*rgszNames*[1] ...*rgszNames*[*cNames* − 1]) to the ID of the member (*rgid*[0]), and to the IDs of the specified parameters (*rgid*[1] ... *rgid*[*cNames* − 1]). The IDs of parameters are 0 for the first parameter in the member function's argument list, 1 for the second, and so on.

    If the type description inherits from another type description, this function is recursive to the base type description, if necessary, to find the item with the requested member ID.

ITypeInfo::GetImplTypeFlags

HRESULT GetImplTypeFlags(
unsigned int *index,*

int* *pImplTypeFlags*

);

Retrieves the IMPLTYPEFLAGS enumeration for one implemented interface or base interface in a type description.

Parameters
index
    Index of the implemented interface or base interface for which to get the flags.

pImplTypeFlags
    On return, pointer to the IMPLTYPEFLAGS enumeration.

Return Value
The return value obtained from the returned HRESULT is one of the following:

Return value	Meaning
S_OK	Success.
E_OUTOFMEMORY	Out of memory.
E_INVALIDARG	One or more of the arguments is invalid.
TYPE_E_INVDATAREAD	The function could not read from the file.
TYPE_E_UNSUPFORMAT	The type library has an older format.
TYPE_E_INVALIDSTATE	The type library could not be opened.
TYPE_E_WRONGTYPEKIND	Type mismatch.

Comments
The flags are associated with the act of inheritance, and not with the inherited interface.

ITypeInfo::GetMops

HRESULT GetMops(
MEMBERID *memid,*
BSTR FAR* *pBstrMops*
);

Retrieves marshaling information.

Parameters

memid
The member ID that indicates which marshaling information is needed.

pBstrMops
On return, contains a pointer to the *opcode* string used in marshaling the fields of the structure described by the referenced type description, or returns Null if there is no information to return.

Return Value

The return value obtained from the returned HRESULT is one of the following:

Return value	Meaning
S_OK	Success.
E_OUTOFMEMORY	Out of memory.
E_INVALIDARG	One or more of the arguments is invalid.
TYPE_E_IOERROR	The function could not read from the file.
TYPE_E_UNSUPFORMAT	The type library has an older format.
TYPE_E_INVALIDSTATE	The type library could not be opened.
TYPE_E_ELEMENTNOTFOUND	The element was not found.
TYPE_E_WRONGTYPEKIND	Type mismatch.

Comments

If the passed-in member ID is MEMBERID_NIL, the function returns the *opcode* string for marshaling the fields of the structure described by the type description. Otherwise, it returns the *opcode* string for marshaling the function specified by the *index*.

If the type description inherits from another type description, this function recurses on the base type description, if necessary, to find the item with the requested member ID.

ITypeInfo::GetNames

HRESULT GetNames(
MEMBERID *memid*,
BSTR FAR* *rgBstrNames*,
unsigned int *cMaxNames*,
unsigned int FAR* *pcNames*
);

Retrieves the variable with the specified member ID (or the name of the property or method and its parameters) that correspond to the specified function ID.

Parameters

memid
    The ID of the member whose name (or names) is to be returned.

rgBstrNames
    Pointer to the caller-allocated array. On return, each of these *lpcName* elements is filled in to point to a BSTR that contains the name (or names) associated with the member.

cMaxNames
    Length of the passed-in *rgBstrNames* array.

pcNames
    On return, points to the number that represents the number of names in *rgBstrNames* array.

Return Value

The return value obtained from the returned HRESULT is one of the following:

Return value	Meaning
S_OK	Success.
E_OUTOFMEMORY	Out of memory.
E_INVALIDARG	One or more of the arguments is invalid.
TYPE_E_IOERROR	The function could not read from the file.
TYPE_E_INVDATAREAD	Invalid data.
TYPE_E_UNSUPFORMAT	The type library has an older format.
TYPE_E_INVALIDSTATE	The type library could not be opened.
TYPE_E_WRONGTYPEKIND	Type mismatch.
TYPE_E_ELEMENTNOTFOUND	The element was not found.

Comments   The caller must release the returned BSTR (Basic string) array.

If the member ID identifies a property that is implemented with property functions, the property name is returned.

For property **get** functions, the names of the function and its parameters are always returned.

For property put and put reference functions, the right side of the assignment is unnamed. If *cMaxNames* is less than is required to return all of the names of the parameters of a function, then only the names of the first *cMaxNames*– 1 parameters are returned. The names of the parameters are returned in the array in the same order that they appear elsewhere in the interface (for example, the same order in the parameter array associated with the FUNCDESC enumeration).

If the type description inherits from another type description, this function is recursive to the base type description, if necessary, to find the item with the requested member ID.

ITypeInfo::GetRefTypeInfo

HRESULT GetRefTypeInfo(
HREFTYPE *hRefType*,
ITypeInfo FAR* FAR* *ppTInfo*
);

If a type description references other type descriptions, it retrieves the referenced type descriptions.

Parameters   *hRefType*
   Handle to the referenced type description to be returned.

ppTInfo
   Points a pointer to a pointer to the referenced type description.

Return Value   The return value obtained from the returned HRESULT is one of the following:

Return value	Meaning
S_OK	Success.
E_OUTOFMEMORY	Out of memory.
E_INVALIDARG	One or more of the arguments is invalid.
TYPE_E_IOERROR	The function could not read from the file.
TYPE_E_INVDATAREAD	Invalid data.

Return value	Meaning
TYPE_E_UNSUPFORMAT	The type library has an older format.
TYPE_E_INVALIDSTATE	The type library could not be opened.
TYPE_E_WRONGTYPEKIND	Type mismatch.
TYPE_E_ELEMENTNOTFOUND	The element was not found.
TYPE_E_REGISTRYACCESS	There was an error accessing the system registration database.
TYPE_E_LIBNOTREGISTERED	The type library was not found in the system registration database.

Comments

On return, the second parameter contains a pointer to a pointer to a type description that is referenced by this type description. A type description must have a reference to each type description that occurs as the type of any of its variables, function parameters, or function return types. For example, if the type of a data member is a record type, the type description for that data member contains the *hRefType* of a referenced type description. To get a pointer to the type description, the reference is passed to **GetRefTypeInfo**.

ITypeInfo::GetRefTypeOfImplType

HRESULT GetRefTypeOfImplType(
unsigned int *index*,
HREFTYPE FAR* *pRefType*
);

If a type description describes a COM class, it retrieves the type description of the implemented interface types. For an interface, **GetRefTypeOfImplType** returns the type information for inherited interfaces, if any exist.

Parameters

index
Index of the implemented type whose handle is returned. The valid range is 0 to the *cImplTypes* field in the TYPEATTR structure.

pRefType
On return, points to a handle for the implemented interface (if any). This handle can be passed to **ITypeInfo::GetRefTypeInfo** to get the type description.

Return Value

The return value obtained from the returned HRESULT is one of the following:

Return value	Meaning
S_OK	Success.
TYPE_E_ELEMENTNOTFOUND	Passed index is outside the range 0 to 1 less than the number of function descriptions.
E_INVALIDARG	One or more of the arguments is invalid.
TYPE_E_IOERROR	The function could not read from the file.
TYPE_E_INVDATAREAD	Invalid data.
TYPE_E_UNSUPFORMAT	The type library has an older format.
TYPE_E_INVALIDSTATE	The type library could not be opened.

Comments   If the TKIND_DISPATCH type description is for a dual interface, the TKIND_INTERFACE type description can be obtained by calling **GetRefTypeOfImplType** with an *index* of –1, and by passing the returned *pRefType* handle to **GetRefTypeInfo** to retrieve the type information.

ITypeInfo::GetTypeAttr

HRESULT GetTypeAttr(
   TYPEATTR FAR* FAR* *ppTypeAttr*
   );

Retrieves a TYPEATTR structure that contains the attributes of the type description.

Parameter   *ppTypeAttr*
      On return, points to a pointer to a structure that contains the attributes of this type description.

Return Value   The return value obtained from the returned HRESULT is one of the following:

Return value	Meaning
S_OK	Success.
E_OUTOFMEMORY	Out of memory.
E_INVALIDARG	One or more of the arguments is invalid.
TYPE_E_IOERROR	The function could not write to the file.
TYPE_E_INVDATAREAD	The function could not read from the file.
TYPE_E_UNSUPFORMAT	The type library has an older format.
TYPE_E_INVALIDSTATE	The type library could not be opened.

Comments   To free the TYPEATTR structure, use **ITypeInfo::ReleaseTypeAttr**.

Example
```
CHECKRESULT(ptypeinfoCur->GetTypeAttr(&ptypeattrCur));
    .
    .
    .
ptypeinfoCur->ReleaseTypeAttr(ptypeattrCur);
```

ITypeInfo::GetTypeComp

HRESULT GetTypeComp(
ITypeComp FAR* FAR* *ppTComp*
);

Retrieves the **ITypeComp** interface for the type description, which enables a client compiler to bind to the type description's members.

Parameter   *ppTComp*
    On return, points to a pointer to the **ITypeComp** of the containing type library.

Return Value   The return value obtained from the returned HRESULT is one of the following:

Return value	Meaning
S_OK	Success.
E_OUTOFMEMORY	Out of memory.
E_INVALIDARG	One or more of the arguments is invalid.
TYPE_E_IOERROR	The function could not read from the file.
TYPE_E_INVDATAREAD	Invalid data.
TYPE_E_UNSUPFORMAT	The type library has an older format.
TYPE_E_INVALIDSTATE	The type library could not be opened.
TYPE_E_WRONGTYPEKIND	Type mismatch.

Comments   A client compiler can use the **ITypeComp** interface to bind to members of the type.

ITypeInfo::GetVarDesc

HRESULT GetVarDesc(
unsigned int *index,*
VARDESC FAR* FAR* *ppVarDesc*
);

Retrieves a VARDESC structure that describes the specified variable.

Parameters

index
    Index of the variable whose description is to be returned. The *index* should be in the range of 0 to 1 less than the number of variables in this type.

ppVarDesc
    On return, points to a pointer to a VARDESC that describes the specified variable.

Return Value

The return value obtained from the returned HRESULT is one of the following:

Return value	Meaning
S_OK	Success.
E_OUTOFMEMORY	Out of memory.
E_INVALIDARG	One or more of the arguments is invalid.
TYPE_E_IOERROR	The function could not read from the file.
TYPE_E_INVDATAREAD	Invalid data.
TYPE_E_UNSUPFORMAT	The type library has an older format.
TYPE_E_INVALIDSTATE	The type library could not be opened.

Comments

To free the VARDESC structure, use **ReleaseVarDesc.**

Example

```
CHECKRESULT(ptypeinfo->GetVarDesc(i, &pvardesc));
idMember = pvardesc->memid;
CHECKRESULT(ptypeinfo->GetDocumentation(idMember, &bstrName, NULL, NULL,
        NULL));
ptypeinfo->ReleaseVarDesc(pvardesc);
```

ITypeInfo::Invoke

HRESULT Invoke(
VOID FAR* *pvInstance,*
MEMBERID *memid,*
unsigned short *wFlags,*
DISPPARAMS FAR* *pDispParams,*
VARIANT FAR* *pVarResult,*
EXCEPINFO FAR* *pExcepInfo,*
unsigned int FAR* *puArgErr*
);

Invokes a method, or accesses a property of an object, that implements the interface described by the type description.

Parameters

pvInstance
Pointer to an instance of the interface described by this type description.

memid
Identifies the interface member.

wFlags
Flags describing the context of the invoke call, as follows:

Value	Description
DISPATCH_METHOD	The member is accessed as a method. If there is ambiguity, both this and the DISPATCH_PROPERTYGET flag can be set.
DISPATCH_PROPERTYGET	The member is retrieved as a property or data member.
DISPATCH_PROPERTYPUT	The member is changed as a property or data member.
DISPATCH_PROPERTYPUTREF	The member is changed by using a reference assignment, rather than a value assignment. This value is only valid when the property accepts a reference to an object.

pDispParams
Points to a structure that contains an array of arguments, an array of DISPIDs for named arguments, and counts of the number of elements in each array.

pVarResult

Should be Null if the caller does not expect any result. Otherwise, it should be a pointer to the location at which the result is to be stored. If *wFlags* specifies DISPATCH_PROPERTYPUT or DISPATCH_PROPERTYPUTREF, *pVarResult*is ignored.

pExcepInfo

Points to an exception information structure, which is filled in only if DISP_E_EXCEPTION is returned. If *pExcepInfo*is Null on input, only an HRESULT error will be returned.

puArgErr

If **Invoke** returns DISP_E_TYPEMISMATCH, *puArgErr* indicates the index (within *rgvarg*) of the argument with incorrect type. If more than one argument returns an error, *puArgErr* indicates only the first argument with an error. Arguments in *pDispParams->rgvarg* appear in reverse order, so the first argument is the one having the highest index in the array. Cannot be Null.

Return Value   The return value obtained from the returned HRESULT is one of the following:

Return value	Meaning
S_OK	Success.
E_INVALIDARG	One or more of the arguments is invalid.
DISP_E_EXCEPTION	The member being invoked has returned an error HRESULT. If the member implements **IErrorInfo**, details are available in the error object. Otherwise, the *pExcepInfo* parameter contains details.
TYPE_E_IOERROR	The function could not read from the file.
TYPE_E_INVDATAREAD	Invalid data.
TYPE_E_UNSUPFORMAT	The type library has an older format.
TYPE_E_REGISTRYACCESS	There was an error accessing the system registration database.
TYPE_E_LIBNOTREGISTERED	The type library was not found in the system registration database.
TYPE_E_INVALIDSTATE	The type library could not be opened.
TYPE_E_WRONGTYPEKIND	Type mismatch.
TYPE_E_ELEMENTNOTFOUND	The element was not found.
TYPE_E_BADMODULEKIND	The module does not support **Invoke**.
Other return codes	Any of the **IDispatch::Invoke** errors may also be returned.

Comments   Use the function **ITypeInfo::Invoke** to access a member of an object or invoke a
method that implements the interface described by this type description. For objects
that support the **IDispatch** interface, you can use **Invoke** to implement
IDispatch::Invoke.

ITypeInfo::Invoke takes a pointer to an instance of the class. Otherwise, its
parameters are the same as **IDispatch::Invoke,** except that **ITypeInfo::Invoke** omits
the *refiid* and *lcid* parameters. When called, **ITypeInfo::Invoke** performs the actions
described by the **IDispatch::Invoke** parameters on the specified instance.

For VTBL interface members, **ITypeInfo::Invoke** passes the LCID of the type
information into parameters tagged with the **lcid** attribute, and the returned value into
the **retval** attribute.

If the type description inherits from another type description, this function recurses on
the base type description to find the item with the requested member ID.

ITypeInfo::ReleaseFuncDesc

HRESULT ReleaseFuncDesc(
FUNCDESC FAR* *pFuncDesc*
);

Releases a FUNCDESC previously returned by **GetFuncDesc**.

Parameter   *pFuncDesc*
Pointer to the FUNCDESC to be freed.

Comments   The function **ReleaseFuncDesc** releases a FUNCDESC that was returned through
ITypeInfo::GetFuncDesc.

Example   `ptypeinfoCur->ReleaseFuncDesc(pfuncdesc);`

ITypeInfo::ReleaseTypeAttr

HRESULT ReleaseTypeAttr(
TYPEATTR FAR* *pTypeAttr*
);

Releases a TYPEATTR previously returned by **GetTypeAttr**.

Parameter   *pTypeAttr*
Pointer to the TYPEATTR to be freed.

Comments   The function **ReleaseTypeAttr** releases a TYPEATTR that was returned through
ITypeInfo::GetTypeAttr.

ITypeInfo::ReleaseVarDesc

HRESULT ReleaseVarDesc(
VARDESC FAR* *pVarDesc*
);

Releases a VARDESC previously returned by **GetVarDesc**.

Parameter   *pVarDesc*
Pointer to the VARDESC to be freed.

Comments   **ReleaseVarDesc** releases a VARDESC that was returned through
ITypeInfo::GetVarDesc.

Example
```
VARDESC     FAR *pVarDesc;
CHECKRESULT(ptypeinfo->GetVarDesc(i, &pvardesc));
idMember = pvardesc->memid;
CHECKRESULT(ptypeinfo->GetDocumentation(idMember, &bstrName, NULL, NULL,
    NULL));
ptypeinfo->ReleaseVarDesc(pvardesc);
```

ITypeInfo2 Interface

An **ITypeInfo** can be cast to an **ITypeInfo2** rather than use the calls **QueryInterface** and **Release.**

ITypeInfo2::GetTypeKind

HRESULT GetTypeKind(
TYPEKIND *pTypeKind*
);

Returns the TYPEKIND enumeration quickly, without doing any allocations.

Parameter

pTypeKind
Reference to a TYPEKIND enumeration.

Return Value

The return value obtained from the returned HRESULT is one of the following:

Return value	Meaning
S_OK	Success.
E_OUTOFMEMORY	Out of memory.
E_INVALIDARG	One or more of the arguments is invalid.

Example

```
HRESULT ITypeInfo2::GetTypeKind(TYPEKIND * ptypekind)
```

ITypeInfo2::GetTypeFlags

HRESULT GetTypeFlags(
unsigned long *pTypeFlags*
);

Returns the type flags without any allocations. This returns a DWORD type flag, which expands the type flags without growing the TYPEATTR (type attribute).

Parameter

pTypeFlags
The DWORD reference to a TYPEFLAG.

Return Value

The return value obtained from the returned HRESULT is one of the following:

Return value	Meaning
S_OK	Success.
E_OUTOFMEMORY	Out of memory.
E_INVALIDARG	One or more of the arguments is invalid.

Example   `HRESULT ITypeInfo2::GetTypeFlags(DWORD * pTypeFlags)`

ITypeInfo2::GetFuncIndexOfMemId

HRESULT GetFuncIndexOfMemId(
MEMBERID *memid*,
INVOKEKIND *invKind*,
unsigned int **pFuncIndex*
);

Binds to a specific member based on a known DISPID, where the member name is not known (for example, when binding to a default member).

Parameter   *memid*
    Member identifier.

invKind
    Invoke kind.

pFuncIndex
    Returns an index into the function.

Return Value   The return value obtained from the returned HRESULT is one of the following:

Return value	Meaning
S_OK	Success.
E_OUTOFMEMORY	Out of memory.
E_INVALIDARG	One or more of the arguments is invalid.

Example
```
ITypeInfo2::GetFuncIndexOfMemId(
MEMID memid,
INVOKEKIND invKind,
UINT * pFuncIndex)
```

ITypeInfo2::GetVarIndexOfMemId

HRESULT GetVarIndexOfMemId(
MEMBERID *memid*,

unsigned int **pVarIndex*

);

Binds to a specific member based on a known DISPID, where the member name is not known (for example, when binding to a default member).

Parameters

memid
    Member identifier.

pVarIndex
    Returns the index.

Return Value

The return value obtained from the returned HRESULT is one of the following:

Return value	Meaning
S_OK	Success.
E_OUTOFMEMORY	Out of memory.
E_INVALIDARG	One or more of the arguments is invalid.

Example

ITypeInfo2::GetVarIndexOfMemId(MEMID memid, UINT * pvarIndex)

ITypeInfo2::GetCustData

HRESULT GetCustData(
REFGUID *guid*,

VARIANT **pVarVal*

);

Gets the custom data.

Parameters

guid
    GUID used to identify the data.

pVarVal
    Where to put the retrieved data.

Return Value   The return value obtained from the returned HRESULT is one of the following:

Return value	Meaning
S_OK	Success.
E_OUTOFMEMORY	Out of memory.
E_INVALIDARG	One or more of the arguments is invalid.

ITypeInfo2::GetAllCustData

HRESULT
CUSTDATA *pCustData*
);

Gets all custom data items for the library.

Parameters   *pCustData*
    Returns a pointer to CUSTDATA (that holds all custom data items).

Return Value   The return value obtained from the returned HRESULT is one of the following:

Return value	Meaning
S_OK	Success.
E_OUTOFMEMORY	Out of memory.
E_INVALIDARG	One or more of the arguments is invalid.

Comments   After the call, the caller needs to release memory used to hold the custom data item by calling **ClearCustData**.

ITypeInfo2::GetAllFuncCustData

HRESULT
unsigned int *index*
CUSTDATA *pCustData*
);

Gets all custom data from the specified function.

Parameters   *index*
                        The index of the function for which to get the custom data.

                        pCustData
                        Returns a pointer to CUSTDATA (that holds all custom data items).

Return Value   The return value obtained from the returned HRESULT is one of the following:

Return value	Meaning
S_OK	Success.
E_OUTOFMEMORY	Out of memory.
E_INVALIDARG	One or more of the arguments is invalid.

Comments   After the call, the caller needs to release memory used to hold the custom data item by calling **ClearCustData**.

ITypeInfo2::GetAllImplTypeCustData

HRESULT GetAllImplTypeCustData(
unsigned int *index*,
CUSTDATA **pCustData*
);

Gets all custom data for the specified implementation type.

Parameters   *index*
                        Index of the implementation type for the custom data.

                        pCustData
                        Returns a pointer to CUSTDATA (that holds all custom data items).

Return Value   The return value obtained from the returned HRESULT is one of the following:

Return value	Meaning
S_OK	Success.
E_OUTOFMEMORY	Out of memory.
E_INVALIDARG	One or more of the arguments is invalid.

ITypeInfo2::GetAllParamCustData

HRESULT GetAllParamCustData(
unsigned int *indexFunc,*
unsigned int *indexParam,*
CUSTDATA **pCustData*
);

Gets all of the custom data for the specified function parameter.

Parameters   *indexFunc*
Index of the function for which to get the custom data.

IndexParam
Index of the parameter of this function for which to get the custom data.

pCustData
Returns a pointer to CUSTDATA (that holds all custom data items).

Return Value   The return value obtained from the returned HRESULT is one of the following:

Return value	Meaning
S_OK	Success.
E_OUTOFMEMORY	Out of memory.
E_INVALIDARG	One or more of the arguments is invalid.

ITypeInfo2::GetAllVarCustData

HRESULT GetAllVarCustData(
unsigned int *index,*
CUSTDATA **pCustData*
);

Gets the variable for the custom data.

Parameters   *index*
Index of the variable for which to get the custom data.

pCustData
Returns a pointer to CUSTDATA (that holds all custom data items).

Return Value
The return value obtained from the returned HRESULT is one of the following:

Return value	Meaning
S_OK	Success.
E_OUTOFMEMORY	Out of memory.
E_INVALIDARG	One or more of the arguments is invalid.

ITypeInfo2::GetFuncCustData

HRESULT GetFuncCustData(
unsigned int *index*,
REFGUID *guid*,
VARIANT **pVarVal*
);

Gets the custom data from the specified function.

Parameters
index
    The index of the function for which to get the custom data.

guid
    The GUID used to identify the data.

pVarVal
    Where to put the data.

Return Value
The return value obtained from the returned HRESULT is one of the following:

Return value	Meaning
S_OK	Success.
E_OUTOFMEMORY	Out of memory.
E_INVALIDARG	One or more of the arguments is invalid.

ITypeInfo2::GetParamCustData

HRESULT GetParamCustData(
unsigned int *indexFunc*,
unsigned int *indexParam*,
REFGUID *guid*,
VARIANT **pVarVal*
);

Gets the specified custom data parameter.

Parameters

indexFunc
Index of the function for which to get the custom data.

IndexParam
Index of the parameter of this function for which to get the custom data.

guid
GUID used to identify the data.

pVarVal
Where to put the retrieved data.

Return Value

The return value obtained from the returned HRESULT is one of the following:

Return value	Meaning
S_OK	Success.
E_OUTOFMEMORY	Out of memory.
E_INVALIDARG	One or more of the arguments is invalid.

ITypeInfo2::GetVarCustData

HRESULT GetVarCustData(
unsigned int *index*,
REFGUID *guid*,
VARIANT **pVarVal*
);

Gets the variable for the custom data.

Parameters	*index* Index of the variable for which to get the custom data. *guid* GUID used to identify the data. *PVarVal* Where to put the retrieved data.

Return Value   The return value obtained from the returned HRESULT is one of the following:

Return value	Meaning
S_OK	Success.
E_OUTOFMEMORY	Out of memory.
E_INVALIDARG	One or more of the arguments is invalid.

ITypeInfo2::GetImplTypeCustData

HRESULT GetImplTypeCustData(
unsigned int *index,*
REFGUID *guid,*
VARIANT **pVarVal*
);

Gets the implementation type of the custom data.

Parameters   *index*
Index of the implementation type for the custom data.

guid
GUID used to identify the data.

pVarVal
Where to put the retrieved data.

Return Value   The return value obtained from the returned HRESULT is one of the following:

Return value	Meaning
S_OK	Success.
E_OUTOFMEMORY	Out of memory.
E_INVALIDARG	One or more of the arguments is invalid.

ITypeInfo2::GetDocumentation2

HRESULT GetDocumentation2(
[in] MEMID *memid,*
[in] LCID *lcid,*
[out] BSTR FAR* *pbstrHelpString,*
[out] unsigned long FAR* *pdwHelpStringContext,*
BSTR FAR* *pbstrHelpStringDll*
);

Retrieves the documentation string, the complete Help file name and path, the localization context to use, and the context ID for the library Help topic in the Help file.

Parameters

memid
Member identifier for the type description.

lcid
Locale identifier (LCID).

pbstrHelpString
Returns a BSTR that contains the name of the specified item. If the caller does not need the item name, then *pbstrHelpString* can be Null.

pdwHelpStringContext
Returns the Help localization context. If the caller does not need the Help context, it can be Null.

pbstrHelpStringDll
Returns a BSTR that contains the fully qualified name of the file containing the DLL used for Help file. If the caller does not need the file name, it can be Null.

Return Value

The return value obtained from the returned HRESULT is one of the following:

Return value	Meaning
S_OK	Success.
STG_E_INSUFFICIENTMEMORY	Out of memory.
E_INVALIDARG	One or more of the arguments is invalid.
TYPE_E_IOERROR	The function could not write to the file.
TYPE_E_INVDATAREAD	The function could not read from the file.
TYPE_E_UNSUPFORMAT	The type library has an older format.

Return value	Meaning
TYPE_E_INVALIDSTATE	The type library could not be opened.
TYPE_E_ELEMENTNOTFOUND	The element was not found.

Comments   Gets information at the type information level (about the type information and its members). The caller should free the BSTR parameters.

This function will call **_DLLGetDocumentation** in the specified DLL to retrieve the desired Help string, if there is a Help string context for this item. If no Help string context exists or an error occurs, then it will defer to the **GetDocumentation** method and return the associated documentation string.

ITypeComp Interface

The **ITypeComp** interface provides a fast way to access information that compilers need when binding to and instantiating structures and interfaces. Binding is the process of mapping names to types and type members.

Implemented by	Used by	Header file name
Oleaut32.dll (32-bit systems)	Tools that need to access the descriptions of objects contained in type libraries.	Oleauto.h
Typelib.dll (16-bit systems)		Dispatch.h

ITypeComp::Bind

HRESULT Bind(
OLECHAR FAR* *szName***,**
unsigned long *lHashVal***,**
unsigned short *wFlags***,**
ITypeInfo FAR*FAR* *ppTInfo***,**
DESCKIND FAR* *pDescKind***,**
BINDPTR FAR* *pBindPtr*
);

Maps a name to a member of a type, or binds global variables and functions contained in a type library.

Parameters

szName
    Name to be bound.

lHashVal
    Hash value for the name computed by **LHashValOfNameSys**.

wFlags
    Flags word containing one or more of the **Invoke** flags defined in the
    INVOKEKIND enumeration. Specifies whether the name was referenced as a
    method or a property. When binding to a variable, specify the flag
    INVOKE_PROPERTYGET. Specify zero to bind to any type of member.

ppTInfo
    If a FUNCDESC or VARDESC was returned, then *ppTInfo* points to a pointer to
    the type description that contains the item to which it is bound.

pDescKind
    Pointer to a DESCKIND enumerator that indicates whether the name bound to is a
    VARDESC, FUNCDESC, or TYPECOMP. If there was no match, points to
    DESCKIND_NONE.

pBindPtr
    On return, contains a pointer to the bound-to VARDESC, FUNCDESC, or
    ITypeComp interface.

Return Value

The return value obtained from the returned HRESULT is one of the following:

Return value	Meaning
S_OK	Success.
E_OUTOFMEMORY	Out of memory.
E_INVALIDARG	One or more of the arguments is invalid.
TYPE_E_IOERROR	The function could not read from the file.
TYPE_E_INVDATAREAD	Invalid data.
TYPE_E_UNSUPFORMAT	The type library has an older format.
TYPE_E_INVALIDSTATE	The type library could not be opened.
TYPE_E_AMBIGUOUSNAME	More than one instance of this name occurs in the type library.

Comments

Use **Bind** for binding to the variables and methods of a type, or for binding to the
global variables and methods in a type library. The returned DESCKIND pointer
pDescKind indicates whether the name was bound to a VARDESC, a FUNCDESC, or
to an **ITypeComp** instance. The returned *pBindPtr* points to the VARDESC,
FUNCDESC, or **ITypeComp**.

If a data member or method is bound to, then *ppTInfo* points to the type description
that contains the method or data member.

If **Bind** binds the name to a nested binding context, it returns a pointer to an **ITypeComp** instance in *pBindPtr* and a Null type description pointer in *ppTInfo*. For example, if the name of a type description is passed for a module (TKIND_MODULE), enumeration (TKIND_ENUM), or coclass (TKIND_COCLASS), **Bind** returns the **ITypeComp** instance of the type description for the module, enumeration, or coclass. This feature supports languages such as Visual Basic that allow references to members of a type description to be qualified by the name of the type description. For example, a function in a module can be referenced by *modulename.functionname*.

The members of TKIND_ENUM, TKIND_MODULE, and TKIND_COCLASS types marked as Application objects can be bound to directly from **ITypeComp,** without specifying the name of the module. The **ITypeComp** of a coclass defers to the **ITypeComp** of its default interface.

As with other methods of **ITypeComp, ITypeInfo,** and **ITypeLib,** the calling code is responsible for releasing the returned object instances or structures. If a VARDESC or FUNCDESC is returned, the caller is responsible for deleting it with the returned type description and releasing the type description instance itself. Otherwise, if an **ITypeComp** instance is returned, the caller must release it.

Special rules apply if you call a type library's **Bind** method, passing it the name of a member of an Application object class (a class that has the TYPEFLAG_FAPPOBJECT flag set). In this case, **Bind** returns DESCKIND_IMPLICITAPPOBJ in *pDescKind,* a VARDESC that describes the Application object in *pBindPtr*, and the **ITypeInfo** of the Application object class in *ppTInfo*. To bind to the object, **ITypeInfo::GetTypeComp** must make a call to get the **ITypeComp** of the Application object class, and then reinvoke its **Bind** method with the name initially passed to the type library's **ITypeComp.**

The caller should use the returned **ITypeInfo** pointer (*ppTInfo*) to get the address of the member.

Note   The *wflags* parameter is the same as the *wflags* parameter in **IDispatch::Invoke.**

ITypeComp::BindType

HRESULT BindType(
OLECHAR FAR* *szName,*
unsigned long *lHashVal,*
ITypeInfo FAR* FAR* *ppTInfo,*
ITypeComp FAR* FAR* *ppTComp*
);

Binds to the type descriptions contained within a type library.

Parameters

szName
Name to be bound.

lHashVal
Hash value for the name computed by **LHashValOfName**.

ppTInfo
On return, contains a pointer to a pointer to an **ITypeInfo** of the type to which the name was bound.

ppTComp
Passes a valid pointer, such as the address of an **ITypeComp*** variable.

Return Value

The return value obtained from the returned HRESULT is one of the following:

Return value	Meaning
S_OK	Success.
E_OUTOFMEMORY	Out of memory.
E_INVALIDARG	One or more of the arguments is invalid.
TYPE_E_IOERROR	The function could not read from the file.
TYPE_E_INVDATAREAD	Invalid data.
TYPE_E_UNSUPFORMAT	The type library has an older format.
TYPE_E_INVALIDSTATE	The type library could not be opened.
TYPE_E_AMBIGUOUSNAME	More than one instance of this name occurs in the type library.

Comments

Use the function **BindType** for binding a type name to the **ITypeInfo** that describes the type. This function is invoked on the **ITypeComp** that is returned by **ITypeLib::GetTypeComp** to bind to types defined within that library. It can also be used in the future for binding to nested types.

Example

```
TypeComp * ptcomp;
        ptemp -> BindType(szName, lhashval, &ptinfo, &ptemp)
```

Overview of Type Compilation and Library Functions

The functions for loading, registering, and querying type libraries are provided by Oleaut32.dll (for 32-bit systems) and Typelib.dll (for 16-bit systems).

Category	Function name	Purpose
Library loading	**LoadTypeLib**	Loads and registers a type library.
	LoadRegTypeLib	Uses registry information to load a type library.
Library registration	**RegisterTypeLib**	Adds information about a type library to the system registry.
	UnRegisterTypeLib	Removes type library information added through **RegisterTypeLib** to allow uninstall procedures.
	LoadTypeLibEx	Loads a type library and (optionally) registers it in the system registry
	QueryPathOfRegTypeLib	Retrieves the path of a registered type library.
Type compilation	**LHashValOfNameSys** **LHashValOfName**	Computes a hash value for a name that can then be passed to **ITypeComp::Bind**, **ITypeComp::BindType**, **ITypeLib::IsName**, or **ITypeLib::FindName**.

LHashValOfName

HRESULT LHashValOfName(
LCID *lcid*,
OLECHAR FAR* *szName*
);

Computes a hash value for a name that can then be passed to ITypeComp::Bind, ITypeComp::BindType, ITypeLib::FindName, or ITypeLib::IsName.

Parameters

lcid
The LCID for the string.

szName
String whose hash value is to be computed.

Return Value

A 32-bit hash value that represents the passed-in name.

Comments

This function is equivalent to **LHashValOfNameSys**. The header file Oleauto.h contains macros that define **LHashValOfName** as **LHashValOfNameSys,** with the target operating system (*syskind*) based on the build preprocessor flags.

LHashValOfName computes a 32-bit hash value for a name that can be passed to **ITypeComp::Bind, ITypeComp::BindType, ITypeLib::FindName,** or **ITypeLib::IsName**. The returned hash value is independent of the case of the characters in *szName*, as long as the language of the name is one of the languages supported by the OLE National Language Specification API. Any two strings that match when a case-insensitive comparison is done using any language produce the same hash value.

LHashValOfNameSys

ULONG LHashValOfNameSys(
SYSKIND *syskind*,
LCID *lcid*,
OLECHAR FAR* *szName*
);

Computes a hash value for a name that can then be passed to **ITypeComp::Bind**, **ITypeComp::BindType**, **ITypeLib::FindName**, or **ITypeLib::IsName**.

Parameters   *syskind*
                       The SYSKIND of the target operating system.

                    lcid
                       The LCID for the string.

                    szName
                       String whose hash value is to be computed.

Return Value   A 32-bit hash value that represents the passed-in name.

LoadTypeLib

HRESULT LoadTypeLib(
OLECHAR FAR* *szFile,*
ITypeLib FAR* FAR* *pptlib*
);

Loads and registers a type library.

Parameters   *szFile*
                       Contains the name of the file from which **LoadTypeLib** should attempt to load a
                       type library.

                    pptlib
                       On return, contains a pointer to a pointer to the loaded type library.

Return Value   The return value obtained from the returned HRESULT is one of the following:

Return value	Meaning
S_OK	Success.
E_OUTOFMEMORY	Out of memory.
E_INVALIDARG	One or more of the arguments is invalid.
TYPE_E_IOERROR	The function could not write to the file.
TYPE_E_INVALIDSTATE	The type library could not be opened.
TYPE_E_INVDATAREAD	The function could not read from the file.

Return value	Meaning
TYPE_E_UNSUPFORMAT	The type library has an older format.
TYPE_E_UNKNOWNLCID	The LCID could not be found in the OLE-supported DLLs.
TYPE_E_CANTLOADLIBRARY	The type library or DLL could not be loaded.
Other return codes	All FACILITY_STORAGE errors can be returned.

Comments   The function **LoadTypeLib** loads a type library (usually created with MkTypLib) that is stored in the specified file. If *szFile* specifies only a file name without any path, **LoadTypeLib** searches for the file and proceeds as follows:

- If the file is a stand-alone type library implemented by Typelib.dll, the library is loaded directly.

- If the file is a DLL or an executable file, it is loaded. By default, the type library is extracted from the first resource of type **ITypeLib**. To load a different type of library resource, append an integer index to *szFile*. For example:

```
LoadTypeLib("C:\MONTANA\EXE\MFA.EXE\3", pptlib)
```
This statement loads the type library resource 3 from the file Mfa.exe file.

- If the file is none of the above, the file name is parsed into a moniker (an object that represents a file-based link source), and then bound to the moniker. This approach allows **LoadTypeLib** to be used on foreign type libraries, including in-memory type libraries. Foreign type libraries cannot reside in a DLL or an executable file. For more information on monikers, see the *OLE Programmer's Reference* in the Win32 SDK.

If the type library is already loaded, **LoadTypeLib** increments the type library's reference count and returns a pointer to the type library.

For backward compatibility, **LoadTypeLib** will register the type library if the path is not specified in the *szFile* parameter. **LoadTypeLib** will not register the type library if the path of the type library is specified. It is recommended that **RegisterTypeLib** be used to register a type library.

LoadTypeLibEx

HRESULT LoadTypeLibEx(
LPCOLESTR *szFile,*
REGKIND *regkind,*
ITYPELIB *pptlib*
);

Loads a type library and (optionally) registers it in the system registry.

Parameters

szFile
Specification for the type library file.

regkind
Identifies the kind of registration to perform for the type library (DEFAULT, REGISTER, or NONE).

pptlib
Reference to the type library being loaded.

Return Value

The return value obtained from the returned HRESULT is one of the following:

Return value	Meaning
S_OK	Success.
E_OUTOFMEMORY	Out of memory.
E_INVALIDARG	One or more of the arguments is invalid.
TYPE_E_IOERROR	The function could not write to the file.
TYPE_E_REGISTRYACCESS	The system registration database could not be opened.
TYPE_E_INVALIDSTATE	The type library could not be opened.

Comments

Enables programmers to specify whether or not the type library should be loaded.

Example

```
typedef enum tagREGKIND
{
    REGKIND_DEFAULT,
    REGKIND_REGISTER,
    REGKIND_NONE
} REGKIND;
```

LoadRegTypeLib

HRESULT LoadRegTypeLib(
REFGUID *rguid*,

unsigned short *wVerMajor*,

unsigned short *wVerMinor*,

LCID *lcid*,

ITypeLib FAR* FAR* *pptlib*

);

Uses registry information to load a type library.

Parameters
rguid
    The GUID of the library being loaded.

wVerMajor
    Major version number of the library being loaded.

wVerMinor
    Minor version number of the library being loaded.

lcid
    National language code of the library being loaded.

pptlib
    On return, points to a pointer to the loaded type library.

Return Value
The return value obtained from the returned HRESULT is one of the following:

Return value	Meaning
S_OK	Success.
E_OUTOFMEMORY	Out of memory.
E_INVALIDARG	One or more of the arguments is invalid.
TYPE_E_IOERROR	The function could not read from the file.
TYPE_E_INVALIDSTATE	The type library could not be opened.
TYPE_E_INVDATAREAD	The function could not read from the file.
TYPE_E_UNSUPFORMAT	The type library has an older format.

Return value	Meaning
TYPE_E_UNKNOWNLCID	The passed in LCID could not be found in the OLE-supported DLLs.
TYPE_E_CANTLOADLIBRARY	The type library or DLL could not be loaded.
Other return codes	All FACILITY_STORAGE and system registry errors can also be returned.

Comments

The function **LoadRegTypeLib** defers to **LoadTypeLib** to load the file.

LoadRegTypeLib compares the requested version numbers against those found in the system registry, and takes one of the following actions:

- If one of the registered libraries exactly matches both the requested major and minor version numbers, then that type library is loaded.

- If one or more registered type libraries exactly match the requested major version number, and has a greater minor version number than that requested, the one with the greatest minor version number is loaded.

- If none of the registered type libraries exactly match the requested major version number (or if none of those that do exactly match the major version number also have a minor version number greater than or equal to the requested minor version number), then **LoadRegTypeLib** returns an error.

RegisterTypeLib

HRESULT RegisterTypeLib(
ITypeLib FAR* *ptlib,*
OLECHAR FAR* *szFullPath,*
OLECHAR FAR* *szHelpDir*
);

Adds information about a type library to the system registry.

Parameters

ptlib
Pointer to the type library being registered.

szFullPath
Fully qualified path specification for the type library being registered.

szHelpDir
Directory in which the Help file for the library being registered can be found. Can be Null.

Return Value

The return value obtained from the returned HRESULT is one of the following:

Return value	Meaning
S_OK	Success.
E_OUTOFMEMORY	Out of memory.
E_INVALIDARG	One or more of the arguments is invalid.
TYPE_E_IOERROR	The function could not write to the file.
TYPE_E_REGISTRYACCESS	The system registration database could not be opened.
TYPE_E_INVALIDSTATE	The type library could not be opened.

Comments

The function **RegisterTypeLib** can be used during application initialization to register the application's type library correctly.

In addition to filling in a complete registry entry under the type library key, **RegisterTypeLib** adds entries for each of the dispinterfaces and Automation-compatible interfaces, including dual interfaces. This information is required to create instances of these interfaces. Coclasses are not registered (that is, **RegisterTypeLib** does not write any values to the CLSID key of the coclass).

UnRegisterTypeLib

> **HRESULT UnRegisterTypeLib(**
> **REFGUID** *libID,*
> **unsigned short** *wVerMajor,*
> **unsigned short** *wVerMinor,*
> **LCID** *lcid,*
> **SYSKIND** *syskind*
> **);**

Removes type library information from the system registry. Use this API to allow applications to properly uninstall themselves. In-process objects typically call this API from **DllUnregisterServer**.

Parameters

libID
    Globally unique identifier.

wVerMajor
    Major version number of the type library being removed.

wVerMinor
    Minor version number of the type library being removed.

lcid
　　Locale identifier.

syskind
　　The target operating system (SYSKIND).

Return Value　　The return value obtained from the returned HRESULT is one of the following:

Return value	Meaning
S_OK	Success.
E_OUTOFMEMORY	Out of memory.
E_INVALIDARG	One or more of the arguments is invalid.
TYPE_E_IOERROR	The function could not write to the file.
TYPE_E_REGISTRYACCESS	The system registration database could not be opened.
TYPE_E_INVALIDSTATE	The type library could not be opened.

Comments　　In-process objects typically call this API from **DllUnregisterServer**.

QueryPathOfRegTypeLib

HRESULT QueryPathOfRegTypeLib(
REFGUID *guid,*
unsigned short *wVerMajor,*
unsigned short *wVerMinor,*
LCID *lcid,*
LPBSTR *lpbstrPathName*
);

Retrieves the path of a registered type library.

Parameters　　*guid*
　　GUID of the library whose path is to be queried.

wVerMajor
　　Major version number of the library whose path is to be queried.

wVerMinor
　　Minor version number of the library whose path is to be queried.

lcid

National language code for the library whose path is to be queried.

lpbstrPathName

Caller-allocated BSTR in which the type library name is returned.

Return Value

The return value obtained from the returned HRESULT is one of the following:

Return value	Meaning
S_OK	Success.

Comments

Returns the fully qualified file name that is specified for the type library in the registry. The caller allocates the BSTR that is passed in, and must free it after use.

C H A P T E R   1 0

Type Building Interfaces

The type building interfaces, **ICreateTypeInfo, ICreateTypeInfo2, ICreateTypeLib** and **ICreateTypeLib2**, are used to build tools that automate the process of generating type descriptions and creating type libraries. The MkTypLib utility and the Microsoft Interface Definition Language (MIDL) compiler, for example, use these interfaces to create type libraries. For more information about type libraries, refer to Chapter 8, "Type Libraries and the Object Description Language."

Generally, it is not necessary to write custom implementations of these interfaces. The compilers use the default implementations that are returned by the **CreateTypeLib** function. To create tools similar to MkTypLib, the default implementations can be called.

Implemented by	Used by	Header file name	Import library name
Oleaut32.dll (32-bit systems)	Applications that expose programmable objects.	Oleauto.h	Oleaut32.lib
Typelib.dll (16-bit systems)		Dispatch.h	Typelib.lib

Overview of Type Building Interfaces

The type building interfaces include the following member functions:

Interface	Member function	Purpose
ICreateTypeInfo	**AddFuncDesc**	Adds a function description as a type description.
	AddImplType	Specifies an inherited interface.

Interface	Member function	Purpose
ICreateTypeInfo	**AddRefTypeInfo**	Adds a type description to those referenced by the type description being created.
	AddVarDesc	Adds a data member description as a type description.
	DefineFuncAsDllEntry	Associates a dynamic-link library (DLL) entry point with a function that has a specified index.
	LayOut	Assigns virtual function table (VTBL) offsets for virtual functions and instance offsets for per-instance data members.
	SetAlignment	Specifies data alignment for types of TKIND_RECORD.
	SetDocString	Sets the documentation string displayed by type browsers.
	SetFuncAndParamNames	Sets the function name and names of its parameters.
	SetFuncDocString	Sets the documentation string for a function.
	SetFuncHelpContext	Sets the Help context identifier (ID) for a function.
	SetGuid	Sets the globally unique identifier (GUID) for the type library.
	SetHelpContext	Sets the Help context ID of the type description.
	SetImplTypeFlags	Sets the attributes for an implemented or inherited interface of a type.
	SetMops	Sets the *opcode* string for a type description.

Interface	Member function	Purpose
	SetTypeDescAlias	Sets the type description for which this type description is an alias, if TYPEKIND=TKIND_ALIAS.
	SetTypeFlags	Sets type flags of the type description that is being created.
	SetVarDocString	Sets the documentation string for a variable.
	SetVarHelpContext	Sets the Help context ID for a variable.
	SetVarName	Sets the name of a variable.
	SetVersion	Sets version numbers for the type description.
ICreateTypeInfo2	DeleteFuncDesc	Deletes a function description specified by the index number.
	DeleteFuncDescByMemId	Deletes the function description specified by *memid*.
	DeleteVarDesc	Deletes the specified VARDESC structure.
	DeleteVarDescByMemId	Deletes the specified VARDESC structure.
	DeleteImplType	Deletes the IMPLTYPE flags for the indexed interface.
	SetCustData	Sets a value for custom data.
	SetHelpStringContext	Sets the context number for the specified Help string.
	SetFuncCustData	Sets a value for a specified custom function.
	SetFuncHelpStringContext	Sets a Help context value for a specified custom function.
	SetName	Sets the name of the typeinfo.

Interface	Member function	Purpose
ICreateTypeInfo2	SetVarCustData	Sets a custom data variable.
	SetParamCustData	Sets the specified parameter for the custom data.
	SetImplTypeCustData	Sets the implementation type for custom data.
	SetVarHelpStringContext	Sets a Help context value for a specified variable.
ICreateTypeLib	CreateTypeInfo	Creates a new type description instance within the type library.
	SaveAllChanges	Saves the **ICreateTypeLib** instance.
	SetDocString	Sets the documentation string for the type library.
	SetGuid	Sets the GUID for the type library.
	SetHelpContext	Sets the Help context ID for general information about the type library in the Help file.
	SetHelpFileName	Sets the Help file name.
	SetLcid	Sets the locale identifier (LCID) code indicating the national language associated with the library.
	SetLibFlags	Sets library flags, such as LIBFLAG_FRESTRICTED.
	SetName	Sets the name of the type library.
	SetVersion	Sets major and minor version numbers for the type library.

Interface	Member function	Purpose
ICreateTypeLib2	**DeleteTypeInfo**	Deletes a specified type information from the type library.
	SetCustData	Sets a value to custom data.
	SetHelpStringContext	Sets the Help string context number.
	SetHelpStringDll	Sets the DLL name to be used for Help string lookup.
	SetName	Sets the name of the type library.

You create an Automation type library by using the **ICreateTypeLib** and **ICreateTypeInfo** interfaces.

In the following example, a type library is created (Hello.tlb) by the MIDL compiler (or MkTypLib.exe), using the following .odl file.

```
[
uuid(2F6CA420-C641-101A-B826-00DD01103DE1),          // LIBID_Hello.
helpstring("Hello 1.0 Type Library"),
lcid(0x0409),
version(1.0)
]
library Hello
{
#ifdef WIN32
importlib("stdole32.tlb");
#else
importlib("stdole.tlb");
#endif


[
uuid(2F6CA422-C641-101A-B826-00DD01103DE1),          // IID_Ihello.
helpstring("Hello Interface")
]
interface IHello : IUnknown
{
[propput] void HelloMessage([in] BSTR Message);
[propget] BSTR HelloMessage(void);
void SayHello(void);
}
```

```
[
uuid(2F6CA423-C641-101A-B826-00DD01103DE1),          // IID_Dhello.
helpstring("Hello Dispinterface")
]
dispinterface DHello
{
interface IHello;
}


 [
uuid(2F6CA421-C641-101A-B826-00DD01103DE1),          // CLSID_Hello.
helpstring("Hello Class")
]
coclass Hello
{
dispinterface DHello;
interface IHello;
}
}
```

Type Information Interfaces and Functions

There are two type information interfaces: **ICreateTypeInfo** and **ICreateTypeInfo2**

ICreateTypeInfo Interface

The **ICreateTypeInfo** interface provides the tools for creating and administering the type information defined through the type description.

ICreateTypeInfo::AddFuncDesc

HRESULT AddFuncDesc(
unsigned int *index,*
FUNCDESC FAR* *pFuncDesc*
);

Adds a function description to the type description.

Parameters

index
    Index of the new FUNCDESC in the type information.

pFuncDesc
    Pointer to a FUNCDESC structure that describes the function. The *bstrIDLInfo* field in the FUNCDESC should be set to Null for future compatibility.

Return Value

The return value of the returned HRESULT is one of the following:

Return value	Meaning
S_OK	Success.
STG_E_INSUFFICIENTMEMORY	Out of memory.
E_OUTOFMEMORY	Out of memory.
E_INVALIDARG	One or more of the arguments is invalid.
E_ACCESSDENIED	Cannot write to the destination.
TYPE_E_WRONGTYPEKIND	Type mismatch.

Comments

The index specifies the order of the functions within the type information. The first function has an index of zero. If an index is specified that exceeds one less than the number of functions in the type information, an error is returned. Calling this function does not pass ownership of the FUNCDESC structure to **ICreateTypeInfo**. Therefore, the caller must still de-allocate the FUNCDESC structure.

The passed-in virtual function table (VTBL) field (*oVft*) of the FUNCDESC is ignored. This attribute is set when **ICreateTypeInfo::LayOut** is called.

The function **AddFuncDesc** uses the passed-in member identifier (ID) fields within each FUNCDESC for classes with TYPEKIND = TKIND_DISPATCH or TKIND_INTERFACE. If the member IDs are set to MEMBERID_NIL, **AddFuncDesc** assigns member IDs to the functions. Otherwise, the member ID fields within each FUNCDESC are ignored.

Any HREFTYPE fields in the FUNCDESC structure must have been produced by the same instance of **ITypeInfo** for which **AddFuncDesc** is called.

The **get** and **put** accessor functions for the same property must have the same dispatch identifier (DISPID).

ICreateTypeInfo::AddImplType

HRESULT AddImplType(
unsigned int *index,*
HREFTYPE *hRefType*
);

Specifies an inherited interface, or an interface implemented by a component object class (coclass).

Parameters	*index*
	Index of the implementation class to be added. Specifies the order of the type relative to the other type.
	hRefType
	Handle to the referenced type description obtained from the **AddRefType** description.
Return Value	The return value of the returned HRESULT is one of the following:

Return value	Meaning
S_OK	Success.
STG_E_INSUFFICIENTMEMORY	Out of memory.
E_OUTOFMEMORY	Out of memory.
E_ACCESSDENIED	Cannot write to the destination.
TYPE_E_WRONGTYPEKIND	Type mismatch.

Comments   To specify an inherited interface, use *index* = 0. For a dispinterface with Syntax 2, call **ICreateTypeInfo::AddImplType** twice, once with *nindex* = 0 for the inherited **IDispatch** and once with *nindex* = 1 for the interface that is being wrapped. For a dual interface, call **ICreateTypeInfo::AddImplType** with *nindex* = -1 for the TKIND_INTERFACE type information component of the dual interface.

ICreateTypeInfo::AddRefTypeInfo

HRESULT AddRefTypeInfo(
ITypeInfo FAR* *pTInfo***,**
HREFTYPE FAR* *phRefType*
);

Adds a type description to those referenced by the type description being created.

Parameters	*pTInfo*
	Pointer to the type description to be referenced.
	phRefType
	On return, pointer to the handle that this type description associates with the referenced type information.
Return Value	The return value of the returned HRESULT is one of the following:

Return value	Meaning
S_OK	Success.
STG_E_INSUFFICIENTMEMORY	Out of memory.
E_OUTOFMEMORY	Out of memory.
E_INVALIDARG	One or more of the arguments is invalid.
E_ACCESSDENIED	Cannot write to the destination.
TYPE_E_WRONGTYPEKIND	Type mismatch.

Comments   The second parameter returns a pointer to the handle of the added type information. If **AddRefTypeInfo** has been called previously for the same type information, the index that was returned by the previous call is returned in *phRefType*. If the referenced type description is in the type library being created, its type information can be obtained by calling **IUnknown::QueryInterface**(IID_ITypeInfo, ...) on the **ICreateTypeInfo** interface of that type description.

ICreateTypeInfo::AddVarDesc

> **HRESULT AddVarDesc(**
> **unsigned int** *index,*
> **VARDESC FAR*** *pVarDesc*
> **);**

Adds a variable or data member description to the type description.

Parameters   *index*
        Index of the variable or data member to be added to the type description.

pVarDesc
        Pointer to the variable or data member description to be added.

Return Value   The return value of the returned HRESULT is one of the following:

Return value	Meaning
S_OK	Success.
STG_E_INSUFFICIENTMEMORY	Out of memory.
E_OUTOFMEMORY	Out of memory.
E_INVALIDARG	One or more of the arguments is invalid.
E_ACCESSDENIED	Cannot write to the destination.
TYPE_E_WRONGTYPEKIND	Type mismatch.

Comments   The index specifies the order of the variables. The first variable has an index of zero. **ICreateTypeInfo::AddVarDesc** returns an error if the specified index is greater than the number of variables currently in the type information. Calling this function does not pass ownership of the VARDESC structure to **ICreateTypeInfo**. The instance field (*oInst*) of the VARDESC structure is ignored. This attribute is set only when **ICreateTypeInfo::LayOut** is called. Also, the member ID fields within the VARDESCs are ignored unless the TYPEKIND of the class is TKIND_DISPATCH.

Any HREFTYPE fields in the VARDESC structure must have been produced by the same instance of **ITypeInfo** for which **AddVarDesc** is called.

AddVarDesc ignores the contents of the *idldesc* field of the ELEMDESC.

ICreateTypeInfo::DefineFuncAsDllEntry

> **HRESULT DefineFuncAsDllEntry(**
> **unsigned int** *index,*
> **OLECHAR FAR*** *szDllName,*
> **OLECHAR FAR*** *szProcName*
> **);**

Associates a DLL entry point with the function that has the specified *index*.

Parameters   *index*
　　Index of the function.

szDllName
　　Name of the DLL that contains the entry point.

szProcName
　　Name of the entry point or an ordinal (if the high word is zero).

Return Value   The return value of the returned HRESULT is one of the following:

Return value	Meaning
S_OK	Success.
STG_E_INSUFFICIENTMEMORY	Out of memory.
E_OUTOFMEMORY	Out of memory.
E_INVALIDARG	One or more of the arguments is invalid.
TYPE_E_ELEMENTNOTFOUND	The element cannot be found.
TYPE_E_WRONGTYPEKIND	Type mismatch.

Comments   If the high word of *szProcName* is zero, then the low word must contain the ordinal of
the entry point; otherwise, *szProcName* points to the zero-terminated name of the
entry point.

ICreateTypeInfo::LayOut

HRESULT LayOut();

Assigns VTBL offsets for virtual functions and instance offsets for per-instance data
members, and creates the two type descriptions for dual interfaces.

Parameters   *None*

Return Value   The return value of the returned HRESULT is one of the following:

Return value	Meaning
S_OK	Success.
STG_E_INSUFFICIENTMEMORY	Out of memory.
E_OUTOFMEMORY	Out of memory.
E_ACCESSDENIED	Cannot write to the destination.
TYPE_E_UNDEFINEDTYPE	Bound to unrecognized type.
TYPE_E_INVALIDSTATE	The state of the type library is not valid for this operation.
TYPE_E_WRONGTYPEKIND	Type mismatch.
TYPE_E_ELEMENTNOTFOUND	The element cannot be found.
TYPE_E_AMBIGUOUSNAME	More than one item exists with this name.
TYPE_E_SIZETOOBIG	The type information is too long.
TYPE_E_TYPEMISMATCH	Type mismatch.

Comments   **LayOut** also assigns member ID numbers to the functions and variables, unless the
TYPEKIND of the class is TKIND_DISPATCH. Call **LayOut** after all members of
the type information are defined, and before the type library is saved.

Use **ICreateTypeLib::SaveAllChanges** to save the type information after calling
LayOut. Other members of the **ICreateTypeInfo** interface should not be called after
calling **LayOut**.

> **Note** Different implementations of **ICreateTypeInfo** or other interfaces that create
> type information are free to assign any member ID numbers, provided that all
> members (including inherited members), have unique IDs. For examples, see the
> **ICreateTypeInfo2** interface later in this chapter.

ICreateTypeInfo::SetAlignment

HRESULT SetAlignment(
unsigned short *cbAlignment*

);

Specifies the data alignment for an item of TYPEKIND=TKIND_RECORD.

Parameter

cbAlignment
Alignment method for the type. A value of 0 indicates alignment on the 64K
boundary; 1 indicates no special alignment. For other values, *n* indicates alignment
on byte *n*.

Return Value

The return value of the returned HRESULT is one of the following:

Return value	Meaning
S_OK	Success.
STG_E_INSUFFICIENTMEMORY	Out of memory.
E_OUTOFMEMORY	Out of memory.
E_ACCESSDENIED	Cannot write to the destination.
TYPE_E_INVALIDSTATE	The state of the type library is not valid for this operation.

Comments

The alignment is the minimum of the natural alignment (for example, byte data on
byte boundaries, word data on word boundaries, and so on), and the alignment
denoted by *cbAlignment*.

ICreateTypeInfo::SetDocString

HRESULT SetDocString(
OLECHAR FAR* *pStrDoc*
);

Sets the documentation string displayed by type browsers.

Parameter *pStrDoc*
Pointer to the documentation string.

Return Value The return value of the returned HRESULT is one of the following:

Return value	Meaning
S_OK	Success.
STG_E_INSUFFICIENTMEMORY	Out of memory.
E_OUTOFMEMORY	Out of memory.
E_ACCESSDENIED	Cannot write to the destination.
TYPE_E_INVALIDSTATE	The state of the type library is not valid for this operation.

Comments The documentation string is a brief description of the type description being created.

ICreateTypeInfo::SetFuncAndParamNames

HRESULT SetFuncAndParamNames(
unsigned int *index,*
OLECHAR FAR* FAR* *rgszNames,*
unsigned int *cNames*
);

Sets the name of a function and the names of its parameters to the names in the array of pointers *rgszNames*.

Parameters   *index*
Index of the function whose function name and parameter names are to be set.

rgszNames
Array of pointers to names. The first element is the function name. Subsequent elements are names of parameters.

cNames
Number of elements in the *rgszNames* array.

Return Value   The return value of the returned HRESULT is one of the following:

Return value	Meaning
S_OK	Success.
STG_E_INSUFFICIENTMEMORY	Out of memory.
E_OUTOFMEMORY	Out of memory.
E_INVALIDARG	One or more of the arguments is invalid.
E_ACCESSDENIED	Cannot write to the destination.
TYPE_E_ELEMENTNOTFOUND	The element cannot be found.

Comments   The function **SetFuncAndParamNames** needs to be used once for each property. The last parameter for **put** and **putref** accessor functions is unnamed.

ICreateTypeInfo::SetFuncDocString

HRESULT SetFuncDocString(
unsigned int *index*,
OLECHAR FAR* *szDocString*
);

Sets the documentation string for the function with the specified *index*.

Parameters   *index*
Index of the function.

szDocString
Pointer to the documentation string.

Return Value   The return value of the returned HRESULT is one of the following:

Return value	Meaning
S_OK	Success.
STG_E_INSUFFICIENTMEMORY	Out of memory.
E_OUTOFMEMORY	Out of memory.
E_INVALIDARG	One or more of the arguments is invalid.
E_ACCESSDENIED	Cannot write to the destination.
TYPE_E_ELEMENTNOTFOUND	The element cannot be found.

Comments   The documentation string is a brief description of the function intended for use by tools such as type browsers. **SetFuncDocString** only needs to be used once for each property, because all property accessor functions are identified by one name.

ICreateTypeInfo::SetFuncHelpContext

HRESULT SetFuncHelpContext(
unsigned int *index,*
unsigned long *dwHelpContext*
);

Sets the Help context ID for the function with the specified *index*.

Parameters   *index*
Index of the function.

dwHelpContext
Help context ID for the Help topic.

Return Value   The return value of the returned HRESULT is one of the following:

Return value	Meaning
S_OK	Success.
STG_E_INSUFFICIENTMEMORY	Out of memory.
E_OUTOFMEMORY	Out of memory.
E_ACCESSDENIED	Cannot write to the destination.
TYPE_E_ELEMENTNOTFOUND	The element cannot be found.
E_INVALIDARG	One or more of the arguments is invalid.

Comments   **SetFuncHelpContext** only needs to be set once for each property, because all property accessor functions are identified by one name.

ICreateTypeInfo::SetGuid

HRESULT SetGuid(
REFGUID *guid*
);

Sets the globally unique identifier (GUID) associated with the type description.

Parameter   *guid*
                    Globally unique ID to be associated with the type description.

Return Value   The return value of the returned HRESULT is one of the following:

Return value	Meaning
S_OK	Success.
STG_E_INSUFFICIENTMEMORY	Out of memory.
E_OUTOFMEMORY	Out of memory.
E_ACCESSDENIED	Cannot write to the destination.

Comments   For an interface, this is an interface ID (IID); for a coclass, it is a class ID (CLSID).
                    For information on GUIDs, see Chapter 8, "Type Libraries and the Object Description
                    Language."

ICreateTypeInfo::SetHelpContext

HRESULT SetHelpContext(
unsigned long *dwHelpContext*
);

Sets the Help context ID of the type information.

Parameter   *dwHelpContext*
                    Handle to the Help context.

Return Value   The return value of the returned HRESULT is one of the following:

Return value	Meaning
S_OK	Success.
STG_E_INSUFFICIENTMEMORY	Out of memory.
E_OUTOFMEMORY	Out of memory.
E_INVALIDARG	One or more of the arguments is invalid.
E_ACCESSDENIED	Cannot write to the destination.

ICreateTypeInfo::SetImplTypeFlags

HRESULT SetImplTypeFlags(
unsigned int *index,*

int *implTypeFlags*

);

Sets the attributes for an implemented or inherited interface of a type.

Parameters

index
    Index of the interface for which to set type flags.

implTypeFlags
    IMPLTYPE flags to be set.

Return Value

The return value of the returned HRESULT is one of the following:

Return value	Meaning
S_OK	Success.
STG_E_INSUFFICIENTMEMORY	Out of memory.
E_OUTOFMEMORY	Out of memory.
E_INVALIDARG	One or more of the arguments is invalid.
E_ACCESSDENIED	Cannot write to the destination.

Comments

SetImplTypeFlags sets the IMPLTYPE flags for the indexed interface. For more information, see the "IMPLTYPEFLAGS" section in Chapter 9, "Type Description Interfaces."

ICreateTypeInfo::SetMops

HRESULT SetMops(
unsigned int *index*
BSTR *bstrMops*
);

Sets the marshaling *opcode* string associated with the type description or the function.

Parameters

index
Index of the member for which to set the *opcode* string. If *index* is –1, sets the *opcode* string for the type description.

bstrMops
The marshaling *opcode* string.

Return Value

The return value of the returned HRESULT is one of the following:

Return value	Meaning
S_OK	Success.
STG_E_INSUFFICIENTMEMORY	Out of memory.
E_OUTOFMEMORY	Out of memory.
E_INVALIDARG	One or more of the arguments is invalid.
E_ACCESSDENIED	Cannot write to the destination.

ICreateTypeInfo::SetTypeDescAlias

HRESULT SetTypeDescAlias(
TYPEDESC FAR* *pTDescAlias*
);

Sets the type description for which this type description is an alias, if TYPEKIND=TKIND_ALIAS.

Parameter

pTDescAlias
Pointer to a type description that describes the type for which this is an alias.

Return Value   The return value of the returned HRESULT is one of the following:

Return value	Meaning
S_OK	Success.
STG_E_INSUFFICIENTMEMORY	Out of memory.
E_OUTOFMEMORY	Out of memory.
E_INVALIDARG	One or more of the arguments is invalid.
E_ACCESSDENIED	Cannot write to the destination.
TYPE_E_WRONGTYPEKIND	Type mismatch.

Comments   To set the type for an alias, call **SetTypeDescAlias** for a type description whose TYPEKIND is TKIND_ALIAS.

ICreateTypeInfo::SetTypeFlags

HRESULT SetTypeFlags(
unsigned int *uTypeFlags*
);

Sets type flags of the type description being created.

Parameter   *uTypeFlags*
Settings for the type flags.

Return Value   The return value of the returned HRESULT is one of the following:

Return value	Meaning
S_OK	Success.
STG_E_INSUFFICIENTMEMORY	Out of memory.
E_OUTOFMEMORY	Out of memory.
E_INVALIDARG	One or more of the arguments is invalid.
E_ACCESSDENIED	Cannot write to the destination.
TYPE_E_WRONGTYPEKIND	Type mismatch.

Comments   Use **SetTypeFlags** to set the flags for the type description. For details, see the "TYPEFLAGS" section in Chapter 9, "Type Description Interfaces."

ICreateTypeInfo::SetVarDocString

HRESULT SetVarDocString(
unsigned int *index,*
OLECHAR FAR* *szDocString*
);

Sets the documentation string for the variable with the specified *index*.

Parameters

index
   Index of the variable being documented.

szDocString
   The documentation string to be set.

Return Value

The return value of the returned HRESULT is one of the following:

Return value	Meaning
S_OK	Success.
STG_E_INSUFFICIENTMEMORY	Out of memory.
E_OUTOFMEMORY	Out of memory.
E_ACCESSDENIED	Cannot write to the destination.
TYPE_E_ELEMENTNOTFOUND	The element was not found.

ICreateTypeInfo::SetVarHelpContext

HRESULT SetVarHelpContext(
unsigned int *index,*
unsigned long *dwHelpContext*
);

Sets the Help context ID for the variable with the specified *index*.

Parameters

index
   Index of the variable described by the type description.

dwHelpContext
   Handle to the Help context ID for the Help topic on the variable.

Return Value   The return value of the returned HRESULT is one of the following:

Return value	Meaning
S_OK	Success.
STG_E_INSUFFICIENTMEMORY	Out of memory.
E_OUTOFMEMORY	Out of memory.
E_ACCESSDENIED	Cannot write to the destination.
TYPE_E_ELEMENTNOTFOUND	The element cannot be found.

ICreateTypeInfo::SetVarName

HRESULT SetVarName(
unsigned int *index,*
OLECHAR FAR* *szName*
);

Sets the name of a variable.

Parameters   *index*
    Index of the variable whose name is being set.

szName
    Name for the variable.

Return Value   The return value of the returned HRESULT is one of the following:

Return value	Meaning
S_OK	Success.
STG_E_INSUFFICIENTMEMORY	Out of memory.
E_OUTOFMEMORY	Out of memory.
E_ACCESSDENIED	Cannot write to the destination.
TYPE_E_ELEMENTNOTFOUND	The element cannot be found.

ICreateTypeInfo::SetVersion

HRESULT SetVersion(wMajorVerNum, wMinorVerNum)·
unsigned short *wMajorVerNum,*

unsigned short *wMinorVerNum*

);

Sets the major and minor version number of the type information.

Parameters

wMajorVerNum
   Major version number for the type.

wMinorVerNum
   Minor version number for the type.

Return Value

The return value of the returned HRESULT is one of the following:

Return value	Meaning
S_OK	Success.
E_ACCESSDENIED	Cannot write to the destination.
TYPE_E_INVALIDSTATE	The state of the type library is not valid for this operation.

ICreateTypeInfo2 Interface

The **ICreateTypeInfo2** interface derives from **ICreateTypeInfo,** and adds methods for deleting items that have been added through **ICreateTypeInfo**.

The **ICreateTypeInfo::LayOut** method provides a way for the creator of the type information to check for any errors. A call to **QueryInterface** can be made to the **ICreateTypeInfo** instance at any time for its **ITypeInfo** interface. Calling any of the methods in the **ITypeInfo** interface that require layout information lays out the type information automatically.

Example

```
interface ICreateTypeInfo2 : ICreateTypeInfo
```

ICreateTypeInfo2::SetName

HRESULT SetName(
OLECHAR FAR* *szName*
);

Sets the name of the typeinfo.

Parameter

szName
    Name to be assigned to the typeinfo.

Return Value

The return value of the returned HRESULT is one of the following:

Return value	Meaning
S_OK	Success.
STG_E_INSUFFICIENTMEMORY	Out of memory.
E_OUTOFMEMORY	Out of memory.
E_INVALIDARG	One or more of the arguments is invalid.
TYPE_E_INVALIDSTATE	The state of the type info is not valid for this operation.

ICreateTypeInfo2::DeleteFuncDesc

HRESULT DeleteFuncDesc(
unsigned int *index*
);

Deletes a function description specified by the index number.

Parameter

index
    Index of the function whose description is to be deleted. The index should be in the range of 0 to 1 less than the number of functions in this type.

Return Value

The return value obtained from the returned HRESULT is one of the following:

Return value	Meaning
S_OK	Success.
E_OUTOFMEMORY	Out of memory.
E_INVALIDARG	One or more of the arguments is invalid.

ICreateTypeInfo2::DeleteFuncDescByMemId

HRESULT DeleteFuncDescByMemId(
MEMBERID *memid,*
INVOKEKIND *invKind*
);

Deletes the function description (FUNCDESC) specified by *memid*.

Parameters   *memid*
Member identifier of the FUNCDESC to delete.

invKind
The type of the invocation.

Return Value   The return value obtained from the returned HRESULT is one of the following:

Return value	Meaning
S_OK	Success.
E_OUTOFMEMORY	Out of memory.
E_INVALIDARG	One or more of the arguments is invalid.

ICreateTypeInfo2::DeleteVarDesc

HRESULT DeleteVarDesc(
unsigned int *index*
);

Deletes the specified VARDESC structure.

Parameter   *index*
Index number of the VARDESC structure.

Return Value   The return value obtained from the returned HRESULT is one of the following:

Return value	Meaning
S_OK	Success.
E_OUTOFMEMORY	Out of memory.

Return value	Meaning
E_INVALIDARG	One or more of the arguments is invalid.
TYPE_E_IOERROR	The function cannot read from the file.
TYPE_E_INVDATAREAD	The function cannot read from the file.
TYPE_E_UNSUPFORMAT	The type library has an old format.
TYPE_E_INVALIDSTATE	The type library cannot be opened.

Example

```
ptypeinfo->DeleteVarDesc(index);
```

ICreateTypeInfo2::DeleteVarDescByMemId

HRESULT DeleteVarDescByMemId(
MEMBERID *memid*
);

Deletes the specified VARDESC structure.

Parameter

memid
　　Member identifier of the VARDESC to be deleted.

Return Value

The return value obtained from the returned HRESULT is one of the following:

Return value	Meaning
S_OK	Success.
E_OUTOFMEMORY	Out of memory.
E_INVALIDARG	One or more of the arguments is invalid.
TYPE_E_IOERROR	The function cannot read from the file.
TYPE_E_INVDATAREAD	The function cannot read from the file.
TYPE_E_UNSUPFORMAT	The type library has an older format.
TYPE_E_INVALIDSTATE	The type library cannot be opened.

ICreateTypeInfo2::DeleteImplType

HRESULT DeleteImplType(
unsigned int *index*
);

Deletes the IMPLTYPE flags for the indexed interface.

Parameter   *index*
                     Index of the interface for which to delete the type flags.

Return Value   The return value obtained from the returned HRESULT is one of the following:

Return value	Meaning
S_OK	Success.
E_OUTOFMEMORY	Out of memory.
E_INVALIDARG	One or more of the arguments is invalid.

ICreateTypeInfo2::SetCustData

HRESULT SetCustData(
REFGUID *guid*,
VARIANT **pVarVal*
);

Sets a value for custom data.

Parameters   *guid*
                     Unique identifier that can be used to identify the data.

                     pVarVal
                     The data to store (any variant except an object).

Return Value   The return value obtained from the returned HRESULT is one of the following:

Return value	Meaning
S_OK	Success.
E_OUTOFMEMORY	Out of memory.
E_INVALIDARG	One or more of the arguments is invalid.

ICreateTypeInfo2::SetHelpStringContext

HRESULT SetHelpStringContext(
DWORD **dwHelpStringContext*
);

Sets the context number for the specified Help string.

Parameter

dwHelpStringContext
    Pointer to the Help string context number.

Return Value

The return value obtained from the returned HRESULT is one of the following:

Return value	Meaning
S_OK	Success.
E_OUTOFMEMORY	Out of memory.
E_INVALIDARG	Argument is invalid.

ICreateTypeInfo2::SetFuncCustData

HRESULT SetFuncCustData(
unsigned int *index,*
REFGUID *guid,*
VARIANT **pVarVal*
);

Sets a value for a specified custom function.

Parameters

index
    The index of the function for which to set the custom data.

guid
    Unique identifier used to identify the data.

pVarVal
    The data to store (any variant except an object).

Return Value

The return value obtained from the returned HRESULT is one of the following:

Return value	Meaning
S_OK	Success.
E_OUTOFMEMORY	Out of memory.
E_INVALIDARG	One or more of the arguments is invalid.

ICreateTypeInfo2::SetFuncHelpStringContext

HRESULT SetFuncHelpStringContext(
unsigned int *index,*

DWORD *dwHelpStringContext,*

);

Sets a Help context value for a specified custom function.

Parameters

index
    The index of the function for which to set the custom data.

dwHelpStringContext
    Help string context for a localized string

Return Value

The return value obtained from the returned HRESULT is one of the following:

Return value	Meaning
S_OK	Success.
E_OUTOFMEMORY	Out of memory.
E_INVALIDARG	One or more of the arguments is invalid.

ICreateTypeInfo2::SetVarCustData

HRESULT SetVarCustData(
unsigned int *index,*
REFGUID *guid,*
VARIANT **pVarVal*
);

Sets a custom data variable.

Parameters

index
 Index of the variable for which to set the custom data.

guid
 Globally unique ID (GUID) used to identify the data.

pVarVal
 Data to store (any legal variant except an object).

Return Value

The return value obtained from the returned HRESULT is one of the following:

Return value	Meaning
S_OK	Success.
E_OUTOFMEMORY	Out of memory.
E_INVALIDARG	One or more of the arguments is invalid.

ICreateTypeInfo2::SetParamCustData

HRESULT SetParamCustData(
unsigned int *indexFunc,*
unsigned int *indexParam,*
REFGUID *guid,*
VARIANT **pVarVal*
);

Sets the specified parameter for the custom data.

Parameters	*indexFunc* Index of the function for which to set the custom data. *indexParam* Index of the parameter of the function for which to set the custom data. *guid* Globally unique identifier (GUID) used to identify the data. *pvarVal* The data to store (any legal variant except an object).
Return Value	The return value obtained from the returned HRESULT is one of the following:

Return value	Meaning
S_OK	Success.
E_OUTOFMEMORY	Out of memory.
E_INVALIDARG	One or more of the arguments is invalid.

ICreateTypeInfo2::SetImplTypeCustData

HRESULT SetImplTypeCustData(
unsigned int *index,*
REFGUID *guid,*
VARIANT **pVarVal,*
);

Sets the implementation type for custom data.

Parameters	*index* Index of the variable for which to set the custom data. *guid* Unique identifier used to identify the data. *pVarVal* Reference to the value of the variable.
Return Value	The return value obtained from the returned HRESULT is one of the following:

Return value	Meaning
S_OK	Success.
E_OUTOFMEMORY	Out of memory.
E_INVALIDARG	One or more of the arguments is invalid.

ICreateTypeInfo2::SetVarHelpStringContext

HRESULT SetVarHelpStringContext(
unsigned int *index,*

DWORD *dwHelpStringContext,*

);

Sets a Help context value for a specified variable.

Parameters   *index*
     The index of the variable.

dwHelpStringContext
     Help string context for a localized string

Return Value   The return value obtained from the returned HRESULT is one of the following:

Return value	Meaning
S_OK	Success.
E_OUTOFMEMORY	Out of memory.
E_INVALIDARG	One or more of the arguments is invalid.

Library Creation APIs, Interfaces and Functions

The following APIs, interfaces and methods support the creation and administration of type libraries and type descriptions.

CreateTypeLib API

HRESULT CreateTypeLib(
SYSKIND *syskind,*

OLECHAR FAR* *szFile,*

ICreateTypeLib FAR* FAR* *ppctlib*

);

Provides access to a new object instance that supports the **ICreateTypeLib** interface.

Parameters

    syskind
        The target operating system for which to create a type library.

    szFile
        The name of the file to create.

    ppctlib
        Pointer to an instance supporting the **ICreateTypeLib** interface.

Return Value

The return value of the returned HRESULT is one of the following:

Return value	Meaning
S_OK	Success.
STG_E_INSUFFICIENTMEMORY	Out of memory.
E_OUTOFMEMORY	Out of memory.
E_INVALIDARG	One or more of the arguments is invalid.
TYPE_E_IOERROR	The function could not create the file.
Other return codes	All FACILITY_STORAGE errors.

Comments

CreateTypeLib sets its output parameter (*ppctlib*) to point to a newly created object that supports the **ICreateTypeLib** interface.

ICreateTypeLib Interface

The **ICreateTypeLib** interface provides the methods for creating and managing the component or file that contains type information. Type libraries are created from type descriptions using the MkTypLib utility or the MIDL compiler. These type libraries are accessed through the **ITypeLib** interface.

ICreateTypeLib::CreateTypeInfo

    HRESULT CreateTypeInfo(
    OLECHAR FAR* *szName,*
    TYPEKIND *tkind,*
    ICreateTypeInfo FAR* FAR* *ppCTInfo*
    );

Creates a new type description instance within the type library.

Parameters

szName
>Name of the new type.

tkind
>TYPEKIND of the type description to be created.

ppCTInfo
>On return, contains a pointer to the type description.

Return Value

The return value of the returned HRESULT is one of the following:

Return value	Meaning
S_OK	Success.
STG_E_INSUFFICIENTMEMORY	Out of memory.
E_OUTOFMEMORY	Out of memory.
E_INVALIDARG	One or more of the arguments is invalid.
TYPE_E_INVALIDSTATE	The state of the type library is not valid for this operation.
TYPE_E_NAMECONFLICT	The provided name is not unique.
TYPE_E_WRONGTYPEKIND	Type mismatch.

Comments

Use the function **CreateTypeInfo** to create a new type description instance within the library. An error is returned if the specified name already appears in the library. Valid *tkind* values are described in the "TYPEKIND" section in Chapter 9, "Type Description Interfaces." To get the type information of the type description that is being created, call **IUnknown::QueryInterface**(IID_ITypeInfo, ...) on the returned **ICreateTypeInfo**. This type information can be used by other type descriptions that reference it by using **ICreateTypeInfo::AddRefTypeInfo.**

ICreateTypeLib::SaveAllChanges

HRESULT SaveAllChanges();

Saves the **ICreateTypeLib** instance following the layout of type information.

Parameters

None.

Return Value

The return value of the returned HRESULT is one of the following:

Return value	Meaning
S_OK	Success.
STG_E_INSUFFICIENTMEMORY	Out of memory.
E_OUTOFMEMORY	Out of memory.

Return value	Meaning
E_INVALIDARG	One or more of the arguments is invalid.
TYPE_E_IOERROR	The function cannot write to the file.
TYPE_E_INVALIDSTATE	The state of the type library is not valid for this operation.
Other return codes	All FACILITY_STORAGE errors.

Comments   You should not call any other **ICreateTypeLib** methods after calling **SaveAllChanges**.

ICreateTypeLib::SetDocString

HRESULT SetDocString(
OLECHAR FAR* *szDoc*
);

Sets the documentation string associated with the library.

Parameter   *szDoc*
    A documentation string that briefly describes the type library.

Return Value   The return value of the returned HRESULT is one of the following:

Return value	Meaning
S_OK	Success.
STG_E_INSUFFICIENTMEMORY	Out of memory.
E_OUTOFMEMORY	Out of memory.
E_INVALIDARG	One or more of the arguments is invalid.

Comments   The documentation string is a brief description of the library intended for use by type information browsing tools.

ICreateTypeLib::SetGuid

HRESULT SetGuid(
REFGUID *guid*
);

Sets the universal unique identifier (UUID) associated with the type library (Also known as the globally unique identifier (GUID)).

Parameter

guid
   The globally unique identifier to be assigned to the library.

Return Value

The return value of the returned HRESULT is one of the following:

Return value	Meaning
S_OK	Success.
STG_E_INSUFFICIENTMEMORY	Out of memory.
E_OUTOFMEMORY	Out of memory.
E_INVALIDARG	One or more of the arguments is invalid.
TYPE_E_INVALIDSTATE	The state of the type library is not valid for this operation.

Comments

Universal unique identifiers (UUIDs) are described in Chapter 8, "Type Libraries and the Object Description Language."

ICreateTypeLib::SetHelpContext

HRESULT SetHelpContext(
unsigned long *dwHelpContext*
);

Sets the Help context ID for retrieving general Help information for the type library.

Parameter

dwHelpContext
   Help context ID to be assigned to the library.

Return Value   The return value of the returned HRESULT is one of the following:

Return value	Meaning
S_OK	Success.
STG_E_INSUFFICIENTMEMORY	Out of memory.
E_OUTOFMEMORY	Out of memory.
E_INVALIDARG	One or more of the arguments is invalid.
TYPE_E_INVALIDSTATE	The state of the type library is not valid for this operation.

Comments   Calling **SetHelpContext** with a Help context of zero is equivalent to not calling it at all, because zero indicates a null Help context.

ICreateTypeLib::SetHelpFileName

HRESULT SetHelpFileName(
OLECHAR FAR* *szHelpFileName*
);

Sets the name of the Help file.

Parameter   *szHelpFileName*
     The name of the Help file for the library.

Return Value   The return value of the returned HRESULT is one of the following:

Return value	Meaning
S_OK	Success.
STG_E_INSUFFICIENTMEMORY	Out of memory.
E_OUTOFMEMORY	Out of memory.
E_INVALIDARG	One or more of the arguments is invalid.
TYPE_E_INVALIDSTATE	The state of the type library is not valid for this operation.

Comments   Each type library can reference a single Help file.

The **GetDocumentation** method of the created **ITypeLib** returns a fully qualified path for the Help file, which is formed by appending the name passed into *szHelpFileName* to the registered Help directory for the type library. The Help directory is registered under:

\TYPELIB\<guid of library>\<Major.Minor version >\HELPDIR

ICreateTypeLib::SetLibFlags

HRESULT SetLibFlags(
unsigned int *uLibFlags*

);

Sets library flags, such as LIBFLAG_FRESTRICTED.

Parameter

uLibFlags
The flags to set for the library.

Return Value

The return value of the returned HRESULT is one of the following:

Return value	Meaning
S_OK	Success.
STG_E_INSUFFICIENTMEMORY	Out of memory.
E_OUTOFMEMORY	Out of memory.
E_INVALIDARG	One or more of the arguments is invalid.
TYPE_E_INVALIDSTATE	The state of the type library is not valid for this operation.

Comments

Valid *uLibFlags* values are listed in "LIBFLAGS," in Chapter 6, "Data Types, Structures, and Enumerations."

ICreateTypeLib::SetLcid

HRESULT SetLcid(
LCID *lcid*

);

Sets the binary Microsoft national language ID associated with the library.

Parameter

lcid
Represents the locale ID for the type library.

Return Value   The return value of the returned HRESULT is one of the following:

Return value	Meaning
S_OK	Success.
STG_E_INSUFFICIENTMEMORY	Out of memory.
E_OUTOFMEMORY	Out of memory.
E_INVALIDARG	One or more of the arguments is invalid.
TYPE_E_INVALIDSTATE	The state of the type library is not valid for this operation.

Comments   For more information on national language IDs, see "Supporting Multiple National Languages," in Chapter 2, "Exposing Automation Objects." For additional information for 16-bit systems, refer to Appendix A, "National Language Support Functions." For 32-bit systems, refer to Windows NT documentation on the National Language Support (NLS) API.

ICreateTypeLib::SetName

HRESULT
OLECHAR FAR* *szName*
);

Sets the name of the type library.

Parameter   *szName*
    Name to be assigned to the library.

Return Value   The return value of the returned HRESULT is one of the following:

Return value	Meaning
S_OK	Success.
STG_E_INSUFFICIENTMEMORY	Out of memory.
E_OUTOFMEMORY	Out of memory.
E_INVALIDARG	One or more of the arguments is invalid.
TYPE_E_INVALIDSTATE	The state of the type library is not valid for this operation.

ICreateTypeLib::SetVersion

HRESULT SetVersion(
unsigned short *wMajorVerNum,*

unsigned short *wMinorVerNum*

);

Sets the major and minor version numbers of the type library.

Parameters   *wMajorVerNum*
Major version number for the library.

wMinorVerNum
Minor version number for the library.

Return Value   The return value of the returned HRESULT is one of the following:

Return value	Meaning
S_OK	Success.
TYPE_E_INVALIDSTATE	The state of the type library is not valid for this operation.

CreateTypeLib2 API

The **CreateTypeLib2** API creates a type library in the current file format.

The file and in-memory format for this current version of Automation makes use of memory-mapped files for 32-bit (and files for the Apple Macintosh). The existing **CreateTypeLib** API is still available for creating a type library in the older format.

HRESULT CreateTypeLib2

SYSKIND *syskind,*

LPOLESTR *szFile,*

ICreateTypeLib2** *ppctlib*

);

ICreateTypeLib2 Interface

ICreateTypeLib2 inherits from **ICreateTypeLib,** and has four member functions. The **ICreateTypeInfo** instance returned from **ICreateTypeLib** can be accessed through a **QueryInterface** call to **ICreateTypeInfo2**.

Example

```
interface ICreateTypeLib2 : ICreateTypeLib
```

ICreateTypeLib2::SetName

HRESULT SetName(
OLECHAR FAR* *szName*
);

Sets the name of the type library.

Parameter

szName
    Name to be assigned to the library.

Return Value

The return value of the returned HRESULT is one of the following:

Return value	Meaning
S_OK	Success.
STG_E_INSUFFICIENTMEMORY	Out of memory.
E_OUTOFMEMORY	Out of memory.
E_INVALIDARG	One or more of the arguments is invalid.
TYPE_E_INVALIDSTATE	The state of the type library is not valid for this operation.

ICreateTypeLib2::DeleteTypeInfo

HRESULT DeleteTypeInfo(
OLECHAR FAR* *szName*
);

Deletes a specified type information from the type library.

Parameter	*szName* Name of the type information to remove.
Return Value	The return value obtained from the returned HRESULT is one of the following:

Return value	Meaning
S_OK	Success.
E_OUTOFMEMORY	Out of memory.
E_INVALIDARG	One or more of the arguments is invalid.

ICreateTypeLib2::SetCustData

HRESULT SetCustData(
REFGUID *guid,*
VARIANT **pVarVal*
);

Sets a value to custom data.

Parameters	*guid* Unique identifier used to identify the data. *pVarVal* The data to store (any variant except an object).
Return Value	The return value obtained from the returned HRESULT is one of the following:

Return value	Meaning
S_OK	Success.
E_OUTOFMEMORY	Out of memory.
E_INVALIDARG	One or more of the arguments is invalid.

ICreateTypeLib2::SetHelpStringContext

HRESULT SetHelpStringContext(
DWORD **dwHelpStringContext*
);

Sets the Help string context number.

Parameter

DwHelpStringContext
The Help string context number.

Return Value

The return value obtained from the returned HRESULT is one of the following:

Return value	Meaning
S_OK	Success.
E_OUTOFMEMORY	Out of memory.
E_INVALIDARG	One or more of the arguments is invalid.

ICreateTypeLib2::SetHelpStringDll

HRESULT SetHelpStringDll(
LPOLESTR *szFileName*
);

Sets the DLL name to be used for Help string lookup (for localization purposes).

Parameter

szFileName
The DLL file name.

Return Value

The return value obtained from the returned HRESULT is one of the following:

Return value	Meaning
S_OK	Success.
E_OUTOFMEMORY	Out of memory.
E_INVALIDARG	One or more of the arguments is invalid.

CHAPTER 11

Error Handling Interfaces

Objects that are invoked through virtual function table (VTBL) binding need to use the Automation error handling interfaces and API functions to define and return error information. In addition to the API functions, the interfaces include the following:

- **IErrorInfo** —Returns information from an error object.

- **ICreateErrorInfo** —Sets error information.

- **ISupportErrorInfo** —Identifies this object as supporting the **IErrorInfo** interface.

- Error handling functions.

This chapter covers the error handling interfaces. The member functions of each interface are listed in the following table.

Category	Member function	Purpose
IErrorInfo	**GetDescription**	Returns a textual description of the error.
	GetGUID	Returns the globally unique identifier (GUID) for the interface that defined the error.
	GetHelpContext	Returns the Help context identifier (ID) for the error.
	GetHelpFile	Returns the path of the Help file that describes the error.
	GetSource	Returns the programmatic identifier (ProgID) for the class or application that returned the error.

Category	Member function	Purpose
ICreateErrorInfo	SetDescription	Sets a textual description of the error.
	SetGUID	Sets the GUID for the interface that defined the error.
	SetHelpContext	Sets the Help context ID for the error.
	SetHelpFile	Sets the path of the Help file that describes the error.
	SetSource	Sets the ProgID for the class or application that returned the error.
ISupportErrorInfo	InterfaceSupportsErrorInfo	Indicates whether an interface supports the **IErrorInfo** interface.
Error handling functions	CreateErrorInfo	Creates a generic error object.
	GetErrorInfo	Retrieves and clears the current error object.
	SetErrorInfo	Sets the current error object.

Returning Error Information

▶   **To return error information**

1. Implement the **ISupportErrorInfo** interface.

2. To create an instance of the generic error object, call the **CreateErrorInfo** function.

3. To set its contents, use the **ICreateErrorInfo** methods.

4. To associate the error object with the current logical thread, call the **SetErrorInfo** function.

The following figure illustrates this procedure.

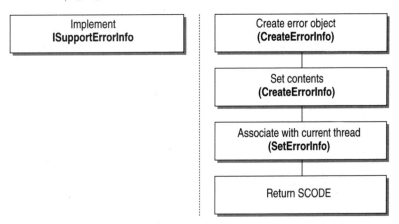

The error handling interfaces create and manage an error object, which provides information about the error. The error object is not the same as the object that encountered the error. It is a separate object associated with the current thread of execution.

Retrieving Error Information

▶ **To retrieve error information**

1. Check whether the returned value represents an error that the object is prepared to handle.

2. Call **QueryInterface** to get a pointer to the **ISupportErrorInfo** interface. Then, call **InterfaceSupportsErrorInfo** to verify that the error was raised by the object that returned it and that the error object pertains to the current error, and not to a previous call.

3. To get a pointer to the error object, call the **GetErrorInfo** function.

4. To retrieve information from the error object, use the **IErrorInfo** methods.

The following figure illustrates this procedure.

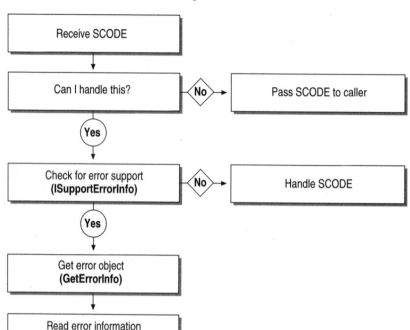

If the object is not prepared to handle the error, but needs to propagate the error information further down the call chain, it should simply pass the return value to its caller. Because the **GetErrorInfo** function clears the error information and passes ownership of the error object to the caller, the function should be called only by the object that handles the error.

IErrorInfo Interface

The **IErrorInfo** interface provides detailed contextual error information.

Implemented by	Used by	Header filename	Import library name
Oleaut32.dll (32-bit systems)	Applications that receive rich information.	Oleauto.h	Oleaut32.lib
Ole2disp.dll (16-bit systems)		Dispatch.h	Oledisp.lib

IErrorInfo::GetDescription

HRESULT GetDescription(
BSTR **pBstrDescription*

);

Returns a textual description of the error.

Parameter

pBstrDescription
    Pointer to a brief string that describes the error.

Return Value

The return value obtained from the returned HRESULT is:

Return value	Meaning
S_OK	Success.

Comments

The text is returned in the language specified by the locale identifier (LCID) that was passed to **IDispatch::Invoke** for the method that encountered the error.

IErrorInfo::GetGUID

HRESULT GetGUID(
GUID **pGUID*

);

Returns the globally unique identifier (GUID) of the interface that defined the error.

Parameter

pGUID
    Pointer to a GUID, or GUID_NULL, if the error was defined by the operating system.

Return Value

The return value obtained from the returned HRESULT is:

Return value	Meaning
S_OK	Success.

Comments   **IErrorInfo::GetGUID** returns the GUID of the interface that defined the error. If the error was defined by the system, **IErrorInfo::GetGUID** returns GUID_NULL.

This GUID does not necessarily represent the source of the error. The source is the class or application that raised the error. Using the GUID, an application can handle errors in an interface, independent of the class that implements the interface.

IErrorInfo::GetHelpContext

HRESULT GetHelpContext(
DWORD *pdwHelpContext*
);

Returns the Help context identifier (ID) for the error.

Parameter   *pdwHelpContext*
Pointer to the Help context ID for the error.

Return Value   The return value obtained from the returned HRESULT is:

Return value	Meaning
S_OK	Success.

Comments   **IErrorInfo::GetHelpContext** returns the Help context ID for the error. To find the Help file to which it applies, use **IErrorInfo::GetHelpFile**.

IErrorInfo::GetHelpFile

HRESULT GetHelpFile(
BSTR *pBstrHelpFile*
);

Returns the path of the Help file that describes the error.

Parameter   *pBstrHelpFile*
Pointer to a string that contains the fully qualified path of the Help file.

Return Value   The return value obtained from the returned HRESULT is:

Return value	Meaning
S_OK	Success.

Comments   **IErrorInfo::GetHelpFile** returns the fully qualified path of the Help file that describes the current error. **IErrorInfo::GetHelpContext** should be used to find the Help context ID for the error in the Help file.

IErrorInfo::GetSource

HRESULT GetSource(
BSTR *pBstrSource*
);

Returns the language-dependent programmatic ID (ProgID) for the class or application that raised the error.

Parameter   *pBstrSource*
Pointer to a string containing a ProgID, in the form *progname.objectname*.

Return Value   The return value obtained from the returned HRESULT is:

Return value	Meaning
S_OK	Success.

Comments   Use **IErrorInfo::GetSource** to determine the class or application that is the source of the error. The language for the returned ProgID depends on the locale ID (LCID) that was passed into the method at the time of invocation.

ICreateErrorInfo Interface

The **ICreateErrorInfo** interface returns error information.

Implemented by	Used by	Header filename	Import library name
Oleaut32.dll (32-bit systems)	Applications that return rich error information.	Oleauto.h	Oleaut32.lib
Oledisp.dll (16-bit systems)		Dispatch.h	Oledisp.lib

ICreateErrorInfo::SetDescription

HRESULT SetDescription(
LPCOLESTR **szDescription*
);

Sets the textual description of the error.

Parameter

szDescription
  A brief, zero-terminated string that describes the error.

Return Value

The return value obtained from the returned HRESULT is one of the following:

Return value	Meaning
S_OK	Success.
E_OUTOFMEMORY	Insufficient memory to complete the operation.

Comments

The text should be supplied in the language specified by the locale ID (LCID) that was passed to the method raising the error. For more information, see "LCID Attribute" in Chapter 8, "Type Libraries and the Object Description Language."

Example

```
hr = CreateErrorInfo(&pcerrinfo);
if (m_excepinfo.bstrDescription)
    pcerrinfo->SetDescription(m_excepinfo.bstrDescription);
```

ICreateErrorInfo::SetGUID

HRESULT SetGUID(
REFGUID *rguid*
);

Sets the globally unique identifier (GUID) of the interface that defined the error.

Parameter

rguid
  The GUID of the interface that defined the error, or GUID_NULL if the error was defined by the operating system.

Return Value   The return value obtained from the returned HRESULT is one of the following:

Return value	Meaning
S_OK	Success.
E_OUTOFMEMORY	Insufficient memory to complete the operation.

Comments   **ICreateErrorInfo::SetGUID** sets the GUID of the interface that defined the error. If the error was defined by the system, set **ICreateErrorInfo::SetGUID** to GUID_NULL.

This GUID does not necessarily represent the source of the error; however, the source is the class or application that raised the error. Using the GUID, applications can handle errors in an interface, independent of the class that implements the interface.

Example
```
hr = CreateErrorInfo(&pcerrinfo);
pcerrinfo->SetGUID(IID_IHello);
```

ICreateErrorInfo::SetHelpContext

HRESULT SetHelpContext(
DWORD *dwHelpContext*
);

Sets the Help context identifier (ID) for the error.

Parameter   *dwHelpContext*
     The Help context ID for the error.

Return Value   The return value obtained from the returned HRESULT is one of the following:

Return value	Meaning
S_OK	Success.
E_OUTOFMEMORY	Insufficient memory to complete the operation.

Comments   **ICreateErrorInfo::SetHelpContext** sets the Help context ID for the error. To establish the Help file to which it applies, use **ICreateErrorInfo::SetHelpFile**.

Example
```
hr = CreateErrorInfo(&pcerrinfo);
pcerrinfo->SetHelpContext(dwhelpcontext);
```

ICreateErrorInfo::SetHelpFile

HRESULT SetHelpFile(
LPCOLESTR *szHelpFile*
);

Sets the path of the Help file that describes the error.

Parameter

szHelpFile
    The fully qualified path of the Help file that describes the error.

Return Value

The return value obtained from the returned HRESULT is one of the following:

Return value	Meaning
S_OK	Success.
E_OUTOFMEMORY	Insufficient memory to complete the operation.

Comments

ICreateErrorInfo::SetHelpFile sets the fully qualified path of the Help file that describes the current error. Use **ICreateErrorInfo::SetHelpContext** to set the Help context ID for the error in the Help file.

Example

```
hr = CreateErrorInfo(&pcerrinfo);
pcerrinfo->SetHelpFile("C:\myapp\myapp.hlp");
```

ICreateErrorInfo::SetSource

HRESULT SetSource(
LPCOLESTR *szSource*
);

Sets the language-dependent programmatic identifier (ProgID) for the class or application that raised the error.

Parameter

szSource
    A ProgID in the form *progname.objectname*.

Return Value

The return value obtained from the returned HRESULT is one of the following:

Return value	Meaning
S_OK	Success.
E_OUTOFMEMORY	Insufficient memory to complete the operation.

Comments

ICreateErrorInfo::SetSource should be used to identify the class or application that is the source of the error. The language for the returned ProgID depends on the locale identifier (LCID) that was passed to the method at the time of invocation.

Example

```
hr = CreateErrorInfo(&pcerrinfo);
if (m_excepinfo.bstrSource)
    pcerrinfo->SetSource(m_excepinfo.bstrSource);
```

ISupportErrorInfo Interface

The **ISupportErrorInfo** interface ensures that error information can be propagated up the call chain correctly. Automation objects that use the error handling interfaces must implement **ISupportErrorInfo.**

Implemented by	Used by	Header filename
Applications that return error information.	Applications that retrieve error information.	Oleauto.h (32-bit systems) Dispatch.h (16-bit systems)

ISupportErrorInfo::InterfaceSupportsErrorInfo

HRESULT InterfaceSupportsErrorInfo(
  REFIID *riid*

  );

Indicates whether or not an interface supports the **IErrorInfo** interface.

Parameter

riid
  Pointer to an interface identifier (IID).

Return Value   The return value obtained from the returned HRESULT is one of the following:

Return value	Meaning
S_OK	Interface supports **IErrorInfo.**
S_FALSE	Interface does not support **IErrorInfo**.

Comments   Objects that support the **IErrorInfo** interface must also implement this interface.

Programs that receive an error return value should call **QueryInterface** to get a pointer to the **ISupportErrorInfo** interface, and then call **InterfaceSupportsErrorInfo** with the *riid* of the interface that returned the return value. If **InterfaceSupportsErrorInfo** returns S_FALSE, then the error object does not represent an error returned from the caller, but from somewhere else. In this case, the error object can be considered incorrect and should be discarded.

If **ISupportErrorInfo** returns S_OK, use the **GetErrorInfo** function to get a pointer to the error object.

Example   The following example implements the **ISupportErrorInfo** for the Lines sample. The **IErrorInfo** implementation also supports the **AddRef**, **Release**, and **QueryInterface** members inherited from the **IUnknown** interface.

```
CSupportErrorInfo::CSupportErrorInfo(IUnknown FAR* punkObject, REFIID
riid)
{
    m_punkObject = punkObject;
    m_iid = riid;
}


STDMETHODIMP
CSupportErrorInfo::QueryInterface(REFIID iid, void FAR* FAR* ppv)
{
    return m_punkObject->QueryInterface(iid, ppv);
}


STDMETHODIMP_(ULONG)
CSupportErrorInfo::AddRef(void)
{
    return m_punkObject->AddRef();
}


STDMETHODIMP_(ULONG)
CSupportErrorInfo::Release(void)
{
    return m_punkObject->Release();
}
```

```
STDMETHODIMP
CSupportErrorInfo::InterfaceSupportsErrorInfo(REFIID riid)
{
    return (riid == m_iid) ? NOERROR : ResultFromScode(S_FALSE);
}
```

Error Handling API Functions

For 32-bit systems, the error handling functions are provided in Oleaut32.dll, the header file is Oleauto.h, and the import library is Oleaut32.lib. For 16-bit systems, the error handling functions are provided in Ole2disp.dll, the header file is Dispatch.h, and the import library is Ole2disp.lib.

CreateErrorInfo

HRESULT CreateErrorInfo(
ICreateErrorInfo *******pperrinfo*

);

Creates an instance of a generic error object.

Parameter

pperrinfo
   Pointer to a system-implemented generic error object.

Return Value

The return value obtained from the returned HRESULT is one of the following:

Return value	Meaning
S_OK	Success.
E_OUTOFMEMORY	Could not create the error object.

Comments

This function returns a pointer to a generic error object, which you can use with **QueryInterface** on **ICreateErrorInfo** to set its contents. You can then pass the resulting object to **SetErrorInfo.** The generic error object implements both **ICreateErrorInfo** and **IErrorInfo**.

Example

```
ICreateErrorInfo *perrinfo;
HRESULT hr;

hr = CreateErrorInfo(&pcerrinfo);
```

GetErrorInfo

HRESULT GetErrorInfo
DWORD *dwReserved*,
IErrorInfo ***pperrinfo
);

Obtains the error information pointer set by the previous call to **SetErrorInfo** in the current logical thread.

Parameters

dwReserved
Reserved for future use. Must be zero.

pperrinfo
Pointer to a pointer to an error object.

Return Value

The return value obtained from the returned HRESULT is one of the following:

Return value	Meaning
S_OK	Success.
S_FALSE	There was no error object to return.

Comments

This function returns a pointer to the most recently set **IErrorInfo** pointer in the current logical thread. It transfers ownership of the error object to the caller, and clears the error state for the thread.

SetErrorInfo

HRESULT SetErrorInfo(
DWORD *dwReserved*,
IErrorInfo ***perrinfo
);

Sets the error information object for the current thread of execution.

Parameters

dwReserved
>   Reserved for future use. Must be zero.

perrinfo
>   Pointer to an error object.

Return Value

The return value obtained from the returned HRESULT is:

Return value	Meaning
S_OK	Success.

Comments

This function releases the existing error information object, if one exists, and sets the pointer to *perrinfo*. Use this function after creating an error object that associates the object with the current thread of execution.

If the property or method that calls **SetErrorInfo** is called by **DispInvoke,** then **DispInvoke** will fill the EXCEPINFO parameter with the values specified in the error information object. **DispInvoke** will return DISP_E_EXCEPTION when the property or method returns a failure return value for **DispInvoke.**

Virtual function table (VTBL) binding controllers that do not use **IDispatch::Invoke** can get the error information object by using **GetErrorInfo**. This allows an object that supports a dual interface to use **SetErrorInfo,** regardless of whether the client uses VTBL binding or **IDispatch**.

Example

```
ICreateErrorInfo *pcerrinfo;
    IErrorInfo *perrinfo;
    HRESULT hr;

hr = CreateErrorInfo(&pcerrinfo);
hr = pcerrinfo->QueryInterface(IID_IErrorInfo, (LPVOID FAR*) &perrinfo);
if (SUCCEEDED(hr))
    {
        SetErrorInfo(0, perrinfo);
        perrinfo->Release();
    }
    pcerrinfo->Release();
```

Appendixes

National Language Support Functions

The National Language Support (NLS) functions provide support for applications that use multiple locales at one time, especially applications that support Automation. Locale information is passed to allow the application to interpret both the member names and the argument data in the proper locale context. The information in this appendix applies only to 16-bit Windows systems. On 32-bit Windows systems, an NLS API is part of the system software.

Implemented by	Used by	Header filename	Import library name
Ole2nls.dll	Applications that support multiple national languages	Olenls.h	Ole2nls.lib

For Automation, applications need to get locale information and to compare and transform strings into the proper format for each locale.

A *locale* is simply user-preference information, represented as a list of values describing the user's language and sublanguage. National language support incorporates several disparate definitions of a locale into one coherent model. This model is designed to be general enough at a low level to support multiple, distinct, high-level functions, such as the ANSI C locale functions.

A *code page* is the mapping between character glyphs (shapes) and the 1-byte or 2-byte numeric values that are used to represent them. Microsoft Windows uses one of several code pages, depending on the installed localized version of Windows. For example, the Russian version uses code page 1251 (Cyrillic), while the English U.S. and Western European versions use code page 1252 (Multilingual). For historical reasons, the Windows code page in effect is referred to as the ANSI code page.

Because only one code page is in effect at a time, it is impossible for a computer running English U.S. Windows to display or print data correctly from the Cyrillic code page. The fonts do not contain the Cyrillic characters. However, it can still manipulate the characters internally, and they will display correctly again if moved back to a machine running Russian Windows.

All NLS functions use the locale identifier (LCID) to identify which code page a piece of text is assumed to lie in. For example, when returning locale information (such as month names) for Russian, the returned string can be meaningfully displayed in the Cyrillic code page only, because other code pages do not contain the appropriate characters. Similarly, when attempting to change the case of a string with the Russian locale, the case-mapping rules assume the characters are in the Cyrillic code page.

These functions can be divided into two categories.

- String transformation—NLS functions support uppercasing, lowercasing, generating sort keys (all locale-dependent), and getting string type information.

- Locale manipulation—NLS functions return information about installed locales for use in string transformations.

Overview of Functions

The following table lists the NLS functions.

Function	Purpose
CompareStringA	Compares two strings of the same locale.
LCMapStringA	Transforms the case or sort order of a string.
GetLocaleInfoA	Retrieves locale information from the user's system.
GetStringTypeA	Retrieves locale type information about each character in a string.
GetSystemDefaultLangID	Retrieves the default language ID (LANGID) from a user's system.[1]
GetSystemDefaultLCID	Retrieves the default LCID from a user's system.
GetUserDefaultLangID	Retrieves the default LANGID from a user's system.
GetUserDefaultLCID	Retrieves the default LCID from a user's system.[1]

[1] Because Windows is a single-user system, **GetUserDefaultLangID** and **GetUserDefaultLCID** return the same information as **GetSystemDefaultLangID** and **GetSystemDefaultLCID**.

Localized Member Names

An application may expose a set of objects whose members have names that differ across localized versions of a product. This poses a problem for programming languages that want to access such objects, because it means that late binding is sensitive to the locale of the application. The **IDispatch** and virtual function table (VTBL) interfaces allow software developers a range of solutions that vary in cost of implementation and quality of national language support. All methods of the **IDispatch** interface that are potentially sensitive to language are passed an LCID.

Following are some of the possible approaches a class implementation may take:

- Accept any LCID and use the same member names in all locales. This is acceptable if the interface will typically be accessed only by advanced users. For example, the member names for OLE interfaces will never be localized.

- Simply return an error (DISP_E_UNKNOWNLCID) if the caller's LCID doesn't match the localized version of the class. This would prevent users from being able to write late-bound code which runs on machines with different localized implementations of the class.

- Recognize the particular version's localized names, as well as one language that is recognized in all versions. For example, a French version might accept French and English names, where English is the language supported in all versions. This would constrain users to use English when writing code that runs in all countries,.

- Accept all LCIDs supported by all versions of the product. This means that the implementation of **GetIDsOfNames** would need to interpret the passed array of names based on the given LCID. This is the preferred solution because users would be able to write code in their national language and run the code on any localized version of the application.

At the very least, the application must check the LCID before interpreting member names. Also note that the meaning of parameters passed to a member function may depend on the caller's national language. For example, a spreadsheet application might interpret the arguments to a **SetFormula** method differently, depending on the LCID.

Locale Identifier (LCID)

The **IDispatch** interface uses the 32-bit Windows definition of a LCID to identify locales. An LCID is a DWORD value that contains the LANGID in the lower word and a reserved value in the upper word. The bits are as follows:

Reserved		LANGID		
31	16	15	0	Bits

This LCID has the components necessary to uniquely identify one of the installed system-defined locales.

```
// LCID creation/extraction macros:
// MAKELCID - construct locale ID from language ID and country code.
```

```
#define MAKELCID(1) ((DWORD)(((WORD)(1))|(((DWORD)((WORD)(0))) << 16)))
```

There are two predefined LCID values. LOCALE_SYSTEM_DEFAULT is the system default locale, and LOCALE_USER_DEFAULT is the current users locale. However, when querying the NLS APIs for information, it is more efficient to query once for the current locale with **GetSystemDefaultLCID** or **GetUserDefaultLCID**, rather than using these constants.

Language Identifier (LANGID)

A LANGID is a 16-bit value that is the combination of a primary and sublanguage ID. The bits are as follows:

Sublanguage ID						Primary Language ID										
15	14	13	12	11	10	9	8	7	6	5	4	3	2	1	0	Bits

Macros are provided for constructing a LANGID and extracting the fields:

LANGID creation/extraction macros include:

- MAKELANGID - construct LANGID from primary LANGID and sublanguage ID.
- PRIMARYLANGID - extract primary LANGID from a LANGID.
- SUBLANGID - extract sublanguage identifier (ID) from a LANGID.
- LANGIDFROMLCID - get the LANGID from an LCID.

```
#define MAKELANGID(p, s)        (((((USHORT)(s)) << 10) | (USHORT)(p))
#define PRIMARYLANGID(lgid)     ((USHORT)(lgid) & 0x3ff)
#define SUBLANGID(lgid)         ((USHORT)(lgid) >> 10)
#define LANGIDFROMLCID(lcid)    ((WORD)(lcid))
```

The following three combinations of primary and sublanguage IDs have special meanings:

PRIMARYLANGID	SUBLANGID	Meaning
LANG_NEUTRAL	SUBLANG_NEUTRAL	Language neutral
LANG_NEUTRAL	SUBLANG_SYS_DEFAULT	System default language
LANG_NEUTRAL	SUBLANG_DEFAULT	User default language

For primary language IDs, the range 0x200 to 0x3ff is user definable. The range 0x000 to 0x1ff is reserved for system use. The following table lists the primary LANGIDs supported by Automation:

Language	PRIMARYLANGID
Neutral	0x00
Chinese	0x04
Czech	0x05
Danish	0x06
Dutch	0x13
English	0x09
Finnish	0x0b
French	0x0c
German	0x07
Greek	0x08
Hungarian	0x0e
Icelandic	0x0F
Italian	0x10

Language	PRIMARYLANGID
Japanese	0x11
Korean	0x12
Norwegian	0x14
Polish	0x15
Portuguese	0x16
Russian	0x19
Serbo Croatian	0x1a
Slovak	0x1b
Spanish	0x0a
Swedish	0x1d
Turkish	0x1F

For sublanguage IDs, the range 0x20 to 0x3f is user definable. The range 0x00 to 0x1f is reserved for system use. The following table lists the sublanguage IDs supported by Automation:

Sublanguage	SUBLANGID
Neutral	0x00
Default	0x01
System Default	0x02
Chinese (Simplified)	0x02
Chinese (Traditional)	0x01
Dutch	0x01
Dutch (Belgian)	0x02
English (U.S.)	0x01
English (U.K.)	0x02
English (Australian)	0x03
English (Canadian)	0x04
English (Irish)	0x06
English (New Zealand)	0x05
French	0x01
French (Belgian)	0x02
French (Canadian)	0x03
French (Swiss)	0x04

Sublanguage	SUBLANGID
German	0x01
German (Swiss)	0x02
German (Austrian)	0x03
Greek	0x01
Icelandic	0x01
Italian	0x01
Italian (Swiss)	0x02
Japanese	0x01
Korean	0x01
Norwegian (Bokmal)	0x01
Norwegian (Nynorsk)	0x02
Portuguese	0x02
Portuguese (Brazilian)	0x01
Serbo Croatian (Latin)	0x01
Spanish (Castilian)1	0x01
Spanish (Mexican)	0x02
Spanish (Modern)1	0x03
Turkish	0x01

1 The only difference between Spanish (Castilian) and Spanish (Modern) is the sort ordering. All of the LCType values are the same.

Locale Constants (LCTYPE)

An LCTYPE is a constant that specifies a particular piece of locale information. For example:

```
typedef  DWORD  LCTYPE;
```

The list of supported LCTYPES follows. All values are null-terminated, variable-length strings. Numeric values are expressed as strings of decimal digits, unless otherwise noted. The values in the brackets indicate the maximum number of characters allowed for the string (including the null termination). If no maximum is indicated, the string may be of variable length.

Constant name	Description
LOCALE_ILANGUAGE	A LANGID represented in hexadecimal digits. See the previous sections. [5]
LOCALE_SLANGUAGE	The full localized name of the language.
LOCALE_SENGLANGUAGE	The full English U.S. name of the language from the ISO Standard 639. This will always be restricted to characters that can be mapped into the ASCII 127-character subset.
LOCALE_SABBREVLANGNAME	The abbreviated name of the language, created by taking the two-letter language abbreviation, as found in ISO Standard 639, and adding a third letter as appropriate to indicate the sublanguage.
LOCALE_SNATIVELANGNAME	The native name of the language.
LOCALE_ICOUNTRY	The country code, based on international phone codes, also referred to as IBM country codes. [6]
LOCALE_SCOUNTRY	The full localized name of the country.
LOCALE_SENGCOUNTRY	The full English U.S. name of the country. This will always be restricted to characters that can be mapped into the ASCII 127-character subset.
LOCALE_SABBREVCTRYNAME	The abbreviated name of the country as found in ISO Standard 3166.
LOCALE_SNATIVECTRYNAME	The native name of the country.
LOCALE_IDEFAULTLANGUAGE	LANGID for the principal language spoken in this locale. This is provided so that partially specified locales can be completed with default values. [5]
LOCALE_IDEFAULTCOUNTRY	Country code for the principal country in this locale. This is provided so that partially specified locales can be completed with default values. [6]
LOCALE_IDEFAULTANSICODEPAGE	The ANSI code page associated with this locale. Format: 4 Unicode decimal digits plus a Unicode null terminator. [10] [6]
LOCALE_IDEFAULTCODEPAGE	The OEM code page associated with the country. [6]
LOCALE_SLIST	Characters used to separate list items. For example, a comma is used in many locales.

Constant name	Description
LOCALE_IMEASURE	This value is 0 for the metric system (S.I.) and 1 for the U.S. system of measurements. [2]
LOCALE_SDECIMAL	Characters used for the decimal separator.
LOCALE_STHOUSAND	Characters used as the separator between groups of digits left of the decimal.
LOCALE_SGROUPING	Sizes for each group of digits to the left of the decimal. An explicit size is required for each group. Sizes are separated by semicolons. If the last value is 0, the preceding value is repeated. To group thousands, specify **3;0**.
LOCALE_IDIGITS	The number of fractional digits. [3]
LOCALE_ILZERO	Whether to use leading zeros in decimal fields. [2] A setting of 0 means use no leading zeros; 1 means use leading zeros.
LOCALE_SNATIVEDIGITS	The ten characters that are the native equivalent of the ASCII 0-9.
LOCALE_INEGNUMBER	Negative number mode. [2]
	"0" (1.1)
	"1" -1.1
	"2" -1.1
	"3" 1.1
	"4" 1.1
LOCALE_SCURRENCY	The string used as the local monetary symbol.
LOCALE_SINTLSYMBOL	Three characters of the International monetary symbol specified in ISO 4217, *Codes for the Representation of Currencies and Funds,* followed by the character separating this string from the amount.
LOCALE_SMONDECIMALSEP	Characters used for the monetary decimal separators.
LOCALE_SMONTHOUSANDSEP	Characters used as monetary separator between groups of digits left of the decimal.

Constant name	Description
LOCALE_SMONGROUPING	Sizes for each group of monetary digits to the left of the decimal. An explicit size is needed for each group. Sizes are separated by semicolons. If the last value is 0, the preceding value is repeated. To group thousands, specify **3;0**.
LOCALE_ICURRDIGITS	Number of fractional digits for the local monetary format. [3]
LOCALE_IINTLCURRDIGITS	Number of fractional digits for the international monetary format. [3]
LOCALE_ICURRENCY	Positive currency mode. [2] 0 Prefix, no separation. 1 Suffix, no separation. 2 Prefix, 1-character separation. 3 Suffix, 1-character separation.
LOCALE_INEGCURR	Negative currency mode. [2] 0 ($1.1) 1 -$1.1 2 $-1.1 3 $1.1- 4 $(1.1$) 5 -1.1$ 6 1.1-$ 7 1.1$- 8 -1.1 $ (space before $) 9 -$ 1.1 (space after $) 10 1.1 $- (space before $)
LOCALE_ICALENDARTYPE	The type of calendar currently in use. [2] 1 Gregorian (as in U.S.) 2 Gregorian (always English strings) 3 Era: Year of the Emperor (Japan) 4 Era: Year of the Republic of China 5 Tangun Era (Korea)

Constant name	Description
LOCALE_IOPTIONALCALENDAR	The additional calendar types available for this LCID. Can be a null-separated list of all valid optional calendars. [2] 0 None available 1 Gregorian (as in U.S.) 2 Gregorian (always English strings) 3 Era: Year of the Emperor (Japan) 4 Era: Year of the Republic of China 5 Tangun Era (Korea)
LOCALE_SDATE	Characters used for the date separator.
LOCALE_STIME	Characters used for the time separator.
LOCALE_STIMEFORMAT	Time-formatting string. [80]
LOCALE_SSHORTDATE	Short Date_Time formatting strings for this locale.
LOCALE_SLONGDATE	Long Date_Time formatting strings for this locale.
LOCALE_IDATE	Short Date format-ordering specifier. [2] 0 Month–Day–Year 1 Day–Month–Year 2 Year–Month–Day
LOCALE_ILDATE	Long Date format ordering specifier. [2] 0 Month–Day–Year 1 Day–Month–Year 2 Year–Month–Day
LOCALE_ITIME	Time format specifier. [2] 0 AM/PM 12-hour format. 1 24-hour format.
LOCALE_ITIMEMARKPOSN	Whether the time marker string (AM|PM) precedes or follows the time string. (The registry value is named **ITimePrefix** for previous Far East version compatibility.) 0 Suffix (9:15 AM). 1 Prefix (AM 9:15).
LOCALE_ICENTURY	Whether to use full 4-digit century. [2] 0 Two digit. 1 Full century.

Constant name	Description
LOCALE_ITLZERO	Whether to use leading zeros in time fields. [2]
	0 No leading zeros. 1 Leading zeros for hours.
LOCALE_IDAYLZERO	Whether to use leading zeros in day fields. [2]
	0 No leading zeros. 1 Leading zeros.
LOCALE_IMONLZERO	Whether to use leading zeros in month fields. [2]
	0 No leading zeros. 1 Leading zeros.
LOCALE_S1159	String for the AM designator.
LOCALE_S2359	String for the PM designator.
LOCALE_IFIRSTWEEKOFYEAR	Specifies which week of the year is considered first. [2]
	0 Week containing 1/1 is the first week of the year.
	1 First full week following 1/1 is the first week of the year.
	2 First week with at least 4 days is the first week of the year.
LOCALE_IFIRSTDAYOFWEEK	Specifies the day considered first in the week. [2]
	0 SDAYNAME1 1 SDAYNAME2 2 SDAYNAME3 3 SDAYNAME4 4 SDAYNAME5 5 SDAYNAME6 6 DAYNAME7
LOCALE_SDAYNAME1	Long name for Monday.
LOCALE_SDAYNAME2	Long name for Tuesday.
LOCALE_SDAYNAME2	Long name for Tuesday.
LOCALE_SDAYNAME3	Long name for Wednesday.
LOCALE_SDAYNAME4	Long name for Thursday.
LOCALE_SDAYNAME5	Long name for Friday.
LOCALE_SDAYNAME6	Long name for Saturday.
LOCALE_SDAYNAME7	Long name for Sunday.

Constant name	Description
LOCALE_SABBREVDAYNAME1	Abbreviated name for Monday.
LOCALE_SABBREVDAYNAME2	Abbreviated name for Tuesday.
LOCALE_SABBREVDAYNAME3	Abbreviated name for Wednesday.
LOCALE_SABBREVDAYNAME4	Abbreviated name for Thursday.
LOCALE_SABBREVDAYNAME5	Abbreviated name for Friday.
LOCALE_SABBREVDAYNAME6	Abbreviated name for Saturday.
LOCALE_SABBREVDAYNAME7	Abbreviated name for Sunday.
LOCALE_SMONTHNAME1	Long name for January.
LOCALE_SMONTHNAME2	Long name for February.
LOCALE_SMONTHNAME3	Long name for March.
LOCALE_SMONTHNAME4	Long name for April.
LOCALE_SMONTHNAME5	Long name for May.
LOCALE_SMONTHNAME6	Long name for June.
LOCALE_SMONTHNAME7	Long name for July.
LOCALE_SMONTHNAME8	Long name for August.
LOCALE_SMONTHNAME9	Long name for September.
LOCALE_SMONTHNAME10	Long name for October.
LOCALE_SMONTHNAME11	Long name for November.
LOCALE_SMONTHNAME12	Long name for December.
LOCALE_SMONTHNAME13	Native name for 13th month, if it exists.
LOCALE_SABBREVMONTHNAME1	Abbreviated name for January.
LOCALE_SABBREVMONTHNAME2	Abbreviated name for February.
LOCALE_SABBREVMONTHNAME3	Abbreviated name for March.
LOCALE_SABBREVMONTHNAME4	Abbreviated name for April.
LOCALE_SABBREVMONTHNAME5	Abbreviated name for May.
LOCALE_SABBREVMONTHNAME6	Abbreviated name for June.
LOCALE_SABBREVMONTHNAME7	Abbreviated name for July.
LOCALE_SABBREVMONTHNAME8	Abbreviated name for August.
LOCALE_SABBREVMONTHNAME9	Abbreviated name for September.
LOCALE_SABBREVMONTHNAME10	Abbreviated name for October.
LOCALE_SABBREVMONTHNAME11	Abbreviated name for November.
LOCALE_SABBREVMONTHNAME12	Abbreviated name for December.
LOCALE_SABBREVMONTHNAME13	Native abbreviated name for 13th month, if it exists.
LOCALE_SPOSITIVESIGN	String value for the positive sign.

Constant name	Description
LOCALE_SNEGATIVESIGN	String value for the negative sign.
LOCALE_IPOSSIGNPOSN	Formatting index for positive values. [2]
	0 Parentheses surround the amount and the monetary symbol.
	1 The sign string precedes the amount and the monetary symbol.
	2 The sign string precedes the amount and the monetary symbol.
	3 The sign string precedes the amount and the monetary symbol.
	4 The sign string precedes the amount and the monetary symbol.
LOCALE_INEGSIGNPOSN	Formatting index for negative values. [2]
	0 Parentheses surround the amount and the monetary symbol.
	1 The sign string precedes the amount and the monetary symbol.
	2 The sign string precedes the amount and the monetary symbol.
	3 The sign string precedes the amount and the monetary symbol.
	4 The sign string precedes the amount and the monetary symbol.
LOCALE_IPOSSYMPRECEDES	If the monetary symbol precedes, 1. If it succeeds a positive amount, 0. [2]
LOCALE_IPOSSEPBYSPACE	If the monetary symbol is separated by a space from a positive amount, 1. Otherwise, 0. [2]
LOCALE_INEGSYMPRECEDES	If the monetary symbol precedes, 1. If it succeeds a negative amount, 0. [2]
LOCALE_INEGSEPBYSPACE	If the monetary symbol is separated by a space from a negative amount, 1. Otherwise, 0. [2]

The following table shows the equivalence between LCTYPE values and the information stored in the [intl] section of Win.ini. These values are retrieved from Win.ini if information for the current system locale is queried. Values for LCTYPEs that are not in the following table do not depend on information stored in Win.ini.

Win.ini settings	LCTYPE
sLanguage[1]	LOCALE_SABBREVLANGNAME
iCountry	LOCALE_ICOUNTRY
sCountry	LOCALE_SCOUNTRY
sList	LOCALE_SLIST
iMeasure	LOCALE_IMEASURE
sDecimal	LOCALE_SDECIMAL
sThousand	LOCALE_STHOUSAND
iDigits	LOCALE_IDIGITS
iLZero	LOCALE_ILZERO
sCurrency	LOCALE_SCURRENCY
iCurrDigits	LOCALE_ICURRDIGITS
iCurrency	LOCALE_ICURRENCY
iNegCurr	LOCALE_INEGCURR
sDate	LOCALE_SDATE
sTime	LOCALE_STIME
sShortDate	LOCALE_SSHORTDATE
sLongDate	LOCALE_SLONGDATE
iDate	LOCALE_IDATE
iTime	LOCALE_ITIME
iTLZero	LOCALE_ITLZERO
s1159	LOCALE_S1159
s2359	LOCALE_S2359

[1] Unlike in Win.ini, values returned by LOCALE_SABBREVLANGNAME are always in uppercase.

CompareStringA

int CompareStringA(LCID lcid
DWORD dwCmpFlags
LPCSTR lpString1
integer cchCount1
LPCSTR lpString2
integer cchCount2
    );

Compares two character strings of the same locale according to the supplied LCID.

Parameters

lcid
    Locale context for the comparison. The strings are assumed to be represented in the default ANSI code page for this locale.

dwCmpFlags
    Flags that indicate the character traits to use or ignore when comparing the two strings. Several flags can be combined , or none can be used. (In the case of this function, there are no illegal combinations of flags.) Compare flags include the following.

Value	Meaning
NORM_IGNORECASE	Ignore case. Default is Off.
NORM_IGNOREKANATYPE	Ignore Japanese hiragana/katakana character differences. Default is Off.
NORM_IGNORENONSPACE	Ignore nonspacing marks (accents, diacritics, and vowel marks). Default is Off.
NORM_IGNORESYMBOLS	Ignore symbols. Default is Off.
NORM_IGNOREWIDTH	Ignore character width. Default is Off.

lpString1 and *lpString2*
    The two strings to be compared.

cchCount1 and *cchCount2*
    The character counts of the two strings. The count does not include the null-terminator (if any). If either *cchCount1* or *cchCount2* is −1, the corresponding string is assumed to be null-terminated, and the length is calculated automatically.

	Value	Meaning
Return Value	0	Failure.
	1	*lpString1* is less than *lpString2*.
	2	*lpString1* is equal to *lpString2*.
	3	*lpString1 is greater than lpString2.*

Comments

When used without any flags, this function uses the same sorting algorithm as *lstrcmp* in the given locale. When used with NORM_IGNORECASE, the same algorithm as *lstrcmpi* is used.

For double-byte character set (DBCS) locales, the flag NORM_IGNORECASE has an effect on all the wide (two-byte) characters as well as the narrow (one-byte) characters. This includes the wide Greek and Cyrillic characters.

In Chinese Simplified, the sorting order used to compare the strings is based on the following sequence: symbols, digit numbers, English letters, and Chinese Simplified characters. The characters within each group sort in character-code order.

In Chinese Traditional, the sorting order used to compare the strings is based on the number of strokes in the characters. Symbols, digit numbers, and English characters are considered to have zero strokes. The sort sequence is symbols, digit numbers, English letters, and Chinese Traditional characters. The characters within each stroke-number group sort in character-code order.

In Japanese, the sorting order used to compare the strings is based on the Japanese 50-on sorting sequence. The Kanji ideographic characters sort in character-code order.

In Japanese, the flag NORM_IGNORENONSPACE has an effect on the daku-on, handaku-on, chou-on, you-on, and soku-on modifiers, and on the repeat kana/kanji characters.

In Korean, the sort order is based on the sequence: symbols, digit numbers, Jaso and Hangeul, Hanja, and English. Within the Jaso-Hangeul group, each Jaso character is followed by the Hangeuls that start with that Jaso. Hanja characters are sorted in Hangeul pronunciation order. Where multiple Hanja have the same Hangeul pronunciation, they are sorted in character-code order.

The NORM_IGNORENONSPACE flag only has an effect for the locales in which accented characters are sorted in a second pass from main characters. All characters in the string are first compared without regard to accents and (if the strings are equal) a second pass over the strings to compare accents is performed. In this case, this flag causes the second pass to not be performed. Some locales sort accented characters in the first pass, in which case this flag will have no effect.

If the return value is 2, the two strings are equal in the collation sense, though not necessarily identical (the case might be ignored, and so on).

If the two strings are of different lengths, they are compared up to the length of the shortest one. If they are equal to that point, the return value will indicate that the longer string is greater.

To maintain the C run-time convention of comparing strings, the value 2 can be subtracted from a non-zero return value. The meaning of < 0, == 0, and > 0 is then consistent with the C run-time conventions.

LCMapStringA

int LCMapStringA(LCID lcid
DWORD dwMapFlags
LPCSTR lpSrcStr
int cchSrc
LPSTR lpDestStr
int cchDest
);

Transforms the case or sort order of a string.

Parameters

lcid

Locale ID context for mapping. The strings are assumed to be represented in the default ANSI code page for this locale.

dwMapFlags

Flags that indicate what type of transformation is to occur during mapping. Several flags can be combined on a single transformation (though some combinations are illegal). Mapping options include the following.

Name	Meaning
LCMAP_LOWERCASE	Lowercase.
LCMAP_UPPERCASE	Uppercase.
LCMAP_SORTKEY	Character sort key.
LCMAP_HALFWIDTH	Narrow characters (where applicable).
LCMAP_FULLWIDTH	Wide characters (where applicable).
LCMAP_HIRAGANA	Hiragana.
LCMAP_KATAKANA	Katakana.
NORM_IGNORECASE	Ignore case. Default is Off.

Name	Meaning
NORM_IGNORENONSPACE	Ignore nonspacing. Default is Off.
NORM_IGNOREWIDTH	Ignore character width. Default is Off.
NORM_IGNOREKANATYPE	Ignore Japanese hiragana/katakana character differences. Default is Off.
NORM_IGNORESYMBOLS	Ignore symbols. Default is Off.

The latter five options (NORM_IGNORECASE, NORM_IGNORENONSPACE, NORM_IGNOREWIDTH, NORM_IGNOREKANATYPE, and NORM_IGNORESYMBOLS) are normalization options that can only be used in combination with the LCMAP_SORTKEY conversion option.

Conversion options can be combined only when they are taken from the following three groups, and then only when there is no more than one option from each group:

- Casing options (LCMAP_LOWERCASE, LCMAP_UPPERCASE)
- Width options (LCMAP_HALFWIDTH, LCMAP_FULLWIDTH)
- Kana options (LCMAP_HIRAGANA, LCMAP_KATAKANA)

lpSrcStr
Pointer to the supplied string to be mapped.

cchSrc
Character count of the input string buffer. If–1, *lpSrcStr* is assumed to be null-terminated and the length is calculated automatically.

lpDestStr
Pointer to the memory buffer that stores the resulting mapped string.

cchDest
Character count of the memory buffer pointed to by *lpDestStr*. If *cchDest* is 0, then the return value of this function is the number of characters required to hold the mapped string. In this case, the *lpDestStr* pointer is not referenced.

Return Value

Value	Meaning
0	Failure.
The number of characters written to *lpDestSt*	Success.

Comments

LCMapStringA maps one character string to another, performing the specified locale-dependent translation.

The flag LCMAP_UPPER produces the same result as **AnsiUpper** in the given locale. The flag LCMAP_LOWER produces the same result as **AnsiLower.** This function always maps a single character to a single character.

The mapped string is null-terminated if the source string is null-terminated.

When used with LCMAP_UPPER and LCMAP_LOWER, the *lpSrcStr* and *lpDestStr* may be the same to produce an in-place mapping. When LCMAP_SORTKEY is used, the *lpSrcStr* and *lpDestStr* pointers may not be the same. In this case, an error will result.

The LCMAP_SORTKEY transforms two strings so that when they are compared with the standard C library function **strcmp** (by strict numerical valuation of their characters), the same order will result, as if the original strings were compared with **CompareStringA**. When LCMAP_SORTKEY is specified, the output string is a string (without Nulls, except for the terminator), but the character values will not be meaningful display values. This is similar behavior to the ANSI C function **strxfrm**.

GetLocaleInfoA

int GetLocaleInfoA(LCID *lcid*
LCTYPE *LCType*
LPSTR *lpLCData*
int *cchData*
        );

Retrieves locale information from the user's system.

Parameters   *lcid*
        The locale ID. The returned string is represented in the default ANSI code page for this locale.

LCType
        Flag that indicates the type of information to be returned by the call. See the listing of constant values defined in this chapter. LOCALE_NOUSEROVERRIDE | LCTYPE indicates that the desired information will always be retrieved from the locale database, even if the LCID is the current one and the user has changed some of the values in the Windows 95 Control Panel. If this flag is not specified, the values in Win.ini take precedence over the database settings when getting values for the current system default locale.

lpLCData
        Pointer to the memory where **GetLocaleInfoA** will return the requested data. This pointer is not referenced if *cchData* is 0.

cchData
        Character count of the supplied *lpLCData* memory buffer. If *cchData* is 0, the return value is the number of characters required to hold the string, including the terminating null character. In this case, *lpLCData* is not referenced.

	Value	Meaning
Return Value	0	Failure.
	The number of characters copied, including the terminating null character	Success.

Comments   **GetLocaleInfoA** returns one of the various pieces of information about a locale by querying the stored locale database or Win.ini. The call also indicates how much memory is necessary to contain the desired information.

The information returned is always a null-terminated string. No integers are returned by this function and numeric values are returned as text. (See the format descriptions under LCTYPE).

GetStringTypeA

BOOL GetStringTypeA(LCID *lcid*
DWORD *dwInfoType*
LPCSTR *lpSrcStr*
int *cchSrc*
LPWORD *lpCharType*
   );

Retrieves locale type information about each character in a string.

Parameters   *lcid*
   Locale context for the mapping. The string is assumed to be represented in the default ANSI code page for this locale.

dwInfoType
   Type of character information to retrieve. The various types are divided into different levels. (See the Comments section for a list of information included in each type). The options are mutually exclusive. The following types are supported:

   • CT_CTYPE1

   • CT_CTYPE2

   • CT_CTYPE3

lpSrcStr
   String for which character types are requested. If *cchSrc* is −1, *lpSrcStr* is assumed to be null-terminated.

cchSrc

> Character count of *lpSrcStr*. If *cchSrc* is −1, *lpSrcStr* is assumed to be null-terminated. This must also be the character count of *lpCharType*.

lpCharType

> Array of the same length as *lpSrcStr* (*cchSrc*). On output, the array contains one word corresponding to each character in *lpSrcStr*.

Return Value

Return value	Meaning
0	Failure.
1	Success.

Comments

The *lpSrcStr* and *lpCharType* pointers cannot be the same. In this case, the error ERROR_INVALID_PARAMETER results.

The character type bits are divided up into several levels. One level's information can be retrieved by a single call.

This function supports three character types:

- Ctype 1
- Ctype 2
- Ctype 3

Ctype 1 character types support ANSI C and POSIX character typing functions. A bitwise OR of these values is returned when *dwInfoType* is set to CT_CTYPE1. For DBCS locales, the Ctype 1 attributes apply to both narrow characters and wide characters. The Japanese hiragana and katakana characters, and the kanji ideograph characters all have the C1_ALPHA attribute.

The following table lists the Ctype 1 character types.

Name	Value	Meaning
C1_UPPER	0x0001	Uppercase1.
C1_LOWER	0x0002	Lowercase1.
C1_DIGIT	0x0004	Decimal digits.
C1_SPACE	0x0008	Space characters.
C1_PUNCT	0x0010	Punctuation.
C1_CNTRL	0x0020	Control characters.
C1_BLANK	0x0040	Blank characters.

Name	Value	Meaning
C1_XDIGIT	0x0080	Hexadecimal digits.
C1_ALPHA	0x0100	Any letter.

1 The Windows version 3.1 functions **IsCharUpper** and **IsCharLower** do not always produce correct results for characters in the range 0x80-0x9f, so they may produce different results than this function for characters in that range. (For example, the German Windows version 3.1 language driver incorrectly reports 0x9a, lowercase s hacek, as uppercase).

Ctype 2 character types support the proper layout of text. For DBCS locales, Ctype 2 applies to both narrow and wide characters. The directional attributes are assigned so that the BiDi layout algorithm standardized by Unicode produces the correct results. For more information on the use of these attributes, see *The Unicode Standard: Worldwide Character Encoding* from Addison-Wesley publishers.

Attribute	Name	Value	Meaning
Strong	C2_LEFTTORIGHT	0x1	Left to right.
	C2_RIGHTTOLEFT	0x2	Right to left.
Weak	C2_EUROPENUMBER	0x3	European number, European digit.
	C2_EUROPESEPARATOR	0x4	European numeric separator.
	C2_EUROPETERMINATOR	0x5	European numeric terminator.
	C2_ARABICNUMBER	0x6	Arabic number.
	C2_COMMONSEPARATOR	0x7	Common numeric separator.
Neutral	C2_BLOCKSEPARATOR	0x8	Block separator.
	C2_SEGMENTSEPARATOR	0x9	Segment separator.
	C2_WHITESPACE	0xA	White space.
	C2_OTHERNEUTRAL	0xB	Other neutrals.
Not applicable	C2_NOTAPPLICABLE	0x0	No implicit direction (for example, control codes).

Ctype 3 character types are general text-processing information. A bitwise OR of these values is returned when *dwInfoType* is set to CT_CTYPE3. For DBCS locales, the Ctype 3 attributes apply to both narrow characters and wide characters. The Japanese hiragana and katakana characters, and the kanji ideograph characters all have the C3_ALPHA attribute.

Name	Value	Meaning
C3_NONSPACING	0x1	Nonspacing mark.
C3_DIACRITIC	0x2	Diacritic nonspacing mark.
C3_VOWELMARK	0x4	Vowel nonspacing mark.
C3_SYMBOL	0x8	Symbol.
C3_KATAKANA	0x10	Katakana character.
C3_HIRAGANA	0x20	Hiragana character.
C3_HALFWIDTH	0x40	Narrow character.
C3_FULLWIDTH	0x80	Wide character.
C3_IDEOGRAPH	0x100	Ideograph.
C3_ALPHA	0x8000	Any letter.
C3_NOTAPPLICABLE	0x0	Not applicable.

GetSystemDefaultLangID

LANGID GetSystemDefaultLangID();

Retrieves the default LANGID from a user's system.

Return Value

Return value	Meaning
0	Failure.
System default LANGID	Success.

Comments

Returns the system default LANGID. For information on how this value is determined, see **GetSystemDefaultLCID** in the following section..

GetSystemDefaultLCID

LCID GetSystemDefaultLCID();

Retrieves the default LCID from a user's system.

	Return value	Meaning
Return Value	0	Failure.
	System default locale ID	Success.

Comments Returns the system default LCID. The return value is determined by examining the values of *sLanguage* and *iCountry* in Win.ini, and comparing the values to those in the stored locale database. If no matching values are found, or the required values cannot be read from Win.ini, or if the stored locale database cannot be loaded, the value 0 is returned.

GetUserDefaultLangID

LANGID GetUserDefaultLangID();

Retrieves the default LANGID from a user's system.

	Value	Meaning
Return Value	0	Failure.
	User default LANGID	Success.

Comments Returns the user default LANGID. On single-user systems, the value returned from this function is always the same as that returned from **GetSystemDefaultLangID**.

GetUserDefaultLCID

LCID GetUserDefaultLCID();

Retrieves the default LCID from a user's system.

	Return value	Meaning
Return Value	0	Failure.
	User default locale ID	Success.

Comments Returns the user default LCID. On single-user systems, the value returned by this function is always the same as that returned from **GetSystemDefaultLCID**.

File Requirements

The file names shown in **bold** are required by your application at run time.

32-bit file names	16-bit file names	Purpose
None	Ole2.reg	Registers OLE and Automation. OLE is a system component on 32-bit systems, therefore, no .reg file is required.
None	**Ole2nls.dll** Ole2nls.lib Olenls.h	Provides functions for applications that support multiple national languages. On 32-bit systems, NLS features are provided by the Win32 NLS API.
Oleprx32.dll	**Ole2prox.dll**	Coordinates object access across processes.
MkTypLib.exe	MkTypLib.exe	Builds type libraries from interface descriptions.
Oleaut32.dll Oleaut32.lib Oleauto.h	**TypeLib.dll** Dispatch.h	Accesses type libraries.
	Ole2disp.dll Ole2disp.lib Dispatch.h	Provides functions for creating ActiveX objects and retrieving active objects at run time. Accesses ActiveX objects by invoking methods and properties.
Ole32.dll Ole32.lib Ole2.h	**Ole2.dll** Ole2.lib Ole2.h	Provides OLE functions that can be used by OLE and ActiveX objects or containers.

32-bit file names	16-bit file names	Purpose
	Compobj.dll	Supports COM creation and access.
	Compobj.lib	
	Ole2.h	
	Compobj.h	
	Storage.dll	Supports access to subfiles, such as type libraries, within compound documents.
	Storage.lib	
	Ole2.h	
	Storage.h	

Information for Visual Basic Programmers

Visual Basic provides full support for Automation. The following table lists how Visual Basic statements translate into OLE APIs.

Visual Basic statement	OLE APIs
CreateObject ("ProgID")	**CLSIDFromProgID**
	CoCreateInstance
	QueryInterface to get **IDispatch** interface.
GetObject ("filename", "ProgID")	**CLSIDFromProgID**
	CoCreateInstance
	QueryInterface for **IPersistFile** interface.
	Load on **IPersistFile** interface.
	QueryInterface to get **IDispatch** interface.
GetObject ("filename")	**CreateBindCtx** creates the bind context for the subsequent functions.
	MkParseDisplayName returns a moniker handle for **BindMoniker**.
	BindMoniker returns a pointer to the **IDispatch** interface.
	Release on moniker handle.
	Release on context.
GetObject ("ProgID")	**CLSIDFromProgID**
	GetActiveObject on class ID.
	QueryInterface to get **IDispatch** interface.
Dim *x* **As New** *interface*	Find CLSID for *interface*.
	CoCreateInstance
	QueryInterface

String Comparisons

This appendix describes how Automation compares strings. These comparisons are important when creating applications that support national language accents and digraphs. The information in this appendix applies to the following:

- **CreateStdDispatch**
- **DispGetIDsOfNames**
- **ITypeLib::FindName**
- **IDispatch::GetIDsOfNames**
- **MkTypLib and the MIDL compiler**

When comparing strings, Automation components use the following rules:

- Comparisons are sensitive to locale, based on the string's locale identifier (LCID). A string must have an LCID that is supported by the application or type library. For more information about locales and LCIDs, refer to the section "Supporting Multiple National Languages," in Chapter 2, "Exposing ActiveX Objects."
- Accent characters are ignored. For example, the string **à** compares the same as **a**.
- Case is ignored. For example, the string **A** compares the same as **a**.
- Comparisons are sensitive to digraphs. For example, the string Æ is not the same as **AE**.
- For Japanese, Korean, and Chinese locales, **ITypeLib::FindName** and **IDispatch::GetIDsOfNames** ignore width and kanatype.

Managing GUIDs

Globally unique identifiers (GUIDs) appear in many places in a typical Automation application. GUID errors can cause persistent bugs. To help avoid GUID problems, this appendix lists all of the places that GUIDs appear in a typical Automation application, describes common characteristics of GUID bugs, and offers some GUID management techniques.

GUIDs are the same as UUIDs (universally unique identifiers). A class identifier (CLSID) is a UUID/GUID that refers to a class.

The System Registry

The system registry is a central repository that contains information about objects. GUIDs are used to index that information. You can view the registration information on your system by running Regedit.exe with the **/v** option:

```
regedit /v
```

Typically, a name is connected with a GUID (for example, Hello.Application maps to a GUID), and the GUID is connected to all the other relevant aspects of the object (for example, the GUID maps to Hello.exe).

GUIDs are created with the tool Guidgen.exe. Running Guidgen.exe produces a very large hexidecimal number that uniquely identifies an object, whether it is a class, interface, library, or some other type of object.

GUID Locations

GUIDs appear in the following locations:

- **.reg files**—When an application is created, usually one or more .reg files are created. The .reg files contain the GUIDs for the classes that an application exposes. These GUIDs are added to the registry when you run Regedit.exe to register the classes, or when you register type information with **LoadTypeLib**.

- **The system registry**—Contains the GUIDs for classes in multiple locations. This is where OLE and applications get information about classes.

- **.odl files**—When objects are described in an Object Description Language (.odl) file, a GUID needs to be provided for each object. Compiling the .odl file with the Microsoft Interface Definition Language (MIDL) compiler or the MkTypLib utility places the GUIDs in a type library, which usually exists as a file with a .tlb extension. If a GUID is changed in an .odl file, you should run MIDL or MkTypLib again.

- **.tlb files**—Type libraries describe classes, and this information includes the GUIDs for the classes. The .tlb files can be browsed using the Tlbrowse.exe sample application supplied with OLE.

- **.h files**—Most application developers will declare class IDs (CLSIDs) for their classes in a header file by using the DEFINE_GUID macro.

Troubleshooting

The following problems are common with GUIDs.

Problem

GetObject can't seem to create an instance of my application.

Solution

Visual Basic uses the OLE calls listed in Appendix C to find the .exe file that creates an application instance. Visual Basic proceeds as follows:

1. Looks up the GUID for the object. (For the Hello application, Visual Basic maps the programmatic ID (ProgID) Hello.Application into a GUID.)

2. Finds the object's server (the Hello.exe for the Hello application).

3. Launches the application.

If an error occurs, check the following:

- Has the .reg file been run?
- Are the entries in the registry correct?
- Do all of the GUIDs match?
- Can the application be launched? The .exe file for the application, listed in the LocalServer entry, should either be on the path or it should be fully specified. For example:

```
c:\ole2\sample\hello\hello.bin
```

Problem

When I use **GetObject,** the application launches, but the **GetObject** call fails.

Solution

Normally, when an application is started, a class factory is registered using **CoRegisterClassObject**. Some applications register their class factories only when launched with the **/Automation** switch. If code was inherited, or a sample was copied, determine whether it checks for this switch. The **/Automation** option might appear in the .reg file, the registry, or in the development environment.

Problem   GetTypeInfoOfGuid() fails to get the type information from my type library.

Solution   When **GetTypeInfoOfGuid** is called, a GUID is provided. If this GUID doesn't match the GUID in the .tlb file, no type information will be returned. The GUID in the code may be declared in a header file. The GUID in the .tlb file can be checked by using Browse.exe, which is provided with OLE, or with the Visual Basic Object Browser.

GUID Management

The problem with managing GUIDs is that they are pervasive, and their length prohibits simple comparisons.

The single most important technique in managing GUIDs is to keep a central list of all the GUIDs that are implemented. For example, use the DEFINE_GUID macro or the Guidgen.exe tool with the **-n** option to generate the required number of GUIDs, and then enter the resulting strings in the first column of a spreadsheet. Each time a new GUID is used, enter a description of its purpose in the second column of the spreadsheet.

Note The DEFINE_GUIDE macro does not generate GUIDs. It defines a 128-bit number to a GUID with a human-readable name.

A central spreadsheet of GUIDs has several advantages:

- Listing all the GUIDs in one location may prevent accidental reuse of a GUID. (This often happens when an application is cloned to create another one.)

- The spreadsheet can be used to compare GUIDs. To check the accuracy of a GUID, you can copy it from the location where it is being used (for example, a .reg file), paste it into the spreadsheet, and then compare the two cells with the = operator.

- A record of GUID usage can be helpful in case of future problems, and this single source of information will be available to find the GUID for an object.

Glossary

A

accessor function
A function that sets or retrieves the value of a property. Most properties have a pair of accessor functions. Properties that are read-only may have only one accessor function.

ActiveX
Microsoft's brand name for the technologies that enable interoperability using the Component Object Model (COM). ActiveX technology includes, but is not limited to, OLE.

ActiveX client
Any program or piece of code that accesses the functionality and the content of an ActiveX or OLE object.

ActiveX component
Physical file that contains classes, which are definitions of objects. For example, a .dll, .exe or .ocx file.

ActiveX control
A user interface element created using ActiveX technology.

ActiveX object
Objects an application or programming tool exposes to ActiveX clients.

Application object
The top-level object in an application's object hierarchy. The Application object identifies the application to the system, and typically becomes active when the application starts. Specified by the **appobj** attribute in the type library.

Automation
COM-based technology that enables interoperability among ActiveX components, including OLE components. Formerly referred to as OLE Automation.

Automation controller
An application, programming tool, or scripting language that accesses Automation objects. Visual Basic is an Automation controller.

Automation object
An instance of a class defined within an application that is exposed for access by other applications or programming tools by Automation interfaces.

Automation server
An application, type library, or other source that makes Automation objects available for programming by other applications, programming tools, or scripting languages.

C

class identifier (CLSID)
A universally unique identifier (UUID) for an application class that identifies an object. An object registers its class identifier (CLSID) in the system registration database so that it can be loaded and programmed by other applications.

class factory
An object that implements the **IClassFactory** interface, which allows it to create other objects of a specific class.

coclass (component class)
Component object class. A top-level object in the object hierarchy.

code page
The mapping between character glyphs (shapes) and the 1-byte or 2-byte numeric values that are used to represent them.

collection object
A grouping of exposed objects. A collection object can address multiple occurrences of an object as a unit (for example, to draw a set of points).

Component Object Model (COM)
The programming model and binary standard on which OLE is based. COM defines how objects and their clients interact within processes or across process boundaries.

compound document
A document that contains data of different formats, such as sound clips, spreadsheets, text, and bitmaps, created by different applications. Compound documents are stored by container applications.

container application
An OLE-based application that provides storage, a display site, and access to a compound document object.

custom interface
A user-defined COM interface that is not defined as part of OLE.

D

Dispatch identifier (DISPID)
The number by which a member function, parameter, or data member of an object is known internally to the **IDispatch** interface.

dispinterface (dispatch interface)
An **IDispatch** interface that responds only to a certain fixed set of names. The properties and methods of the dispinterface are not in the virtual function table (VTBL) for the object.

dual interface
An interface that supports both **IDispatch** and VTBL binding.

E

event
An action recognized by an object, such as clicking the mouse or pressing a key, and for which you can write code to respond. In Automation, an event is a method that is called, rather than implemented, by an Automation object.

event sink
A function that handles events. The code associated with a Visual Basic form, which contains event handlers for one or more controls, is an event sink.

event source
A control that experiences events and calls an event handler to dispose of them.

exposed object
See Automation object.

H

HRESULT
A value returned from a function call to an interface, consisting of a severity code, context information, a facility code, and a status code that describes the result. For 16-bit Windows systems, the HRESULT is an opaque result handle defined to be zero for a successful return from a function, and nonzero if error or status information is to be returned. To convert an HRESULT into a more detailed SCODE (or return value), applications call **GetSCode()**. *See SCODE.*

I

ID binding
The ability to bind member names to dispatch identifiers (DISPIDs) at compile time (for example, by obtaining the IDs from a type library). This approach eliminates the need for calls to **IDispatch::GetIDsOfNames,** and results in improved performance over late-bound calls. *See also late binding and VTBL binding.*

in-place activation
The ability to activate an object from within an OLE control and to associate a verb with that activation (for example, edit, play, change). Sometimes referred to as in-place editing or visual editing.

in-process server
An object application that runs in the same process space as the Automation controller.

interfaces
One or more well-defined base classes providing member functions that, when implemented in an application, provide a specific service. Interfaces may include compiled support functions to simplify their implementation.

L

late binding
The ability to bind member names to dispatch identifiers (IDs) at run time, rather than at compile time. *See also ID binding and VTBL binding.*

LCID (locale identifier)
A 32-bit value that identifies the human language preferred by a user, region, or application.

locale
User-preference information, represented as a list of values describing the user's language and sublanguage.

M

MkTypLib utility
A library creation utility that compiles scripts written in the Object Description Language. This utility is obsolete; the Microsoft Interface Definition Language (MIDL) compiler should be used instead of MkTypLib.

marshaling
The process of packaging and sending interface parameters across process boundaries.

member function
One of a group of related functions that make up an interface. *See also method and property.*

method
A member function of an exposed object that performs some action on the object, such as saving it to disk.

MIDL compiler
The Microsoft Interface Definition Library (MIDL) compiler can be used to generate a type library. For information about the MIDL compiler, refer to the *Microsoft Interface Definition Language Programmer's Guide and Reference* in the Win32 Software Development Kit (SDK) section of the Microsoft Developer's Network (MSDN).

multiple-document interface (MDI) application
An application that can support multiple documents from one application instance. MDI object applications can simultaneously service a user and one or more embedding containers. *See also single-document interface (SDI) application.*

N

naming guidelines
Recommendations meant to improve consistency and readability across applications.

O

object
A unit of information that resides in a compound document and whose behavior is constant no matter where it is located or used.

Object Description Language (ODL)
A scripting language used to describe exposed libraries, objects, types, and interfaces. ODL scripts are compiled into type libraries by the MkTypLib tool.

OLE
Microsoft's object-based technology for sharing information and services across process and machine boundaries (object linking and embedding).

out-of process server
An object application implemented in an executable file that runs in a separate process space from the Automation controller.

P

programmable object
See Automation object.

programmatic identifier (ProgID)
An application's unique name that is mapped to the system registry by the class identifier (CLSID). For example, registering Microsoft Excel associates a CLSID with the ProgID Excel.Application.

property
A data member of an exposed object. Properties are set or returned by means of get and put accessor functions.

proxy
An interface-specific object that packages parameters for that interface in preparation for a remote method call. A proxy runs in the address space of the sender and communicates with a corresponding stub in the receiver's address space. *See also stub, marshaling, and unmarshaling.*

R

running object table (ROT)
A globally accessible table on each computer that keeps track of all COM objects in the running state that can be identified by a moniker. Moniker providers register an object in the table, which increments the object's reference count. Before the object can be destroyed, its moniker must be released from the table.

S

safe array
An array that contains information about the number of dimensions and the bounds of its dimensions. Safe arrays are passed by **IDispatch::Invoke** within VARIANTARGs. Their base type is VT_tag | VT_ARRAY.

SCODE
A DWORD value that is used in 16-bit systems to pass detailed information to the caller of an interface member or API function. The status codes for OLE interfaces and APIs are defined in FACILITY_ITF. *See HRESULT.*

single-document interface (SDI) application
An application that can support only one document at a time. Multiple instances of an SDI application must be started to service both an embedded object and a user. *See also multiple-document interface (MDI) application.*

standard objects
A set of objects defined by Automation, including the following: **Application**, **Document**, **Documents**, and **Font**.

stub
An interface-specific object that unpackages the parameters for that interface after they are marshaled across the process boundary, and makes the requested method call. The stub runs in the address space of the receiver and communicates with a corresponding proxy in the sender's address space. *See proxy, marshaling, and unmarshaling.*

T

type description
The information used to build the type information for one or more aspects of an application's interface. Type descriptions are written in Object Description Language (ODL), and include both programmable and nonprogrammable interfaces.

type information
Information that describes the interfaces of an application. Type information is created from type descriptions using OLE Automation tools, such as MkTypLib or the **CreateDispTypeInfo** function. Type information can be accessed through the **ITypeInfo** interface.

type information element
A unit of information identified by one of these statements in a type description: **typedef, enum, struct, module, interface, dispinterface,** or **coclass**.

type library
A file or component within another file that contains type information about exposed objects. Type libraries are created using either the MkTypLib utility or the MIDL compiler, and can be accessed through the **ITypeLib** interface.

U

unmarshaling
The process of unpackaging parameters that have been sent across process boundaries.

V

Value property
The property that defines the default behavior of an object when no other methods or properties are specified. Indicate the Value property by specifying the **default** attribute in ODL.

virtual function table (VTBL)
A table of function pointers, such as an implementation of a class in C++. The pointers in the VTBL point to the members of the interfaces that an object supports.

VTBL binding
A process that allows an ActiveX client to call a method or property accessor function directly without using the **IDispatch** interface. VTBL binding is faster than both ID binding and late binding because the access is direct. *See also late binding and ID binding.*

Index

COM
without the
complexity.

Inside
COM
Microsoft's Component Object Model

The C++ Programmer's Key
to the Distributed
Architecture
of the Future:
• ActiveX Controls
• OLE Components
• Reusable Objects
• Automation

Dale Rogerson

Microsoft Press

U.S.A.	**$34.99**
U.K.	£32.99 [V.A.T. included]
Canada	$46.99
ISBN 1-57231-349-8	

The Component Object Model (COM) isn't just another standard. It's the basis of Microsoft's approach to distributed computing. It's also the method for customizing Microsoft® applications, present and future. And it's the foundation of OLE and ActiveX™. In short, COM is a major key to the future of development. And this is the book that unlocks COM. In it, you'll discover:

- A clear and simple, practical guide to building elegant, robust, portable COM components
- An eye-opening presentation of how accessible COM can be—especially for those already familiar with C++
- An insightful, progressive view of COM design
- Plenty of illustrations in the form of code samples

INSIDE COM is for intermediate to advanced C++ programmers; beginning to advanced COM, ActiveX, and OLE programmers; academics with an interest in component design; and even programmers who want to use COM when it's ported to UNIX, MVS, and other environments. To put it simply, if you work with COM, then INSIDE COM was written for you.

Microsoft Press

The superfast way to get to Java!